Volume 2
by
Hiromu Muto

HAMBURG // LONDON // LOS ANGELES // TOKYO

Never Give Up Vol. 2
created by Hiromu Muto

Translation - Mike Kiefl
English Adaptation - Jodi Bryson
Retouch and Lettering - Alyson Stetz
Production Artist - Jihye "Sophia" Hong
Cover Design - James Lee

Editor - Julie Taylor
Digital Imaging Manager - Chris Buford
Production Manager - Liz Brizzi
Managing Editor - Lindsey Johnston
VP of Production - Ron Klamert
Publisher - Mike Kiley
Editor-in-Chief - Rob Tokar
President and C.O.O. - John Parker
C.E.O. and Chief Creative Officer - Stuart Levy

A  Manga

TOKYOPOP Inc.
5900 Wilshire Blvd. Suite 2000
Los Angeles, CA 90036

E-mail: info@TOKYOPOP.com
Come visit us online at www.TOKYOPOP.com

ISBN: 1-59816-166-0
First TOKYOPOP printing: July 2006
10 9 8 7 6 5 4 3 2 1
Printed in the USA

NEVER GIVE UP™

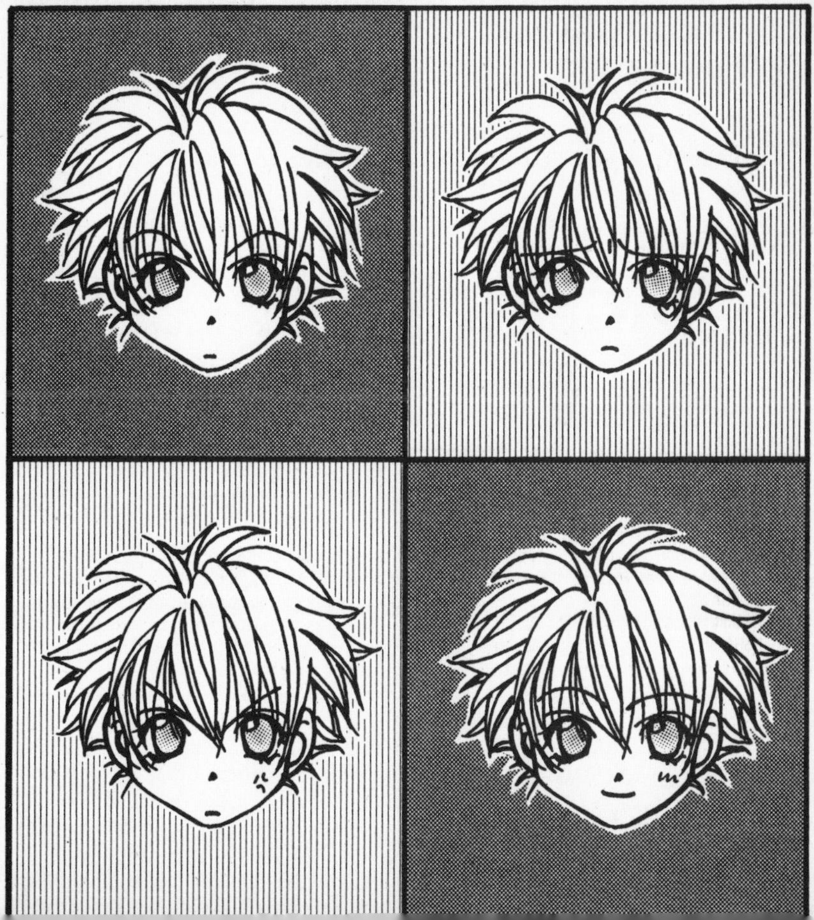

Contents

Chapter 7...6

Chapter 8 39

Chapter 9 69

Chapter 10 99

Chapter 11 131

Chapter 12 161

Secrets of the Muto Household 192

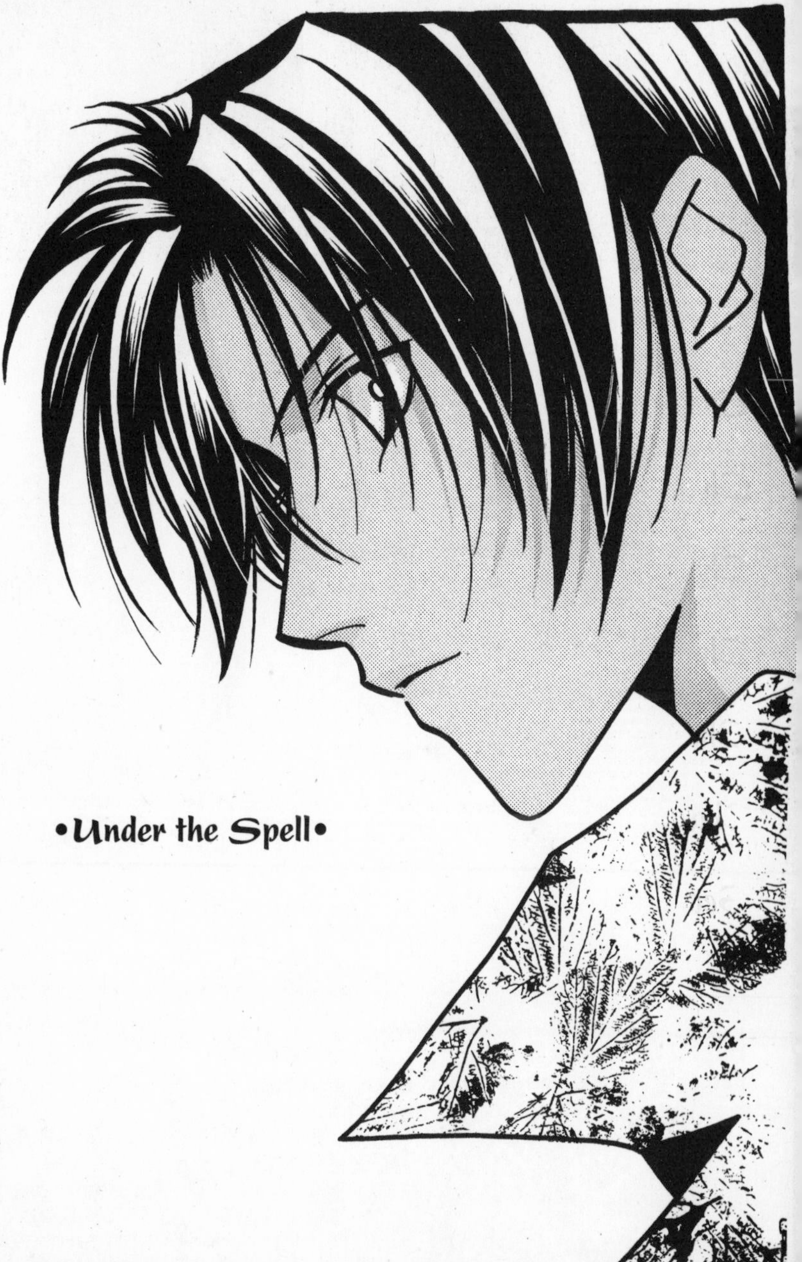

•Under the Spell•

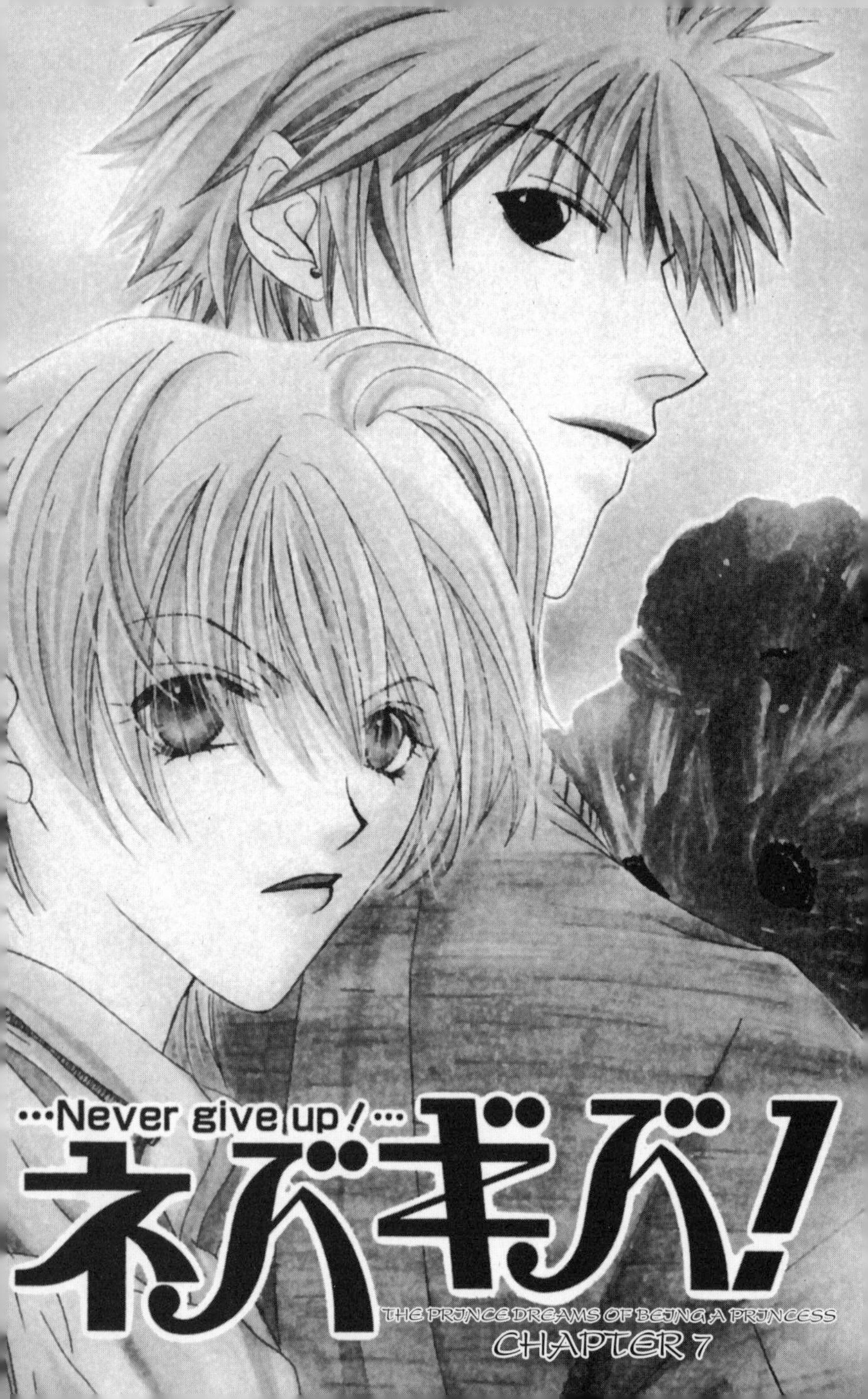
…Never give up!…
ネバギバ!
THE PRINCE DREAMS OF BEING A PRINCESS
CHAPTER 7

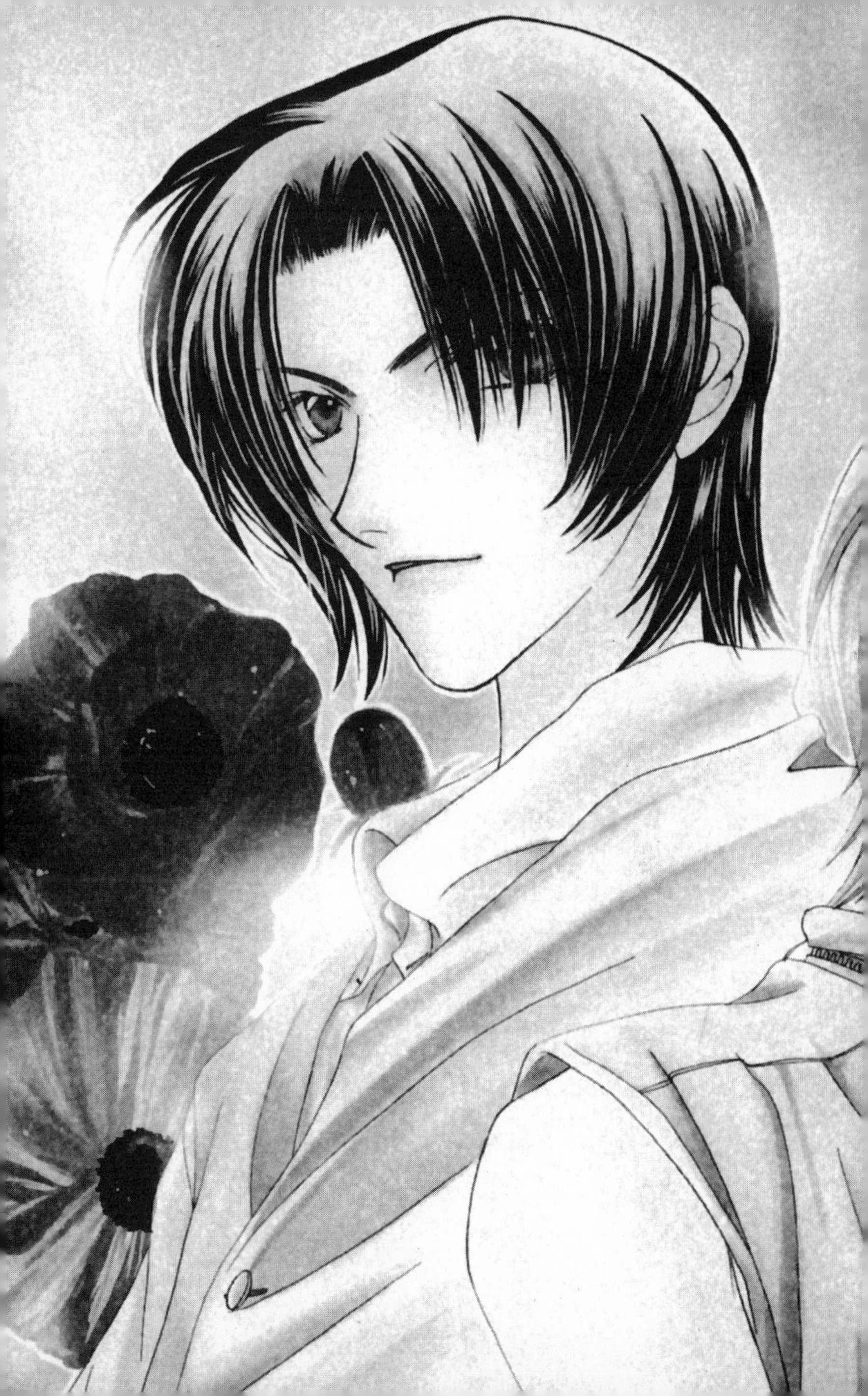

•The Final Tease•

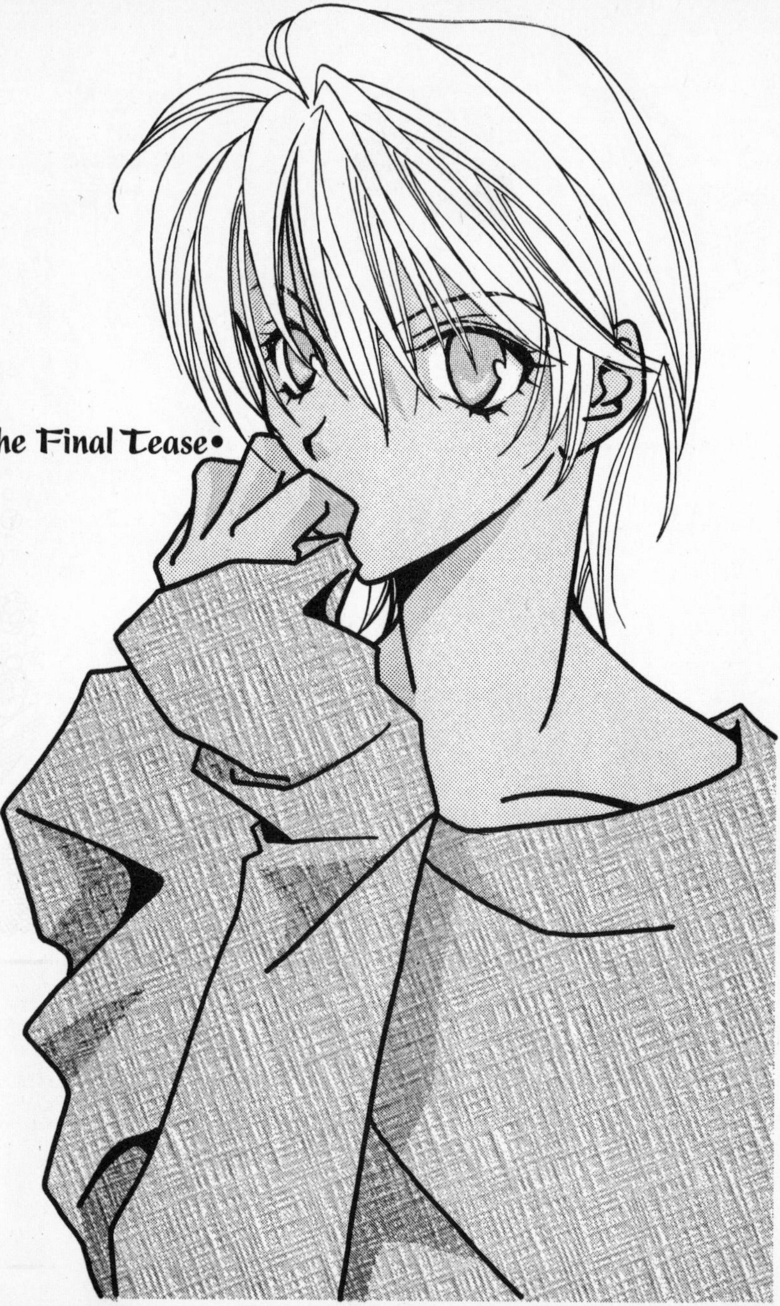

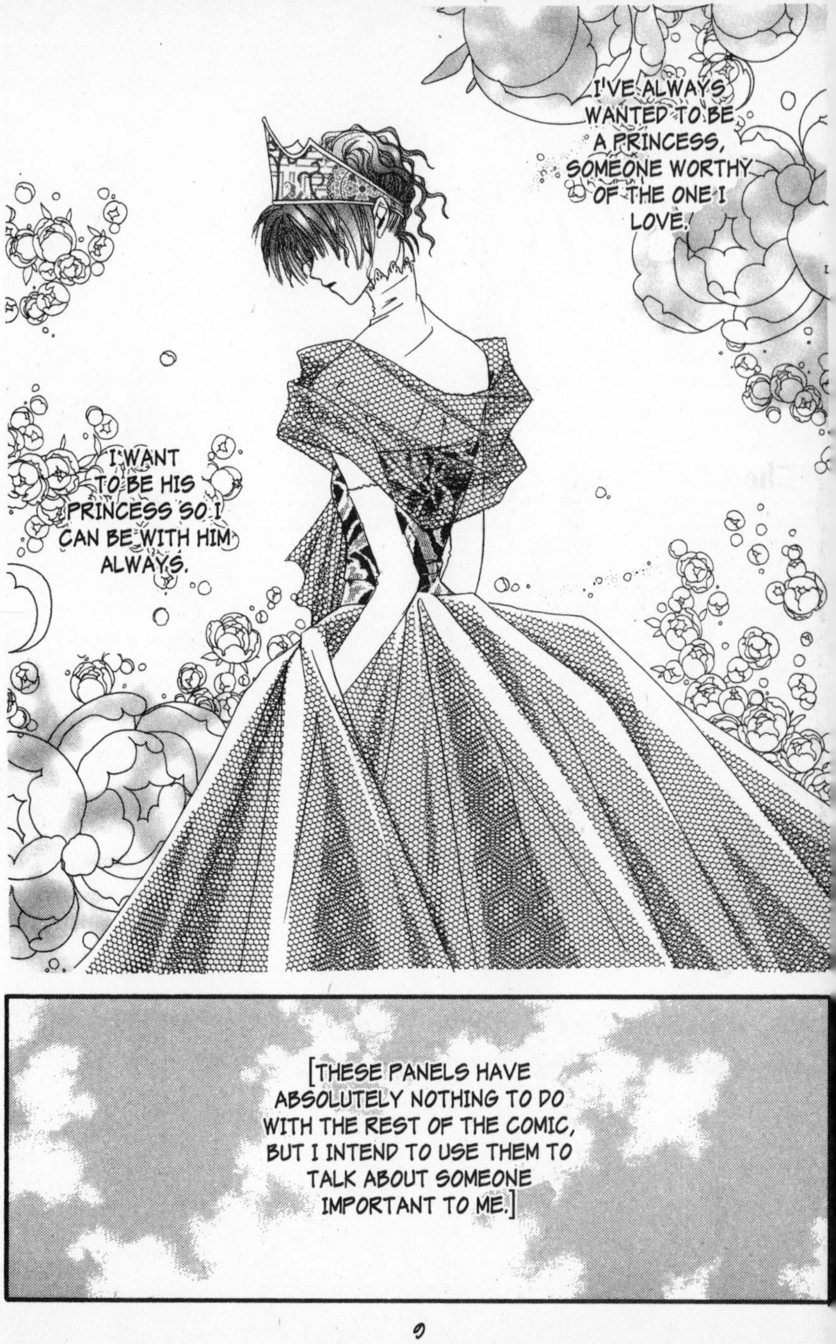
I'VE ALWAYS WANTED TO BE A PRINCESS, SOMEONE WORTHY OF THE ONE I LOVE.
I WANT TO BE HIS PRINCESS SO I CAN BE WITH HIM ALWAYS.
[THESE PANELS HAVE ABSOLUTELY NOTHING TO DO WITH THE REST OF THE COMIC, BUT I INTEND TO USE THEM TO TALK ABOUT SOMEONE IMPORTANT TO ME.]

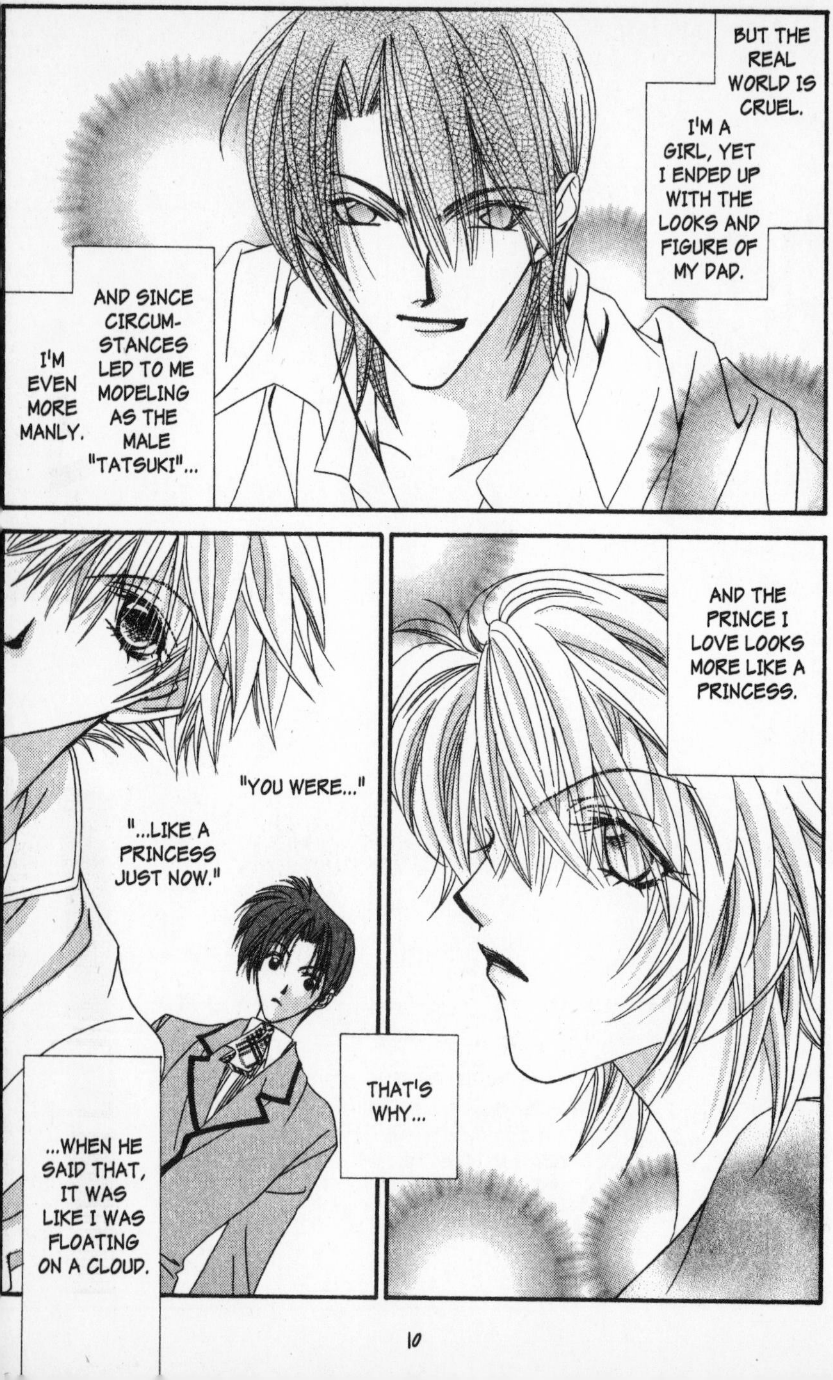
BUT THE REAL WORLD IS CRUEL.
I'M A GIRL, YET I ENDED UP WITH THE LOOKS AND FIGURE OF MY DAD.
AND SINCE CIRCUM-STANCES LED TO ME MODELING AS THE MALE "TATSUKI"...
I'M EVEN MORE MANLY.
AND THE PRINCE I LOVE LOOKS MORE LIKE A PRINCESS.
THAT'S WHY...
"YOU WERE..."
"...LIKE A PRINCESS JUST NOW."
...WHEN HE SAID THAT, IT WAS LIKE I WAS FLOATING ON A CLOUD.

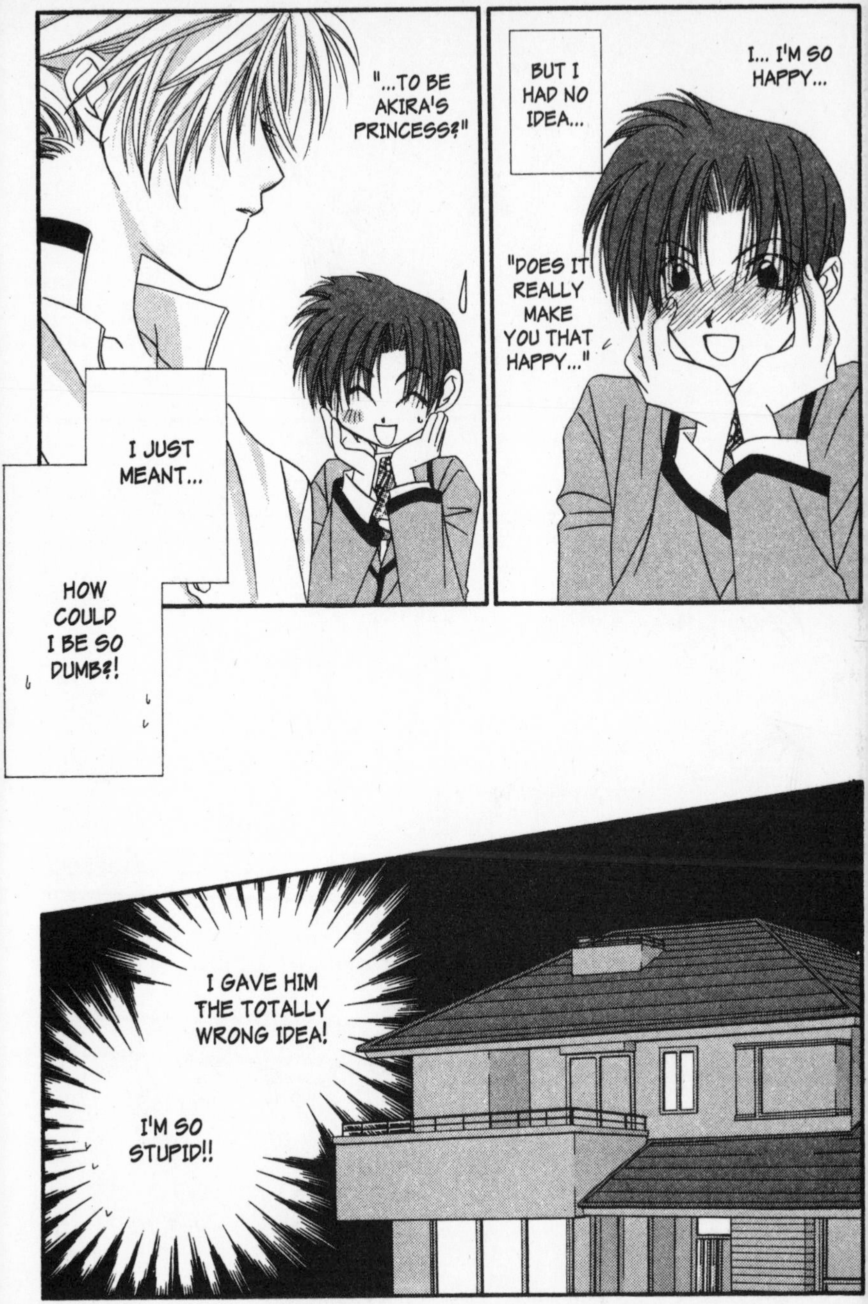
I... I'M SO HAPPY...
BUT I HAD NO IDEA...
"DOES IT REALLY MAKE YOU THAT HAPPY..."
"...TO BE AKIRA'S PRINCESS?!"
I JUST MEANT...
HOW COULD I BE SO DUMB?!
I GAVE HIM THE TOTALLY WRONG IDEA!
I'M SO STUPID!!

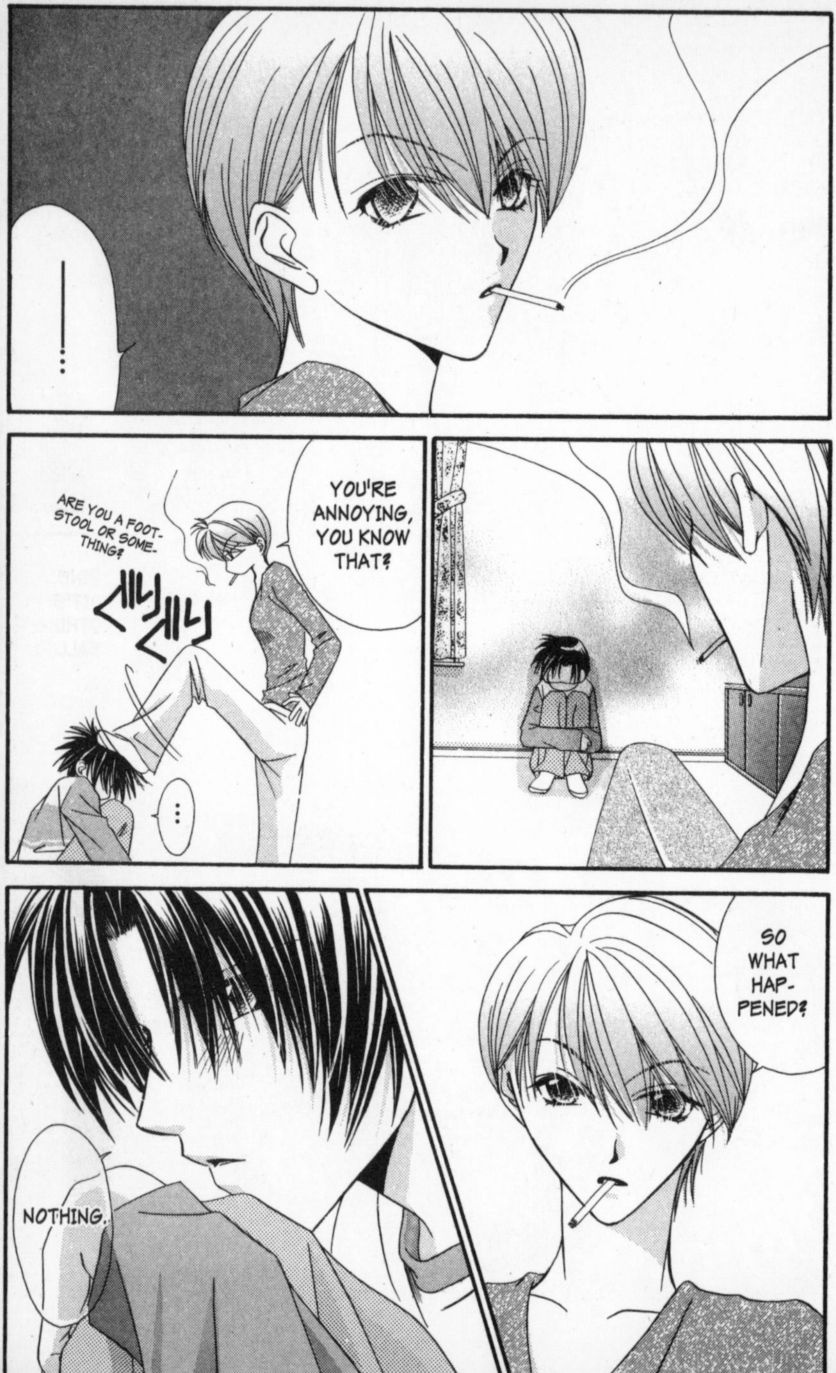

—...
YOU'RE ANNOYING, YOU KNOW THAT?
ARE YOU A FOOT-STOOL OR SOME-THING?
ぐりぐり
...
SO WHAT HAP-PENED?
NOTHING.

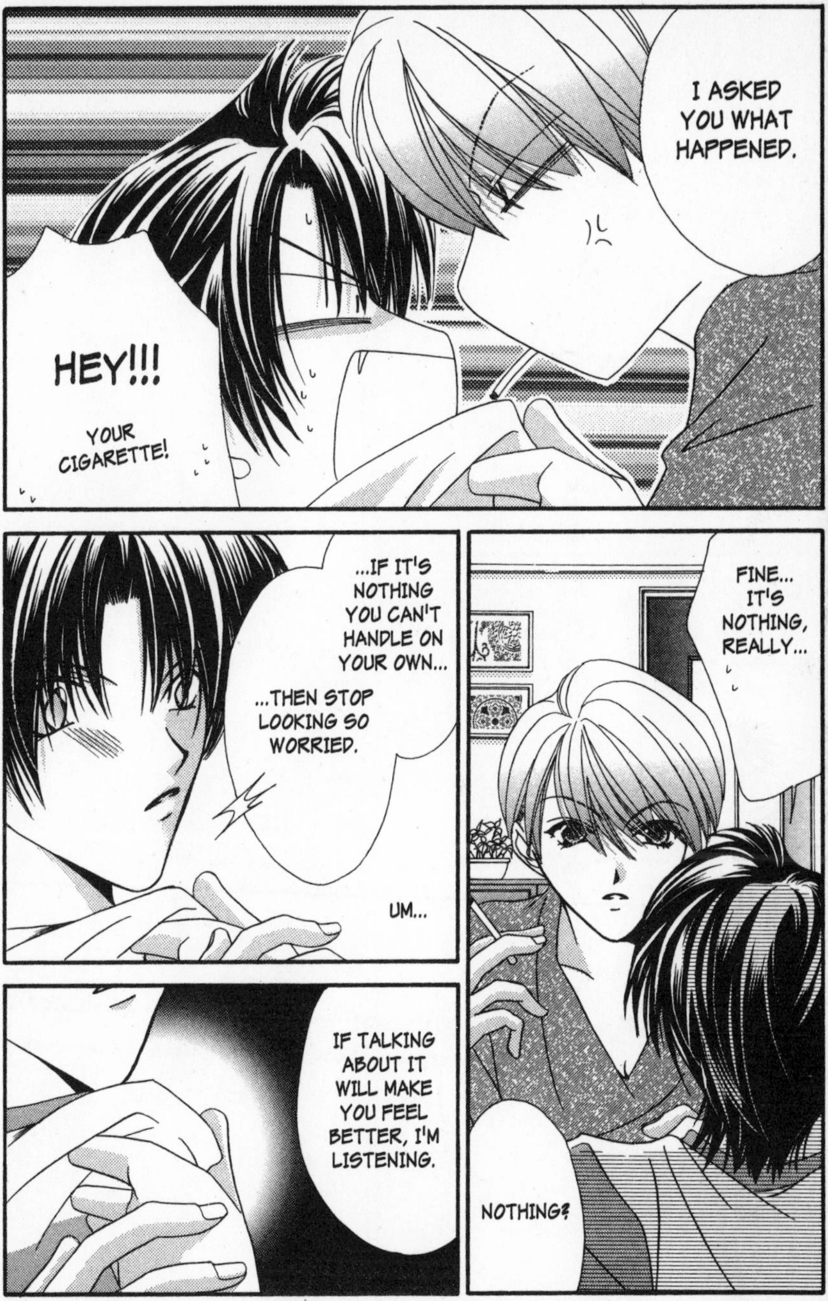
I ASKED YOU WHAT HAPPENED.
HEY!!!
YOUR CIGARETTE!
FINE... IT'S NOTHING, REALLY...
NOTHING?
...IF IT'S NOTHING YOU CAN'T HANDLE ON YOUR OWN...
...THEN STOP LOOKING SO WORRIED.
UM...
IF TALKING ABOUT IT WILL MAKE YOU FEEL BETTER, I'M LISTENING.

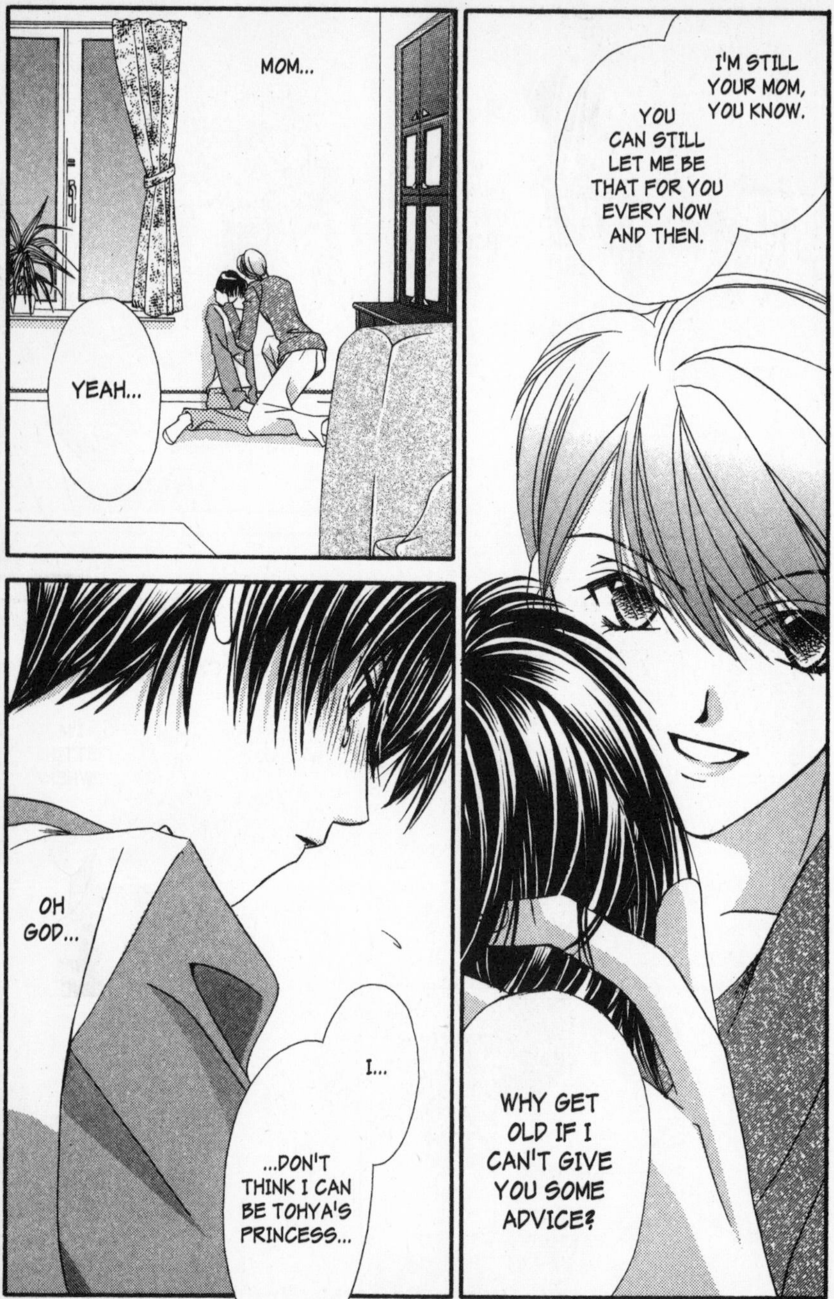
I'M STILL YOUR MOM, YOU KNOW.
YOU CAN STILL LET ME BE THAT FOR YOU EVERY NOW AND THEN.
WHY GET OLD IF I CAN'T GIVE YOU SOME ADVICE?
MOM...
YEAH...
OH GOD...
I...
...DON'T THINK I CAN BE TOHYA'S PRINCESS...

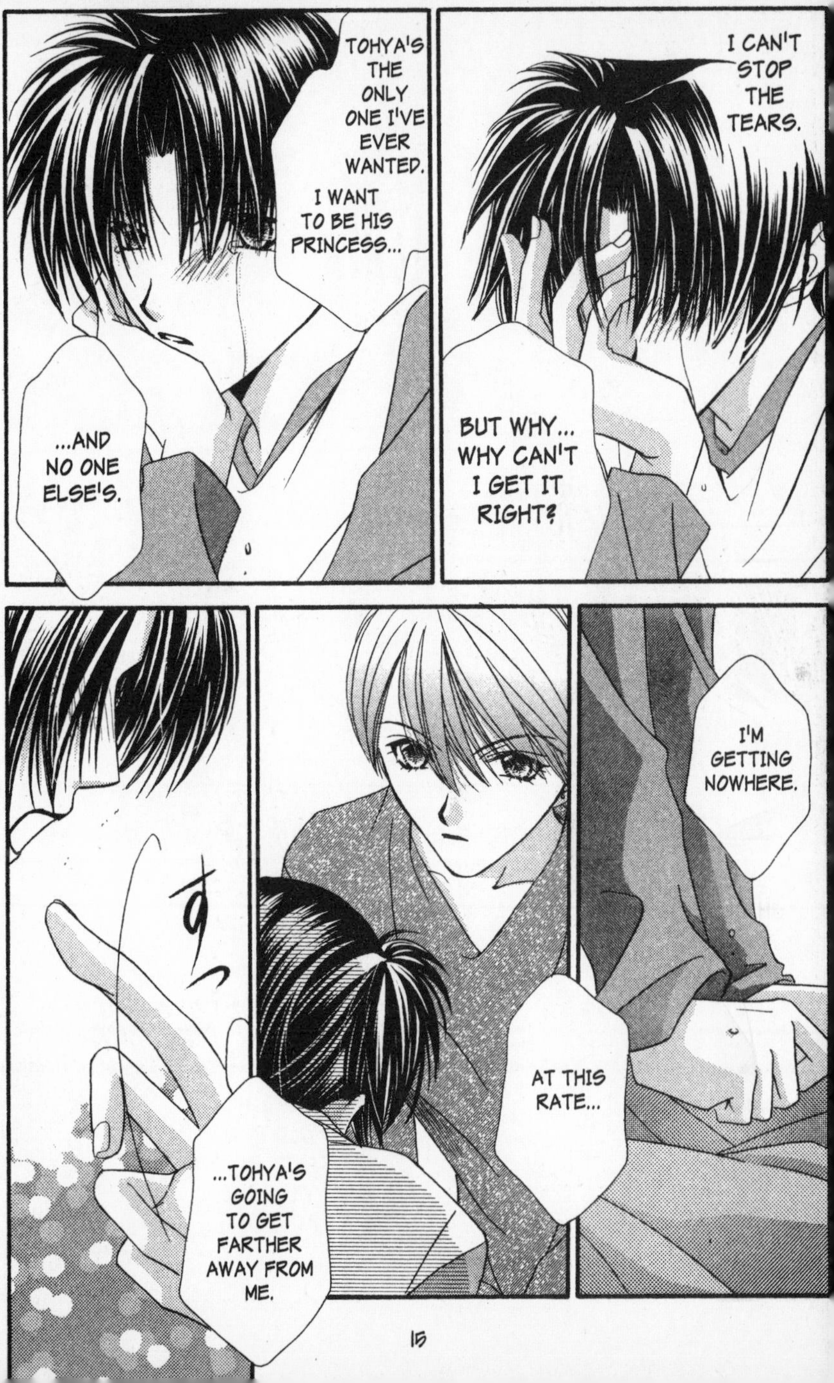
I CAN'T STOP THE TEARS.
BUT WHY... WHY CAN'T I GET IT RIGHT?
TOHYA'S THE ONLY ONE I'VE EVER WANTED.
I WANT TO BE HIS PRINCESS...
...AND NO ONE ELSE'S.
I'M GETTING NOWHERE.
AT THIS RATE...
...TOHYA'S GOING TO GET FARTHER AWAY FROM ME.
すっ

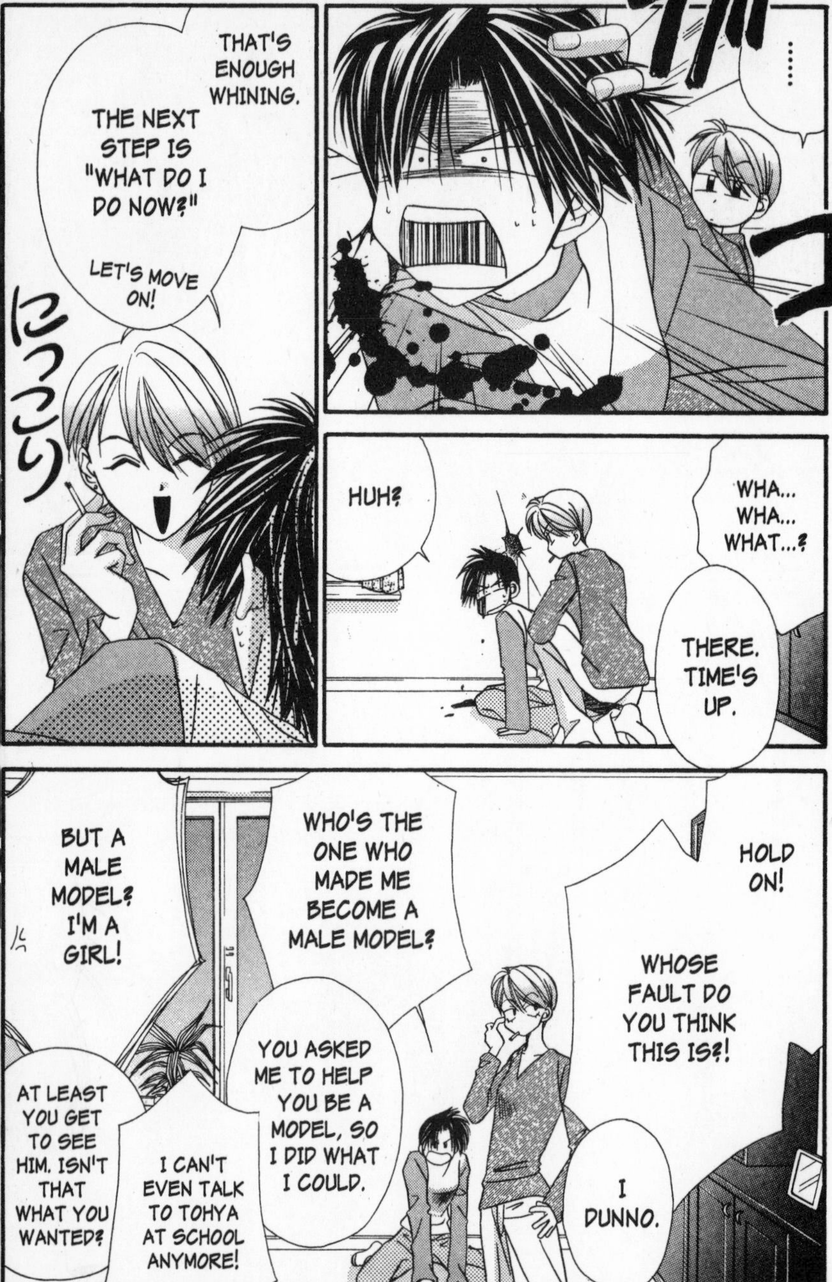
......
WHA... WHA... WHAT...?
THERE. TIME'S UP.
HUH?
THAT'S ENOUGH WHINING.
THE NEXT STEP IS "WHAT DO I DO NOW?"
LET'S MOVE ON!
にっこり
HOLD ON!
WHOSE FAULT DO YOU THINK THIS IS?!
I DUNNO.
WHO'S THE ONE WHO MADE ME BECOME A MALE MODEL?
YOU ASKED ME TO HELP YOU BE A MODEL, SO I DID WHAT I COULD.
BUT A MALE MODEL? I'M A GIRL!
I CAN'T EVEN TALK TO TOHYA AT SCHOOL ANYMORE!
AT LEAST YOU GET TO SEE HIM. ISN'T THAT WHAT YOU WANTED?

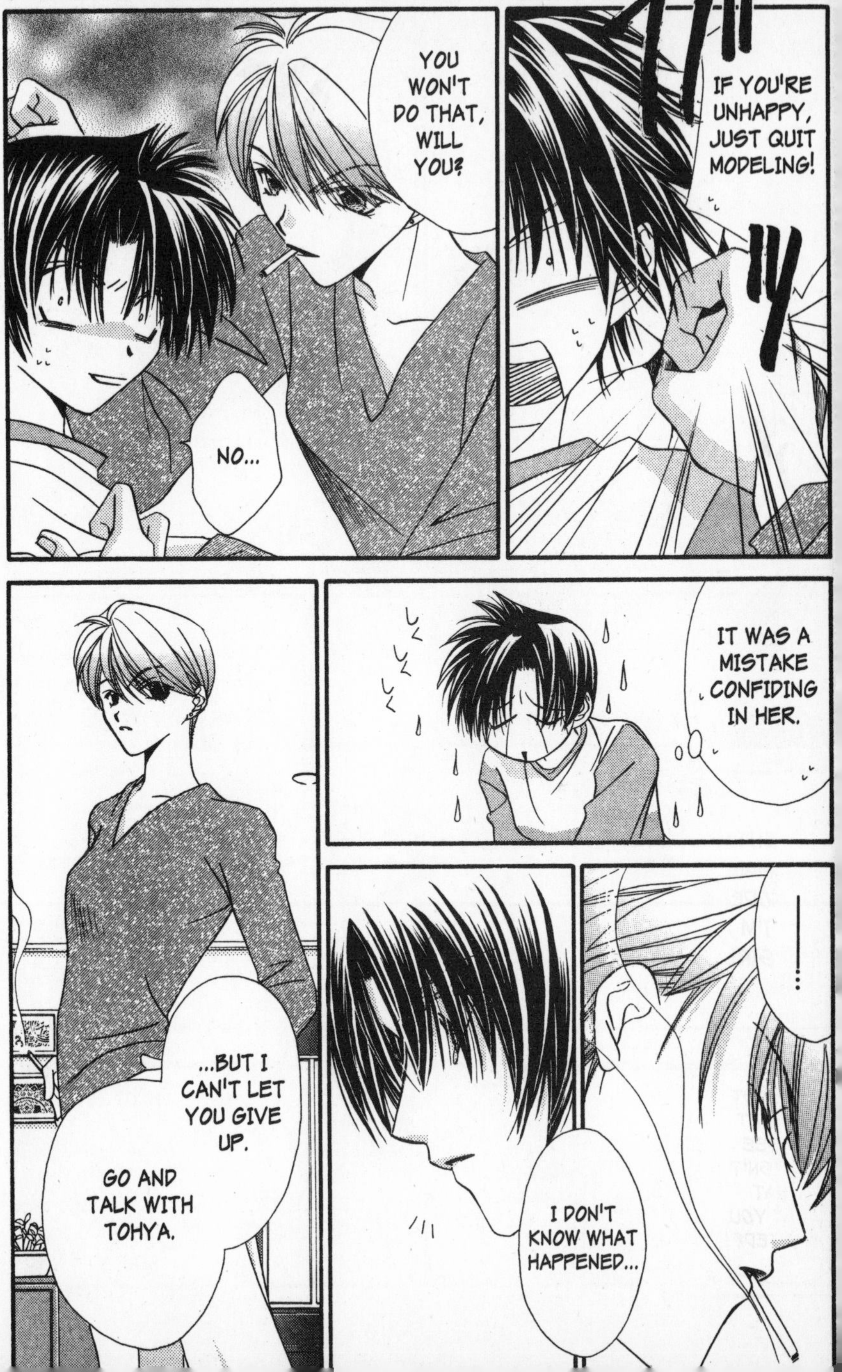
IF YOU'RE UNHAPPY, JUST QUIT MODELING!
YOU WON'T DO THAT, WILL YOU?
NO...
IT WAS A MISTAKE CONFIDING IN HER.
......!
I DON'T KNOW WHAT HAPPENED...
...BUT I CAN'T LET YOU GIVE UP.
GO AND TALK WITH TOHYA.

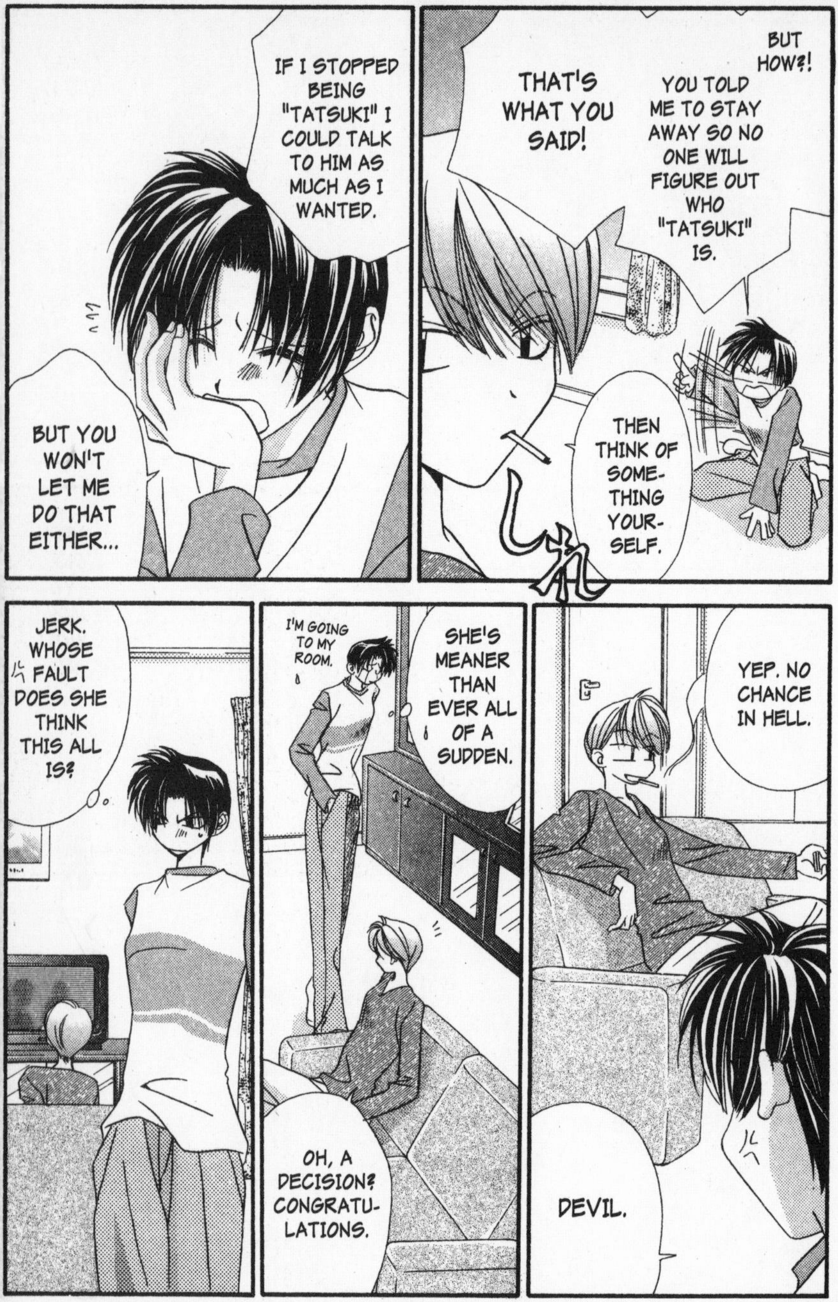
BUT HOW?!
YOU TOLD ME TO STAY AWAY SO NO ONE WILL FIGURE OUT WHO "TATSUKI" IS.
THAT'S WHAT YOU SAID!
THEN THINK OF SOME-THING YOUR-SELF.
IF I STOPPED BEING "TATSUKI" I COULD TALK TO HIM AS MUCH AS I WANTED.
BUT YOU WON'T LET ME DO THAT EITHER...
YEP. NO CHANCE IN HELL.
DEVIL.
SHE'S MEANER THAN EVER ALL OF A SUDDEN.
I'M GOING TO MY ROOM.
OH, A DECISION? CONGRATU-LATIONS.
JERK. WHOSE FAULT DOES SHE THINK THIS ALL IS?

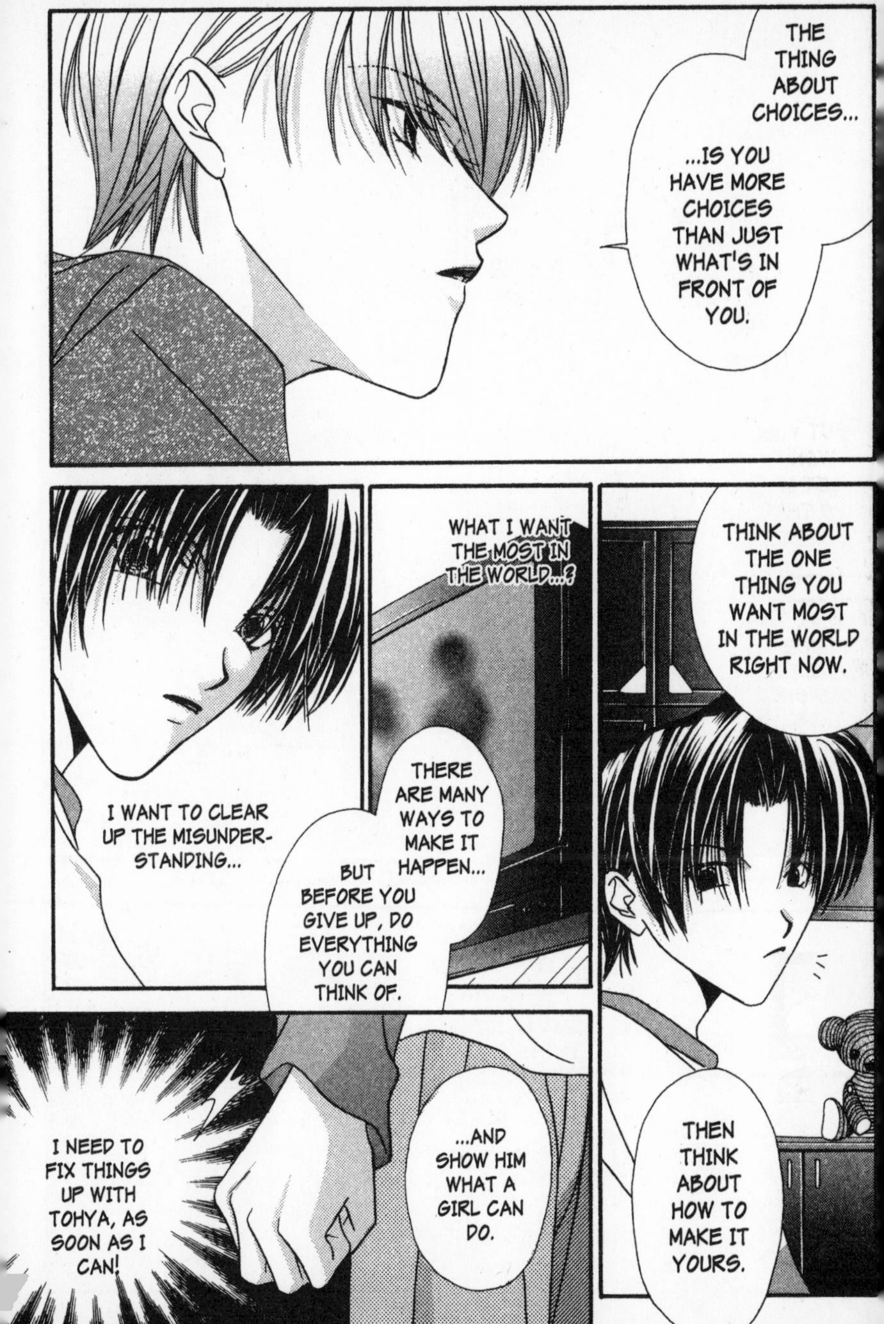
THE THING ABOUT CHOICES...
...IS YOU HAVE MORE CHOICES THAN JUST WHAT'S IN FRONT OF YOU.
THINK ABOUT THE ONE THING YOU WANT MOST IN THE WORLD RIGHT NOW.
THEN THINK ABOUT HOW TO MAKE IT YOURS.
WHAT I WANT THE MOST IN THE WORLD...?
THERE ARE MANY WAYS TO MAKE IT HAPPEN...
BUT BEFORE YOU GIVE UP, DO EVERYTHING YOU CAN THINK OF.
I WANT TO CLEAR UP THE MISUNDER-STANDING...
...AND SHOW HIM WHAT A GIRL CAN DO.
I NEED TO FIX THINGS UP WITH TOHYA, AS SOON AS I CAN!

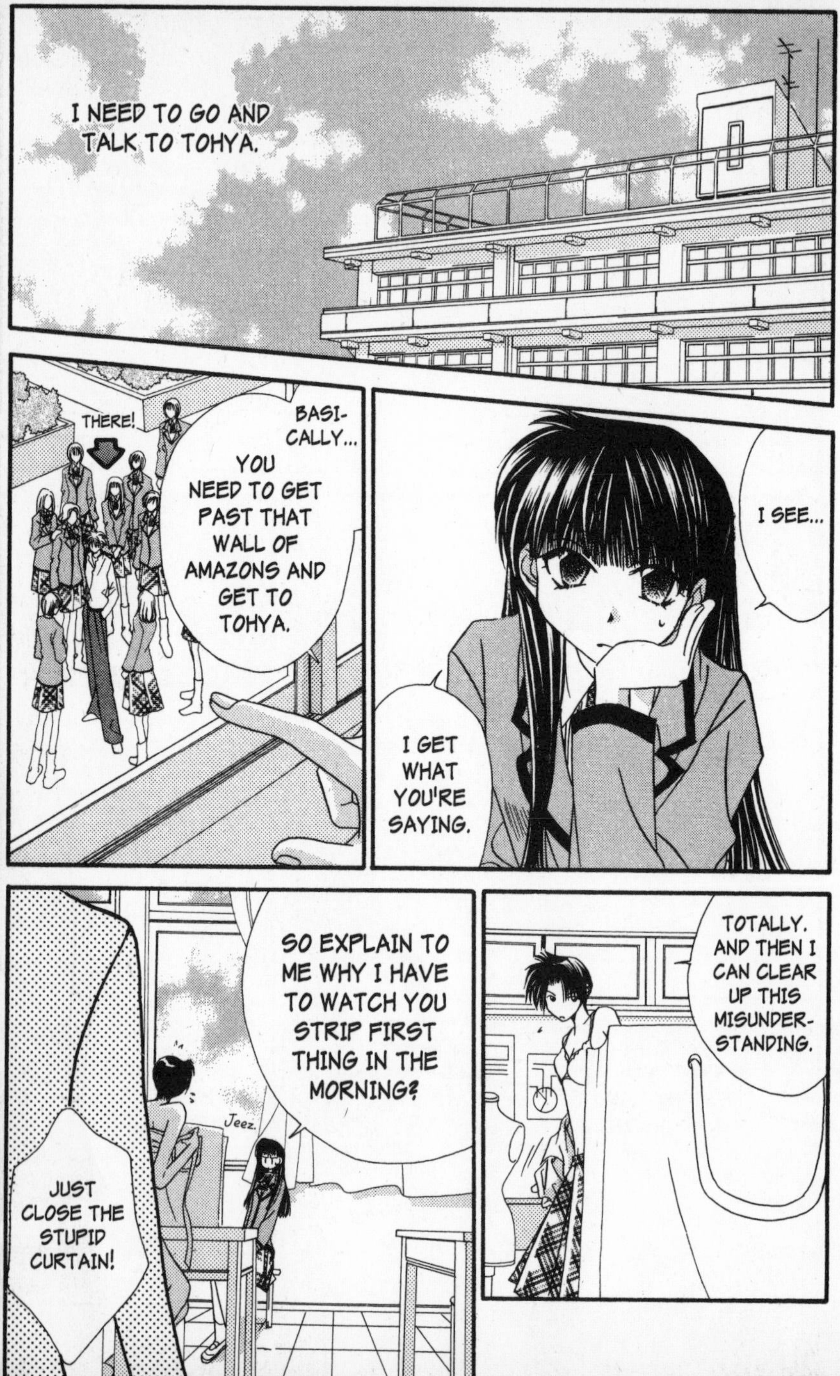
I NEED TO GO AND TALK TO TOHYA.
I SEE...
I GET WHAT YOU'RE SAYING.
BASI-CALLY...
YOU NEED TO GET PAST THAT WALL OF AMAZONS AND GET TO TOHYA.
THERE!
TOTALLY. AND THEN I CAN CLEAR UP THIS MISUNDER-STANDING.
SO EXPLAIN TO ME WHY I HAVE TO WATCH YOU STRIP FIRST THING IN THE MORNING?
Jeez.
JUST CLOSE THE STUPID CURTAIN!

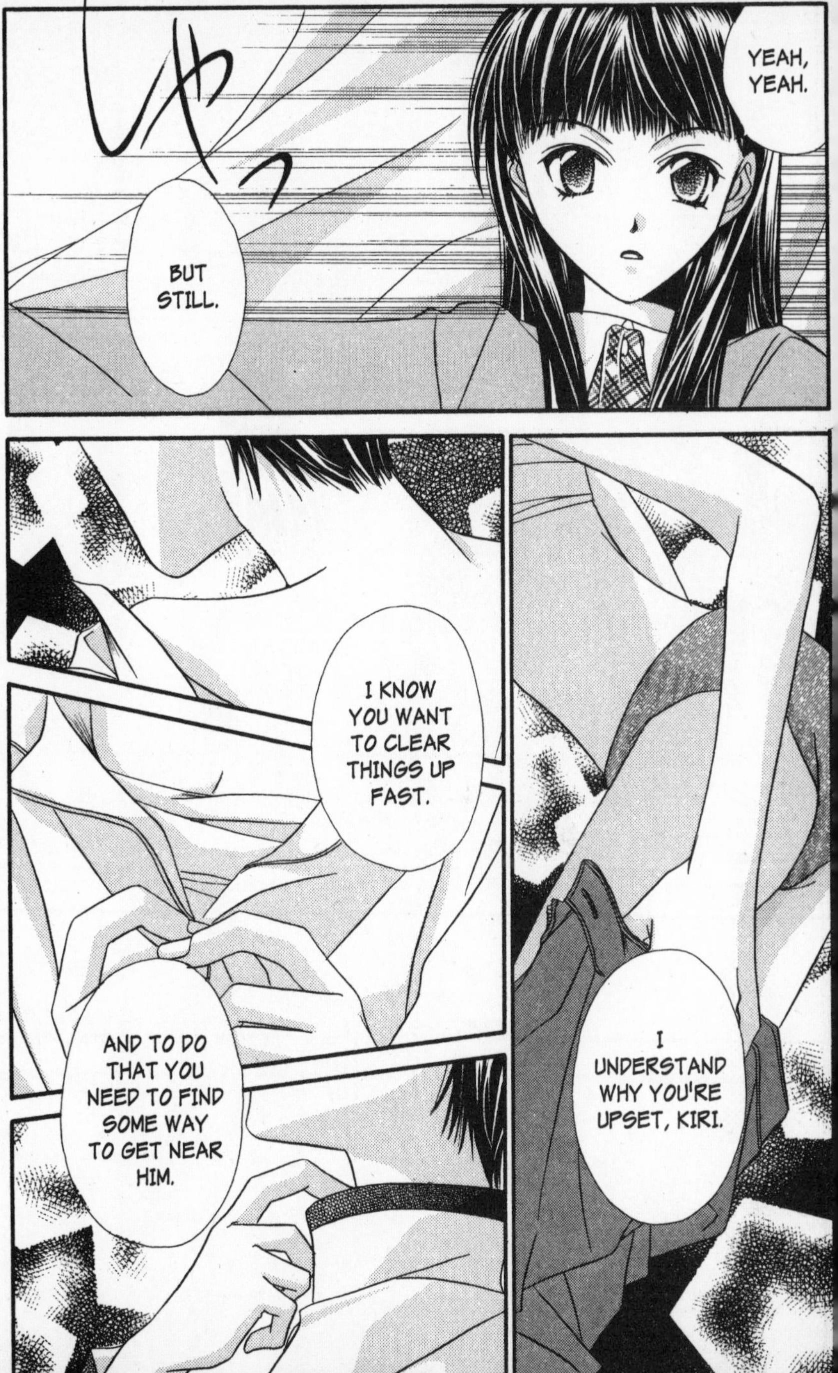
YEAH, YEAH.
BUT STILL.
I UNDERSTAND WHY YOU'RE UPSET, KIRI.
I KNOW YOU WANT TO CLEAR THINGS UP FAST.
AND TO DO THAT YOU NEED TO FIND SOME WAY TO GET NEAR HIM.

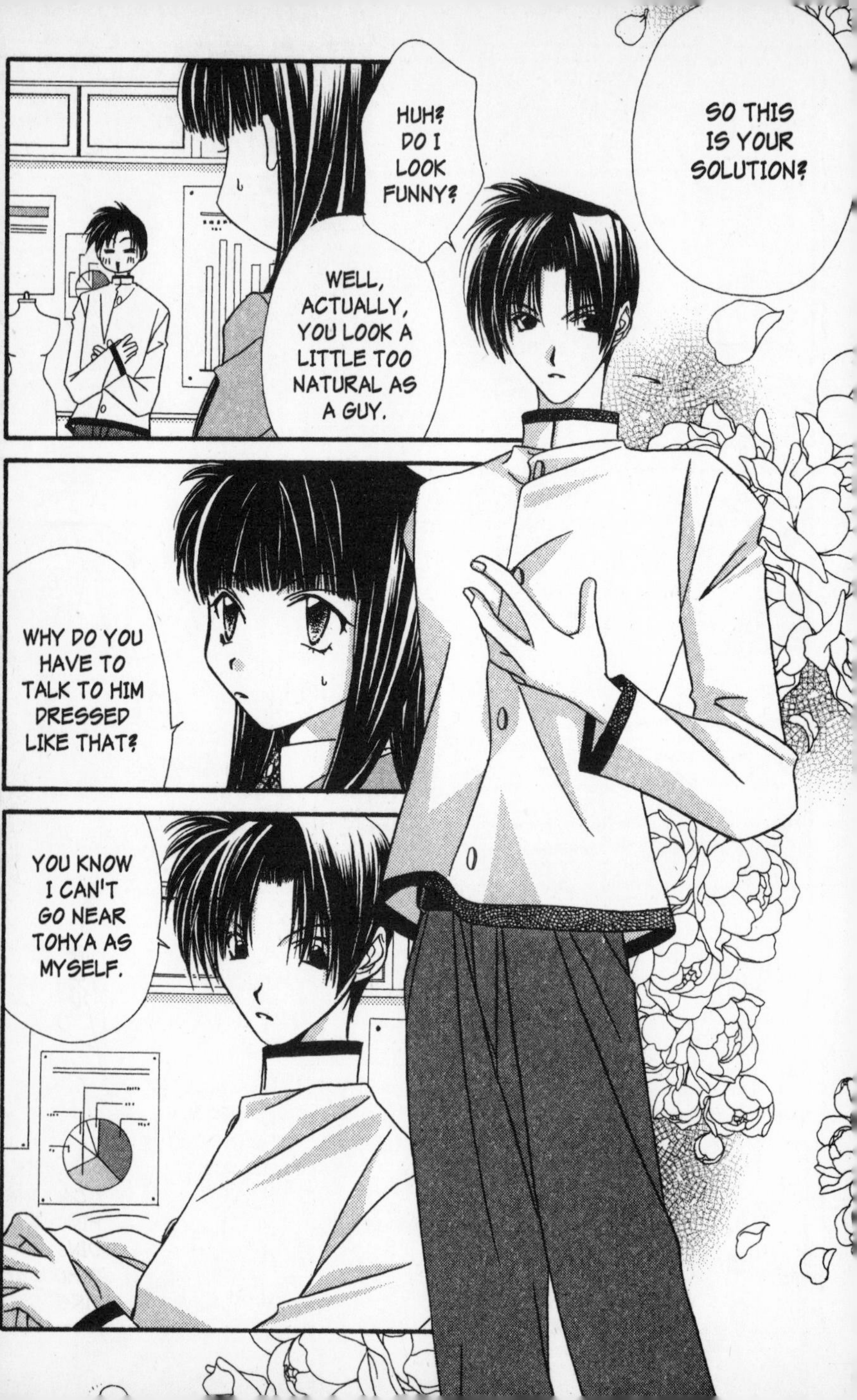
SO THIS IS YOUR SOLUTION?
HUH? DO I LOOK FUNNY?
WELL, ACTUALLY, YOU LOOK A LITTLE TOO NATURAL AS A GUY.
WHY DO YOU HAVE TO TALK TO HIM DRESSED LIKE THAT?
YOU KNOW I CAN'T GO NEAR TOHYA AS MYSELF.

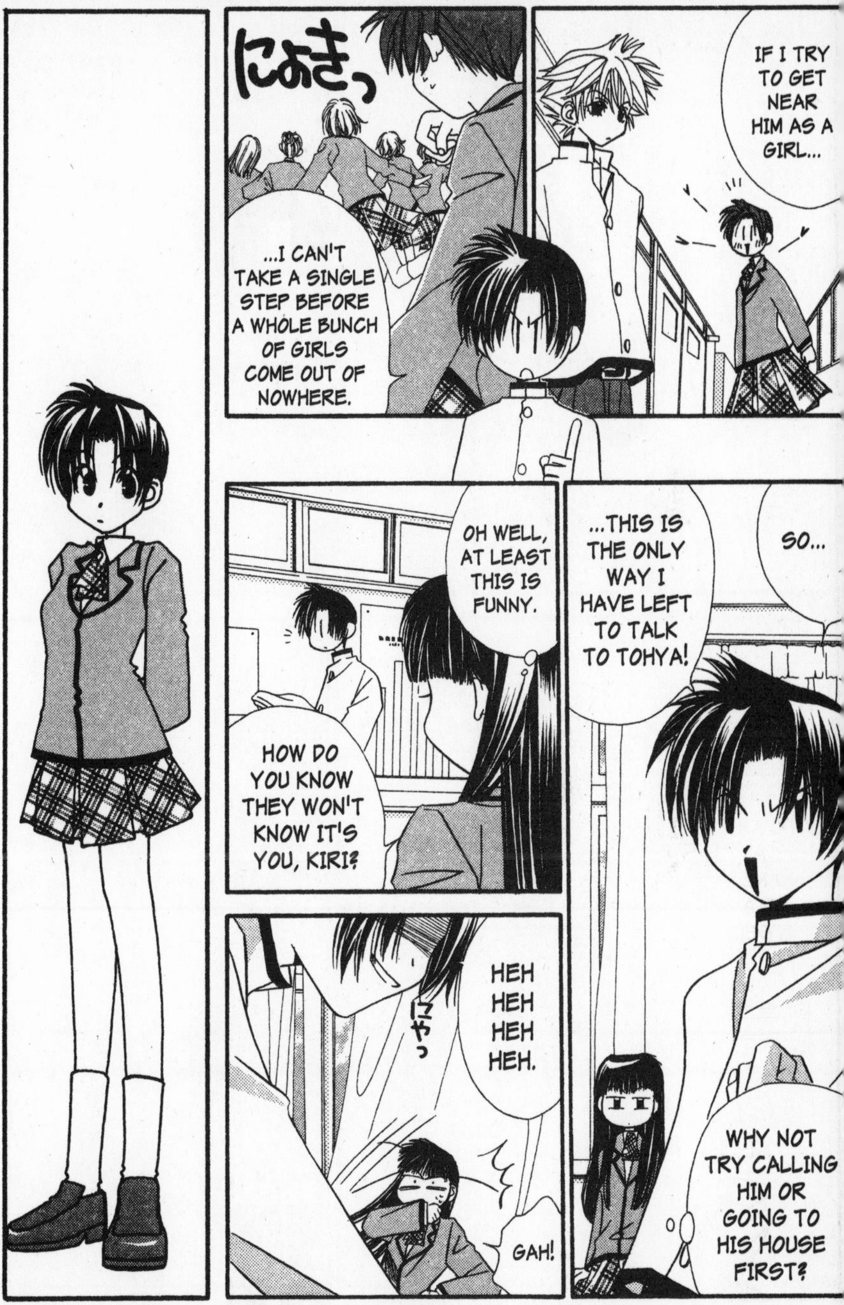
IF I TRY TO GET NEAR HIM AS A GIRL...
にょきっ
...I CAN'T TAKE A SINGLE STEP BEFORE A WHOLE BUNCH OF GIRLS COME OUT OF NOWHERE.
SO...
...THIS IS THE ONLY WAY I HAVE LEFT TO TALK TO TOHYA!
WHY NOT TRY CALLING HIM OR GOING TO HIS HOUSE FIRST?
OH WELL, AT LEAST THIS IS FUNNY.
HOW DO YOU KNOW THEY WON'T KNOW IT'S YOU, KIRI?
にやっ
HEH HEH HEH HEH.
GAH!

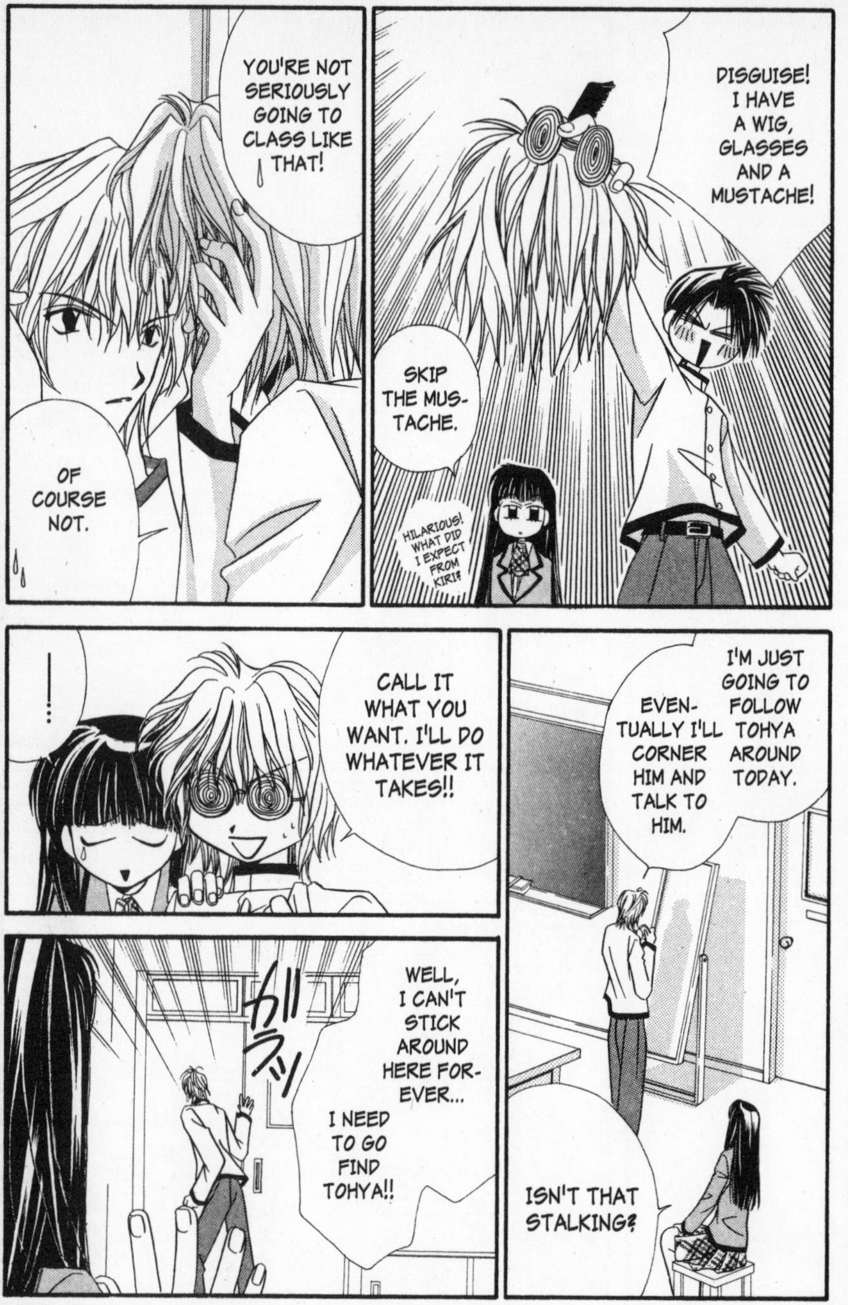
DISGUISE! I HAVE A WIG, GLASSES AND A MUSTACHE!
SKIP THE MUS-TACHE.
HILARIOUS! WHAT DID I EXPECT FROM KIRI?
YOU'RE NOT SERIOUSLY GOING TO CLASS LIKE THAT!
OF COURSE NOT.
I'M JUST GOING TO FOLLOW TOHYA AROUND TODAY.
EVEN-TUALLY I'LL CORNER HIM AND TALK TO HIM.
ISN'T THAT STALKING?
CALL IT WHAT YOU WANT. I'LL DO WHATEVER IT TAKES!!
—!
ガラッ
WELL, I CAN'T STICK AROUND HERE FOR-EVER...
I NEED TO GO FIND TOHYA!!

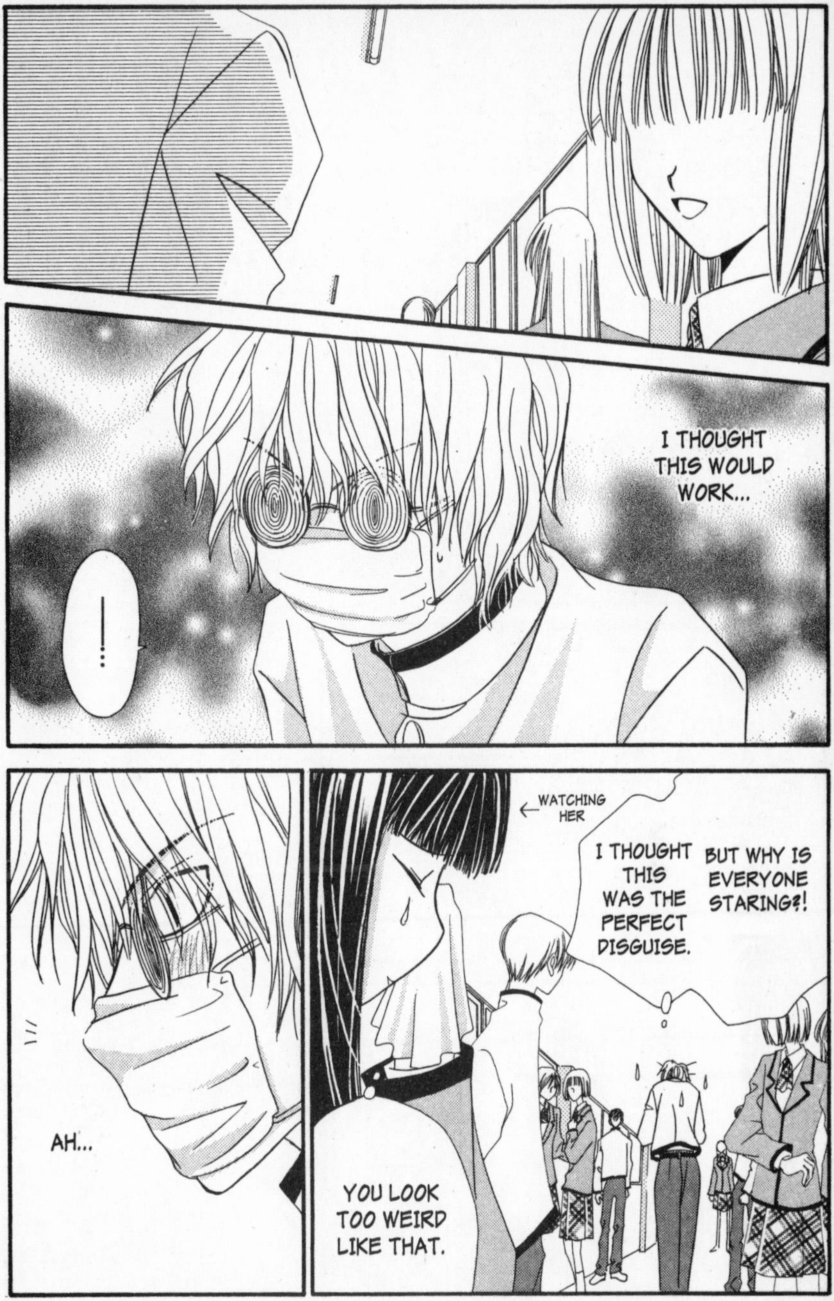
I THOUGHT THIS WOULD WORK...
!...
WATCHING HER
I THOUGHT THIS WAS THE PERFECT DISGUISE. BUT WHY IS EVERYONE STARING?!
YOU LOOK TOO WEIRD LIKE THAT.
AH...

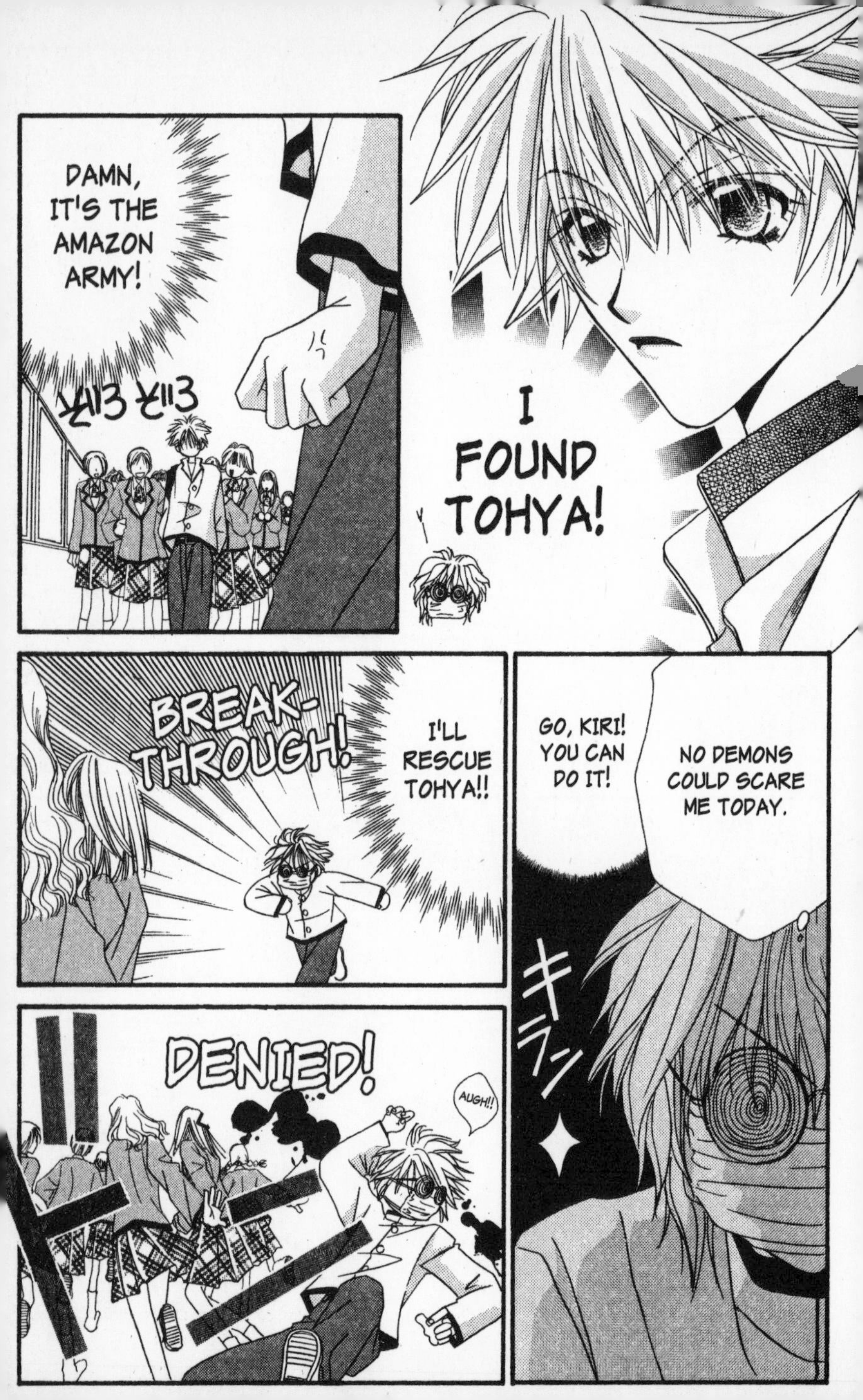
I FOUND TOHYA!
DAMN, IT'S THE AMAZON ARMY!
ぞろぞろ
NO DEMONS COULD SCARE ME TODAY.
GO, KIRI! YOU CAN DO IT!
キラン
BREAK-THROUGH!
I'LL RESCUE TOHYA!!
DENIED!
AUGH!!

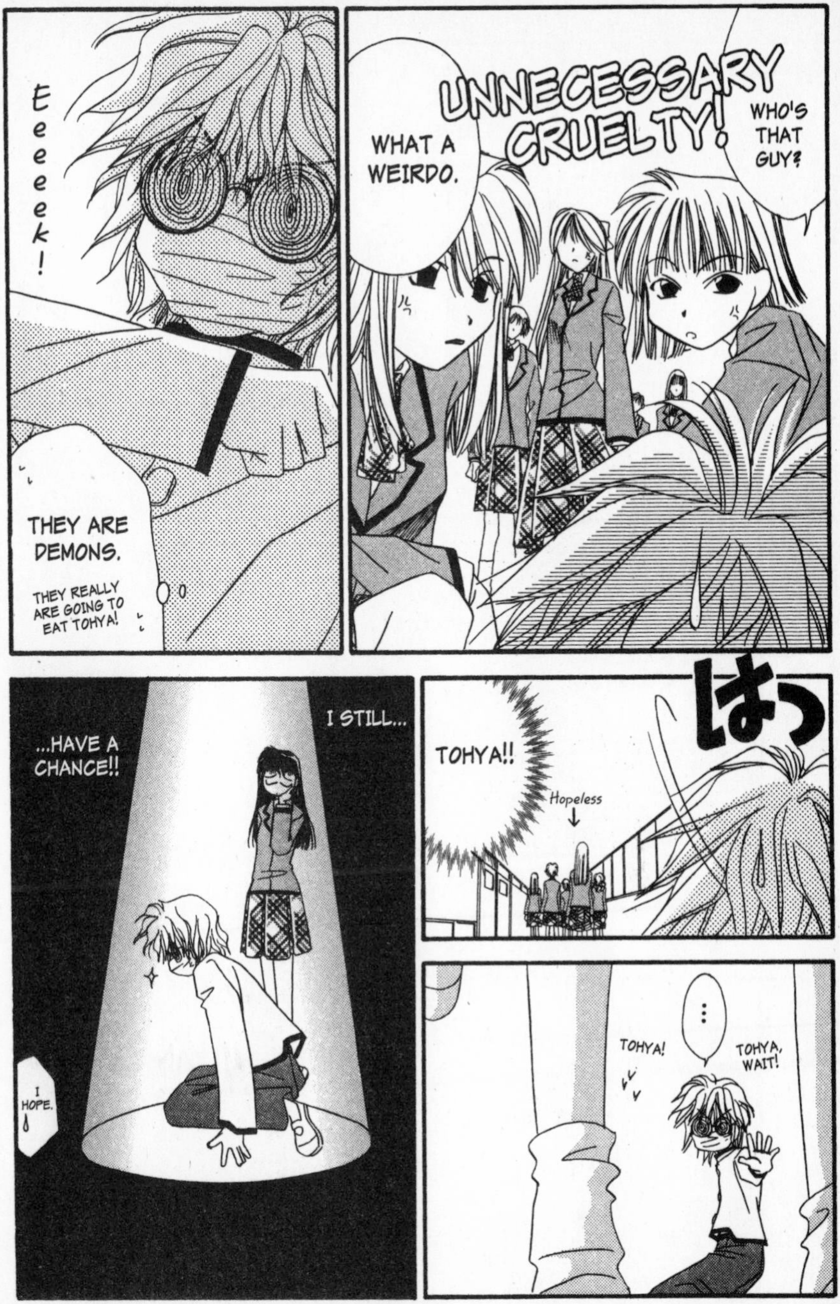
WHO'S THAT GUY?
UNNECESSARY CRUELTY!
WHAT A WEIRDO.
Eeeeek!
THEY ARE DEMONS.
THEY REALLY ARE GOING TO EAT TOHYA!
はっ
TOHYA!!
Hopeless
TOHYA, WAIT!
...
TOHYA!
I STILL...
...HAVE A CHANCE!!
I HOPE.

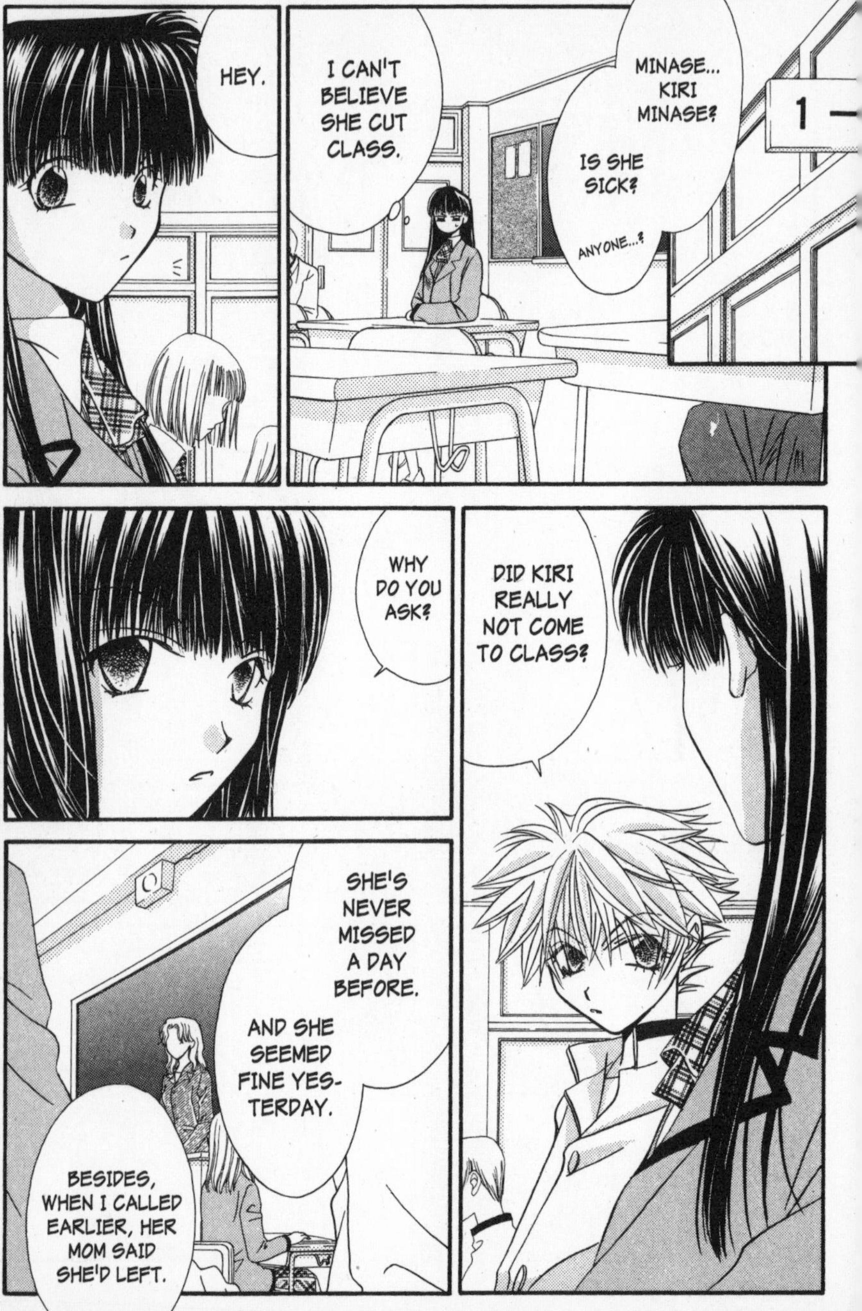
MINASE... KIRI MINASE?
IS SHE SICK?
ANYONE...?
I CAN'T BELIEVE SHE CUT CLASS.
HEY.
DID KIRI REALLY NOT COME TO CLASS?
WHY DO YOU ASK?
SHE'S NEVER MISSED A DAY BEFORE.
AND SHE SEEMED FINE YES-TERDAY.
BESIDES, WHEN I CALLED EARLIER, HER MOM SAID SHE'D LEFT.

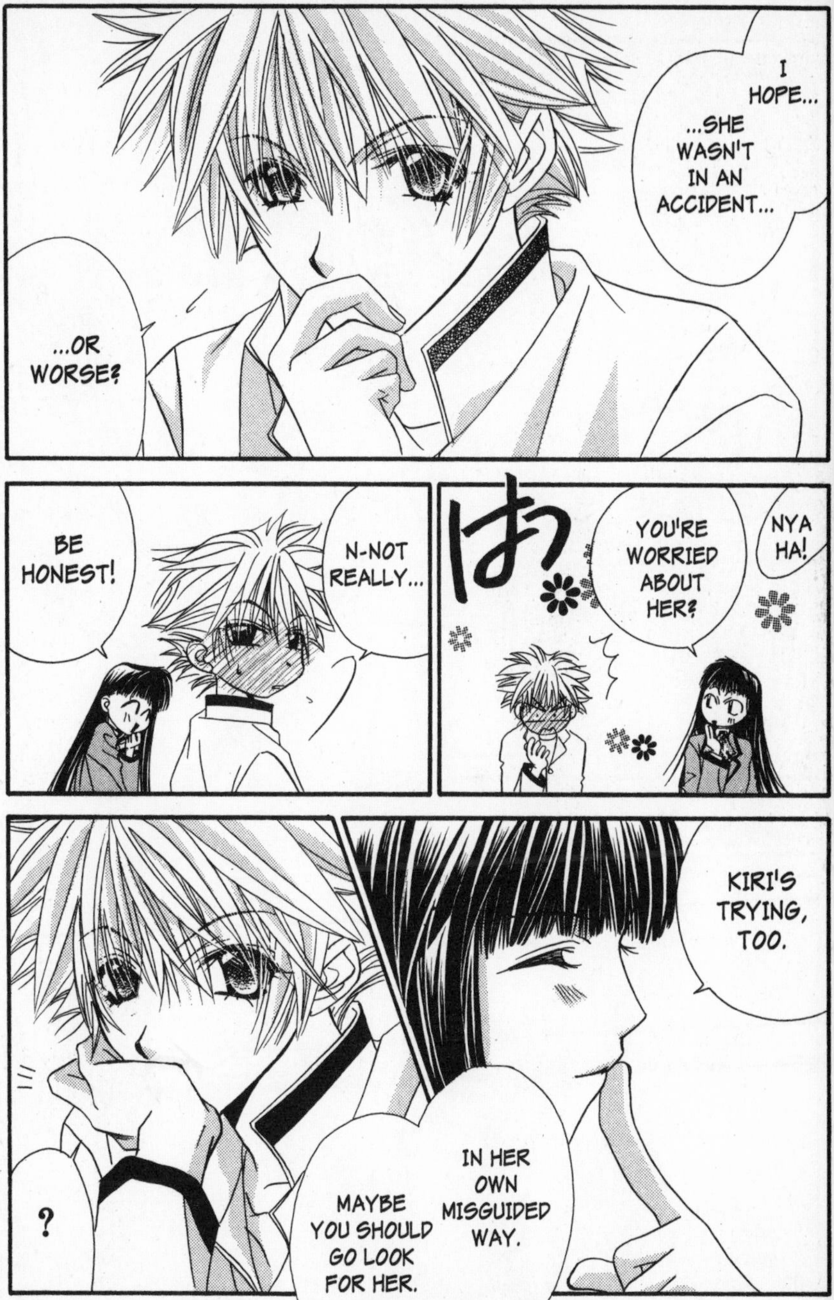
I HOPE...
...SHE WASN'T IN AN ACCIDENT...
...OR WORSE?
NYA HA!
YOU'RE WORRIED ABOUT HER?
は
N-NOT REALLY...
BE HONEST!
KIRI'S TRYING, TOO.
IN HER OWN MISGUIDED WAY.
MAYBE YOU SHOULD GO LOOK FOR HER.
?

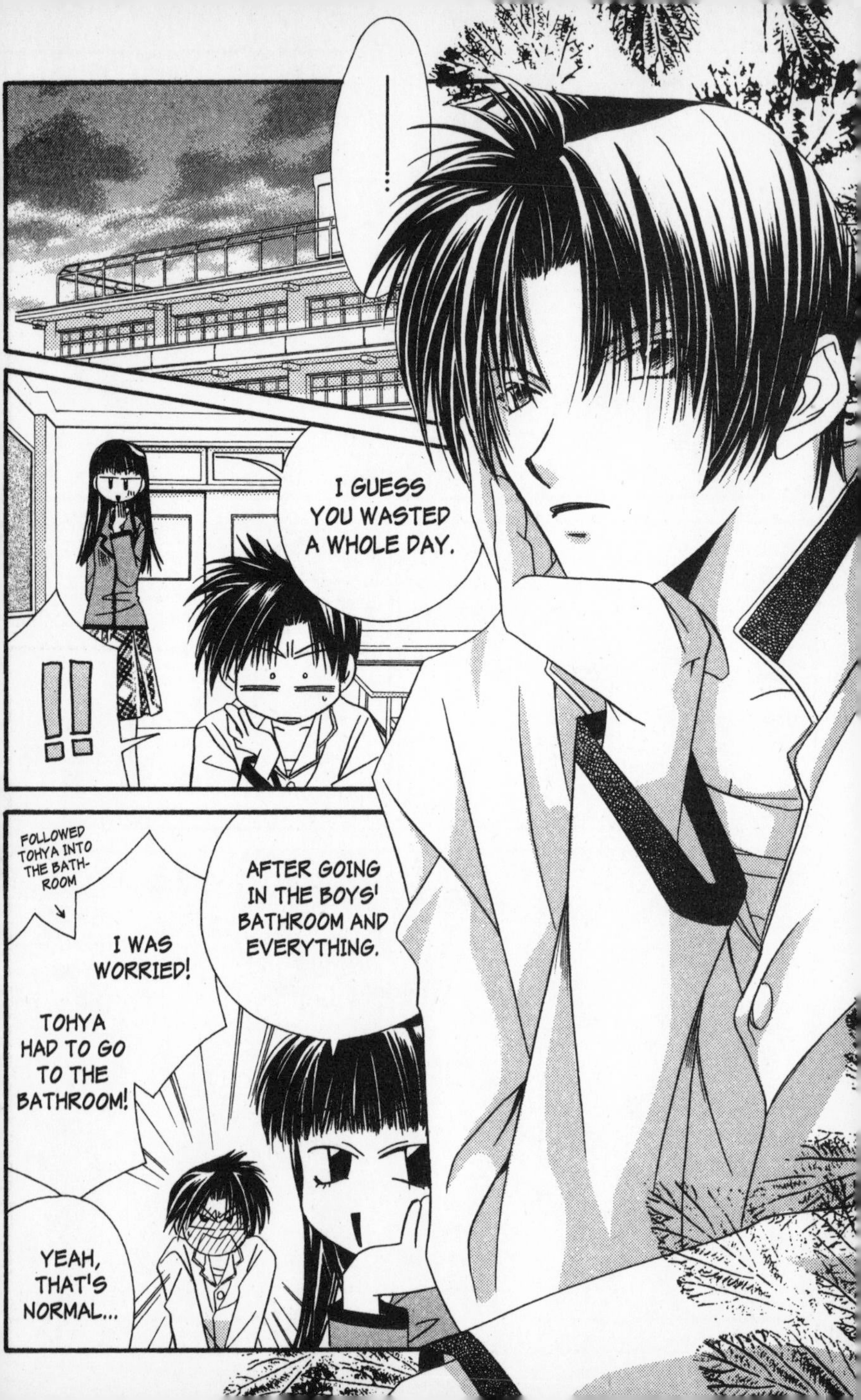
......!
I GUESS YOU WASTED A WHOLE DAY.
AFTER GOING IN THE BOYS' BATHROOM AND EVERYTHING.
!!
I WAS WORRIED!
TOHYA HAD TO GO TO THE BATHROOM!
FOLLOWED TOHYA INTO THE BATH-ROOM
YEAH, THAT'S NORMAL...

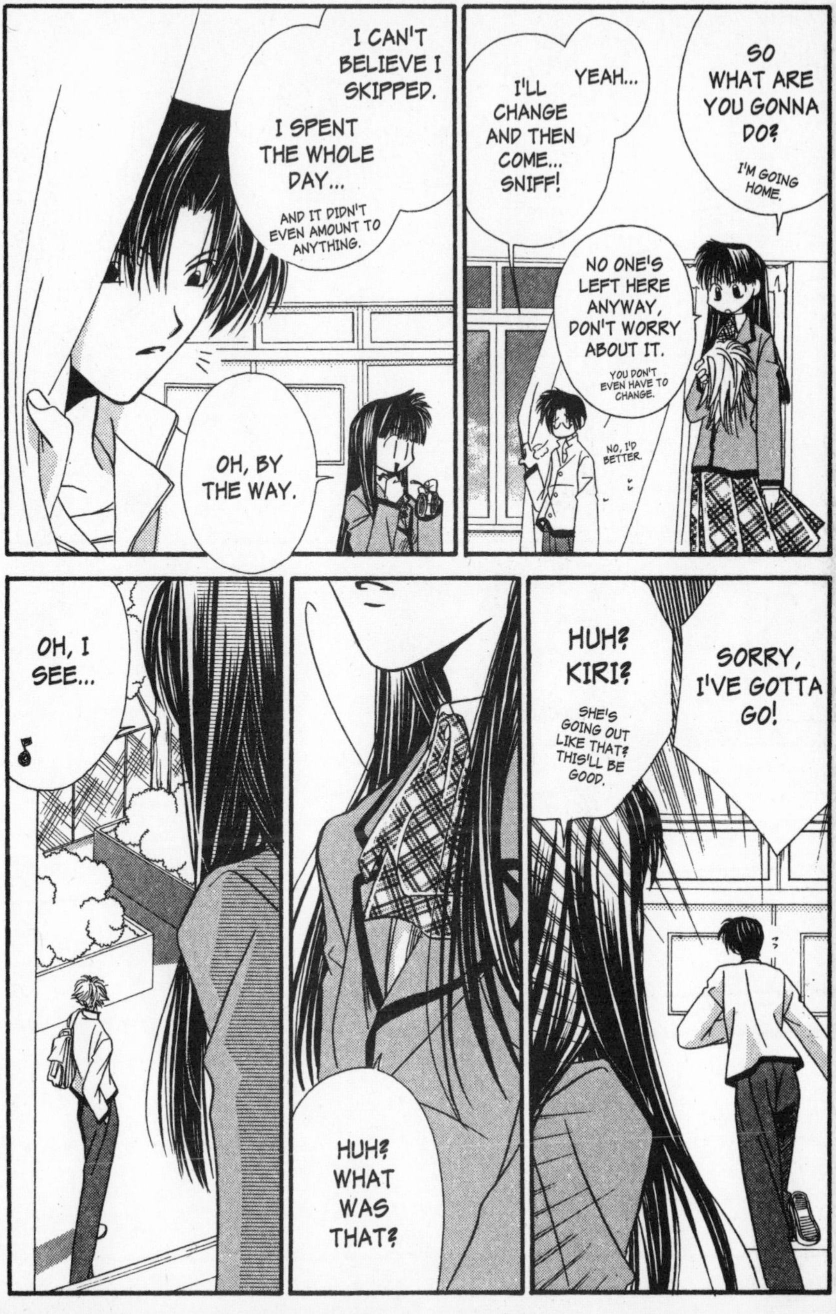
SO WHAT ARE YOU GONNA DO?
I'M GOING HOME.
YEAH... I'LL CHANGE AND THEN COME... SNIFF!
NO ONE'S LEFT HERE ANYWAY, DON'T WORRY ABOUT IT.
YOU DON'T EVEN HAVE TO CHANGE.
NO, I'D BETTER.
I CAN'T BELIEVE I SKIPPED.
I SPENT THE WHOLE DAY...
AND IT DIDN'T EVEN AMOUNT TO ANYTHING.
OH, BY THE WAY.
SORRY, I'VE GOTTA GO!
HUH? KIRI?
SHE'S GOING OUT LIKE THAT? THIS'LL BE GOOD.
HUH? WHAT WAS THAT?
OH, I SEE...

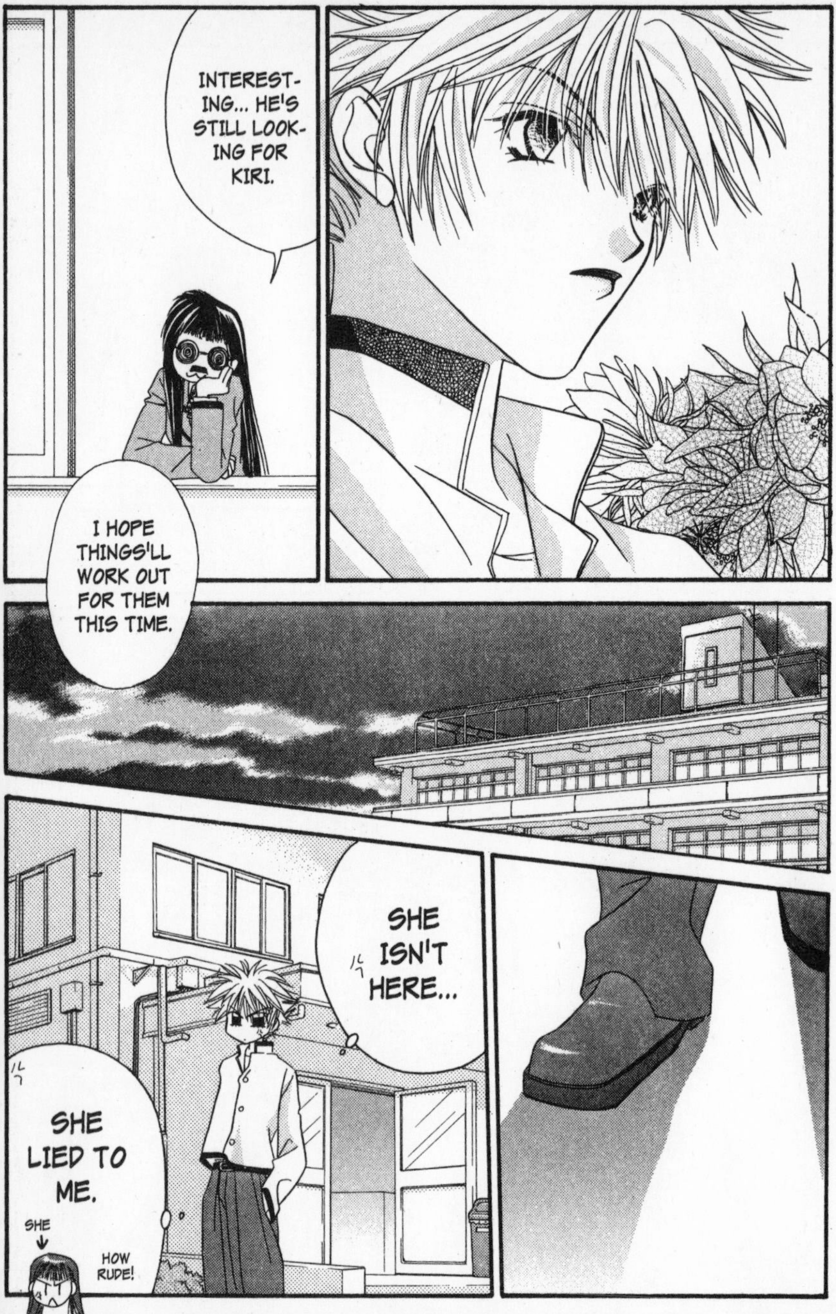
INTEREST-ING... HE'S STILL LOOK-ING FOR KIRI.
I HOPE THINGS'LL WORK OUT FOR THEM THIS TIME.
SHE ISN'T HERE...
SHE LIED TO ME.
SHE
HOW RUDE!

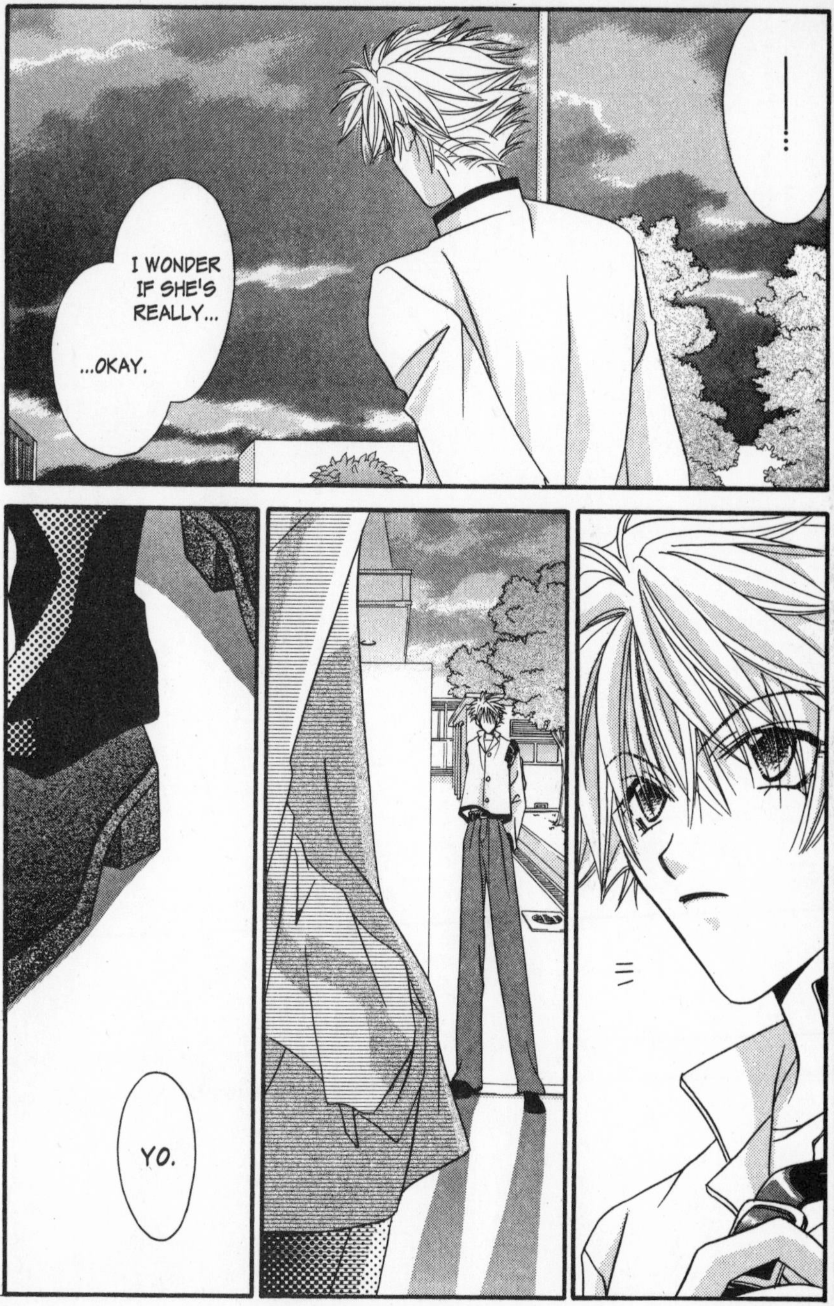
—...
I WONDER IF SHE'S REALLY...
...OKAY.
YO.

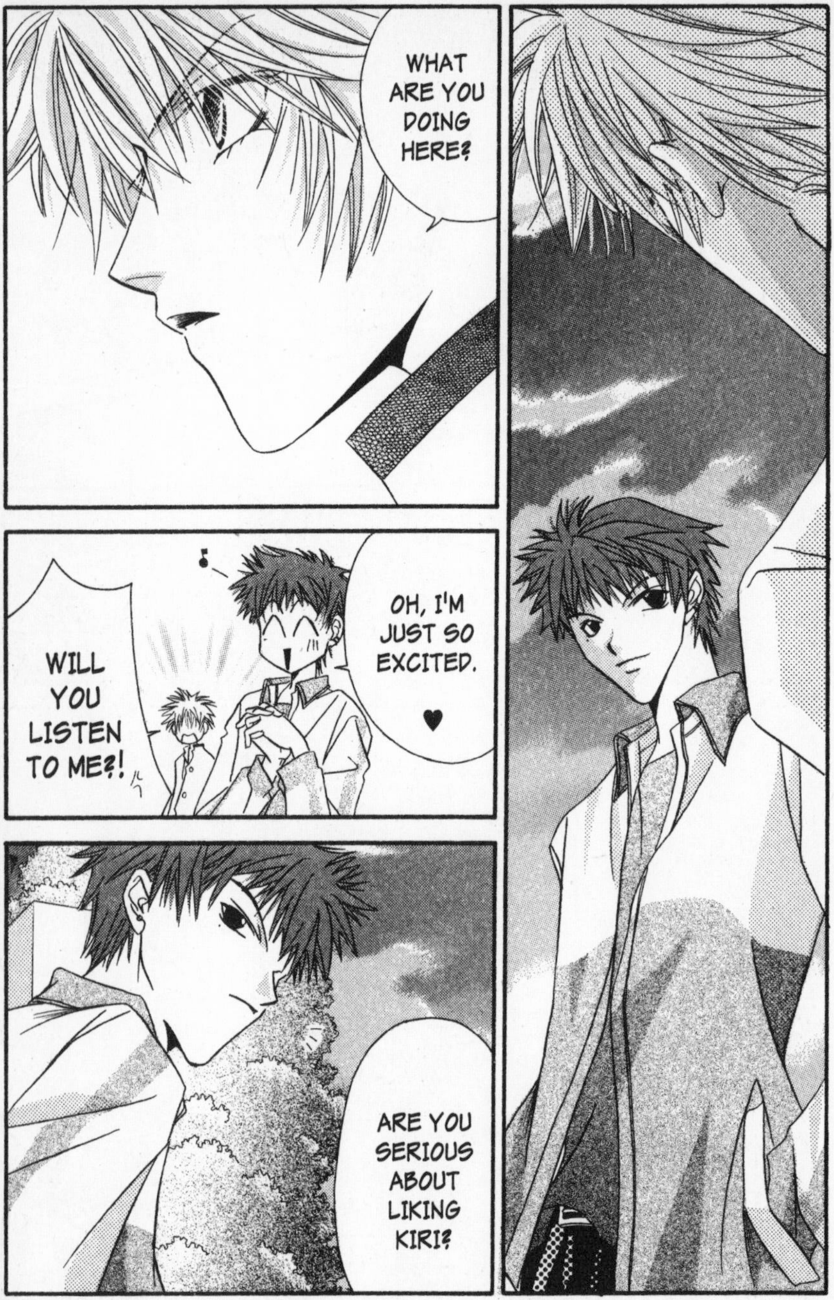
WHAT ARE YOU DOING HERE?
OH, I'M JUST SO EXCITED. ♥
WILL YOU LISTEN TO ME?!
ARE YOU SERIOUS ABOUT LIKING KIRI?

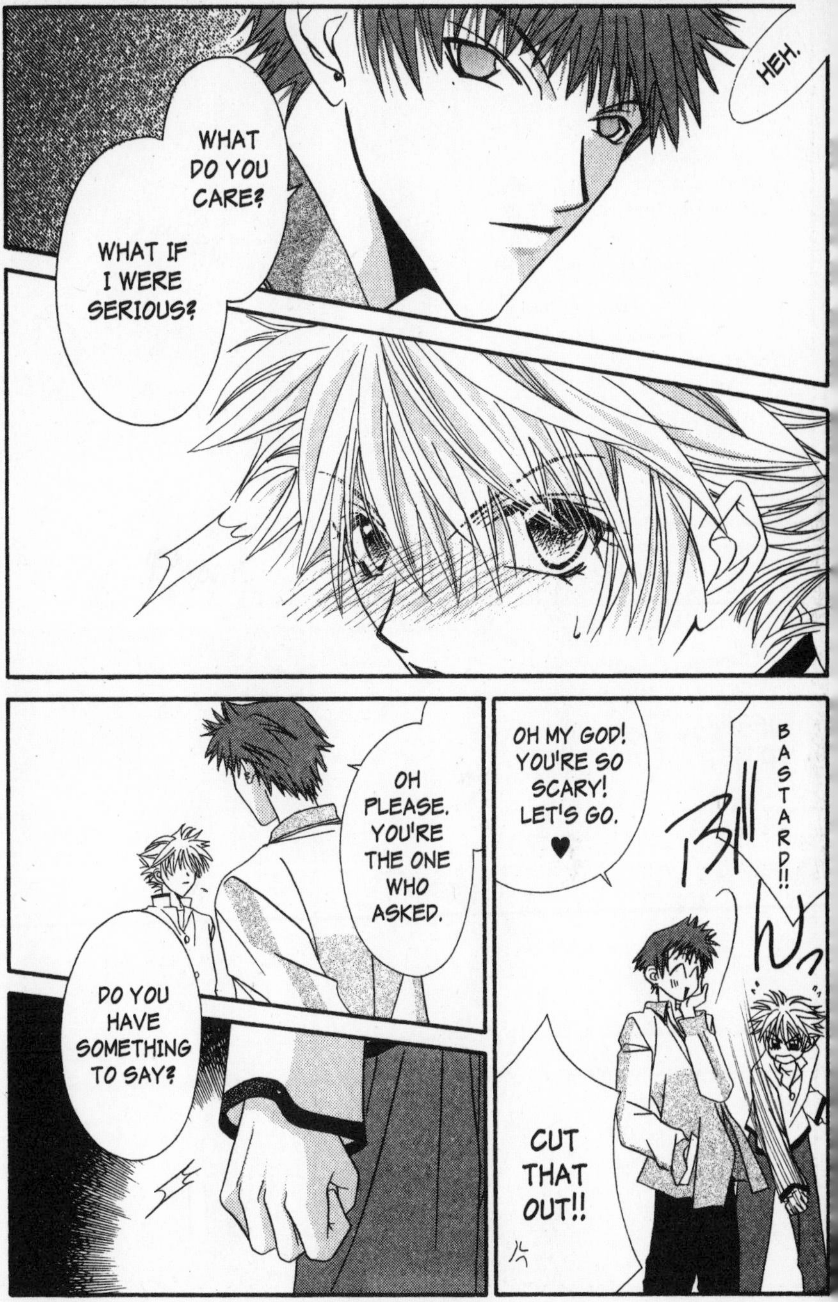
HEH.
WHAT DO YOU CARE?
WHAT IF I WERE SERIOUS?
OH MY GOD! YOU'RE SO SCARY! LET'S GO. ♥
BASTARD!!
CUT THAT OUT!!
OH PLEASE. YOU'RE THE ONE WHO ASKED.
DO YOU HAVE SOMETHING TO SAY?

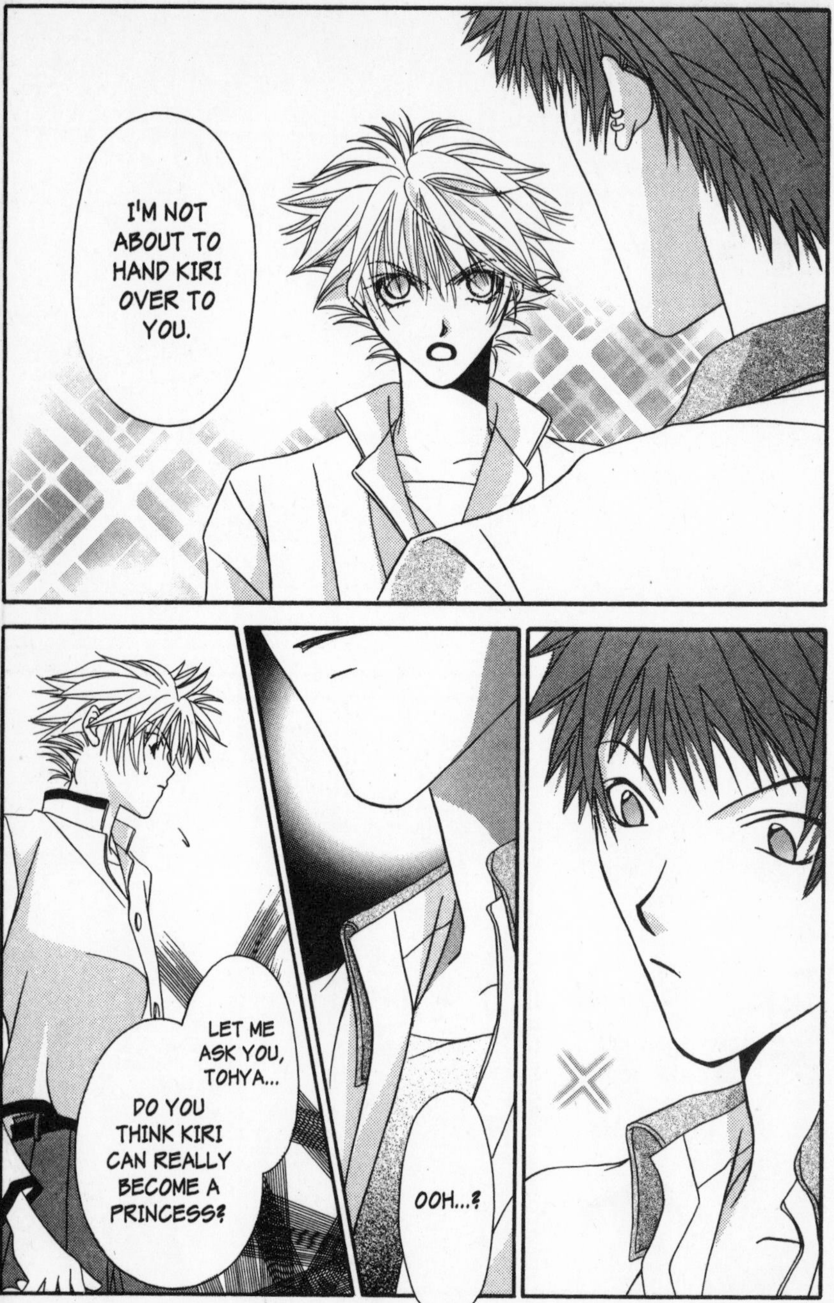
I'M NOT ABOUT TO HAND KIRI OVER TO YOU.
OOH...?
LET ME ASK YOU, TOHYA...
DO YOU THINK KIRI CAN REALLY BECOME A PRINCESS?

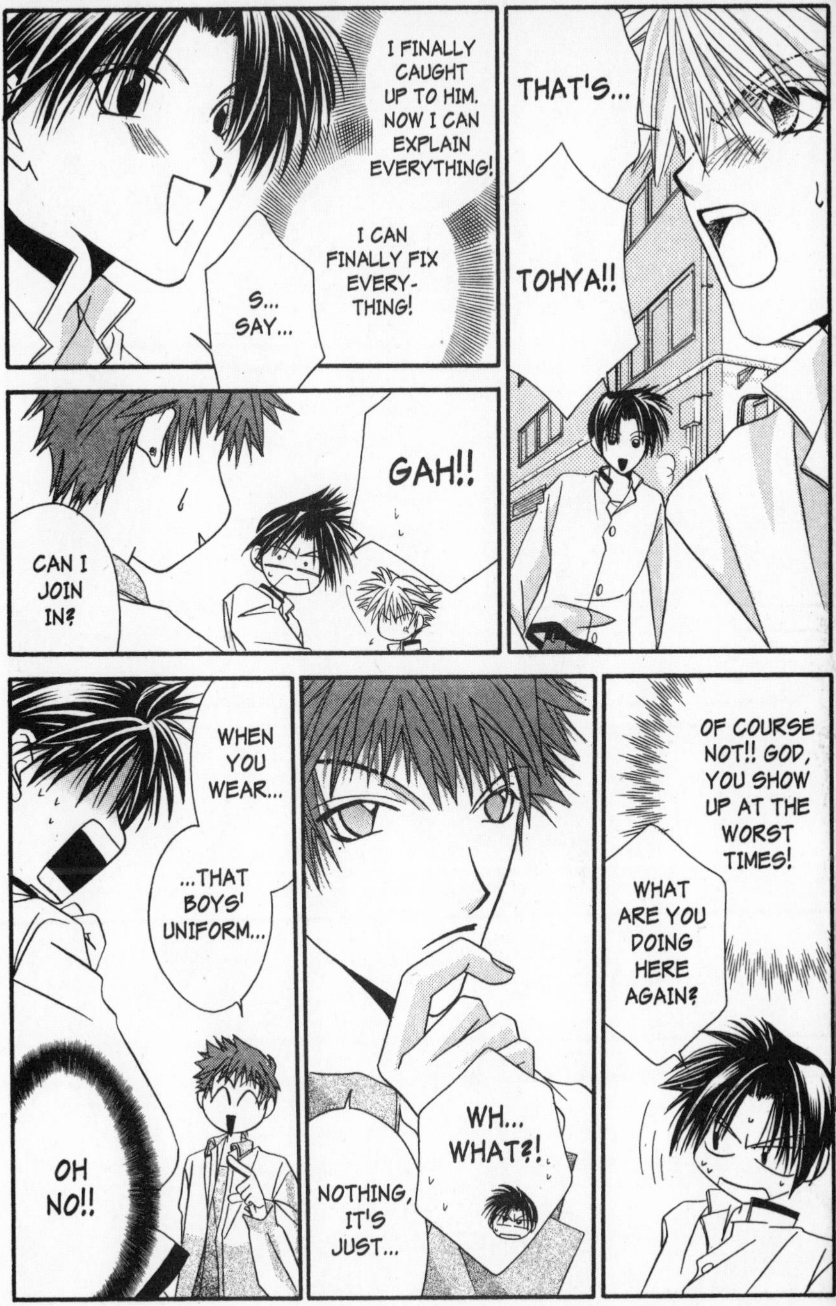
THAT'S...
TOHYA!!
I FINALLY CAUGHT UP TO HIM. NOW I CAN EXPLAIN EVERYTHING!
I CAN FINALLY FIX EVERYTHING!
S... SAY...
GAH!!
CAN I JOIN IN?
OF COURSE NOT!! GOD, YOU SHOW UP AT THE WORST TIMES!
WHAT ARE YOU DOING HERE AGAIN?
WH... WHAT?!
NOTHING, IT'S JUST...
WHEN YOU WEAR...
...THAT BOYS' UNIFORM...
OH NO!!

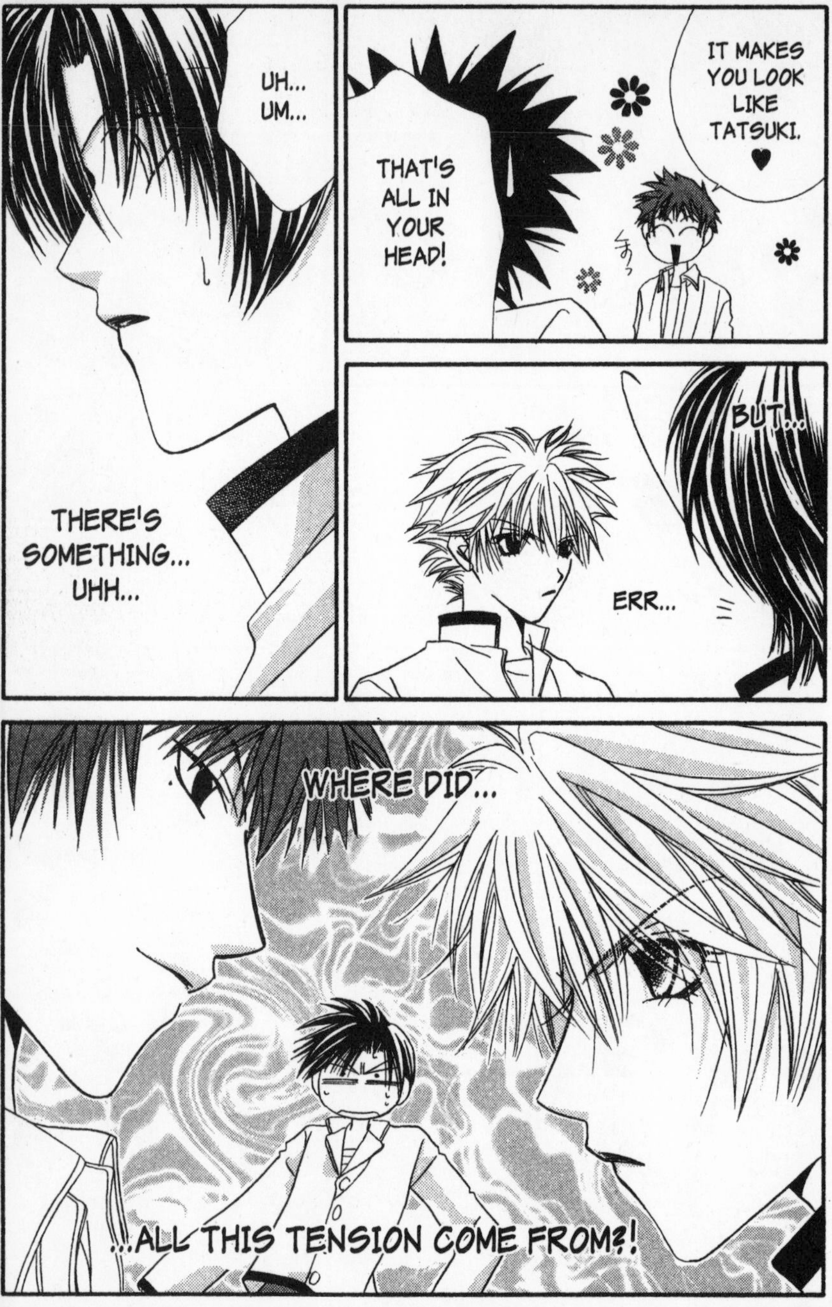
IT MAKES YOU LOOK LIKE TATSUKI. ♥
THAT'S ALL IN YOUR HEAD!
BUT...
ERR...
UH... UM...
THERE'S SOMETHING... UHH...
WHERE DID...
...ALL THIS TENSION COME FROM?!

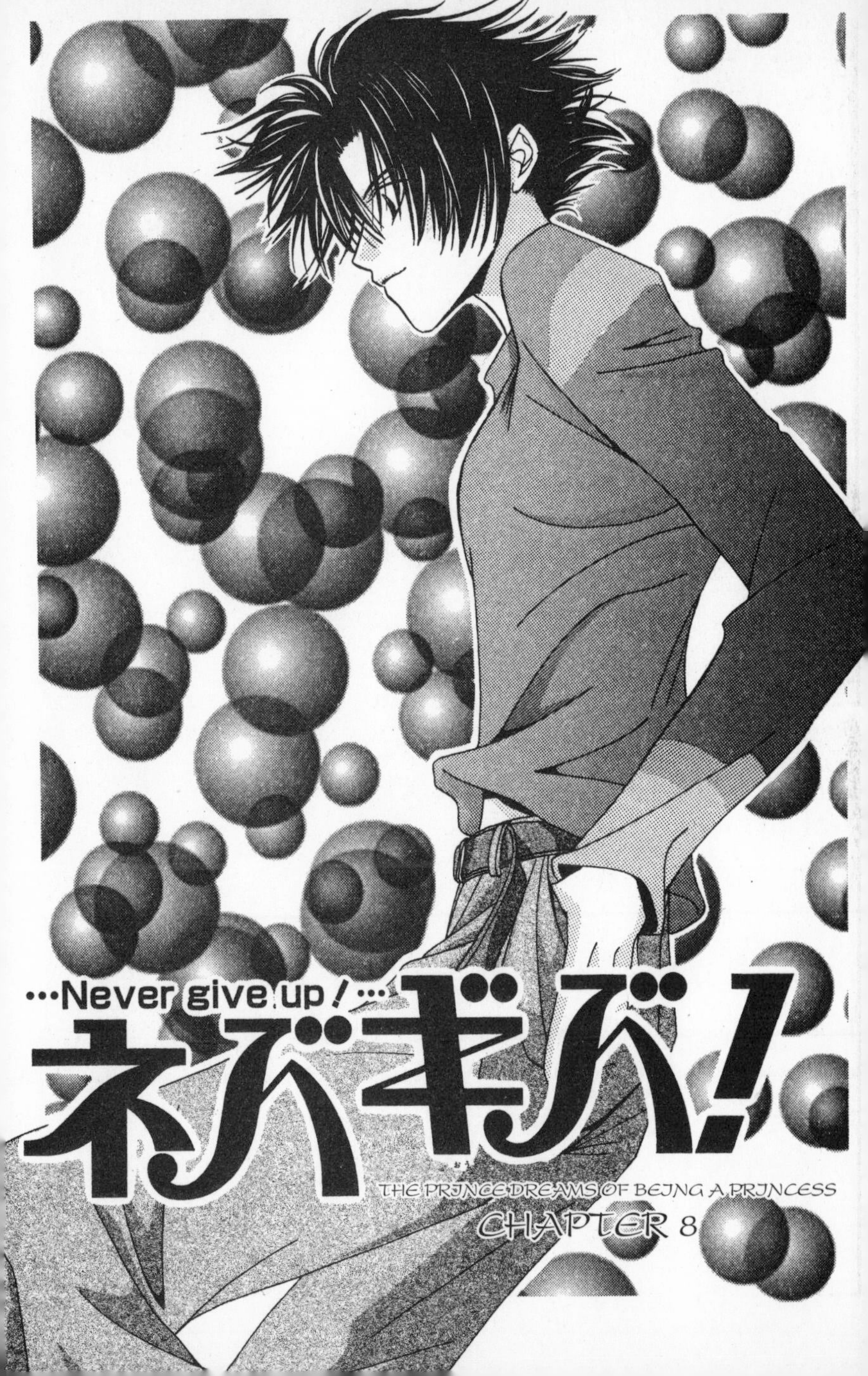
…Never give up!…
ネバギバ!
THE PRINCE DREAMS OF BEING A PRINCESS
CHAPTER 8

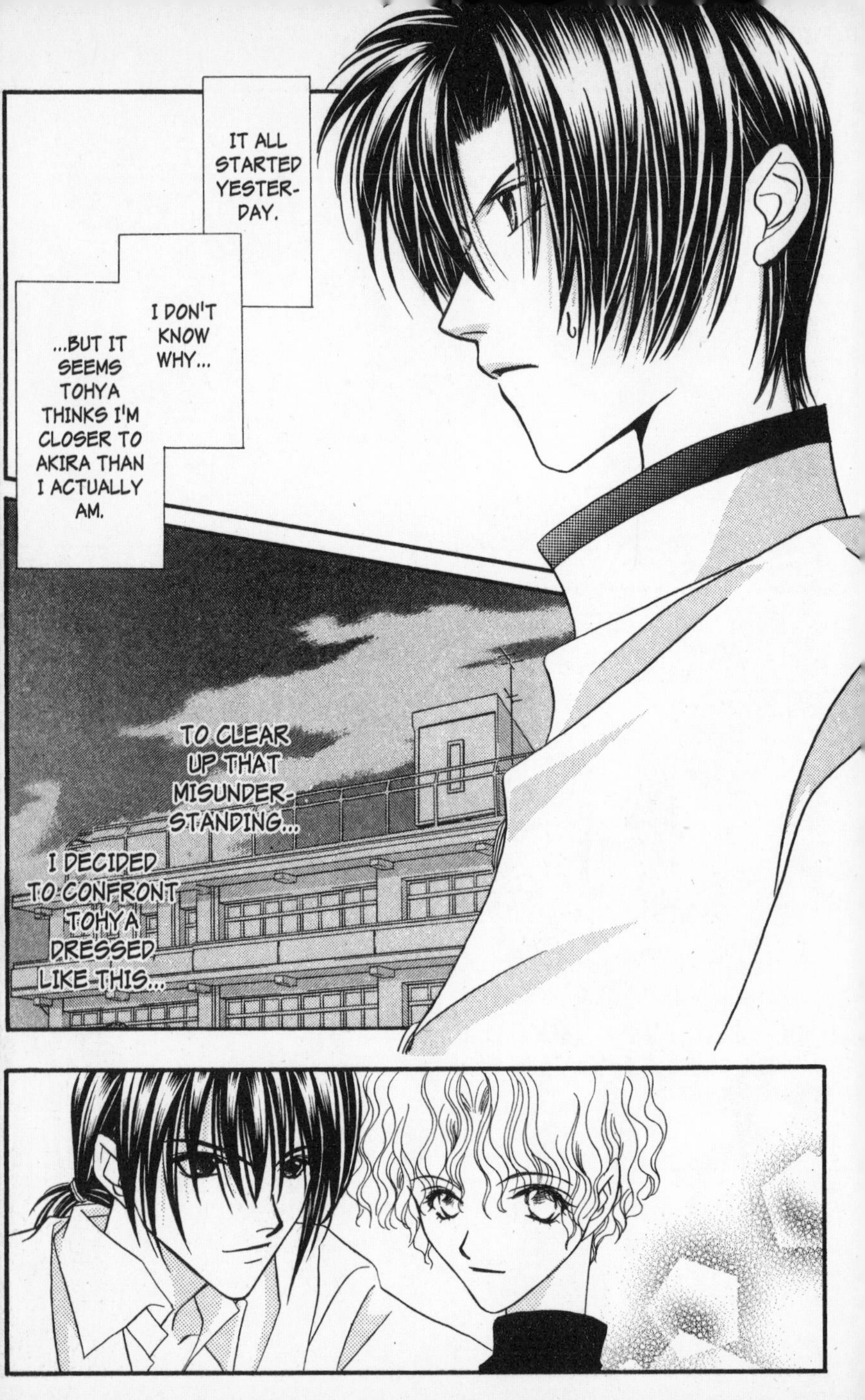
IT ALL STARTED YESTER-DAY.
I DON'T KNOW WHY...
...BUT IT SEEMS TOHYA THINKS I'M CLOSER TO AKIRA THAN I ACTUALLY AM.
TO CLEAR UP THAT MISUNDER-STANDING...
I DECIDED TO CONFRONT TOHYA DRESSED LIKE THIS...

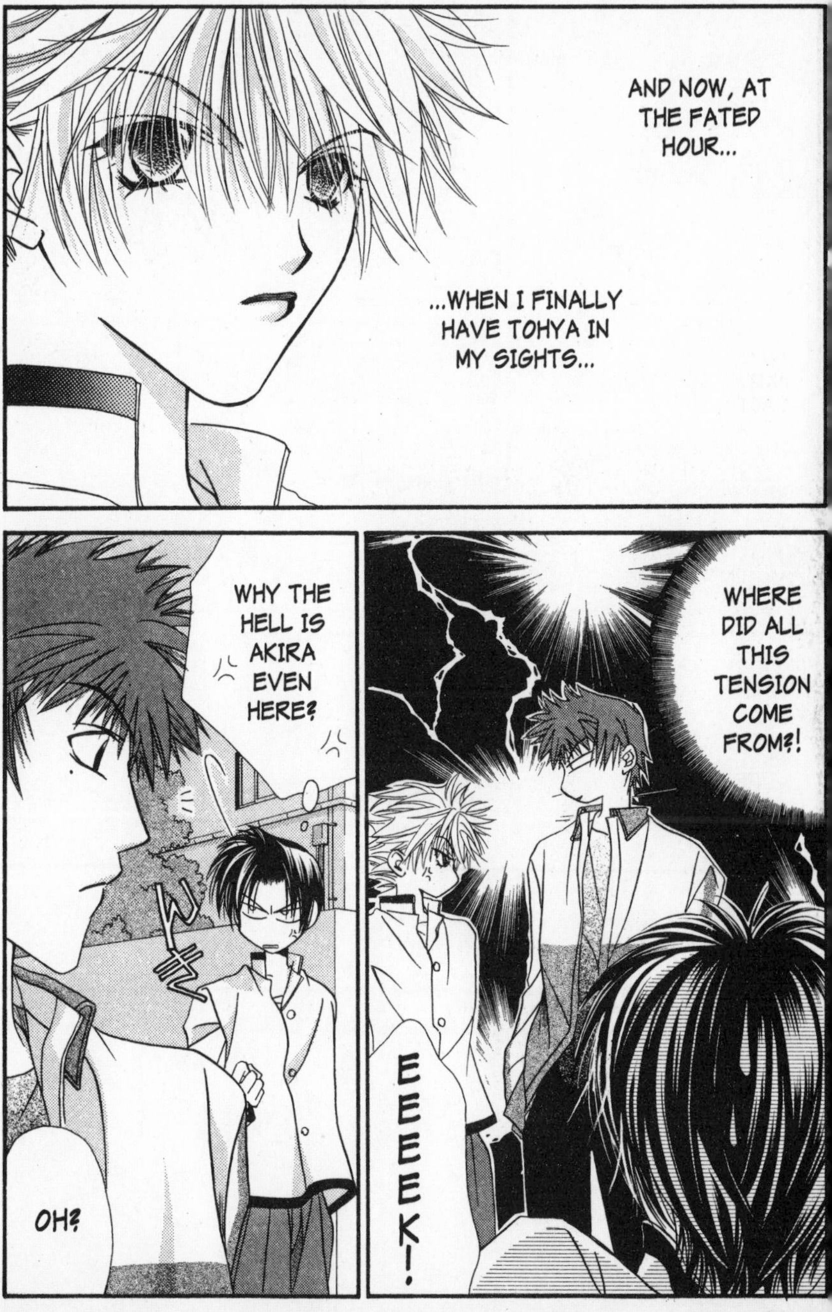
AND NOW, AT THE FATED HOUR...
...WHEN I FINALLY HAVE TOHYA IN MY SIGHTS...
WHERE DID ALL THIS TENSION COME FROM?!
EEEEEK!
WHY THE HELL IS AKIRA EVEN HERE?
OH?

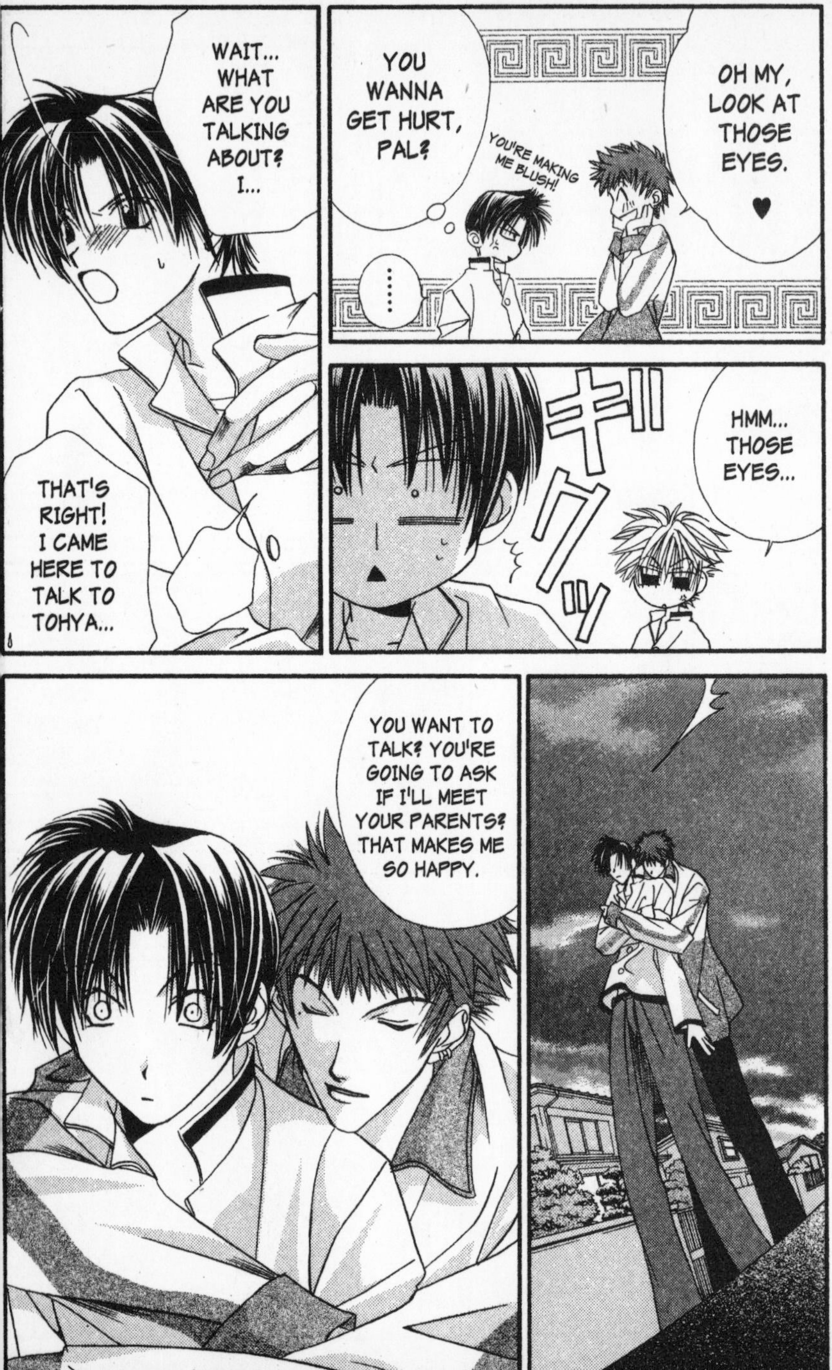
OH MY, LOOK AT THOSE EYES. ♥
YOU'RE MAKING ME BLUSH!
YOU WANNA GET HURT, PAL?
......
HMM... THOSE EYES...
ギクッ
WAIT... WHAT ARE YOU TALKING ABOUT? I...
THAT'S RIGHT! I CAME HERE TO TALK TO TOHYA...
YOU WANT TO TALK? YOU'RE GOING TO ASK IF I'LL MEET YOUR PARENTS? THAT MAKES ME SO HAPPY.

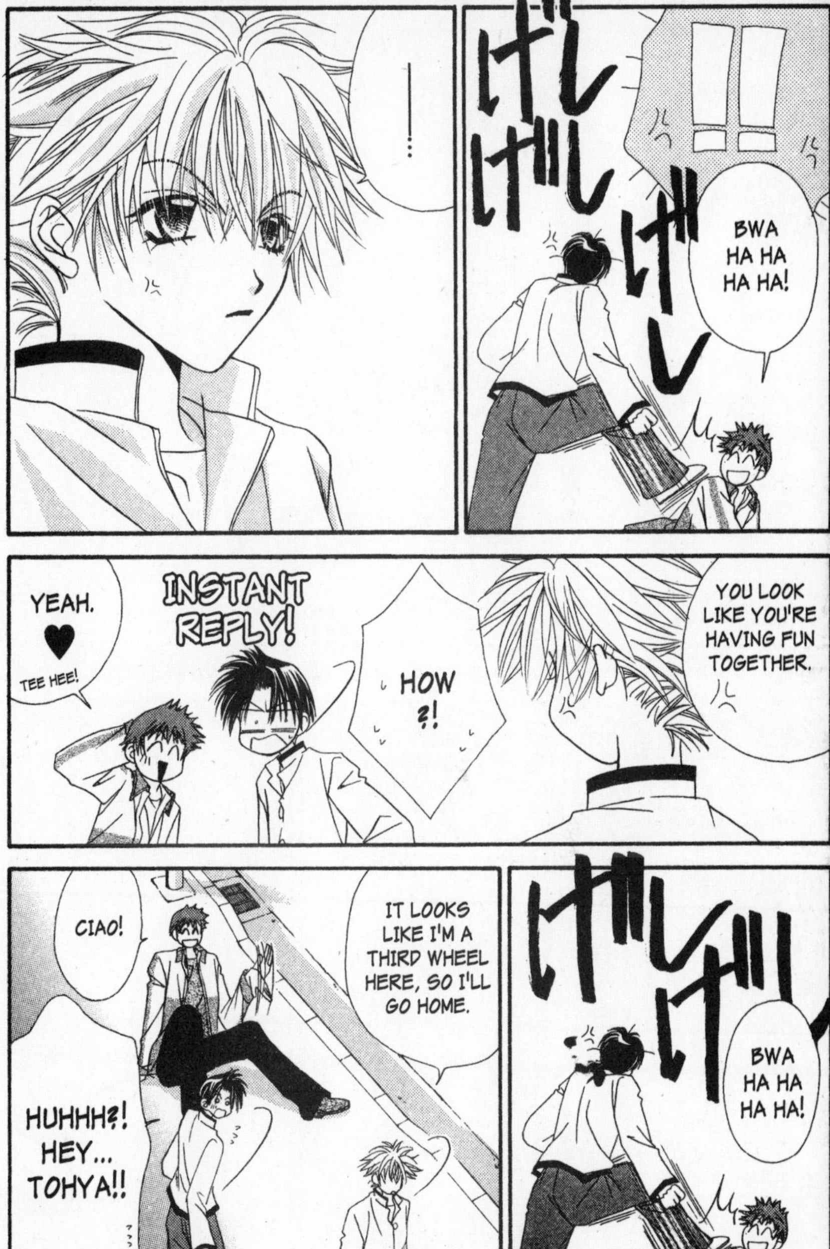
げしげしげし
!!
BWA HA HA HA HA!
......
YOU LOOK LIKE YOU'RE HAVING FUN TOGETHER.
HOW ?!
INSTANT REPLY!
YEAH. ♥
TEE HEE!
げしげしげし
BWA HA HA HA HA!
IT LOOKS LIKE I'M A THIRD WHEEL HERE, SO I'LL GO HOME.
CIAO!
HUHHH?! HEY... TOHYA!!

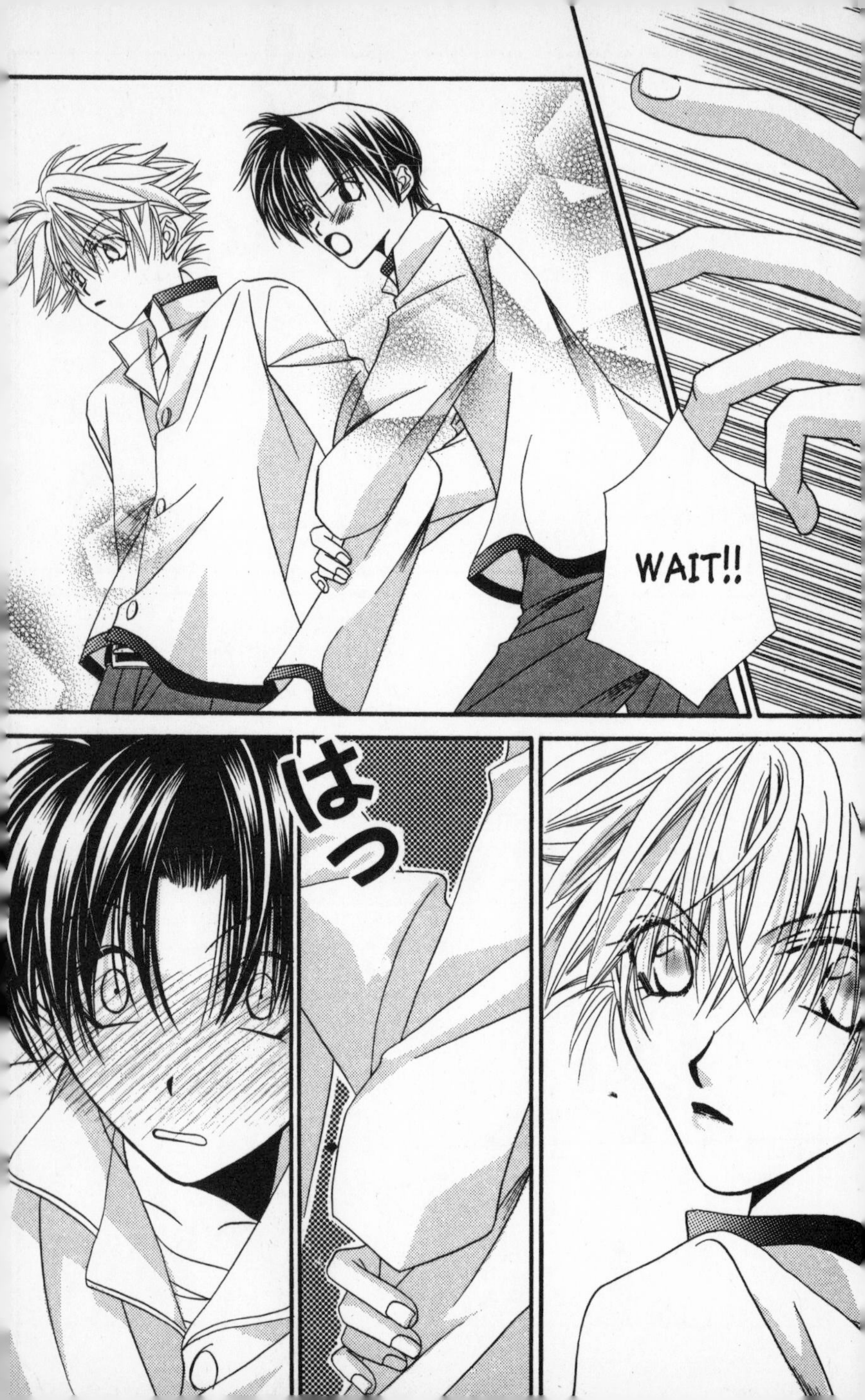
WAIT!!
はっ

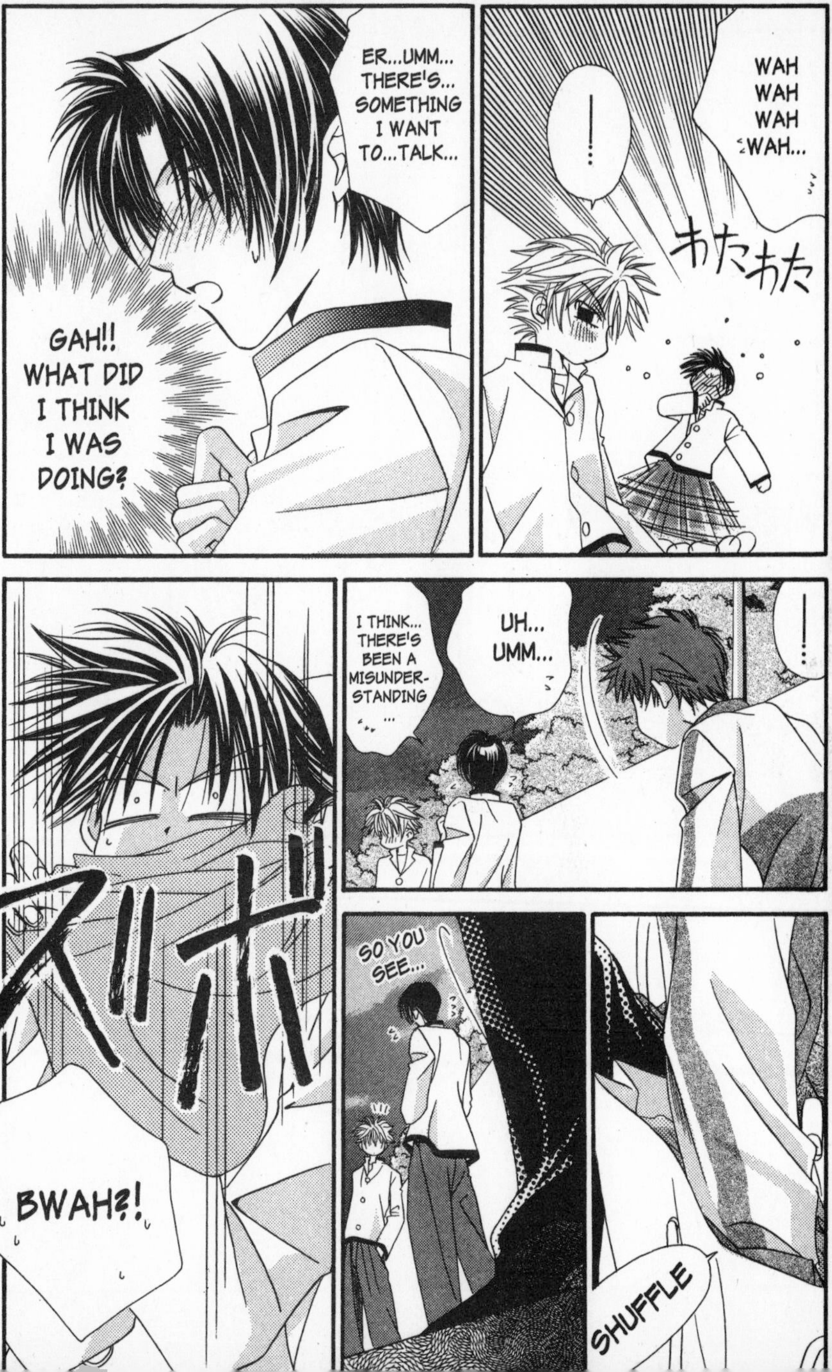
WAH WAH WAH WAH...
!...
わたわた
ER...UMM... THERE'S... SOMETHING I WANT TO...TALK...
GAH!! WHAT DID I THINK I WAS DOING?
!...
UH... UMM...
I THINK... THERE'S BEEN A MISUNDER-STANDING ...
SHUFFLE
SO YOU SEE...
BWAH?!

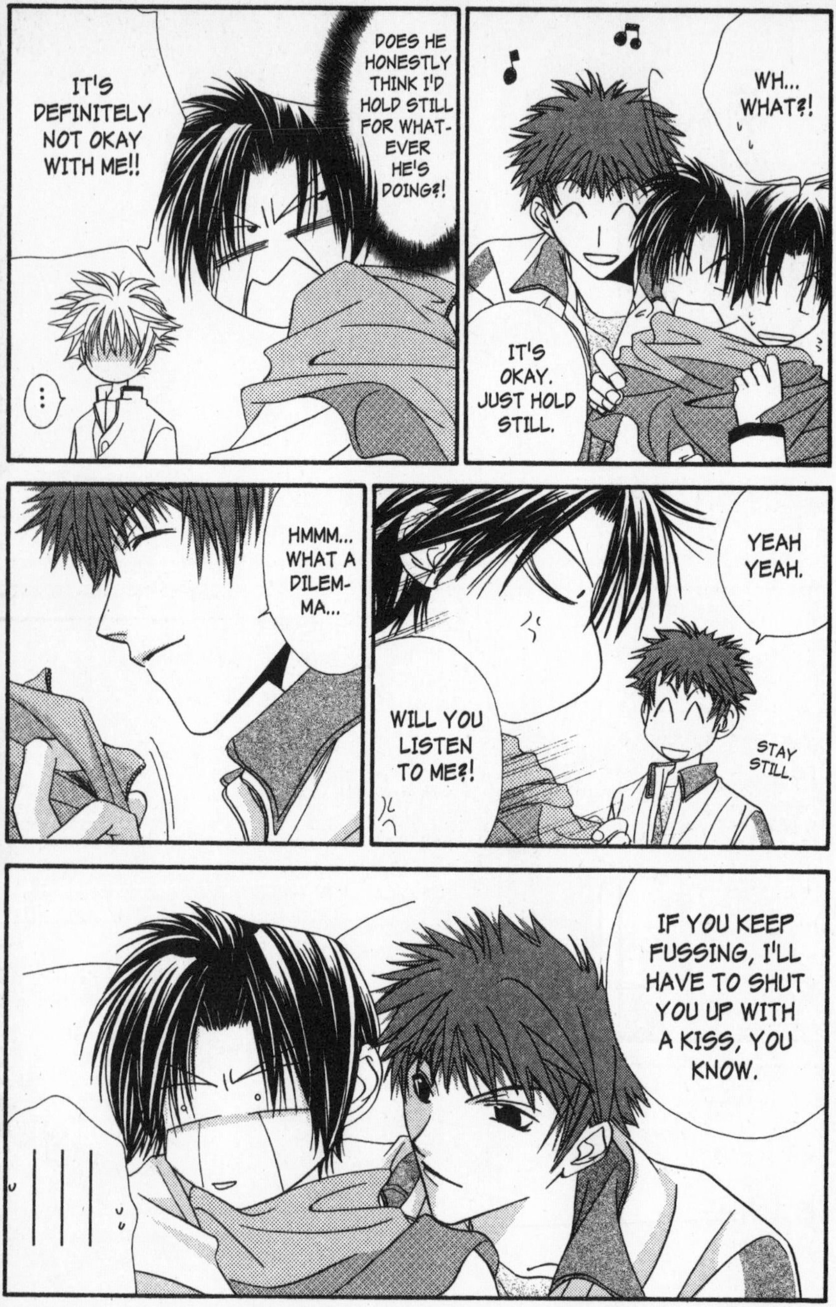
WH... WHAT?!
IT'S OKAY. JUST HOLD STILL.
DOES HE HONESTLY THINK I'D HOLD STILL FOR WHATEVER HE'S DOING?!
IT'S DEFINITELY NOT OKAY WITH ME!!
...
YEAH YEAH.
STAY STILL.
WILL YOU LISTEN TO ME?!
HMMM... WHAT A DILEMMA...
IF YOU KEEP FUSSING, I'LL HAVE TO SHUT YOU UP WITH A KISS, YOU KNOW.

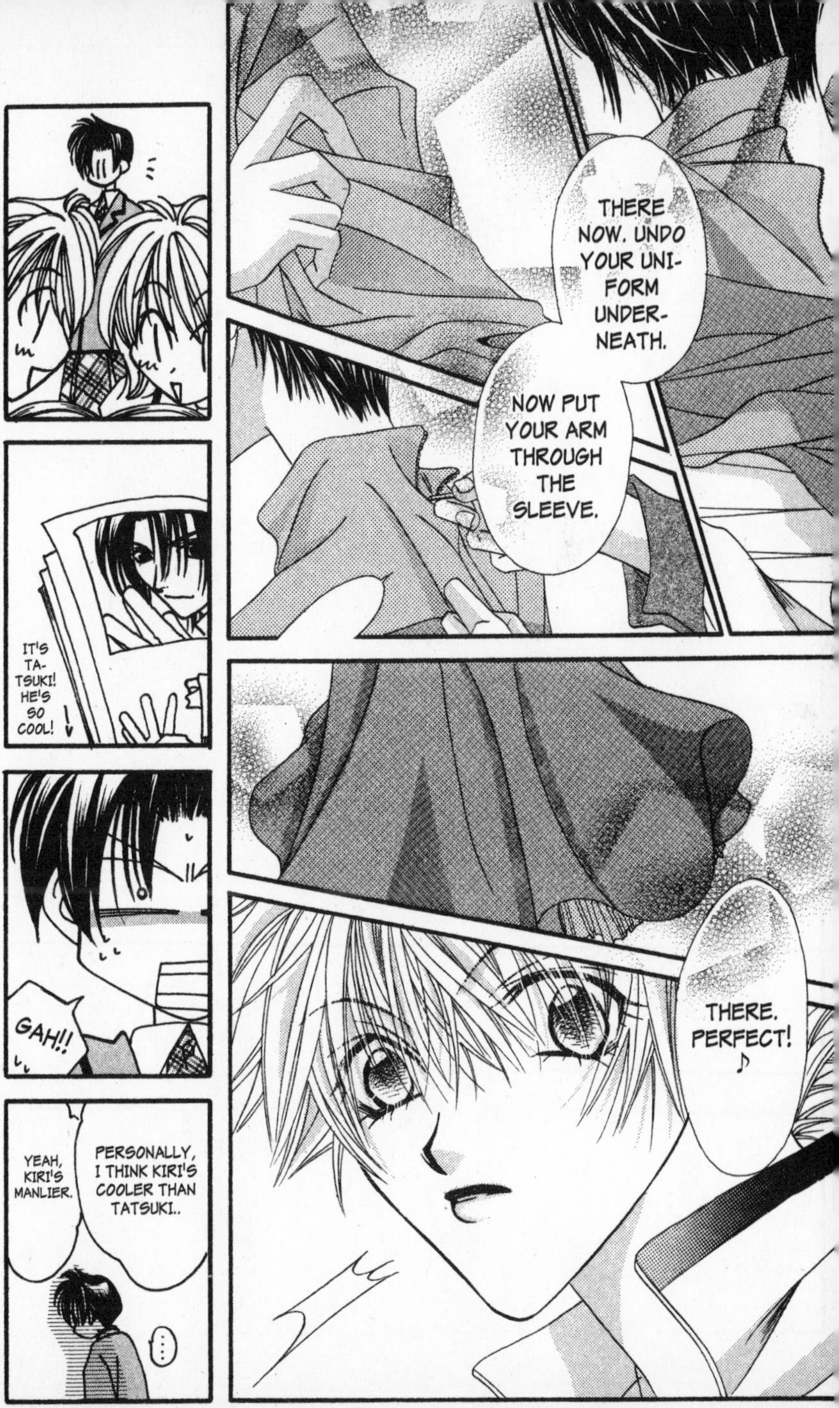
THERE NOW. UNDO YOUR UNIFORM UNDERNEATH.
NOW PUT YOUR ARM THROUGH THE SLEEVE.
THERE. PERFECT! ♪
IT'S TATSUKI! HE'S SO COOL!
GAH!!
PERSONALLY, I THINK KIRI'S COOLER THAN TATSUKI..
YEAH, KIRI'S MANLIER.
...

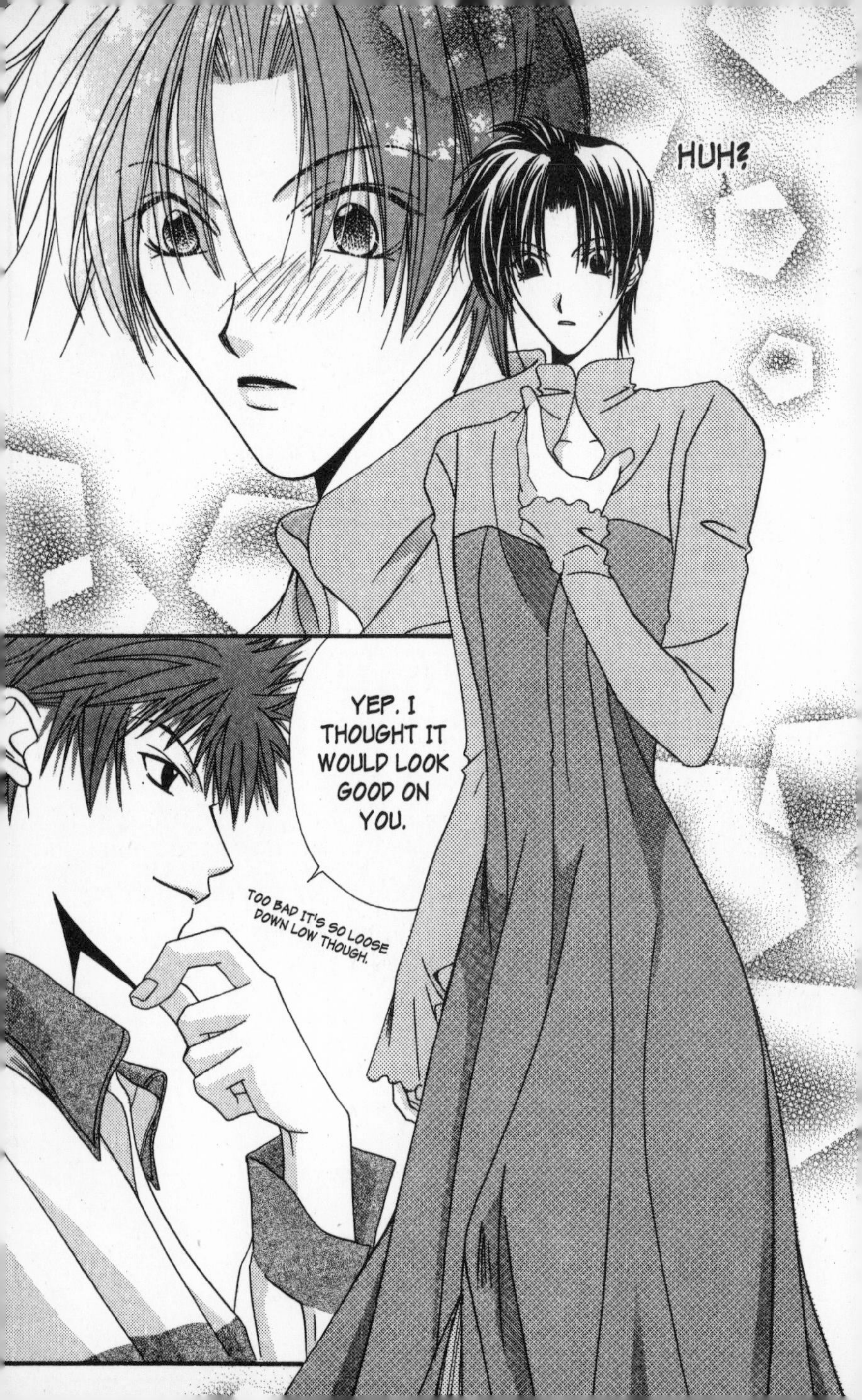
HUH?
YEP. I THOUGHT IT WOULD LOOK GOOD ON YOU.
TOO BAD IT'S SO LOOSE DOWN LOW THOUGH.

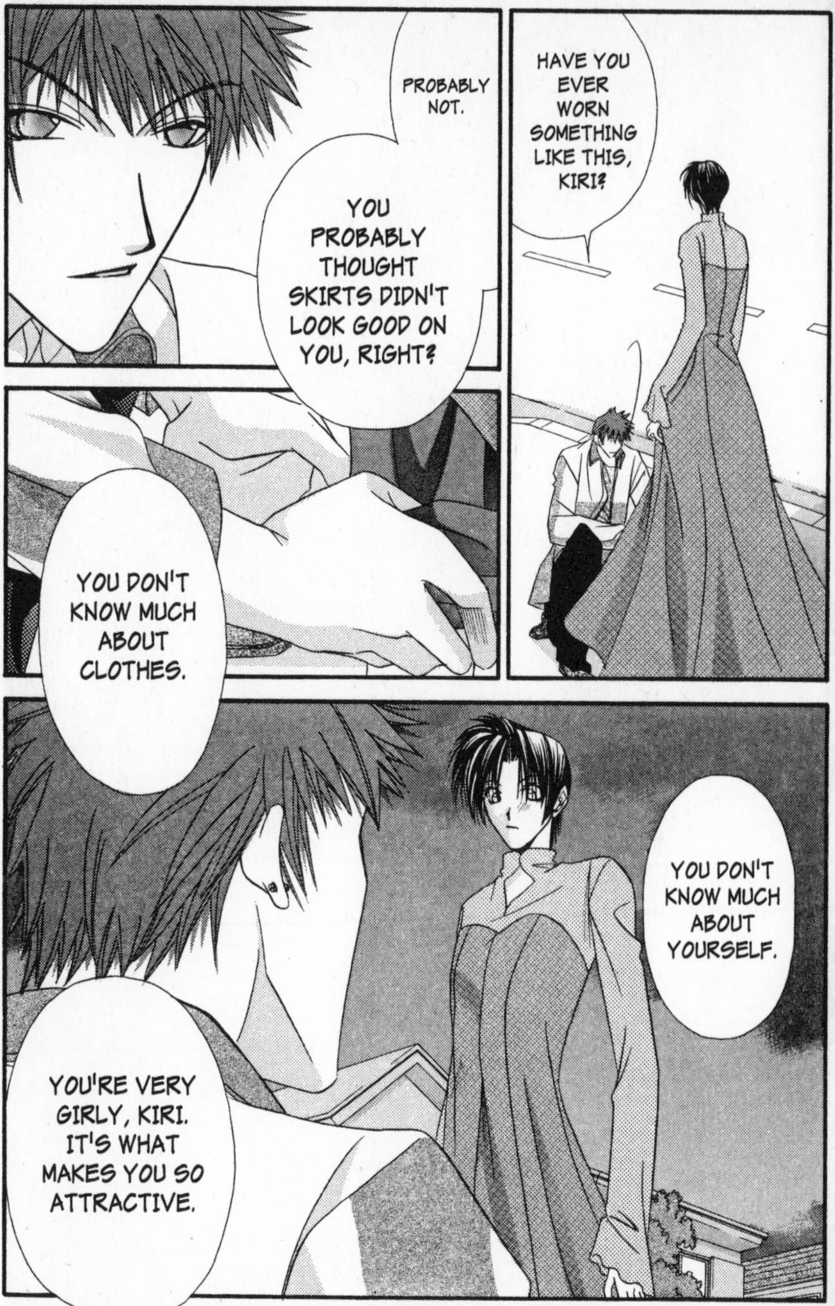
HAVE YOU EVER WORN SOMETHING LIKE THIS, KIRI?
PROBABLY NOT.
YOU PROBABLY THOUGHT SKIRTS DIDN'T LOOK GOOD ON YOU, RIGHT?
YOU DON'T KNOW MUCH ABOUT CLOTHES.
YOU DON'T KNOW MUCH ABOUT YOURSELF.
YOU'RE VERY GIRLY, KIRI. IT'S WHAT MAKES YOU SO ATTRACTIVE.

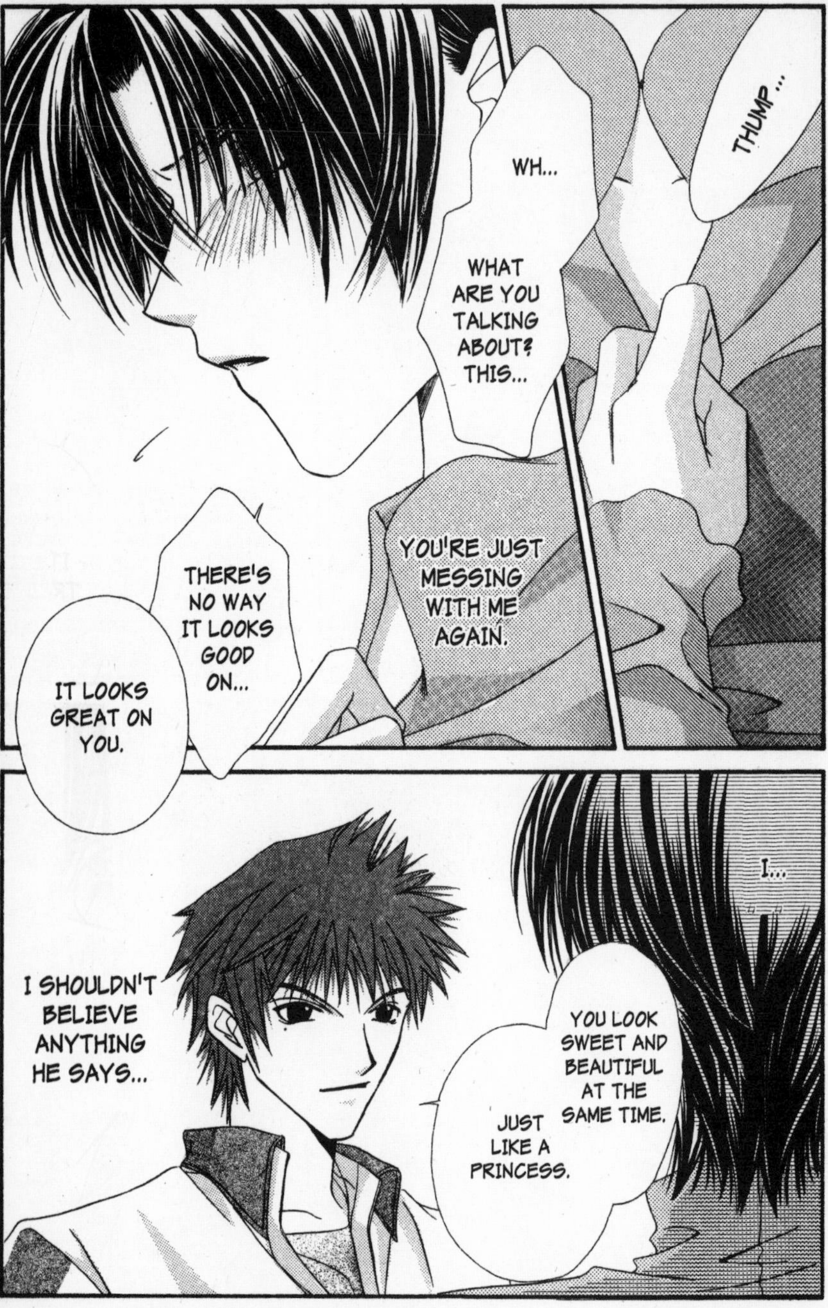
THUMP...
WH...
WHAT ARE YOU TALKING ABOUT? THIS...
YOU'RE JUST MESSING WITH ME AGAIN.
THERE'S NO WAY IT LOOKS GOOD ON...
IT LOOKS GREAT ON YOU.
I...
YOU LOOK SWEET AND BEAUTIFUL AT THE SAME TIME.
JUST LIKE A PRINCESS.
I SHOULDN'T BELIEVE ANYTHING HE SAYS...

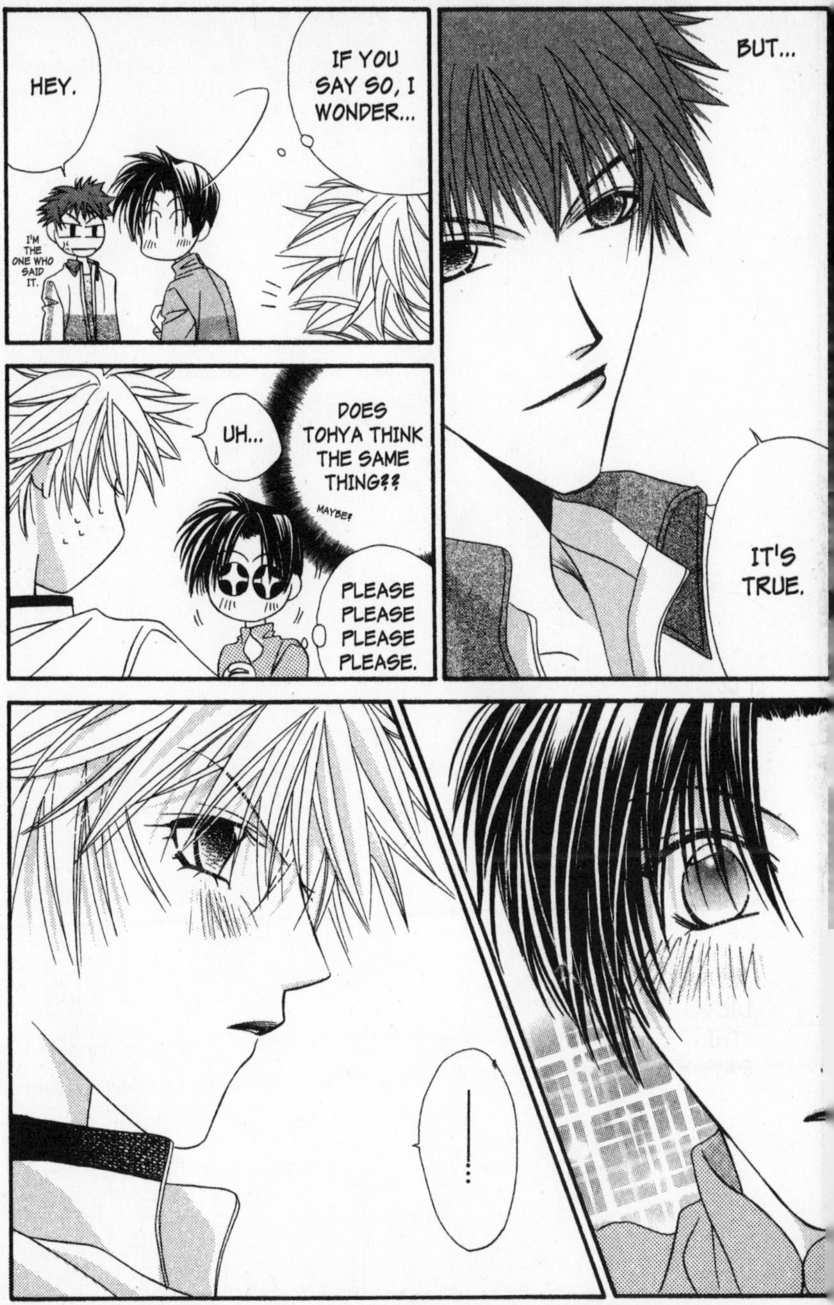
BUT...
IT'S TRUE.
IF YOU SAY SO, I WONDER...
HEY.
I'M THE ONE WHO SAID IT.
DOES TOHYA THINK THE SAME THING??
UH...
MAYBE?
PLEASE PLEASE PLEASE PLEASE.
—...

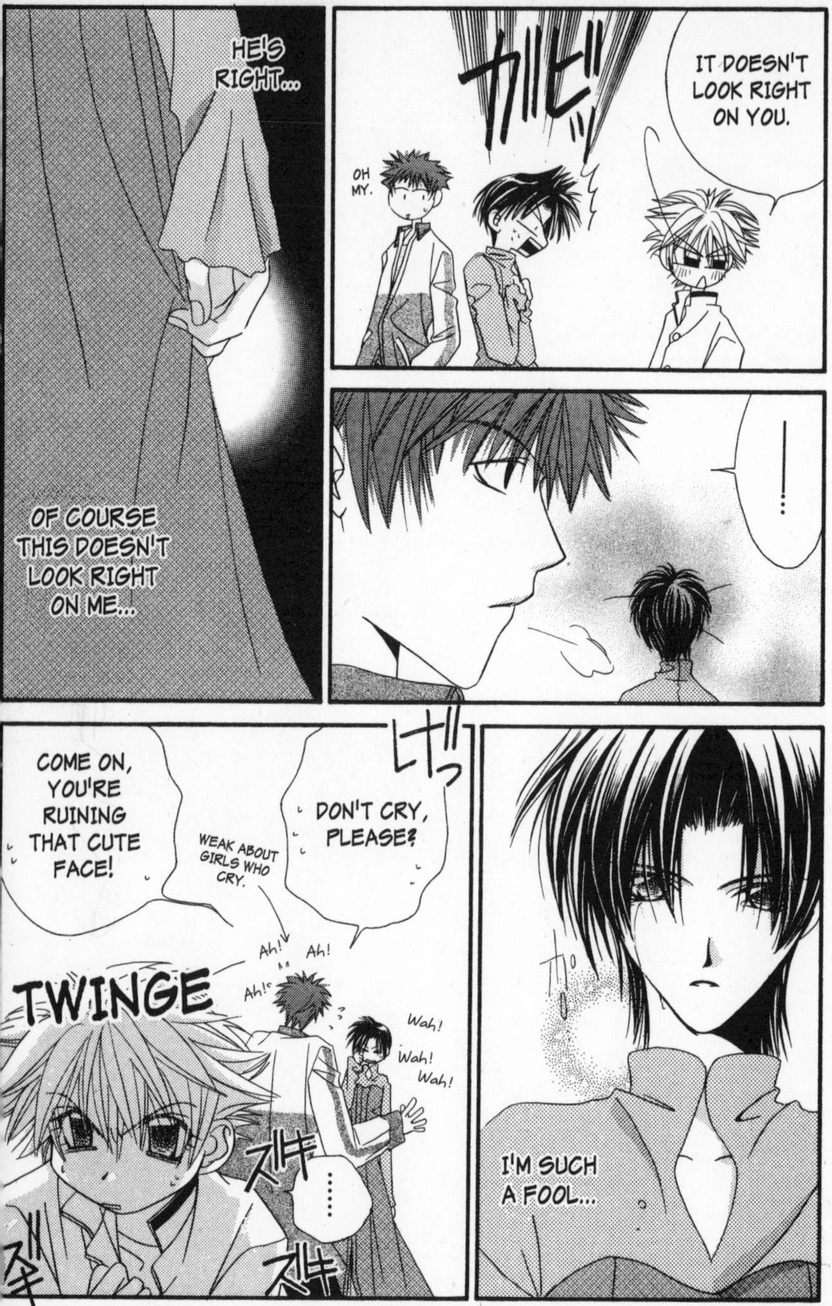
IT DOESN'T LOOK RIGHT ON YOU.
OH MY.
!......
HE'S RIGHT...
OF COURSE THIS DOESN'T LOOK RIGHT ON ME...
I'M SUCH A FOOL...
DON'T CRY, PLEASE?
COME ON, YOU'RE RUINING THAT CUTE FACE!
WEAK ABOUT GIRLS WHO CRY.
Ah! Ah! Ah!
Wah! Wah! Wah!
TWINGE
......

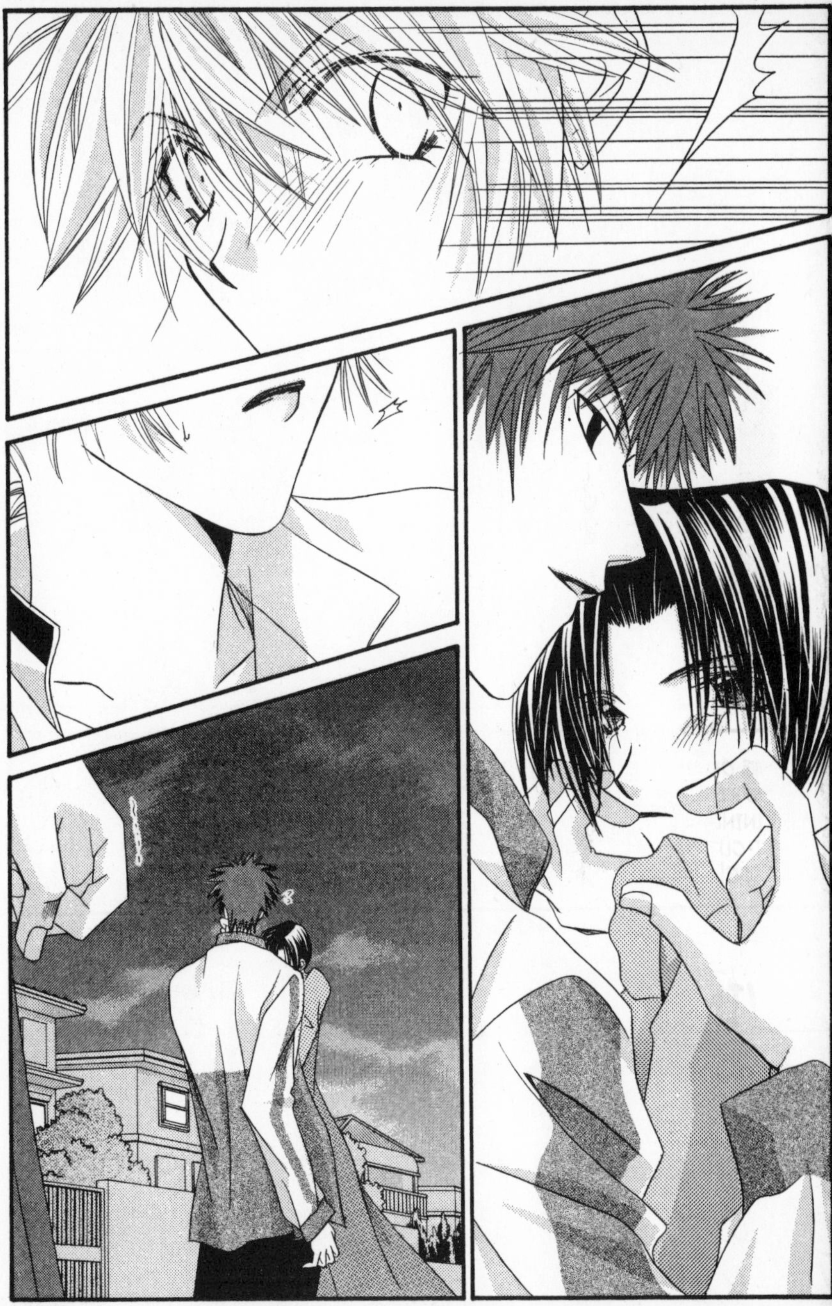

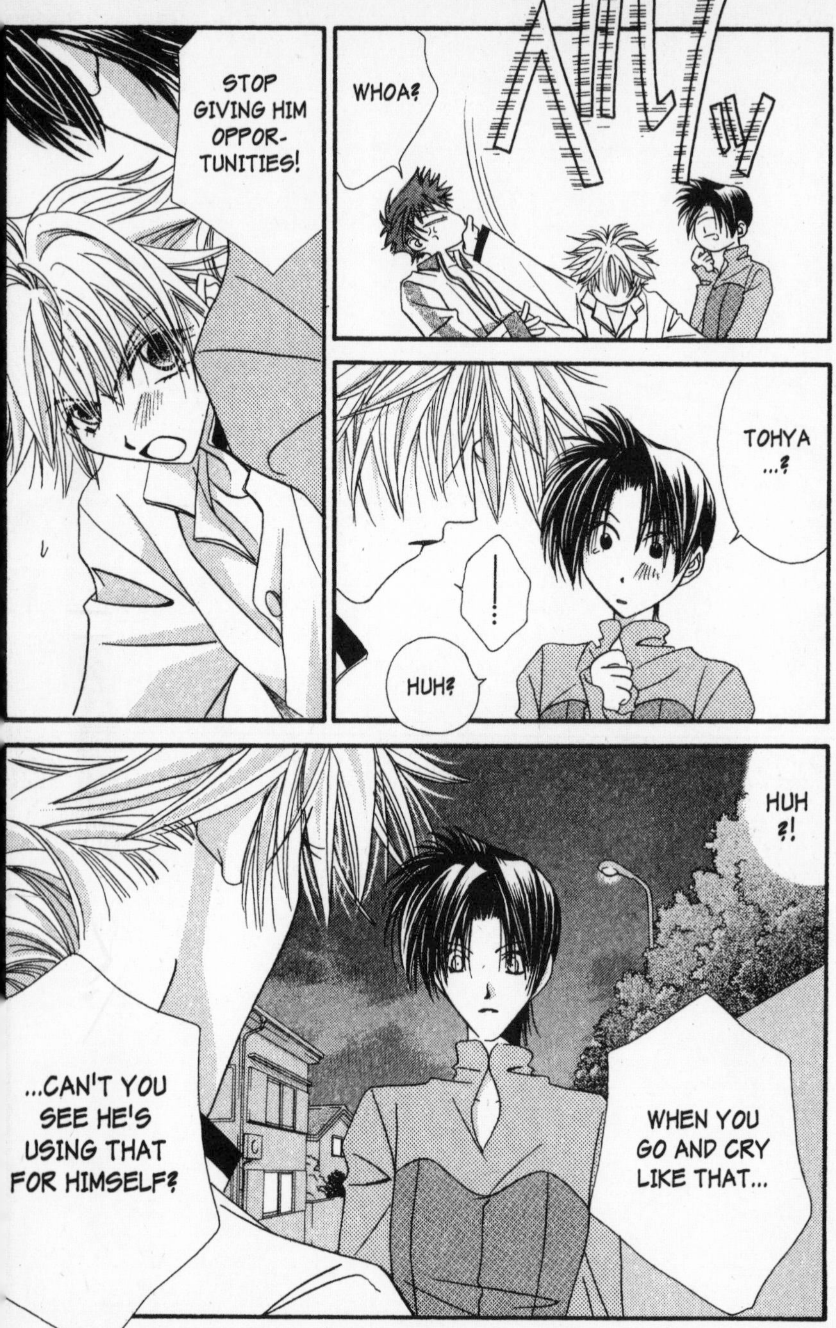
WHOA?
TOHYA ...?
!...
HUH?
STOP GIVING HIM OPPOR-TUNITIES!
HUH ?!
WHEN YOU GO AND CRY LIKE THAT...
...CAN'T YOU SEE HE'S USING THAT FOR HIMSELF?

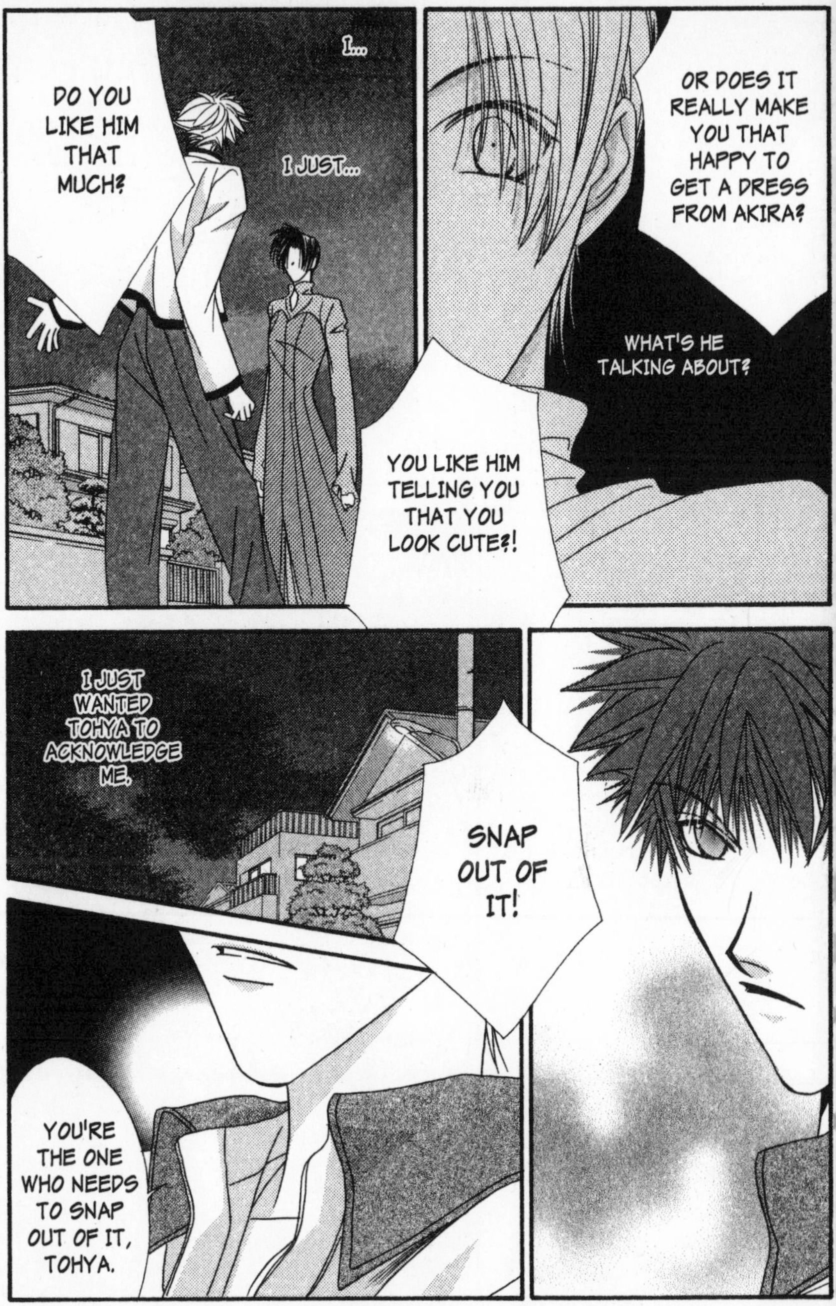
OR DOES IT REALLY MAKE YOU THAT HAPPY TO GET A DRESS FROM AKIRA?
WHAT'S HE TALKING ABOUT?
YOU LIKE HIM TELLING YOU THAT YOU LOOK CUTE?!
I...
I JUST...
DO YOU LIKE HIM THAT MUCH?
SNAP OUT OF IT!
I JUST WANTED TOHYA TO ACKNOWLEDGE ME.
YOU'RE THE ONE WHO NEEDS TO SNAP OUT OF IT, TOHYA.

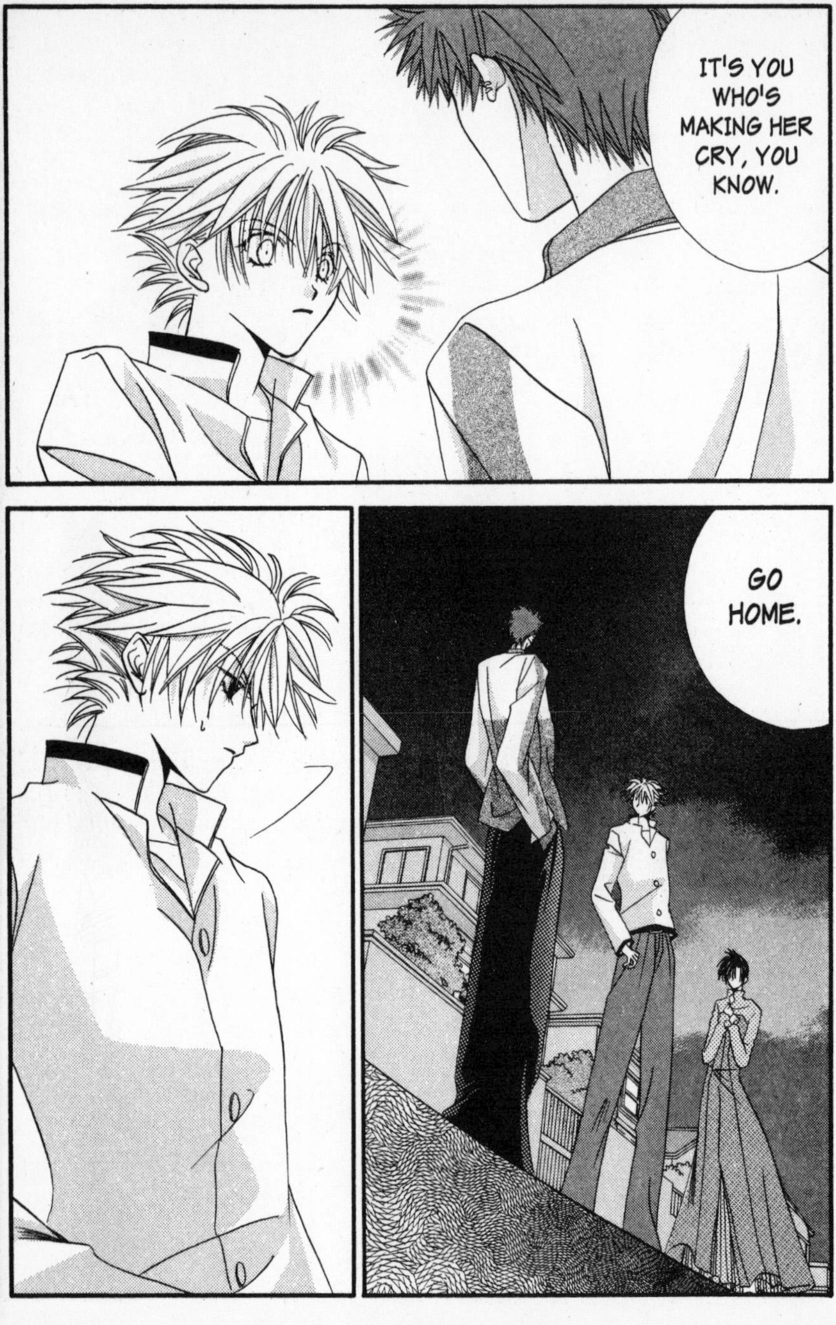
IT'S YOU WHO'S MAKING HER CRY, YOU KNOW.
GO HOME.

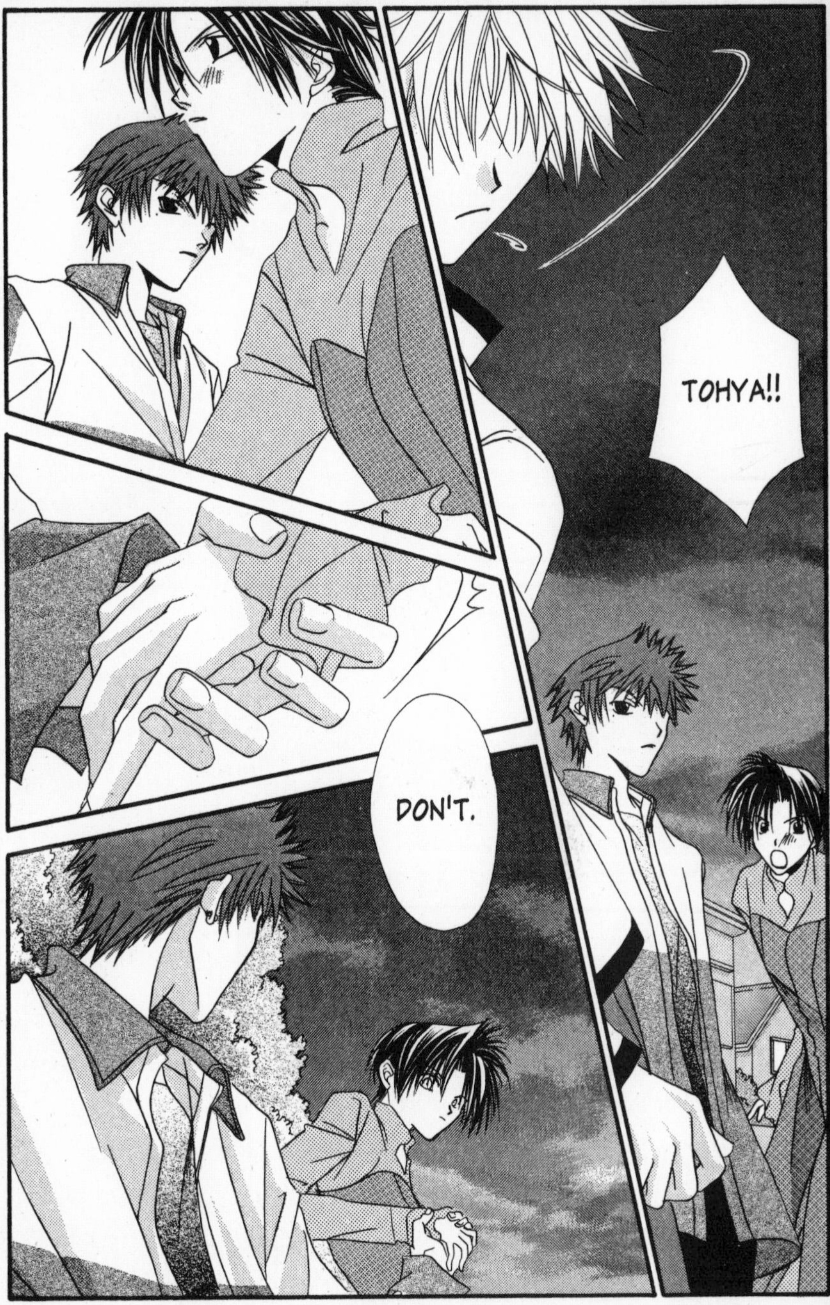
TOHYA!!
DON'T.

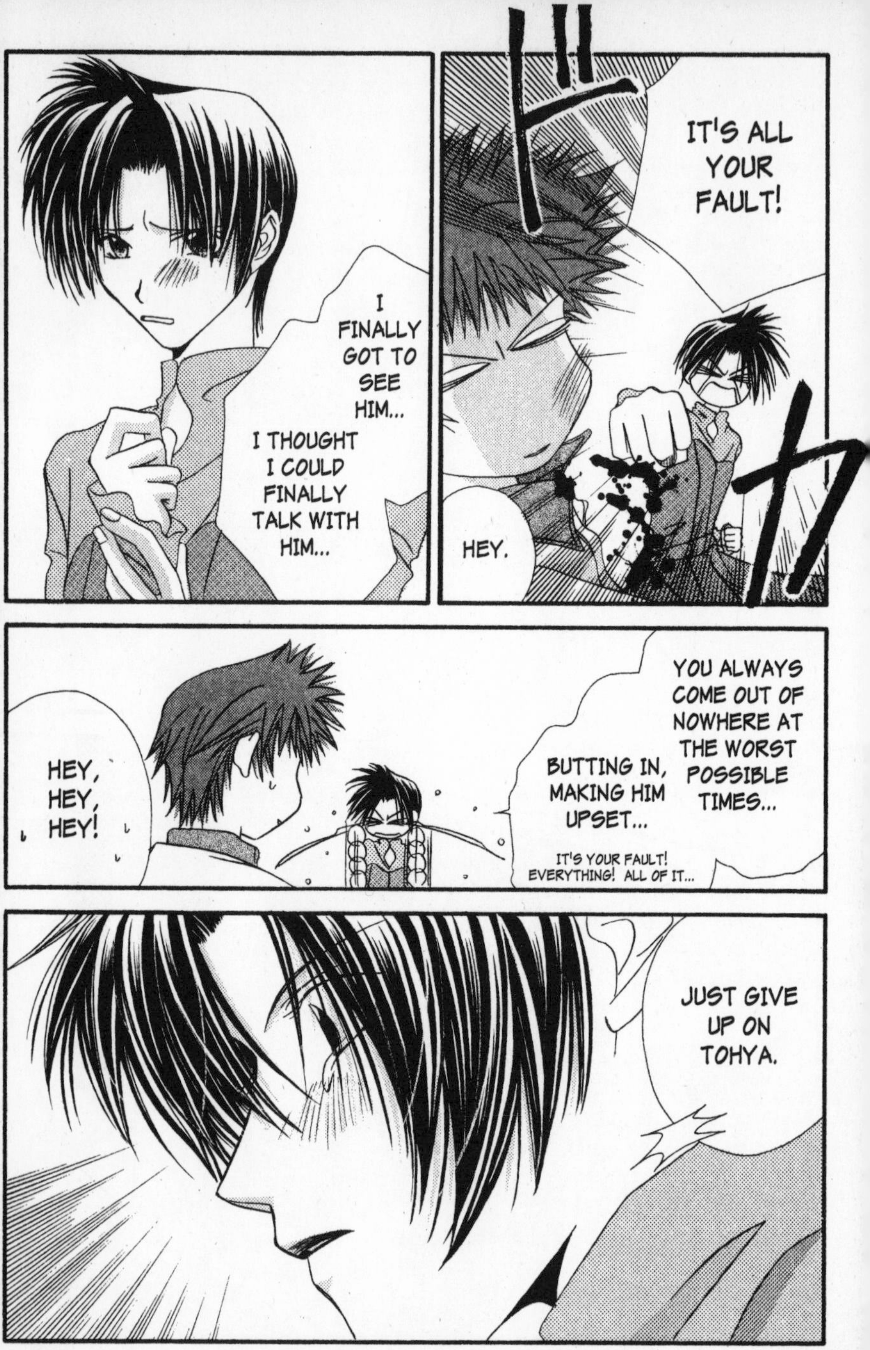
IT'S ALL YOUR FAULT!
ドカ
HEY.
I FINALLY GOT TO SEE HIM...
I THOUGHT I COULD FINALLY TALK WITH HIM...
YOU ALWAYS COME OUT OF NOWHERE AT THE WORST POSSIBLE TIMES...
BUTTING IN, MAKING HIM UPSET...
IT'S YOUR FAULT! EVERYTHING! ALL OF IT...
HEY, HEY, HEY!
JUST GIVE UP ON TOHYA.

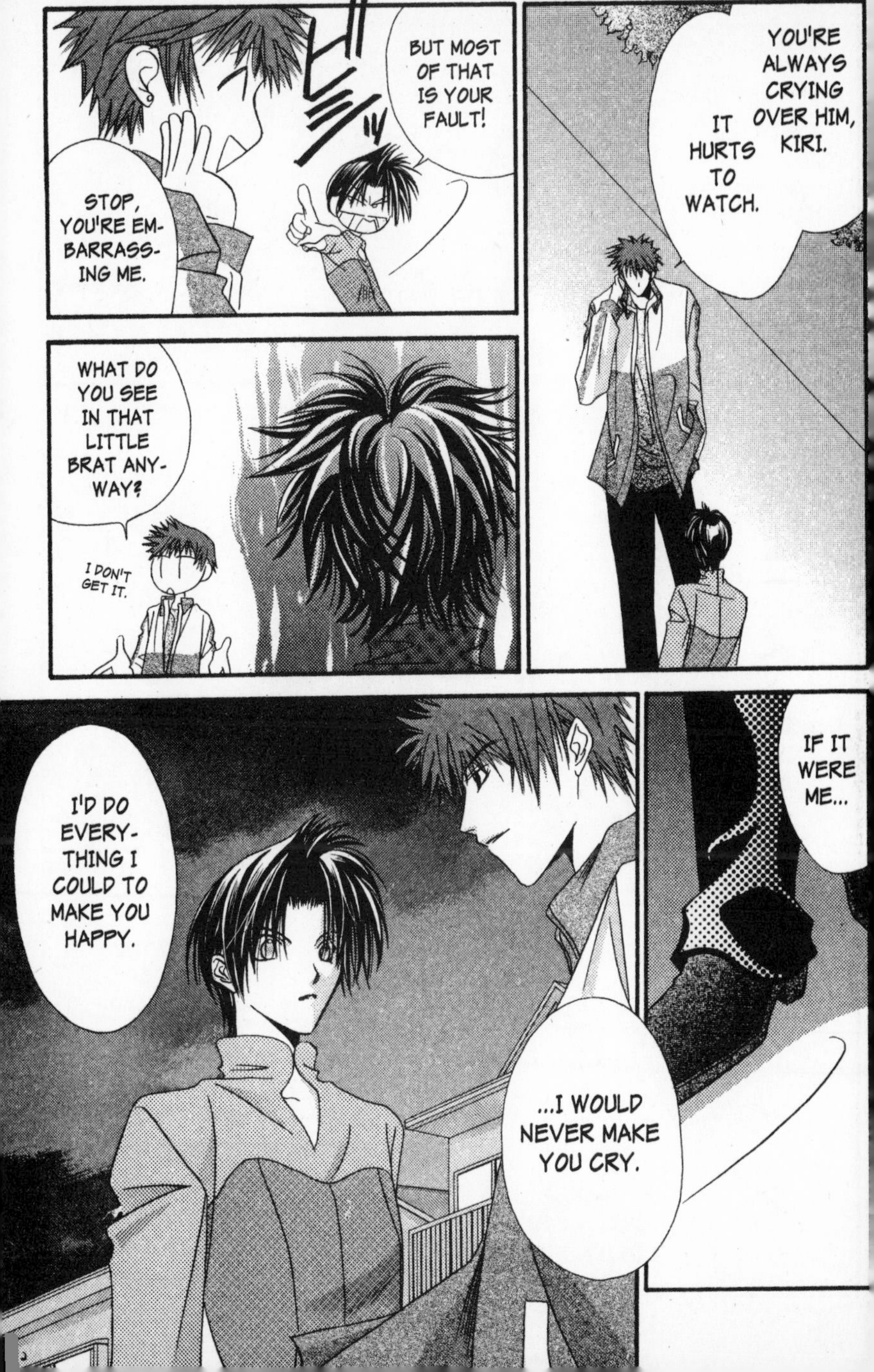

YOU'RE ALWAYS CRYING OVER HIM, KIRI.
IT HURTS TO WATCH.
BUT MOST OF THAT IS YOUR FAULT!
STOP, YOU'RE EM-BARRASS-ING ME.
WHAT DO YOU SEE IN THAT LITTLE BRAT ANY-WAY?
I DON'T GET IT.
IF IT WERE ME...
...I WOULD NEVER MAKE YOU CRY.
I'D DO EVERY-THING I COULD TO MAKE YOU HAPPY.

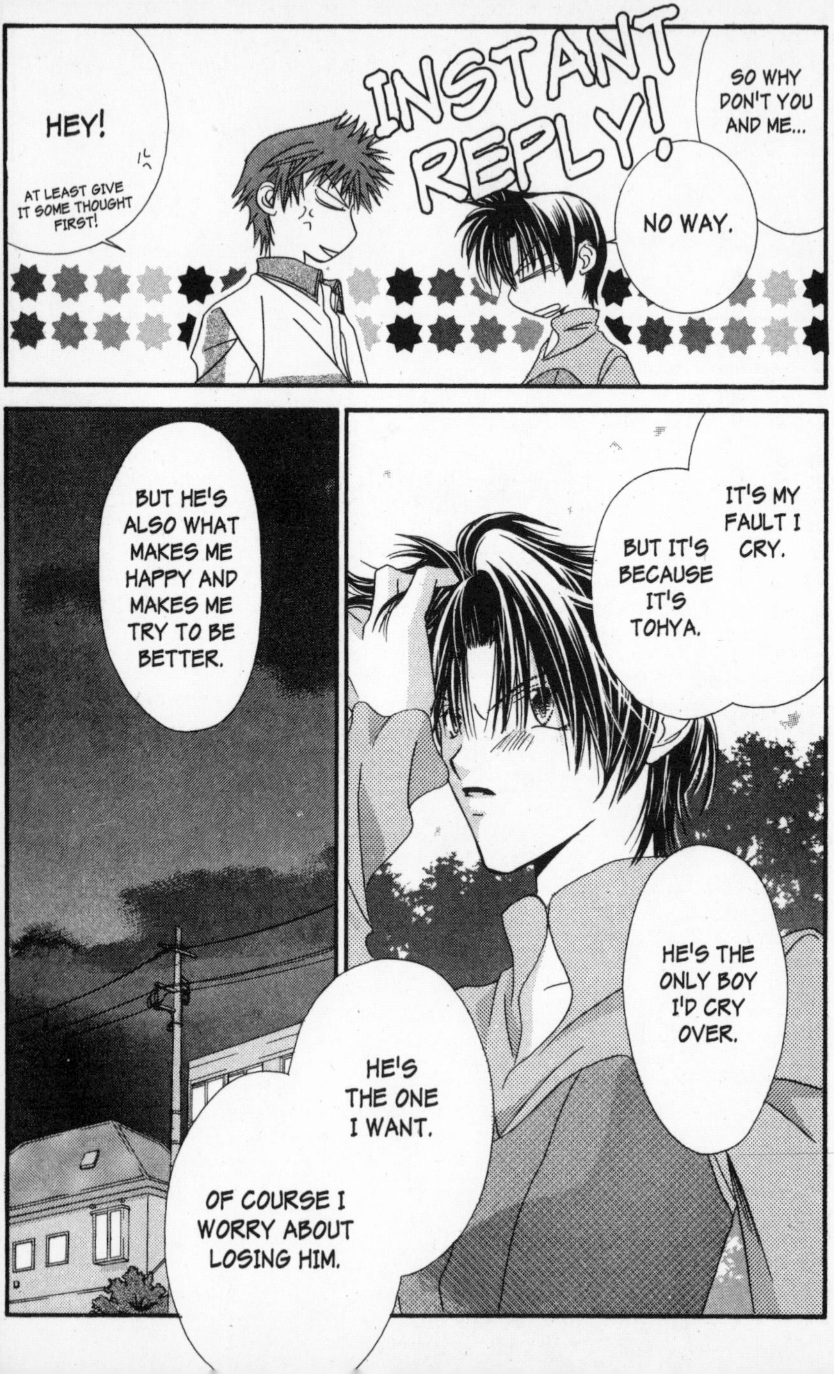
SO WHY DON'T YOU AND ME...
NO WAY.
INSTANT REPLY!
HEY!
AT LEAST GIVE IT SOME THOUGHT FIRST!
IT'S MY FAULT I CRY.
BUT IT'S BECAUSE IT'S TOHYA.
HE'S THE ONLY BOY I'D CRY OVER.
HE'S THE ONE I WANT.
OF COURSE I WORRY ABOUT LOSING HIM.
BUT HE'S ALSO WHAT MAKES ME HAPPY AND MAKES ME TRY TO BE BETTER.

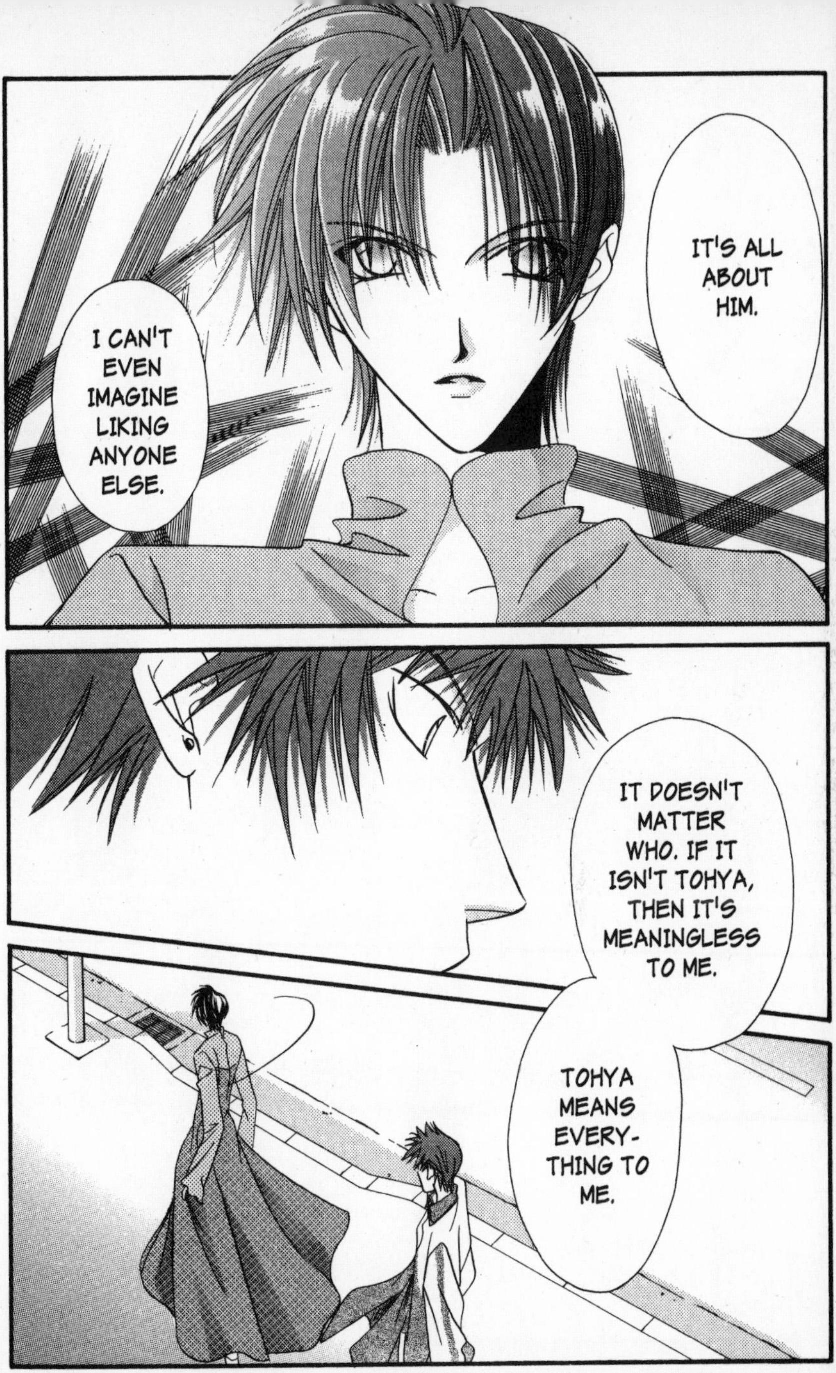
IT'S ALL ABOUT HIM.
I CAN'T EVEN IMAGINE LIKING ANYONE ELSE.
IT DOESN'T MATTER WHO. IF IT ISN'T TOHYA, THEN IT'S MEANINGLESS TO ME.
TOHYA MEANS EVERY-THING TO ME.

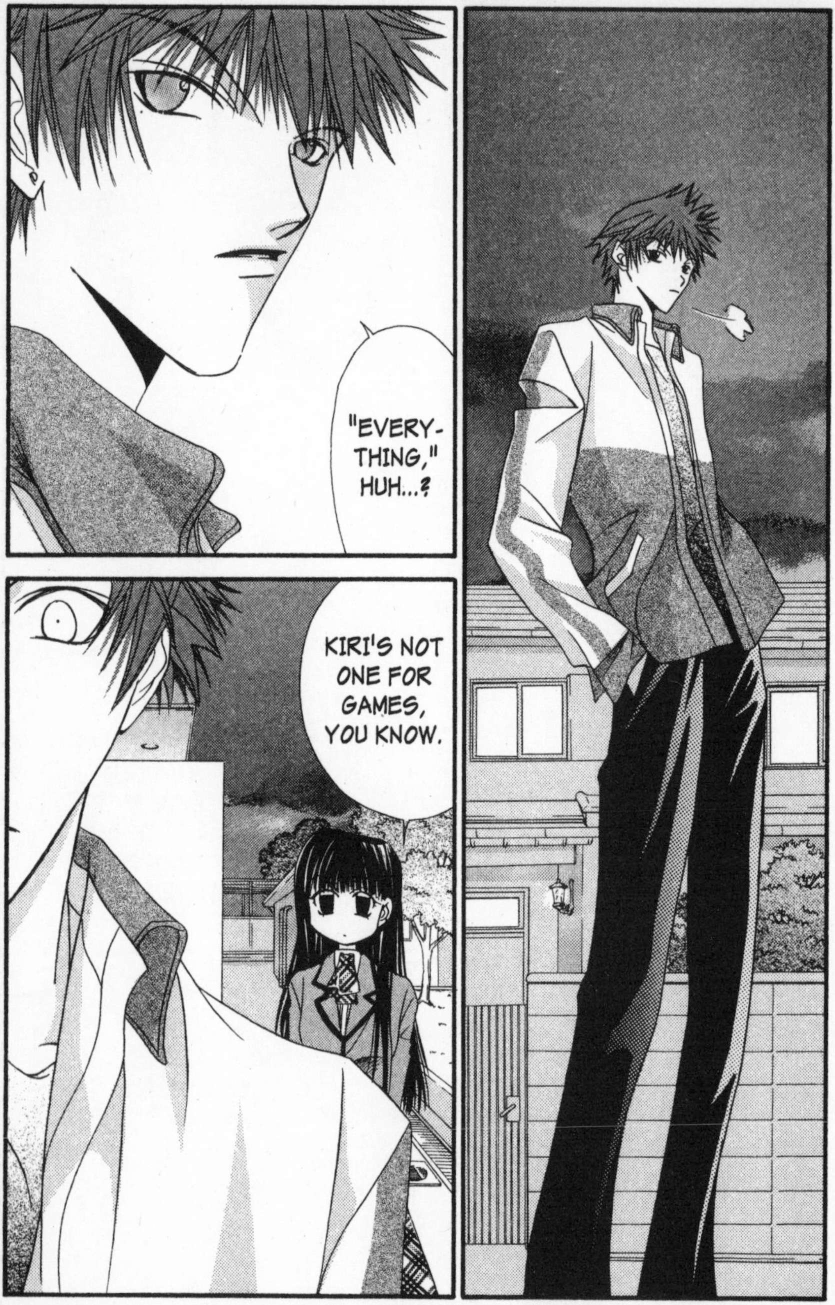
"EVERY-THING," HUH...?
KIRI'S NOT ONE FOR GAMES, YOU KNOW.

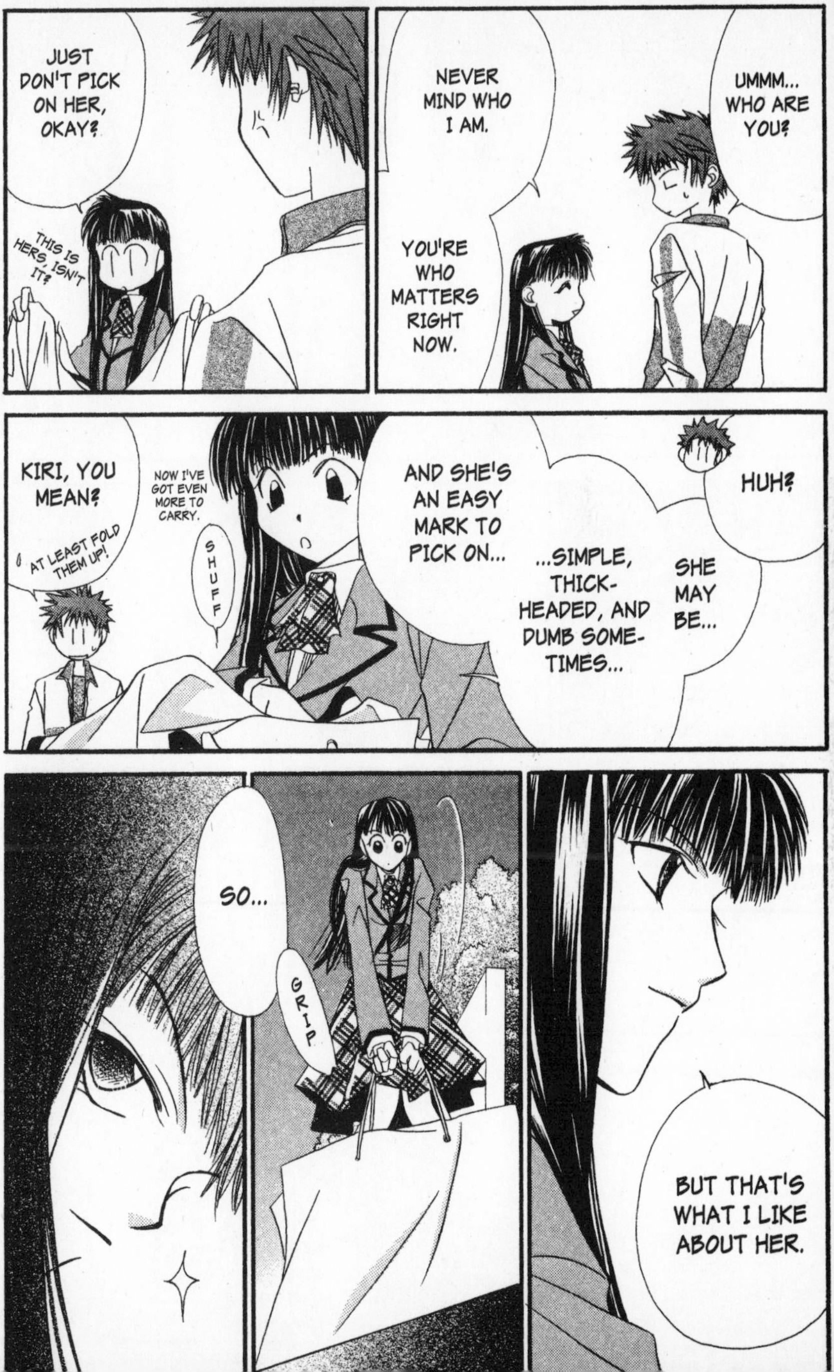
UMMM... WHO ARE YOU?
NEVER MIND WHO I AM.
YOU'RE WHO MATTERS RIGHT NOW.
JUST DON'T PICK ON HER, OKAY?
THIS IS HERS, ISN'T IT?
HUH?
SHE MAY BE...
...SIMPLE, THICK-HEADED, AND DUMB SOME-TIMES...
AND SHE'S AN EASY MARK TO PICK ON...
SHUFF
NOW I'VE GOT EVEN MORE TO CARRY.
KIRI, YOU MEAN?
AT LEAST FOLD THEM UP!
BUT THAT'S WHAT I LIKE ABOUT HER.
SO...
GRIP

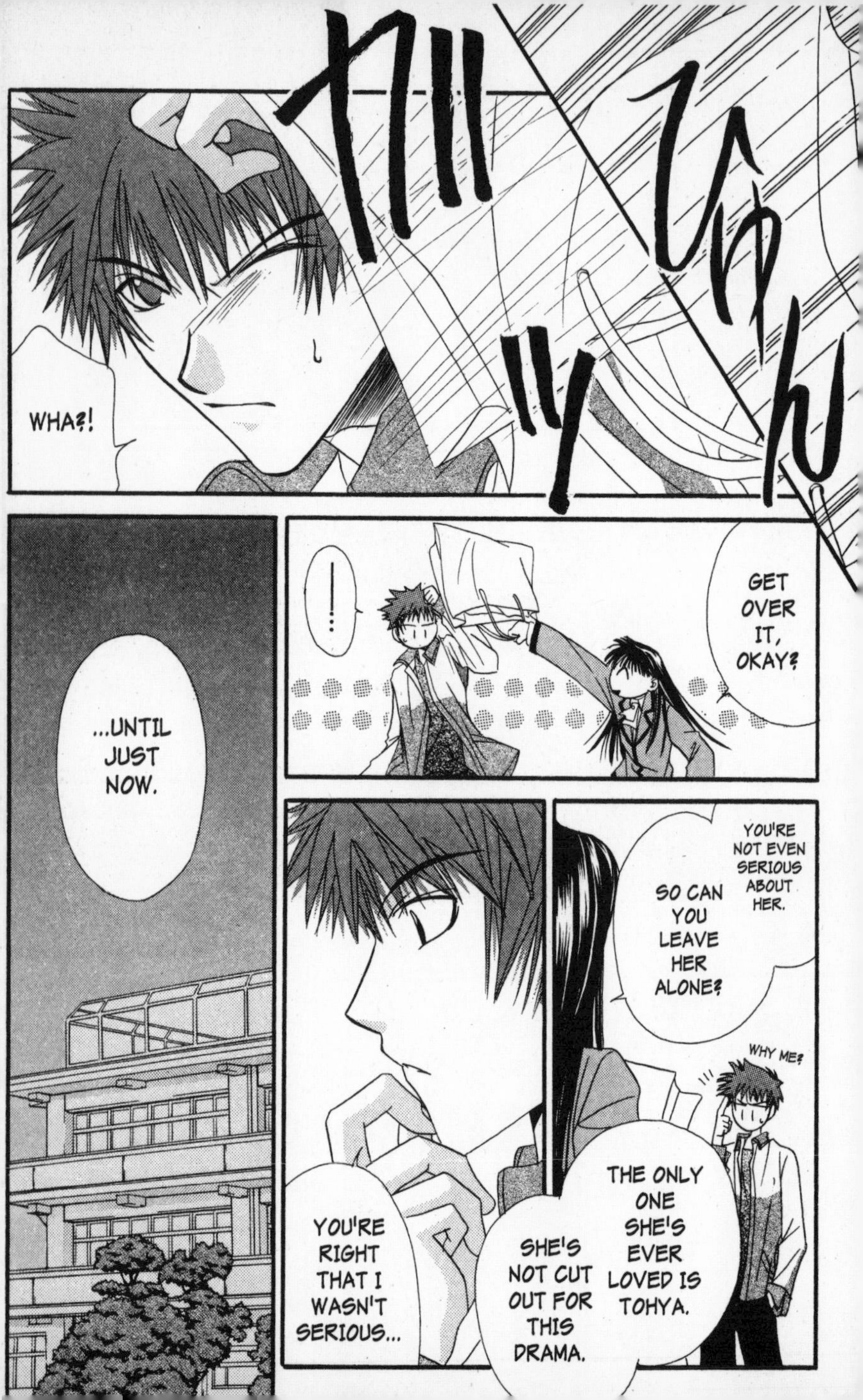

ひゅん
WHA?!
GET OVER IT, OKAY?
!
YOU'RE NOT EVEN SERIOUS ABOUT HER.
SO CAN YOU LEAVE HER ALONE?
WHY ME?
THE ONLY ONE SHE'S EVER LOVED IS TOHYA.
SHE'S NOT CUT OUT FOR THIS DRAMA.
YOU'RE RIGHT THAT I WASN'T SERIOUS...
...UNTIL JUST NOW.

"UNTIL JUST NOW."

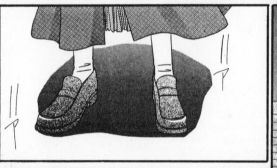

IT'S HARD TO RUN IN THIS!

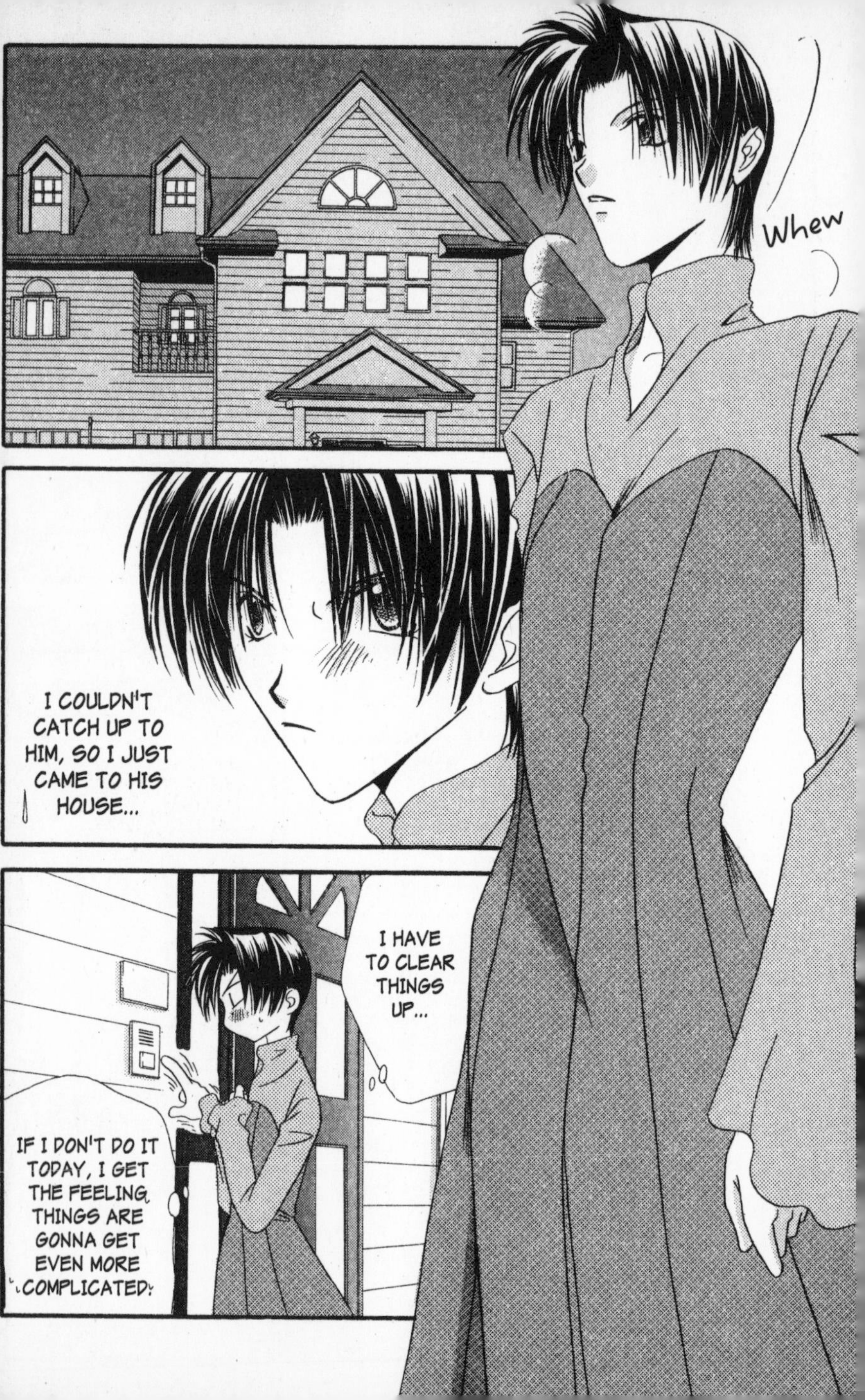
Whew
I COULDN'T CATCH UP TO HIM, SO I JUST CAME TO HIS HOUSE...
I HAVE TO CLEAR THINGS UP...
IF I DON'T DO IT TODAY, I GET THE FEELING THINGS ARE GONNA GET EVEN MORE COMPLICATED.

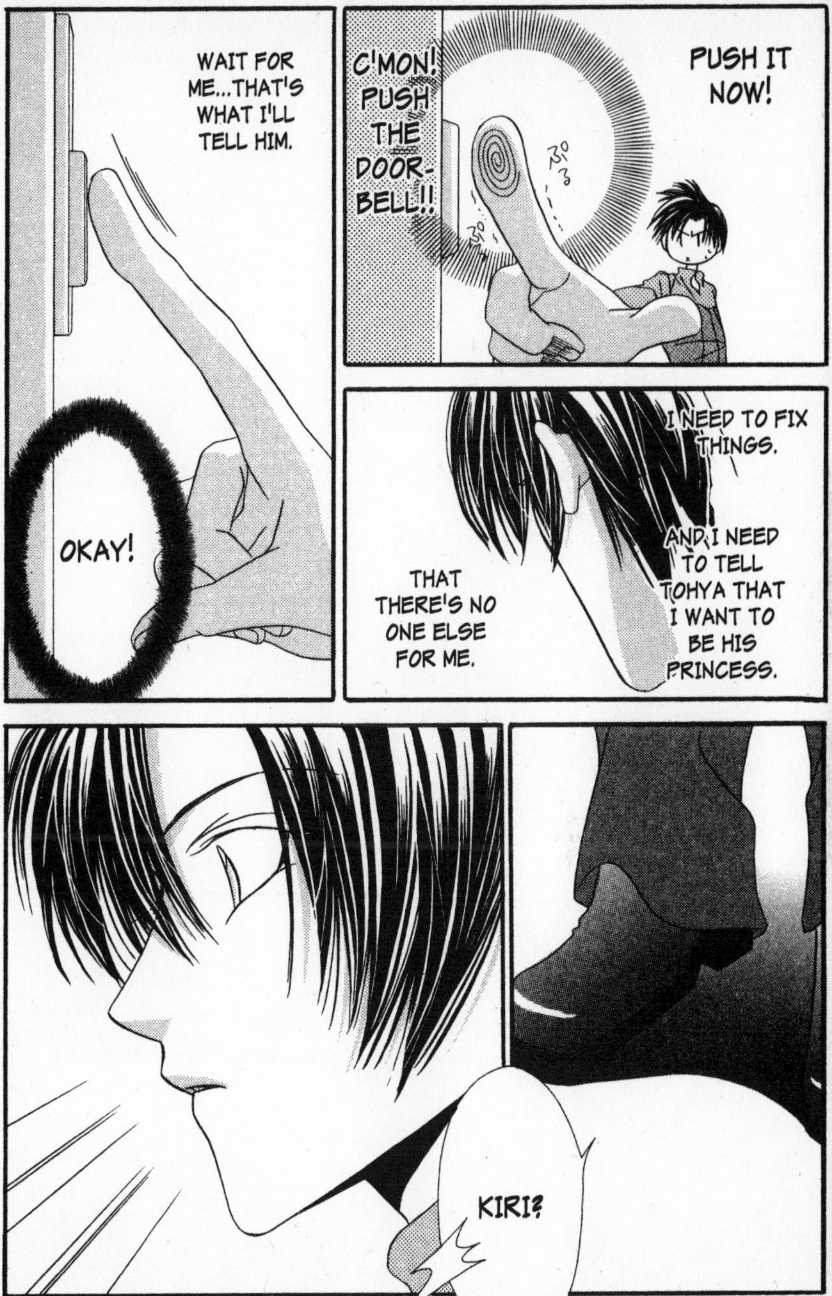
PUSH IT NOW!
C'MON! PUSH THE DOOR-BELL!!
I NEED TO FIX THINGS.
AND I NEED TO TELL TOHYA THAT I WANT TO BE HIS PRINCESS.
THAT THERE'S NO ONE ELSE FOR ME.
WAIT FOR ME...THAT'S WHAT I'LL TELL HIM.
OKAY!
KIRI?

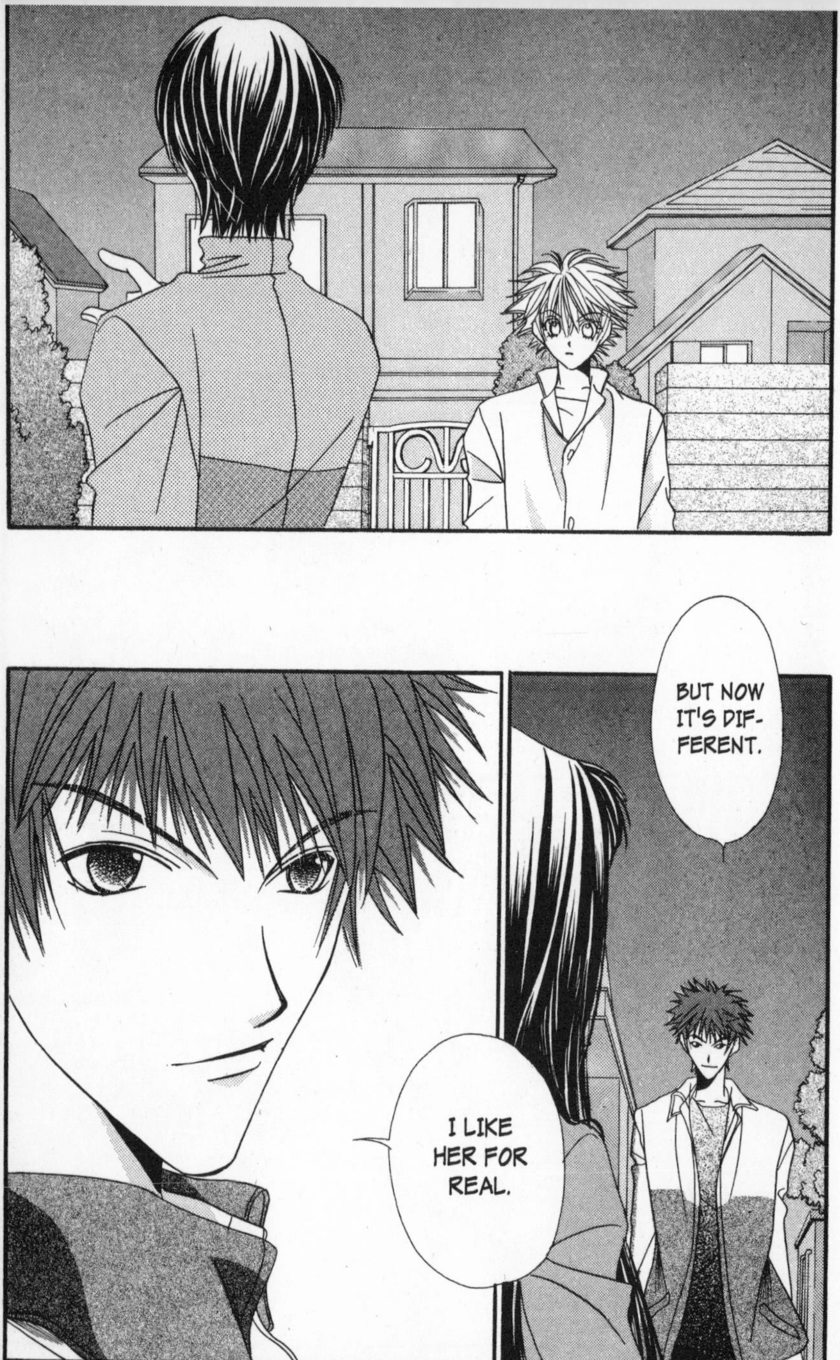
BUT NOW IT'S DIF-FERENT.
I LIKE HER FOR REAL.

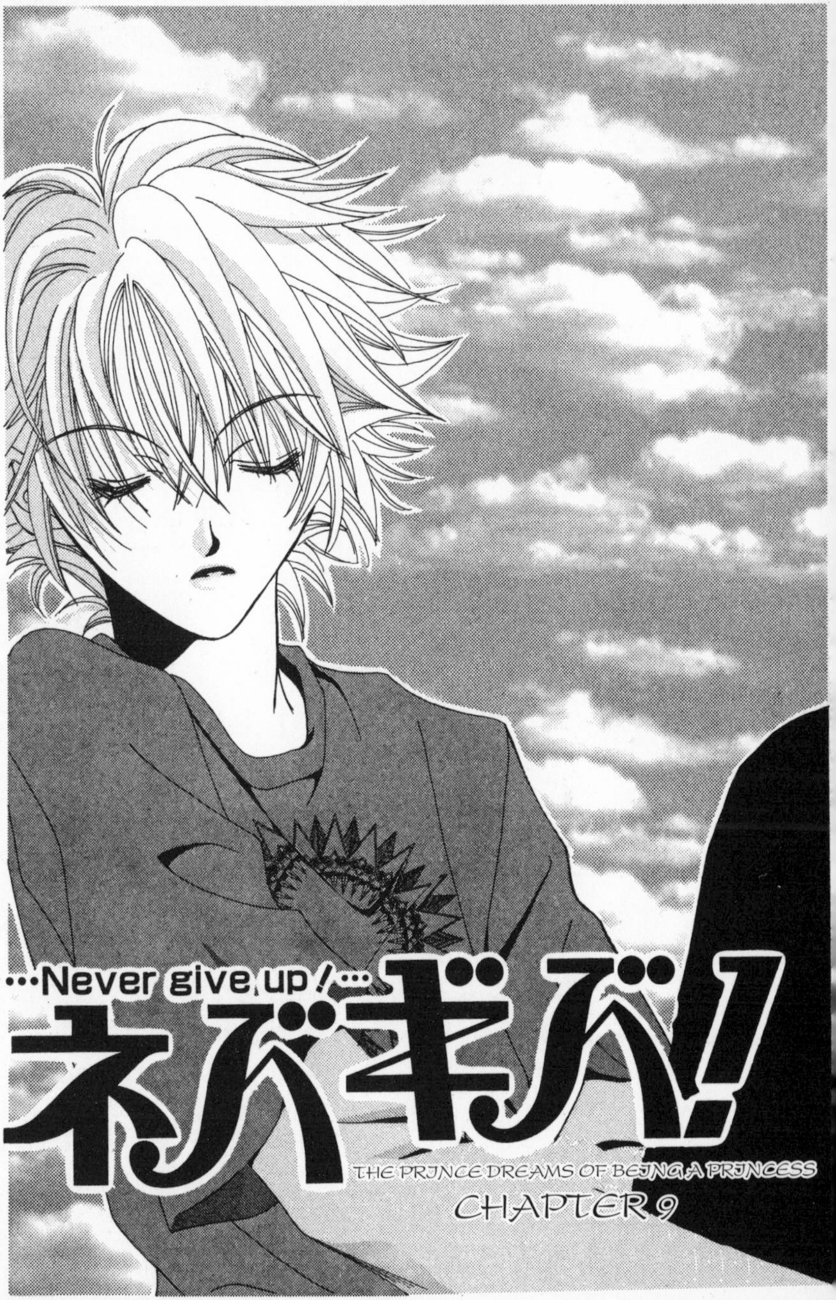
…Never give up!…
ネバギバ!
THE PRINCE DREAMS OF BEING A PRINCESS
CHAPTER 9

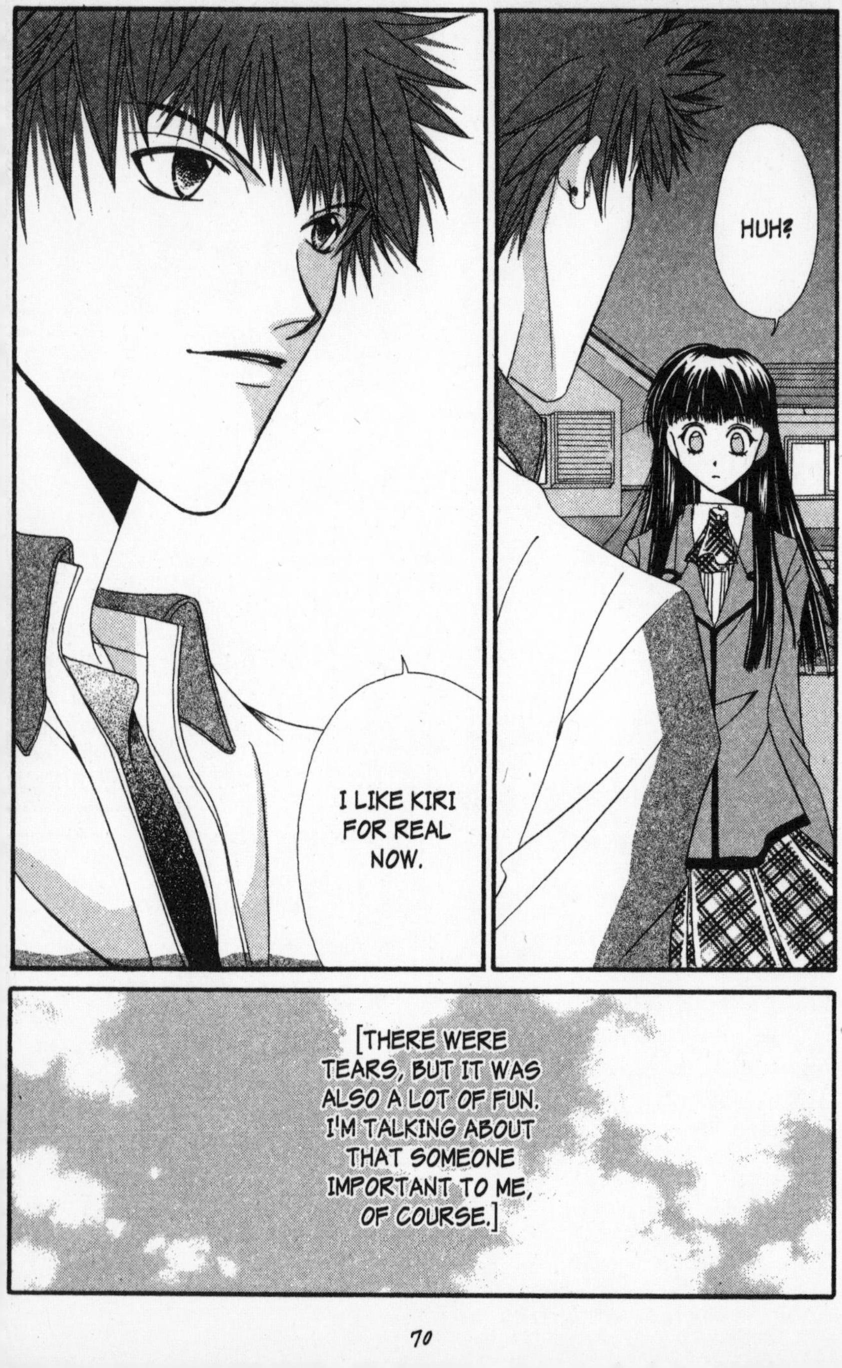
HUH?
I LIKE KIRI FOR REAL NOW.
[THERE WERE TEARS, BUT IT WAS ALSO A LOT OF FUN. I'M TALKING ABOUT THAT SOMEONE IMPORTANT TO ME, OF COURSE.]

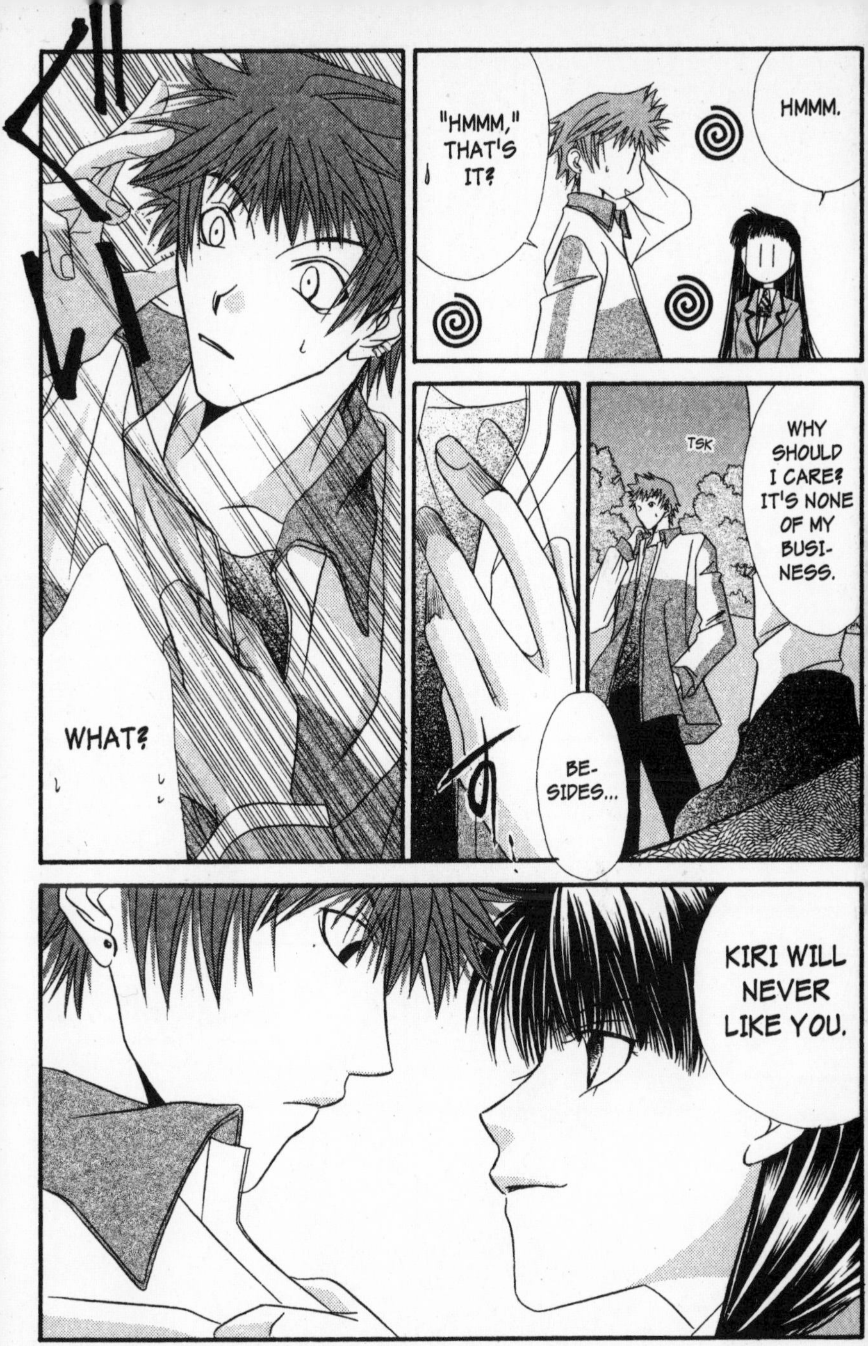
HMMM.
"HMMM," THAT'S IT?
TSK
WHY SHOULD I CARE? IT'S NONE OF MY BUSI-NESS.
BE-SIDES...
WHAT?
KIRI WILL NEVER LIKE YOU.

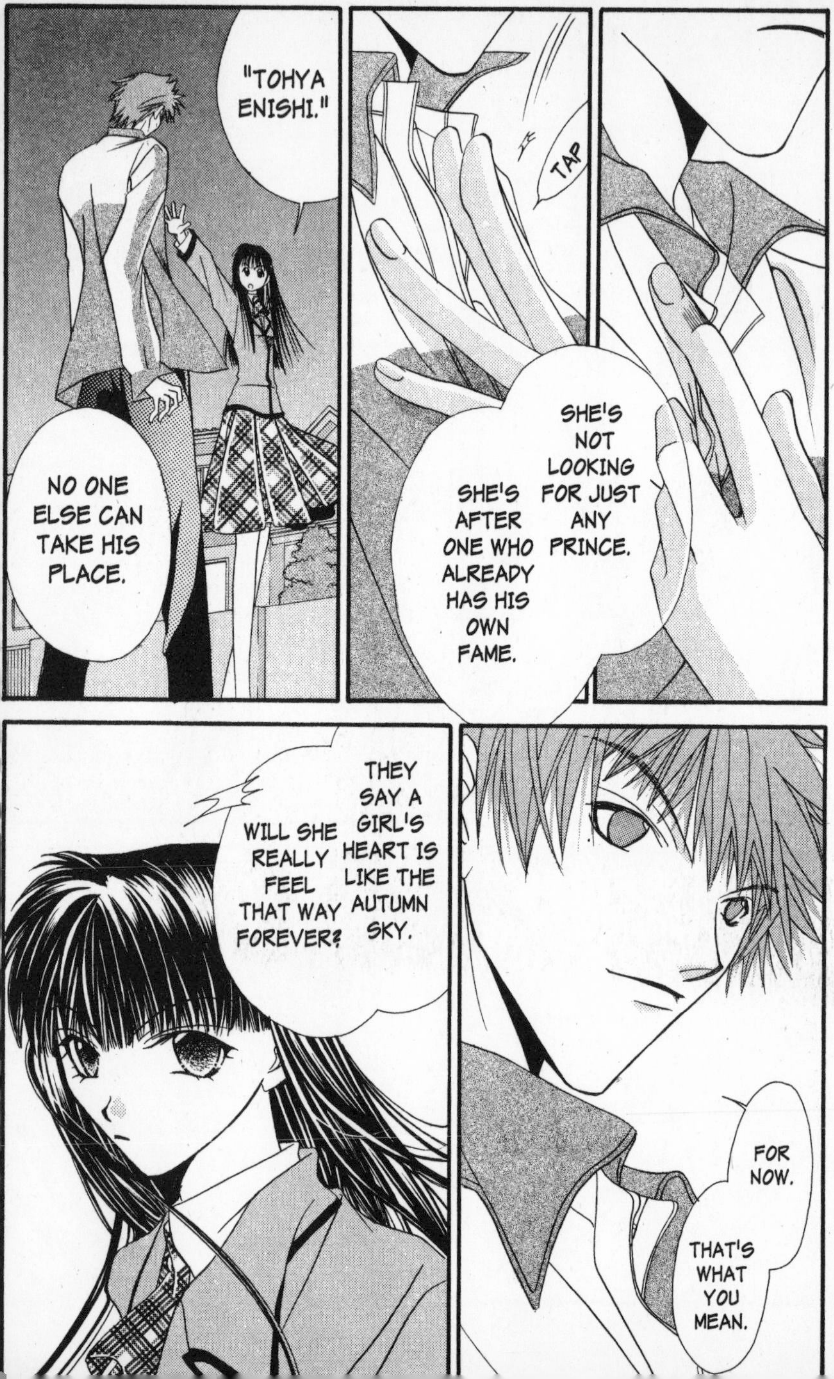
TAP
SHE'S NOT LOOKING FOR JUST ANY PRINCE.
SHE'S AFTER ONE WHO ALREADY HAS HIS OWN FAME.
"TOHYA ENISHI."
NO ONE ELSE CAN TAKE HIS PLACE.
FOR NOW.
THAT'S WHAT YOU MEAN.
THEY SAY A GIRL'S HEART IS LIKE THE AUTUMN SKY.
WILL SHE REALLY FEEL THAT WAY FOREVER?

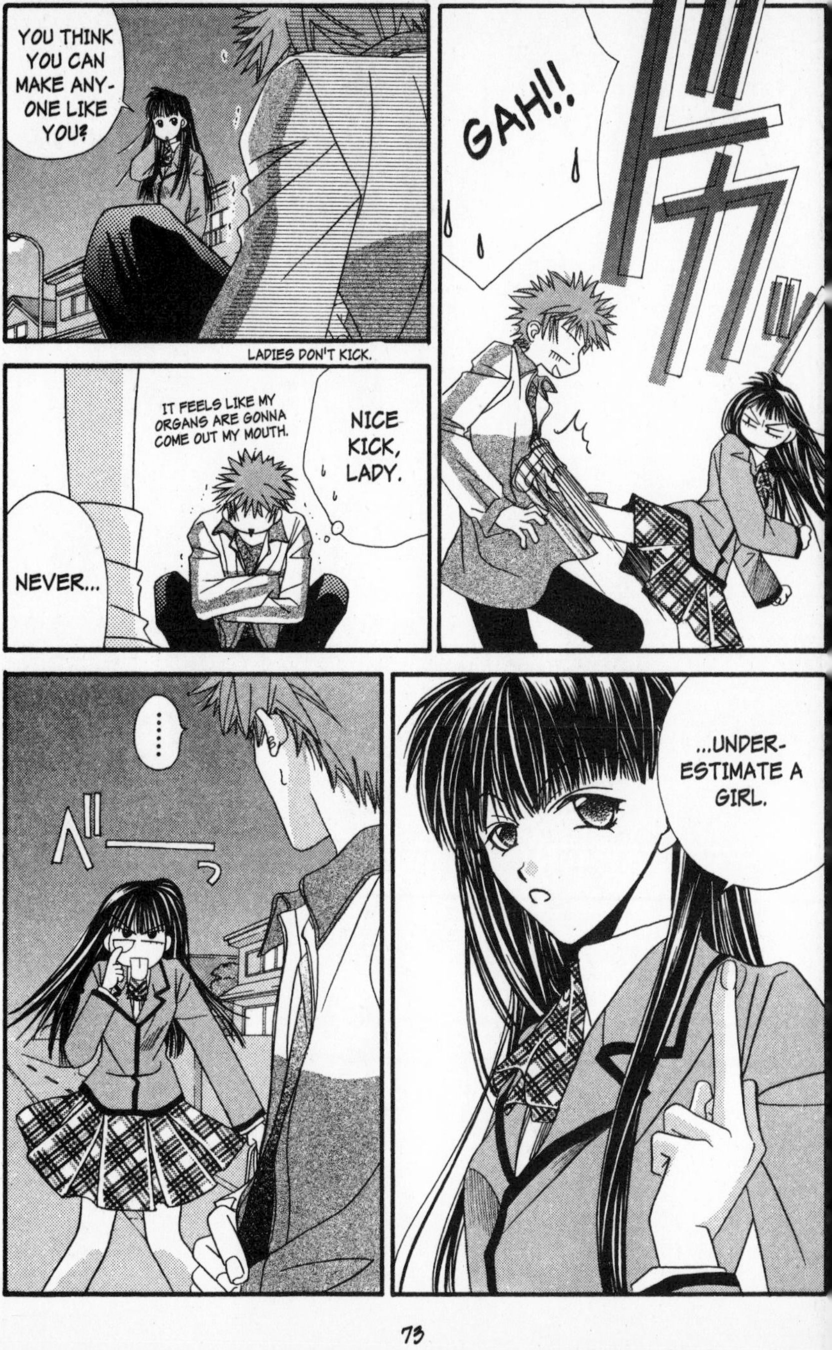
ドカッ
GAH!!
YOU THINK YOU CAN MAKE ANY-ONE LIKE YOU?
LADIES DON'T KICK.
NICE KICK, LADY.
IT FEELS LIKE MY ORGANS ARE GONNA COME OUT MY MOUTH.
NEVER...
...UNDER-ESTIMATE A GIRL.
......
べーっ

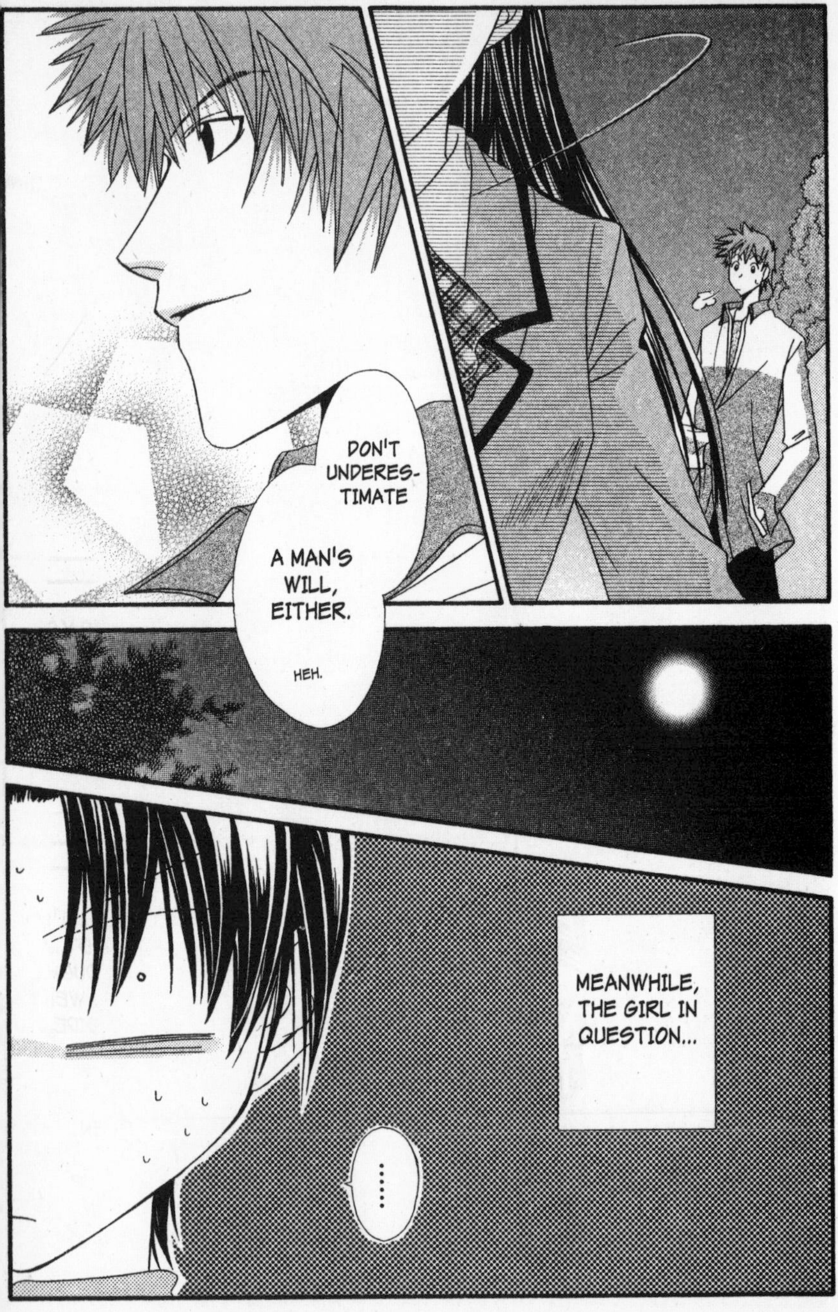
DON'T UNDERES-TIMATE
A MAN'S WILL, EITHER.
HEH.
MEANWHILE, THE GIRL IN QUESTION...
......

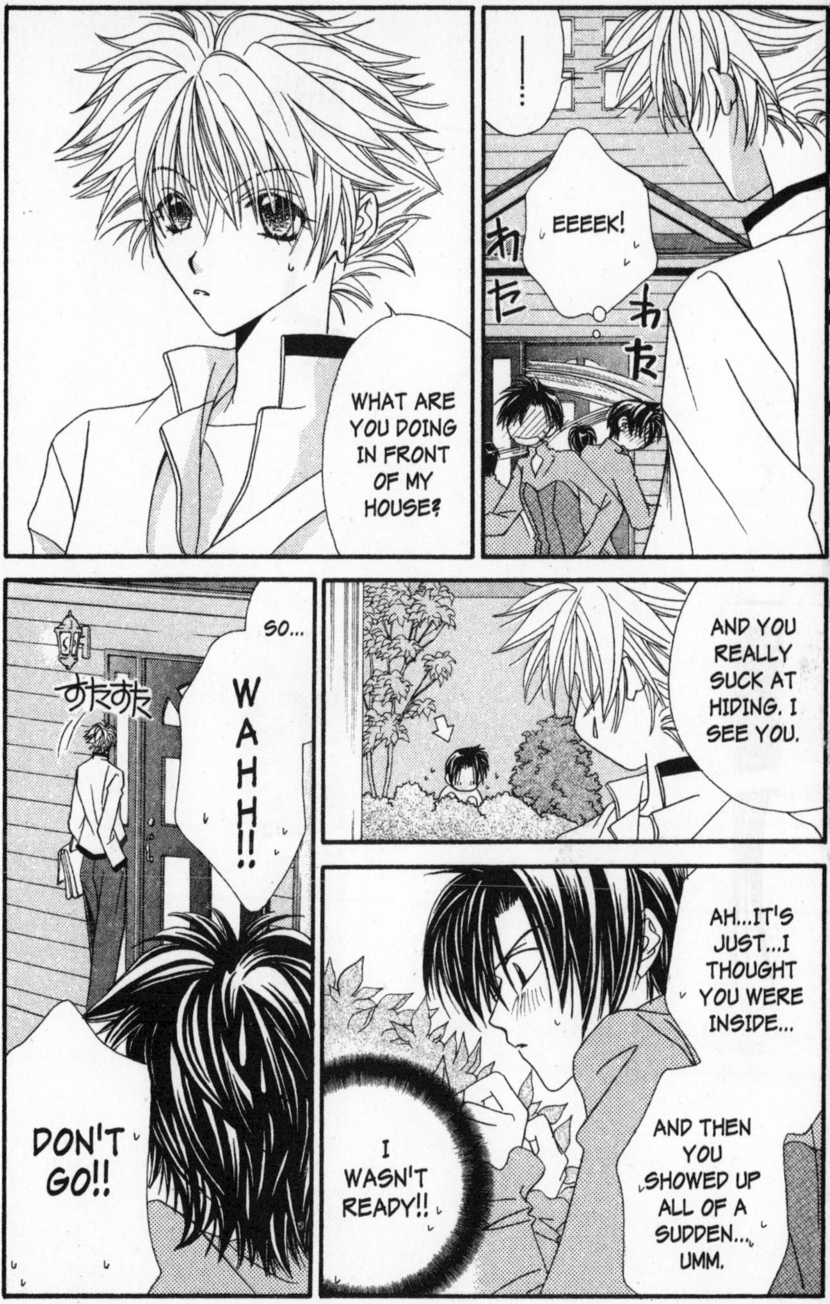

!...
EEEEK!
わた
わた
WHAT ARE YOU DOING IN FRONT OF MY HOUSE?
AND YOU REALLY SUCK AT HIDING. I SEE YOU.
AH...IT'S JUST...I THOUGHT YOU WERE INSIDE...
AND THEN YOU SHOWED UP ALL OF A SUDDEN... UMM.
I WASN'T READY!!
SO...
すたすた
WAHH!!
DON'T GO!!

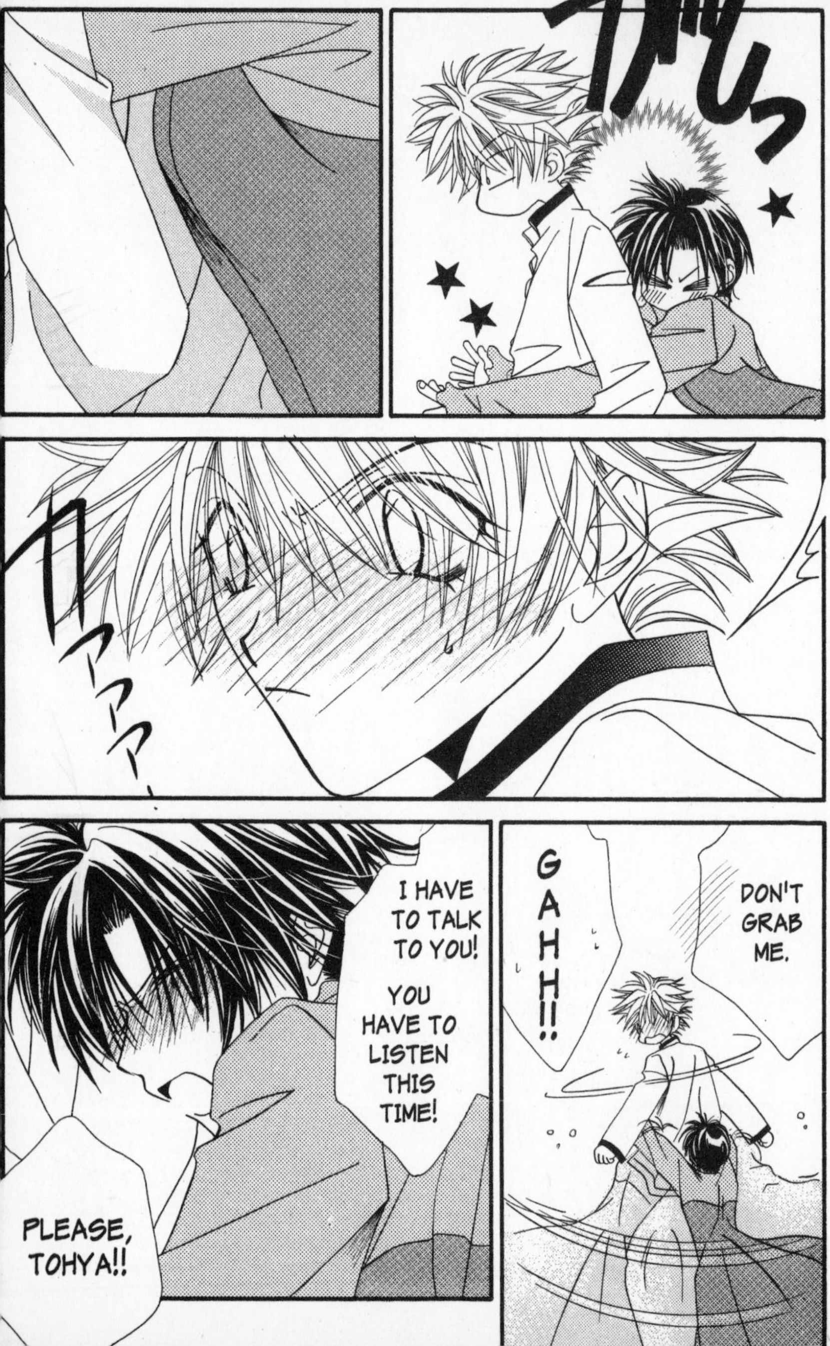

ガしっ
カァァァ
DON'T GRAB ME.
GAHH!!
I HAVE TO TALK TO YOU!
YOU HAVE TO LISTEN THIS TIME!
PLEASE, TOHYA!!

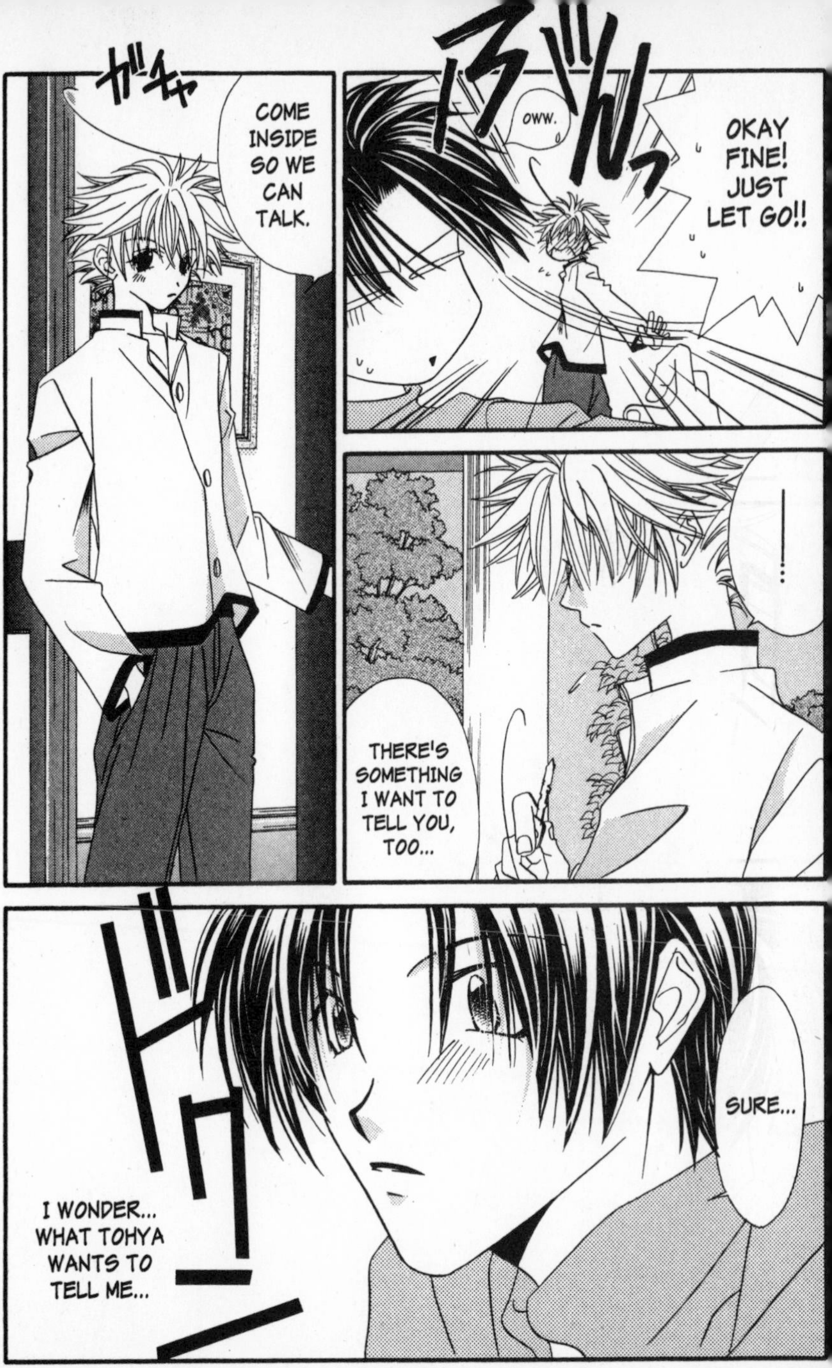
OKAY FINE! JUST LET GO!!
OWW.
...!
THERE'S SOMETHING I WANT TO TELL YOU, TOO...
ガチャ
COME INSIDE SO WE CAN TALK.
SURE...
I WONDER... WHAT TOHYA WANTS TO TELL ME...

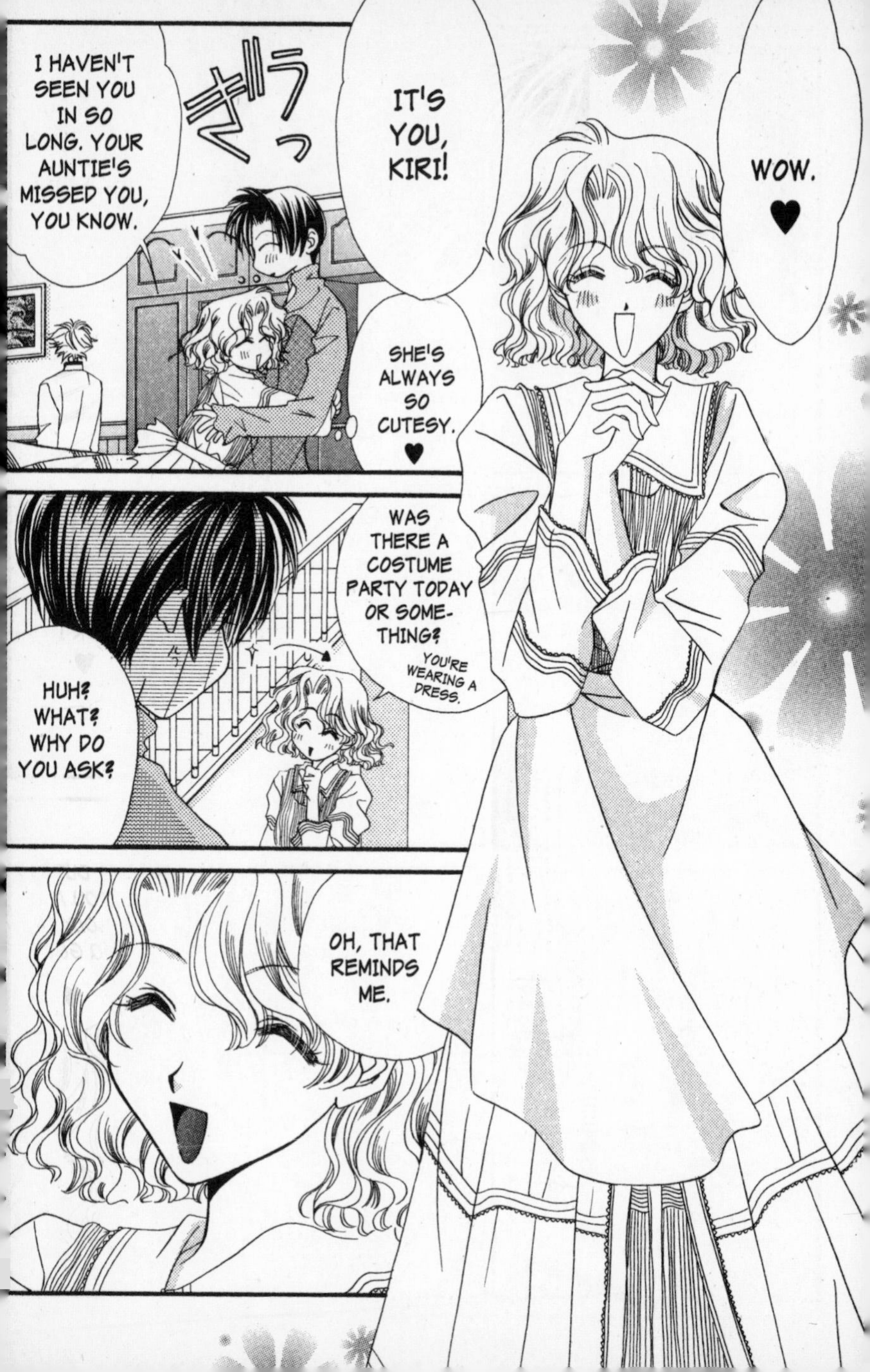
WOW. ♥
IT'S YOU, KIRI!
I HAVEN'T SEEN YOU IN SO LONG. YOUR AUNTIE'S MISSED YOU, YOU KNOW.
SHE'S ALWAYS SO CUTESY. ♥
WAS THERE A COSTUME PARTY TODAY OR SOME-THING?
YOU'RE WEARING A DRESS.
HUH? WHAT? WHY DO YOU ASK?
OH, THAT REMINDS ME.

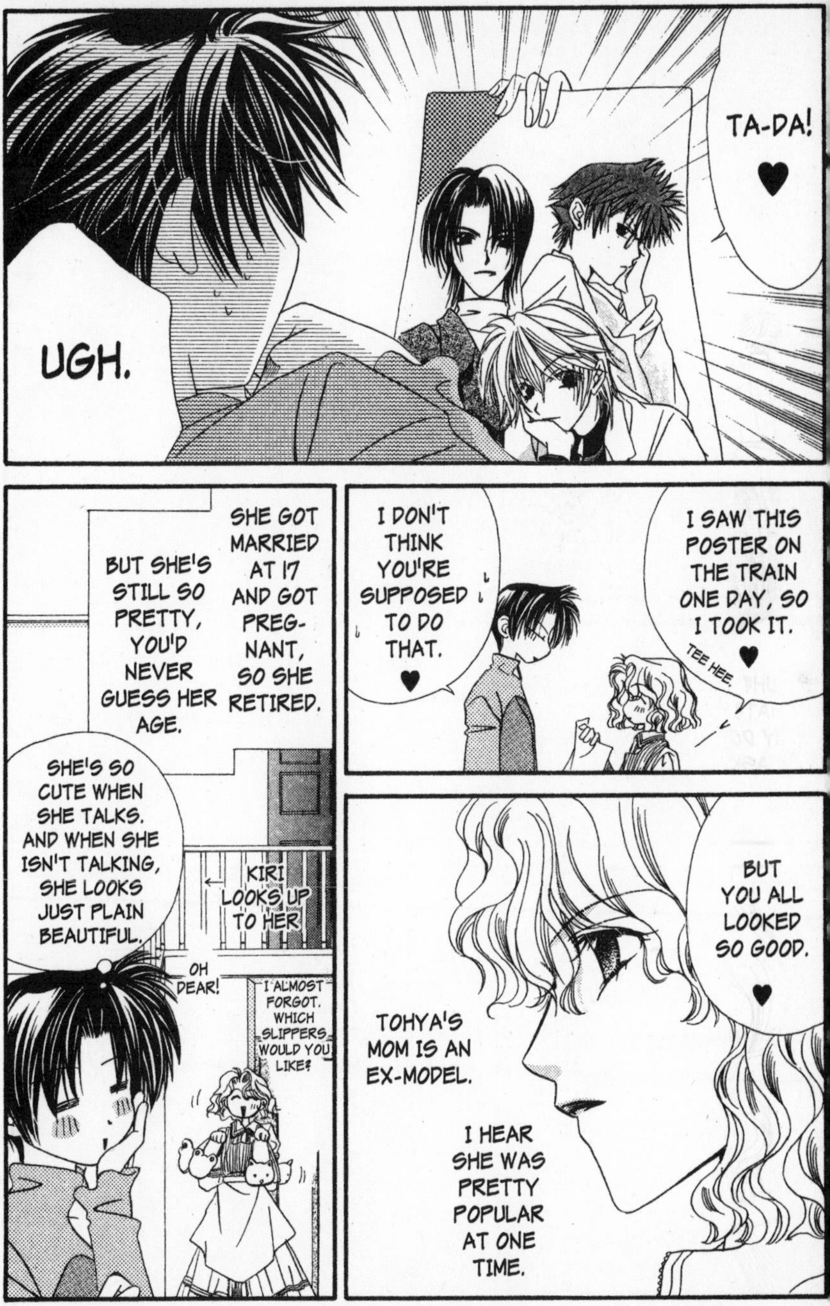
TA-DA! ♥
UGH.
I SAW THIS POSTER ON THE TRAIN ONE DAY, SO I TOOK IT. ♥
TEE HEE.
I DON'T THINK YOU'RE SUPPOSED TO DO THAT. ♥
BUT YOU ALL LOOKED SO GOOD. ♥
TOHYA'S MOM IS AN EX-MODEL.
I HEAR SHE WAS PRETTY POPULAR AT ONE TIME.
SHE GOT MARRIED AT 17 AND GOT PREGNANT, SO SHE RETIRED.
BUT SHE'S STILL SO PRETTY, YOU'D NEVER GUESS HER AGE.
SHE'S SO CUTE WHEN SHE TALKS. AND WHEN SHE ISN'T TALKING, SHE LOOKS JUST PLAIN BEAUTIFUL.
KIRI LOOKS UP TO HER
OH DEAR!
I ALMOST FORGOT. WHICH SLIPPERS WOULD YOU LIKE?

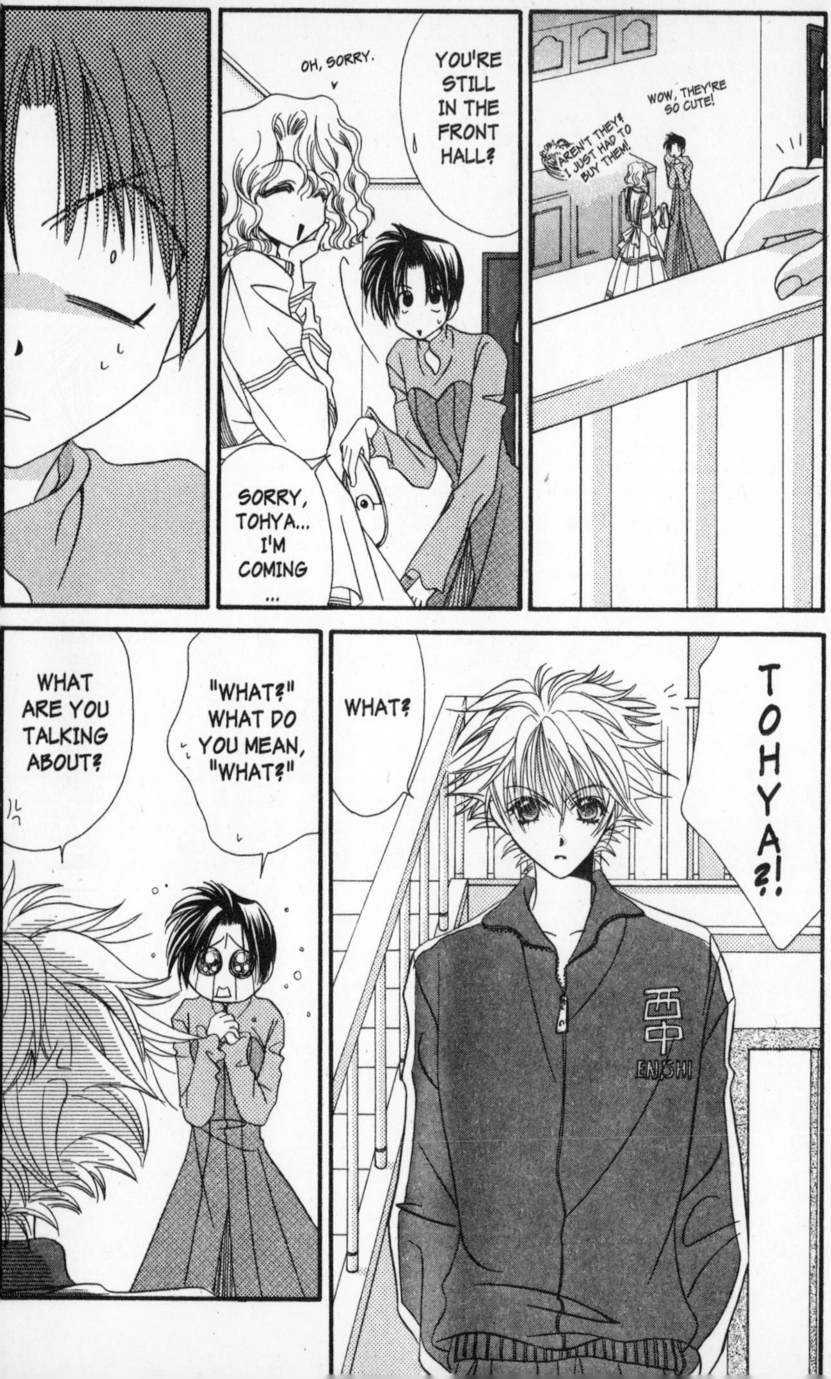
WOW, THEY'RE SO CUTE!
AREN'T THEY? I JUST HAD TO BUY THEM!
YOU'RE STILL IN THE FRONT HALL?
OH, SORRY.
SORRY, TOHYA... I'M COMING ...
TOHYA?!
WHAT?
"WHAT?" WHAT DO YOU MEAN, "WHAT?"
WHAT ARE YOU TALKING ABOUT?

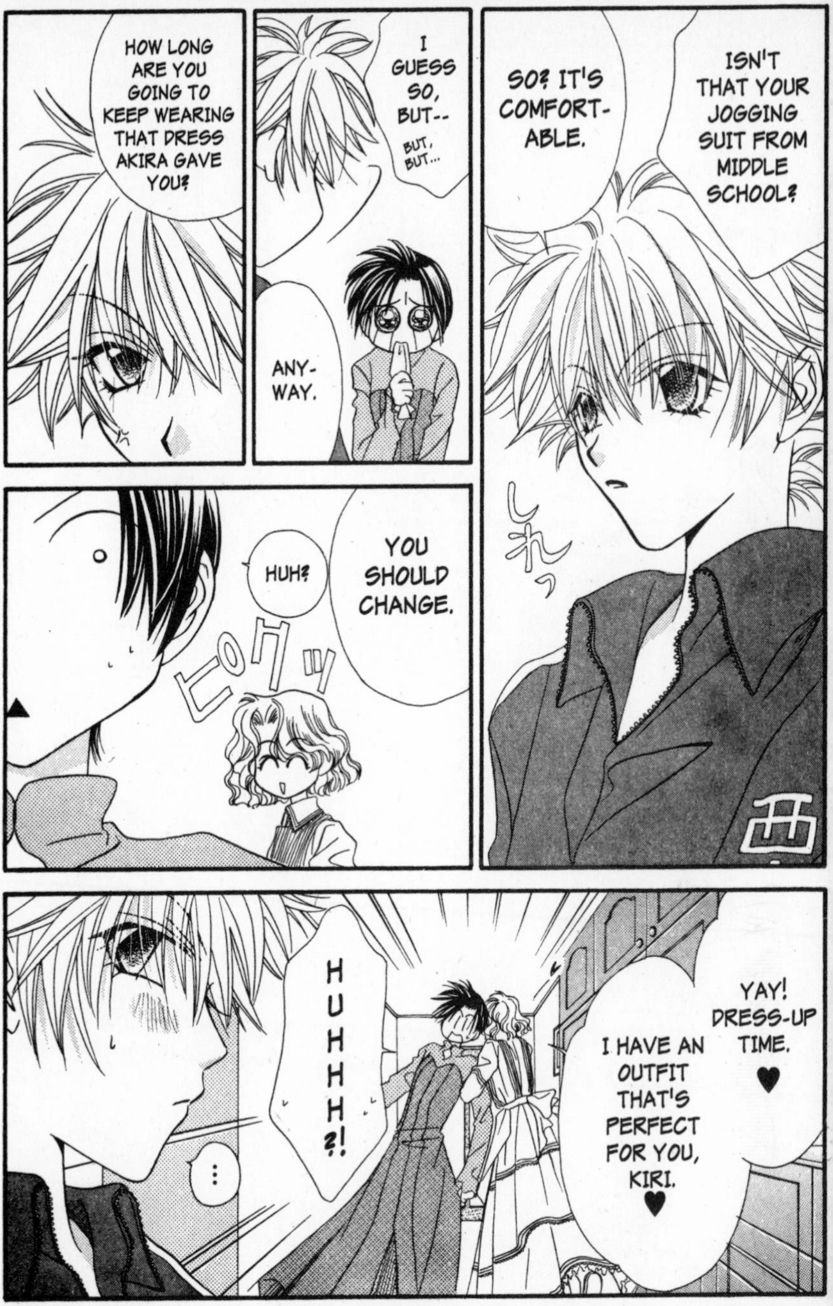
ISN'T THAT YOUR JOGGING SUIT FROM MIDDLE SCHOOL?
SO? IT'S COMFORT-ABLE.
しれっ
I GUESS SO, BUT--
BUT, BUT...
ANY-WAY.
HOW LONG ARE YOU GOING TO KEEP WEARING THAT DRESS AKIRA GAVE YOU?
YOU SHOULD CHANGE.
HUH?
ピクッ
YAY! DRESS-UP TIME. ♥
I HAVE AN OUTFIT THAT'S PERFECT FOR YOU, KIRI. ♥
HUHHHH?!
...

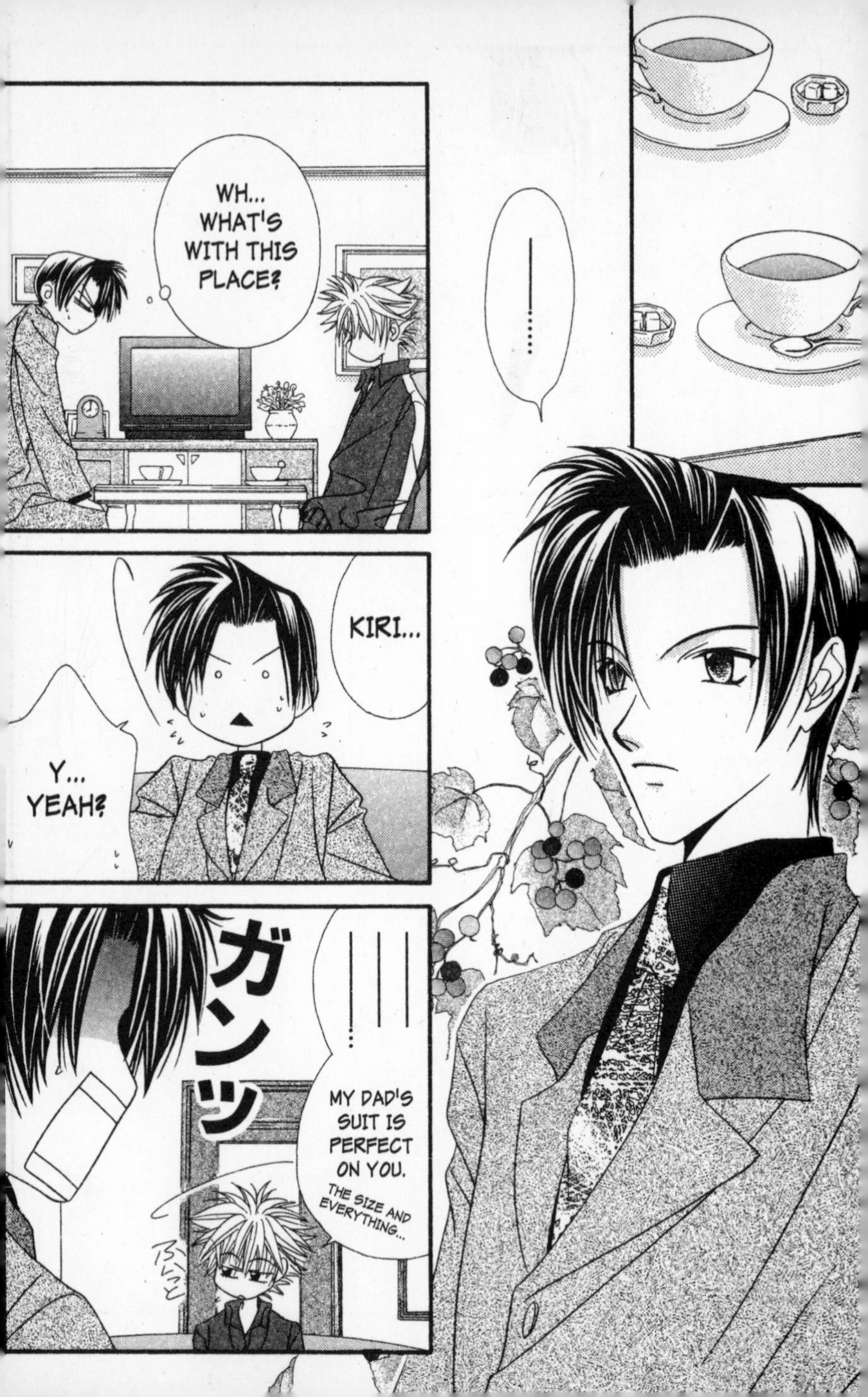

—......
WH... WHAT'S WITH THIS PLACE?
KIRI...
Y... YEAH?
ガンッ
——......
MY DAD'S SUIT IS PERFECT ON YOU.
THE SIZE AND EVERYTHING...

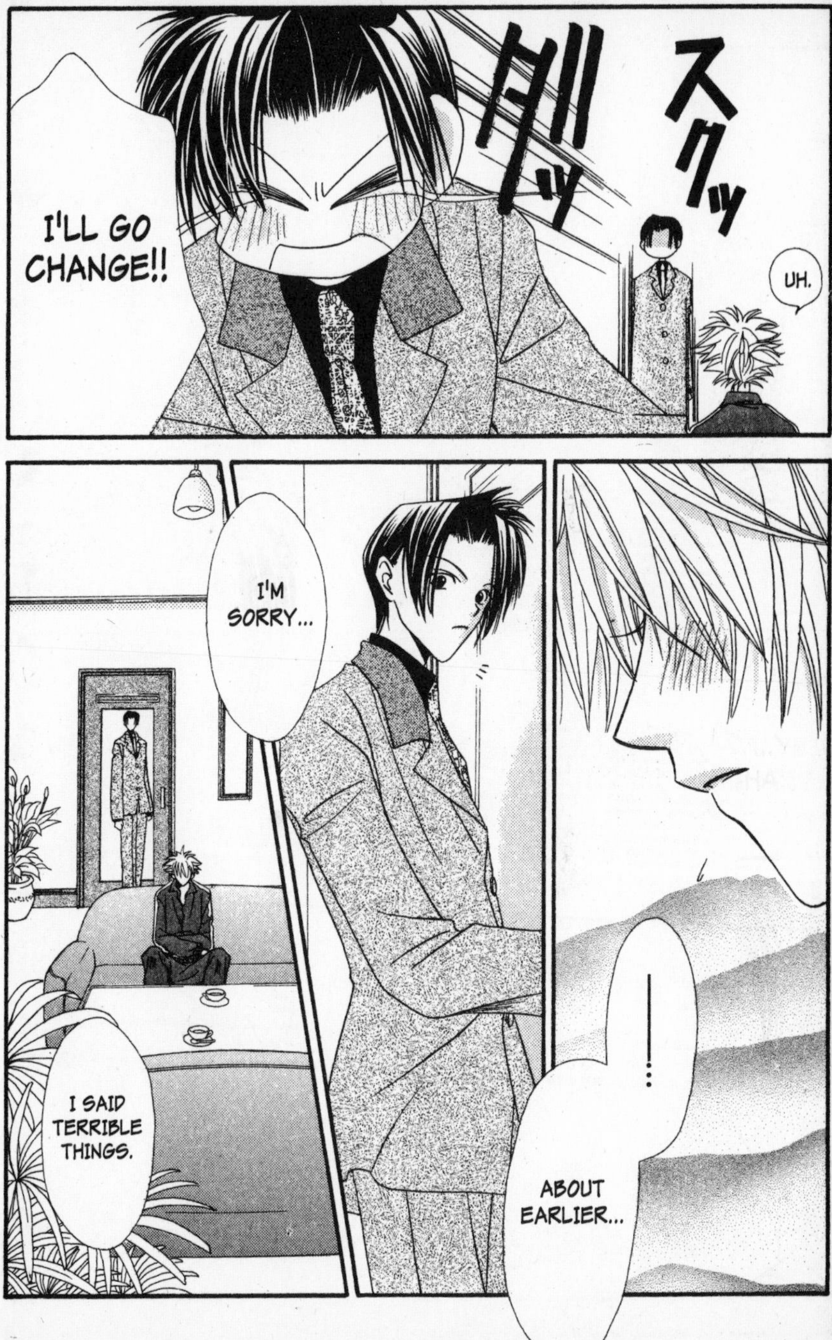
スクッ
I'LL GO CHANGE!!
ダッ
UH.
―……
ABOUT EARLIER...
I'M SORRY...
I SAID TERRIBLE THINGS.

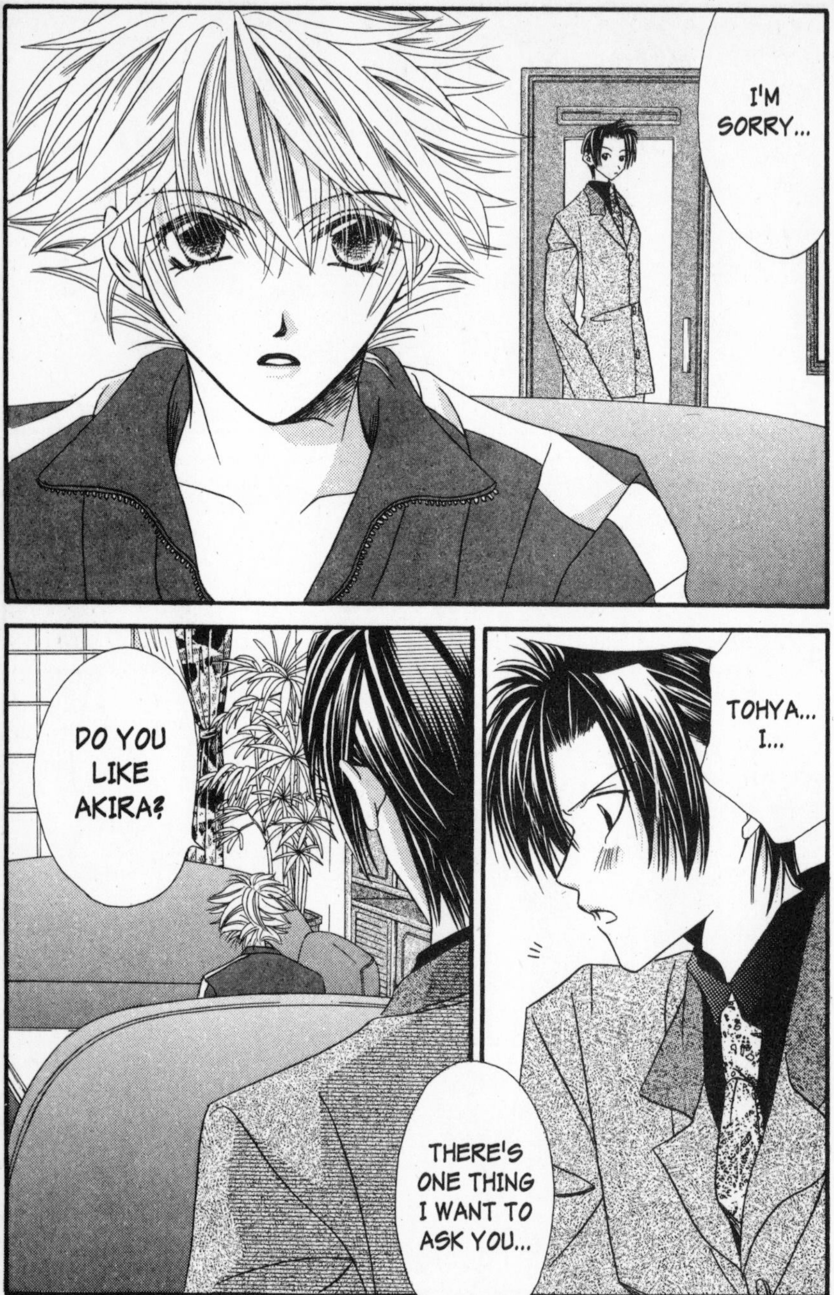
I'M SORRY...
TOHYA... I...
THERE'S ONE THING I WANT TO ASK YOU...
DO YOU LIKE AKIRA?

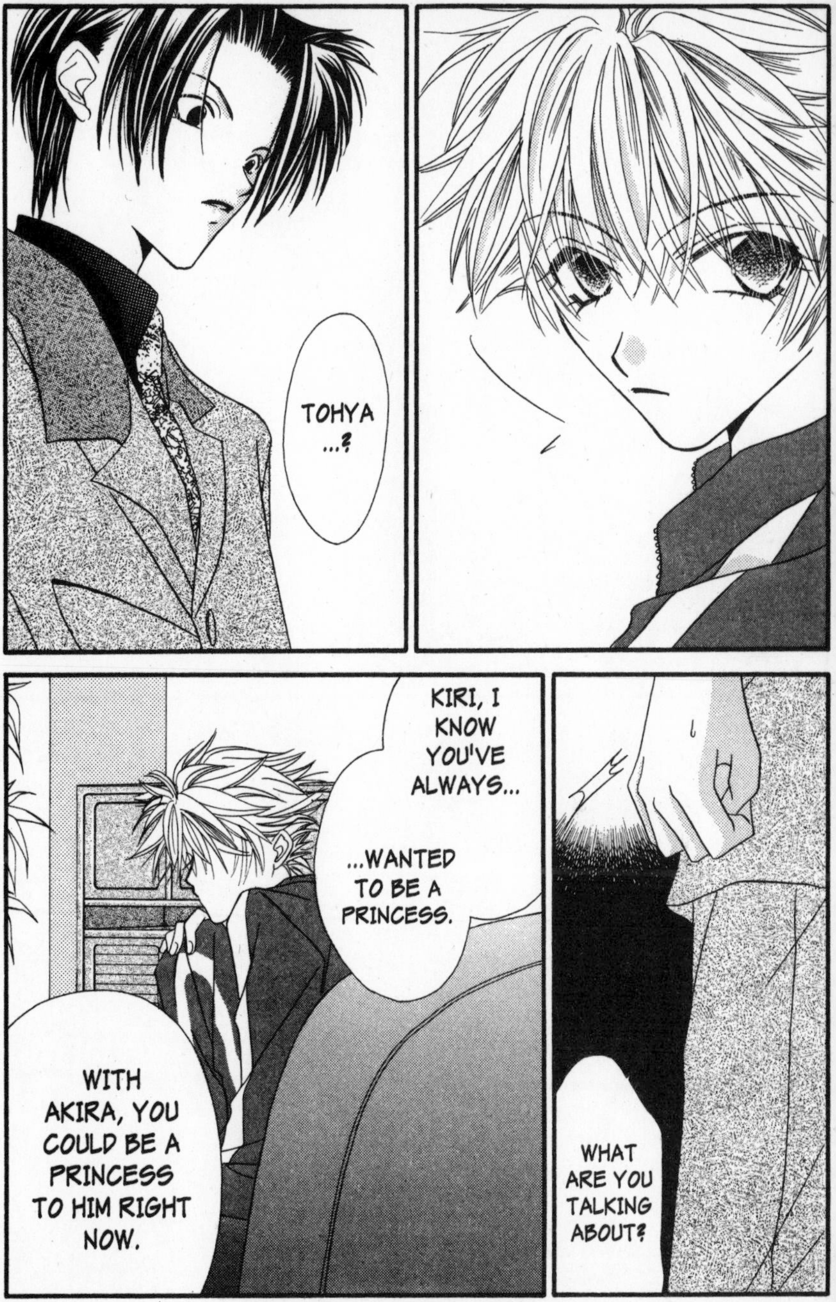
TOHYA ...?
WHAT ARE YOU TALKING ABOUT?
KIRI, I KNOW YOU'VE ALWAYS...
...WANTED TO BE A PRINCESS.
WITH AKIRA, YOU COULD BE A PRINCESS TO HIM RIGHT NOW.

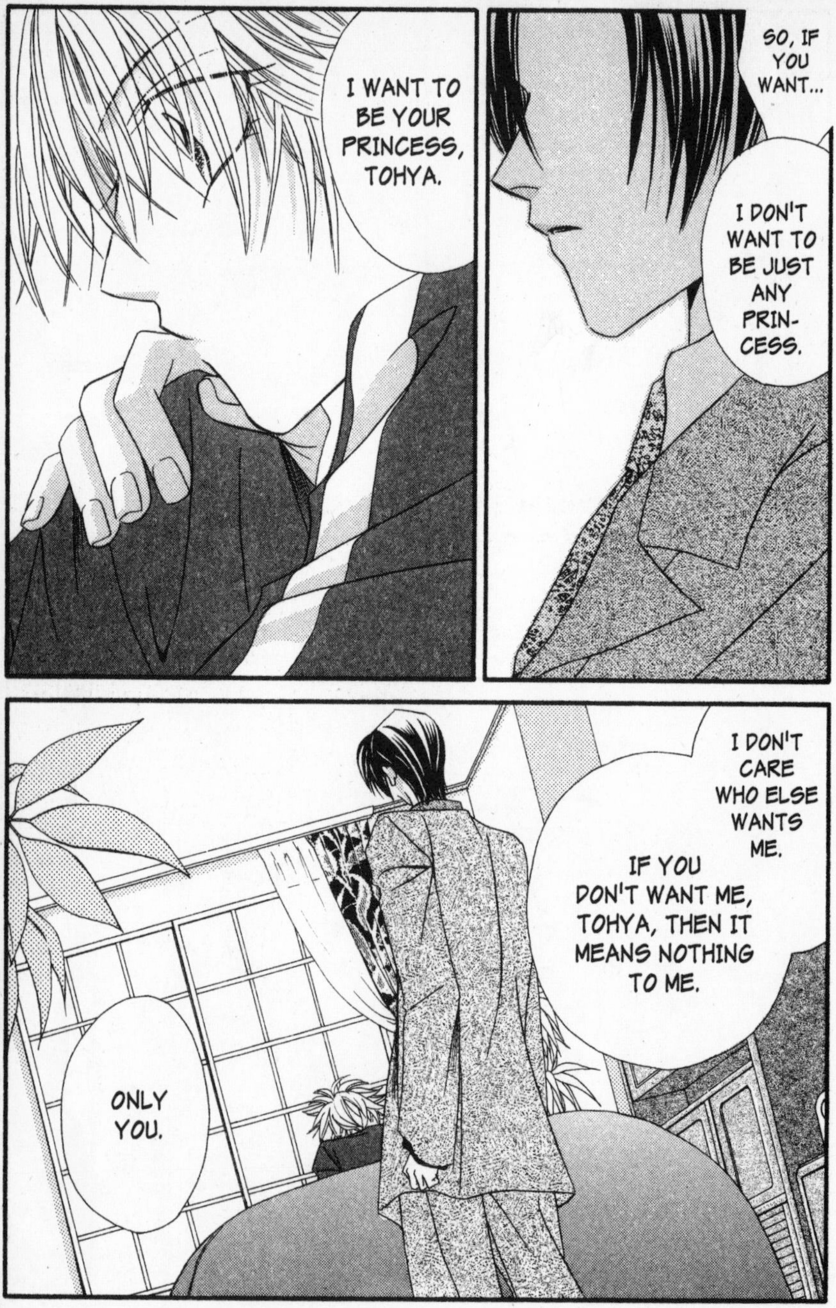
SO, IF YOU WANT...
I DON'T WANT TO BE JUST ANY PRIN- CESS.
I WANT TO BE YOUR PRINCESS, TOHYA.
I DON'T CARE WHO ELSE WANTS ME.
IF YOU DON'T WANT ME, TOHYA, THEN IT MEANS NOTHING TO ME.
ONLY YOU.

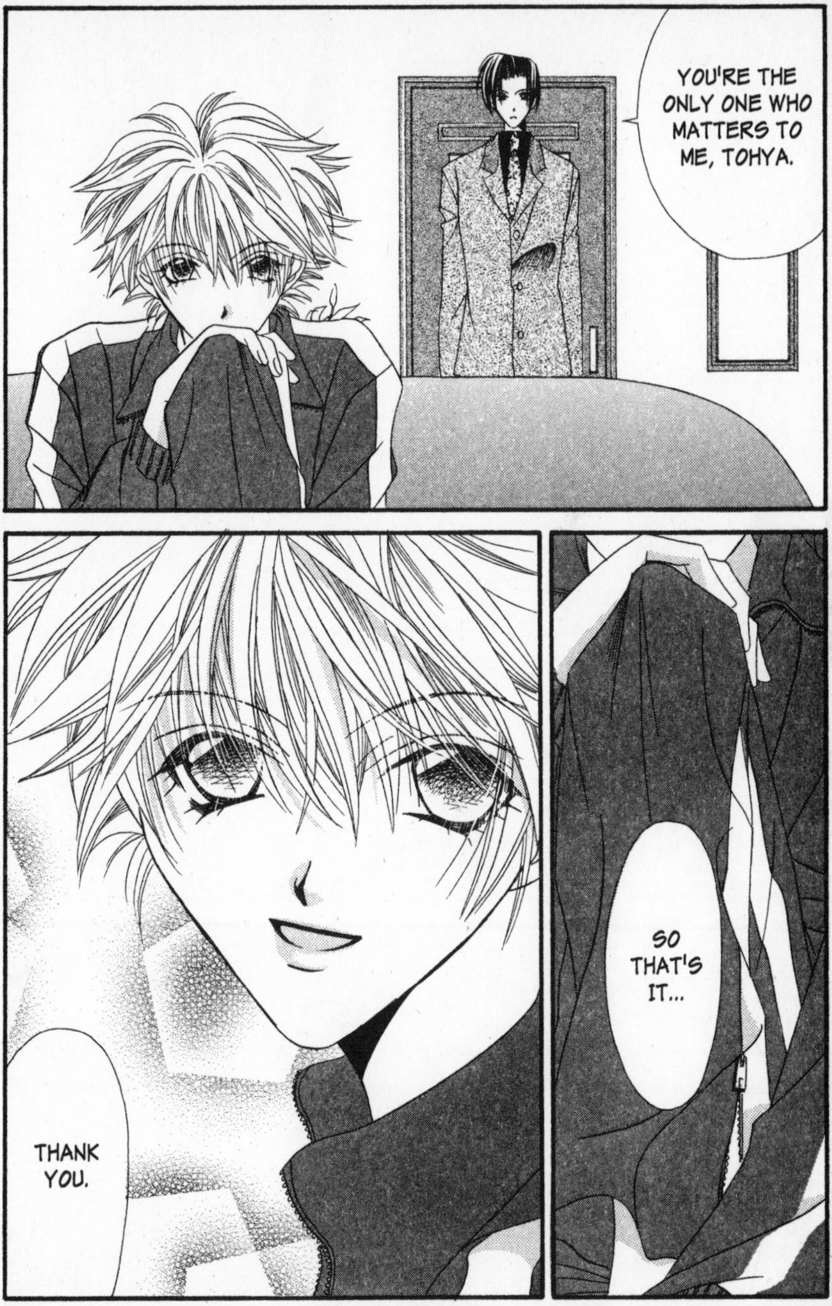
YOU'RE THE ONLY ONE WHO MATTERS TO ME, TOHYA.
SO THAT'S IT...
THANK YOU.

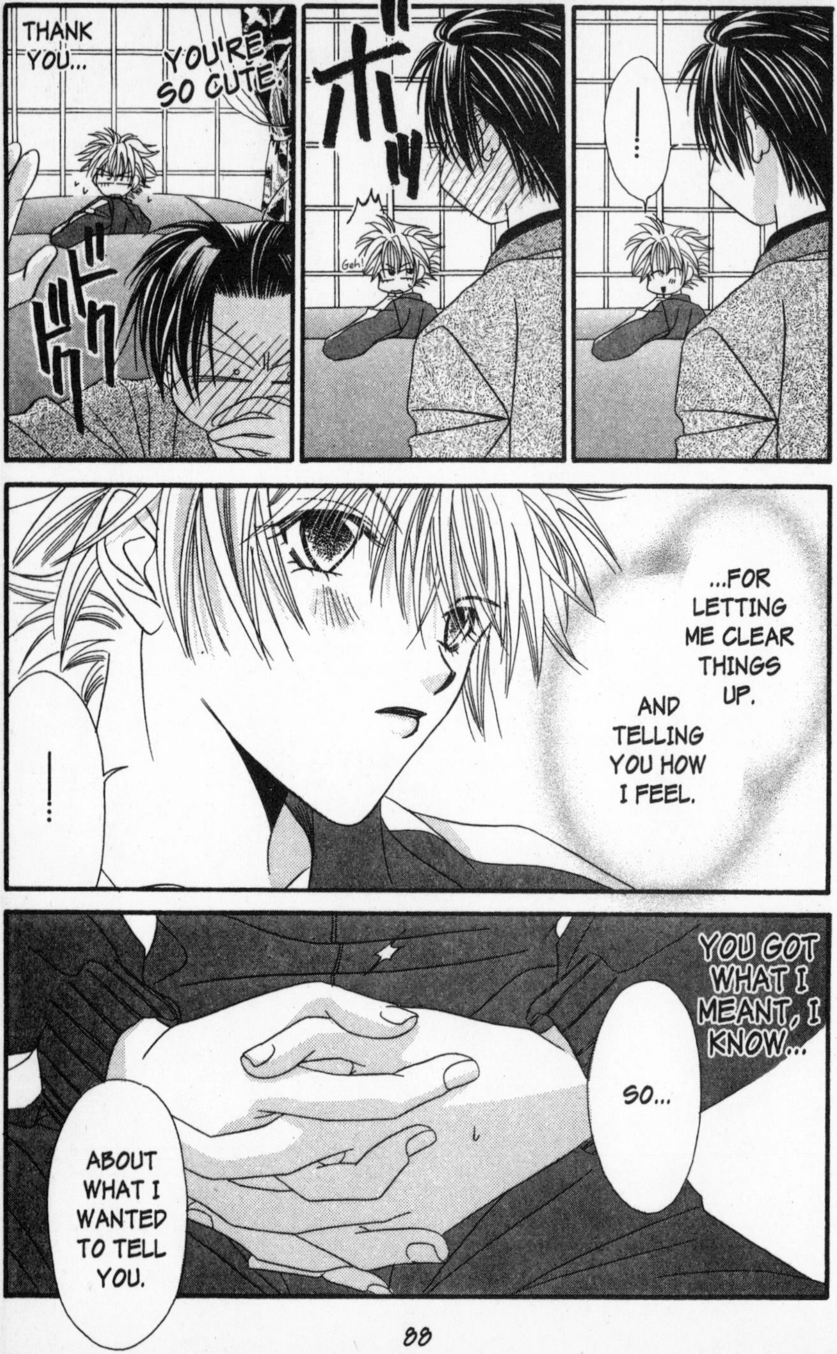
!...
ボッ
Geh!
THANK YOU...
YOU'RE SO CUTE.
ドクッ
...FOR LETTING ME CLEAR THINGS UP.
AND TELLING YOU HOW I FEEL.
!...
YOU GOT WHAT I MEANT, I KNOW...
SO...
ABOUT WHAT I WANTED TO TELL YOU.

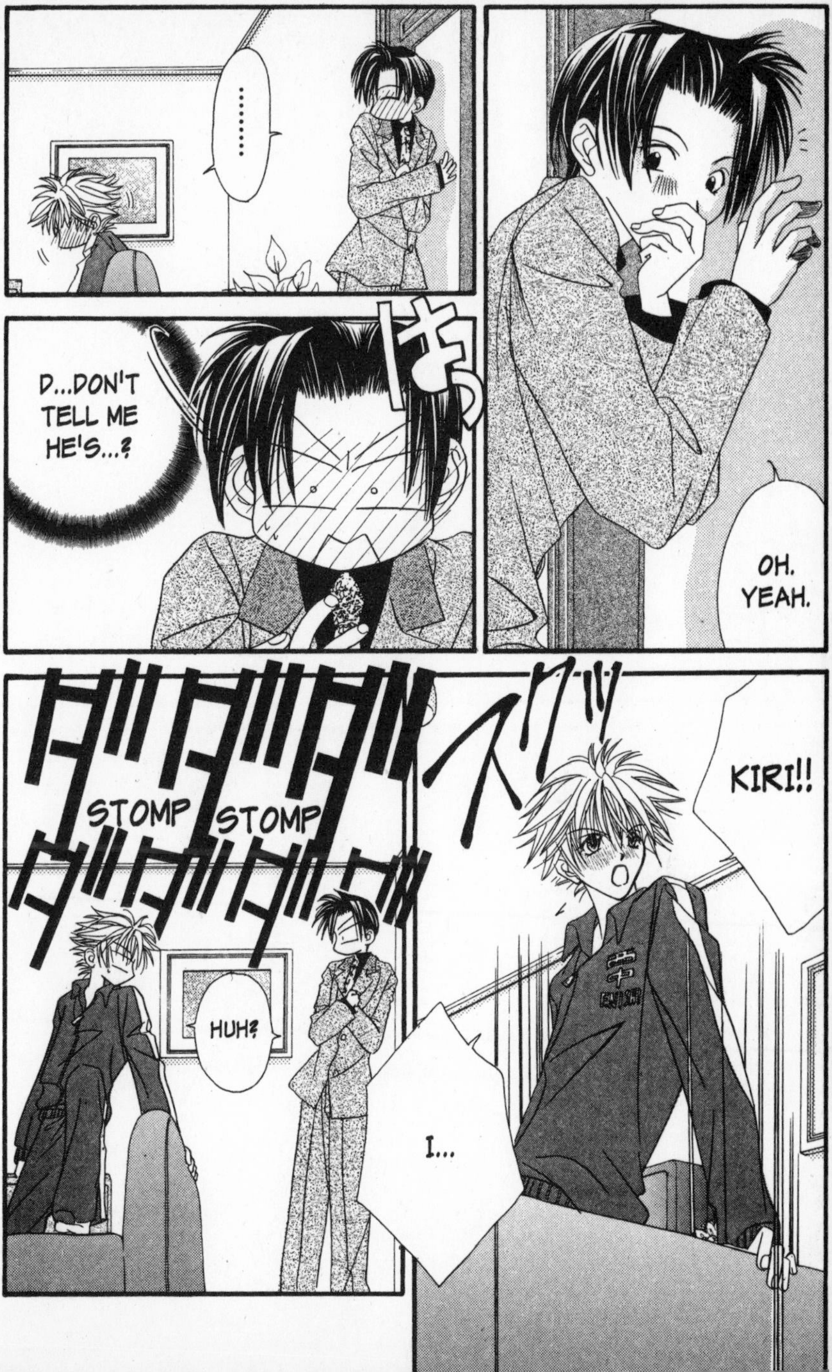
OH. YEAH.
......
はっ
D...DON'T TELL ME HE'S...?
KIRI!!
スクッ
I...
STOMP STOMP
HUH?

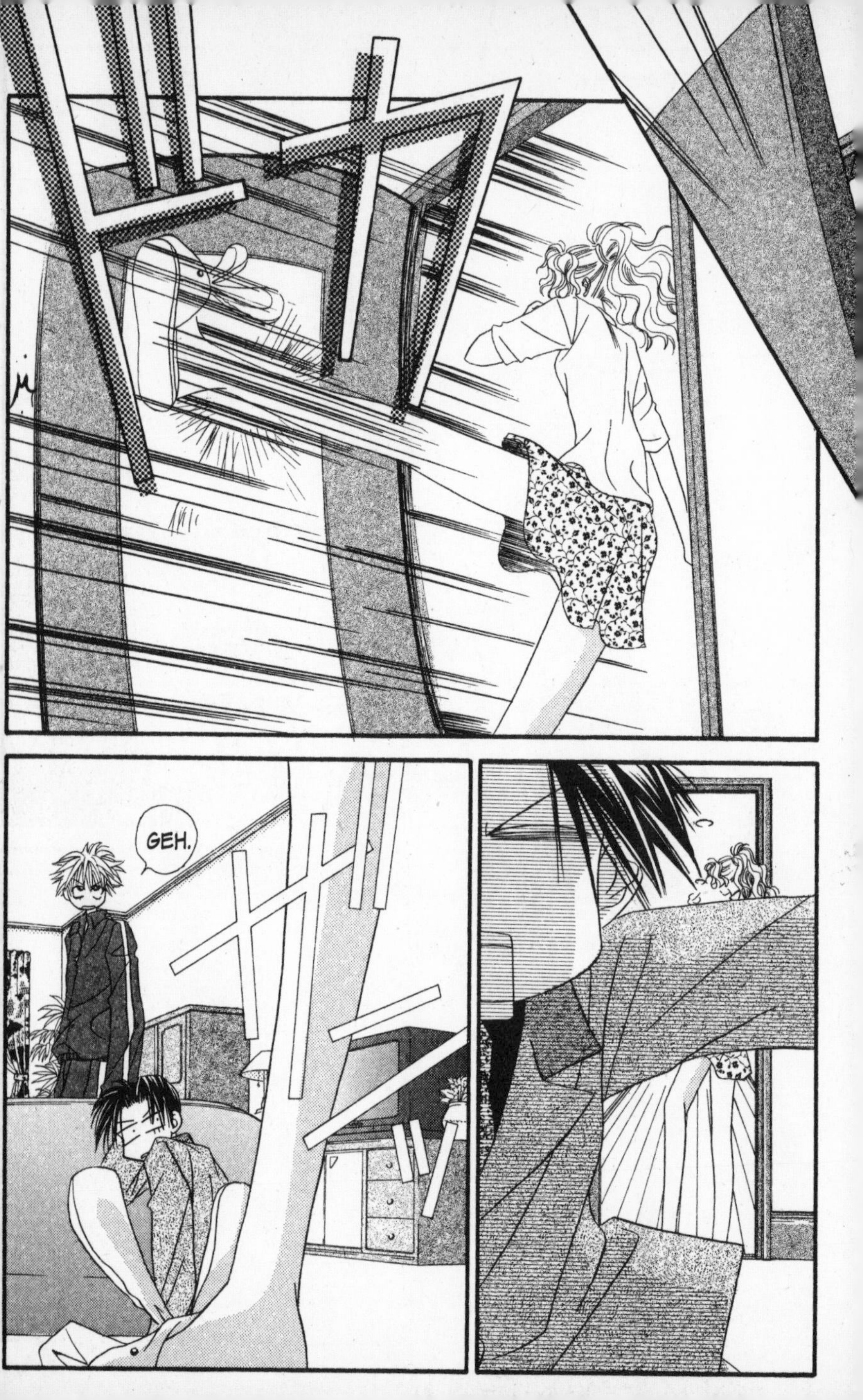
GEH.

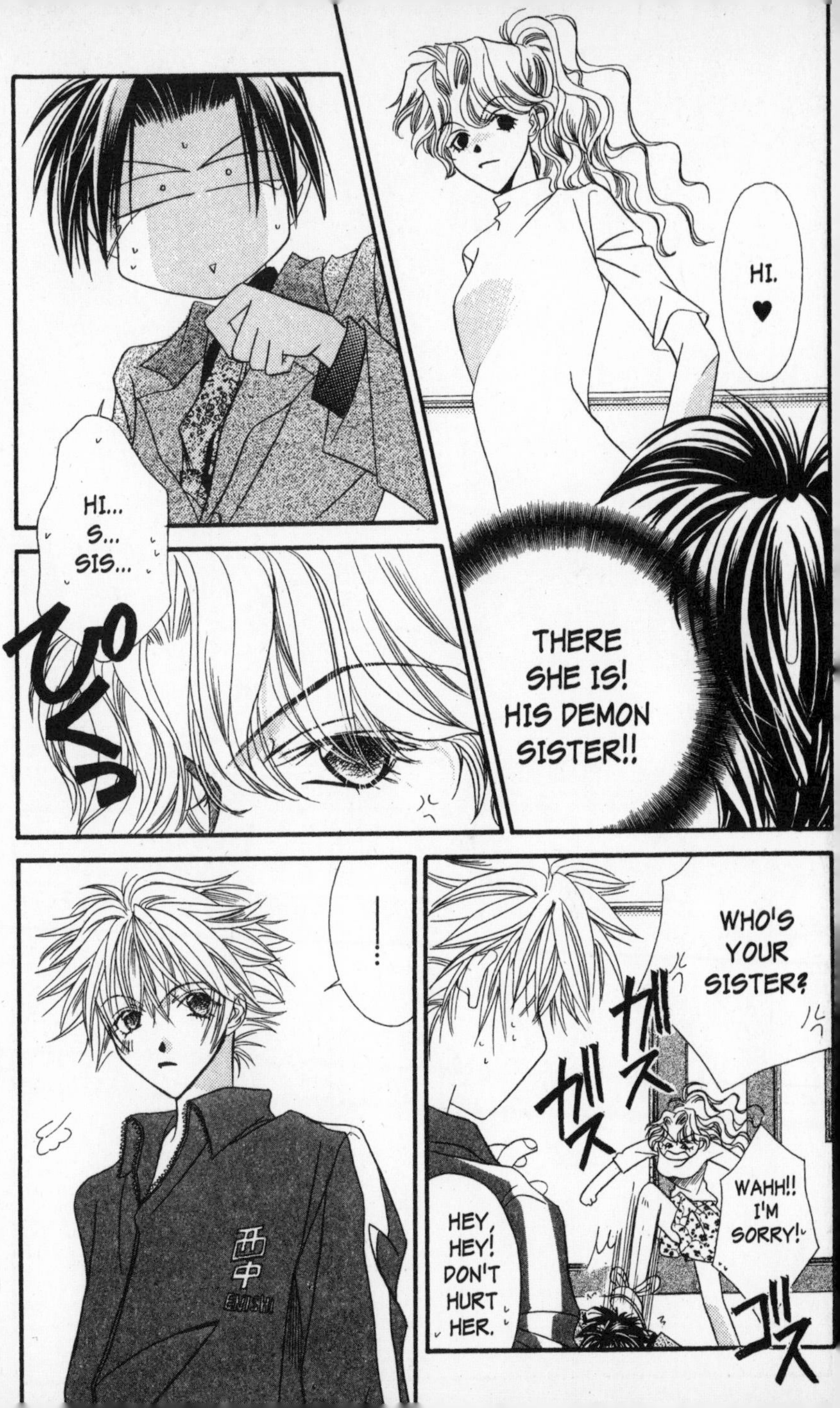
HI. ♥
THERE SHE IS! HIS DEMON SISTER!!
HI... S... SIS...
ぴくっ
WHO'S YOUR SISTER?
ガス ゲス
WAHH!! I'M SORRY!
HEY, HEY! DON'T HURT HER.
ゴス
......!
西中

SIGH.

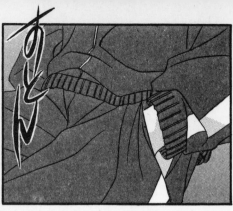

HUH?!

YOU PISSED TOHYA OFF, DIDN'T YOU?

FREEZE

CUT IT OUT.

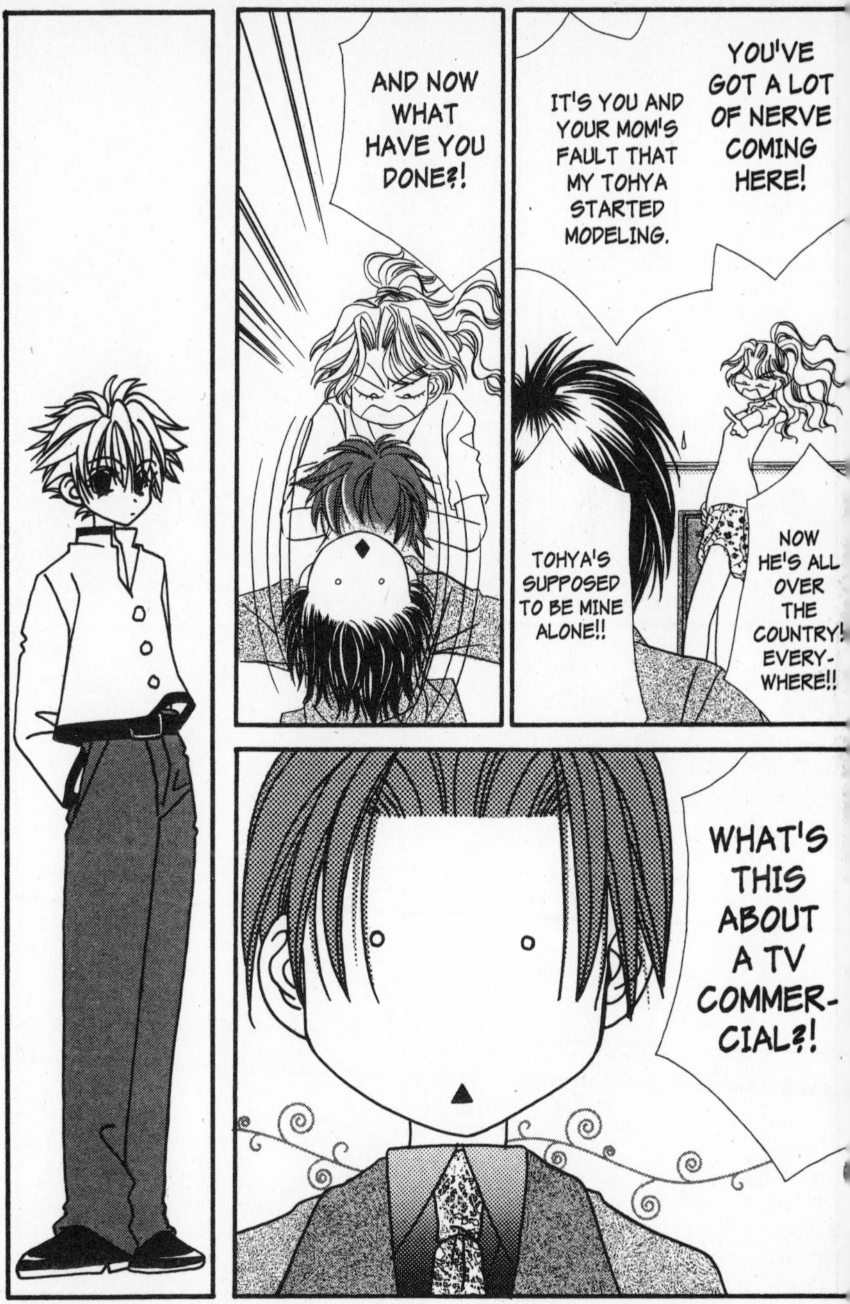
YOU'VE GOT A LOT OF NERVE COMING HERE!
IT'S YOU AND YOUR MOM'S FAULT THAT MY TOHYA STARTED MODELING.
NOW HE'S ALL OVER THE COUNTRY! EVERY-WHERE!!
TOHYA'S SUPPOSED TO BE MINE ALONE!!
AND NOW WHAT HAVE YOU DONE?!
WHAT'S THIS ABOUT A TV COMMER-CIAL?!

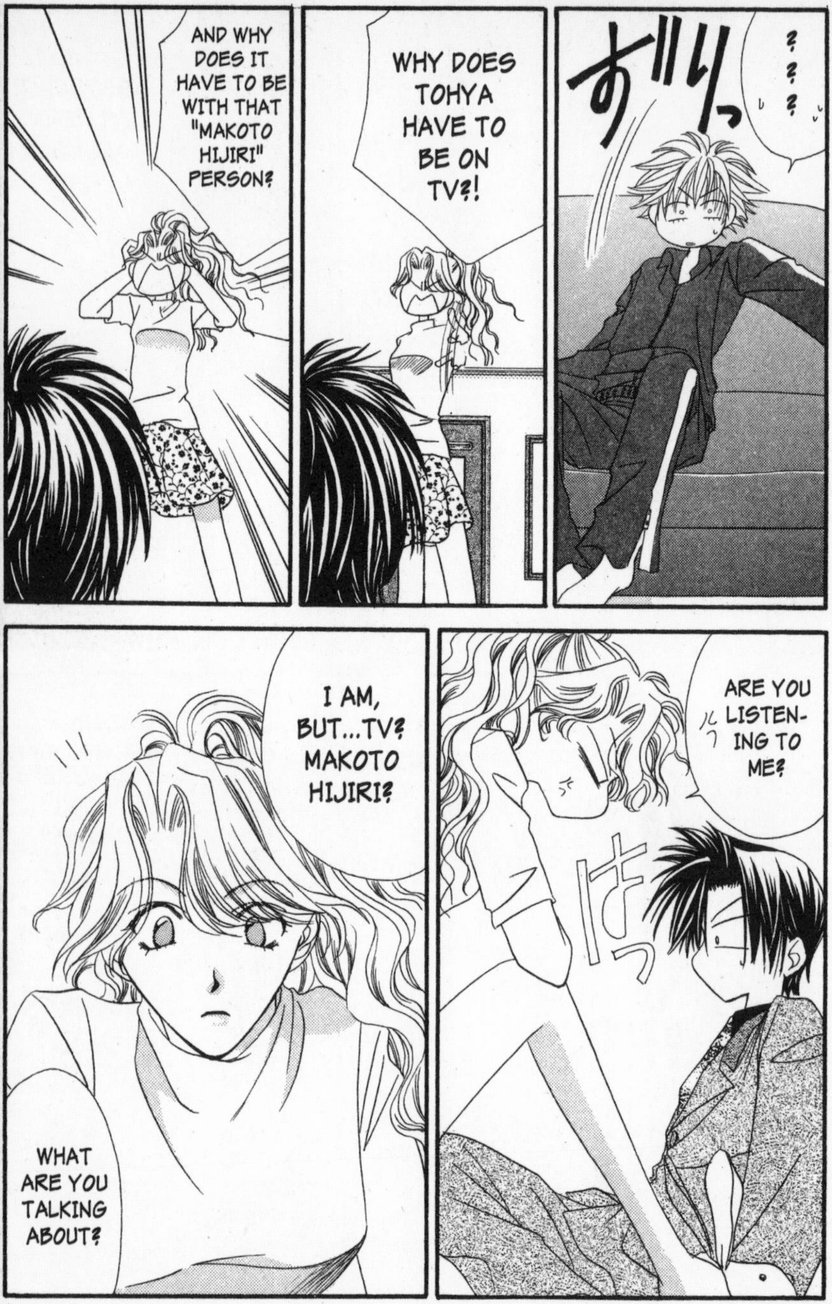
ずりっ
???
WHY DOES TOHYA HAVE TO BE ON TV?!
AND WHY DOES IT HAVE TO BE WITH THAT "MAKOTO HIJIRI" PERSON?
ARE YOU LISTENING TO ME?
はっ
I AM, BUT...TV? MAKOTO HIJIRI?
WHAT ARE YOU TALKING ABOUT?

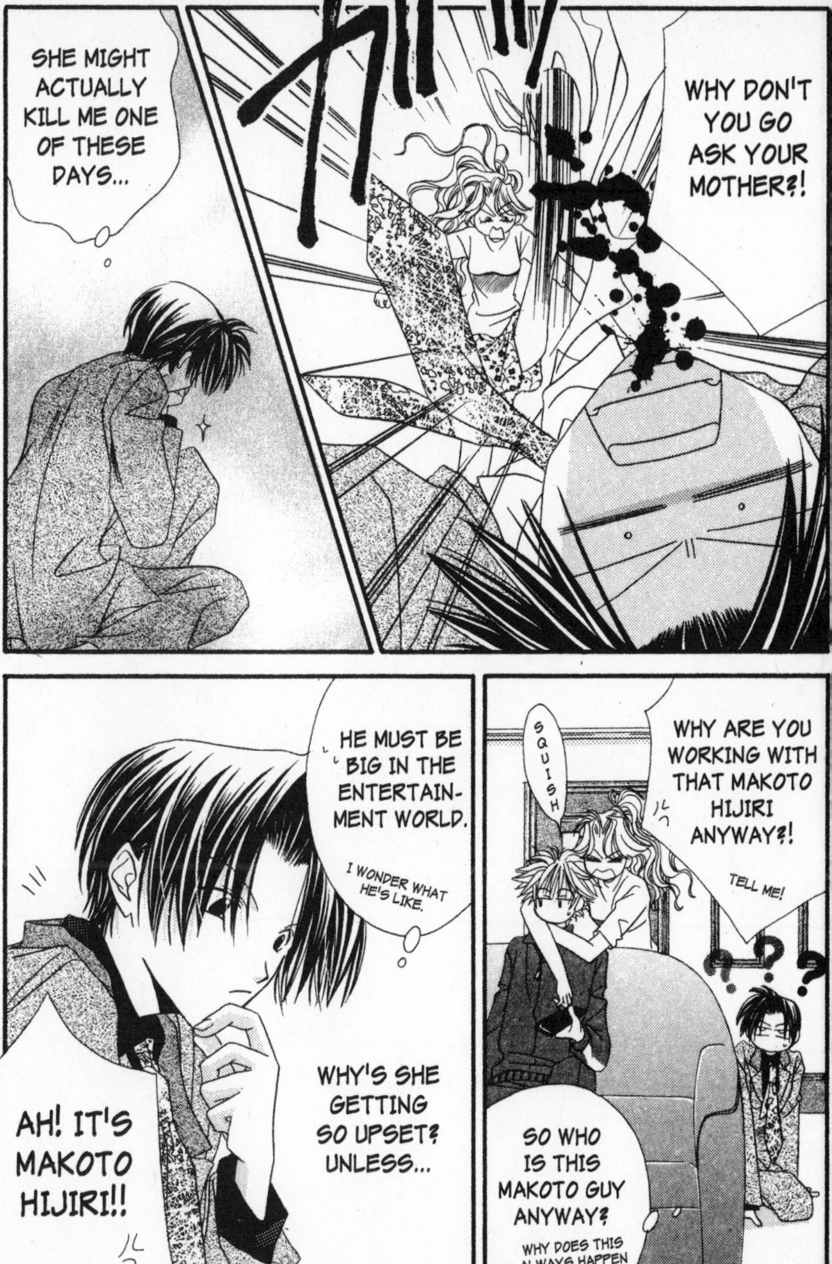
WHY DON'T YOU GO ASK YOUR MOTHER?!
SHE MIGHT ACTUALLY KILL ME ONE OF THESE DAYS...
SQUISH
WHY ARE YOU WORKING WITH THAT MAKOTO HIJIRI ANYWAY?!
TELL ME!
SO WHO IS THIS MAKOTO GUY ANYWAY?
WHY DOES THIS ALWAYS HAPPEN TO ME...?
HE MUST BE BIG IN THE ENTERTAINMENT WORLD.
I WONDER WHAT HE'S LIKE.
WHY'S SHE GETTING SO UPSET? UNLESS...
AH! IT'S MAKOTO HIJIRI!!

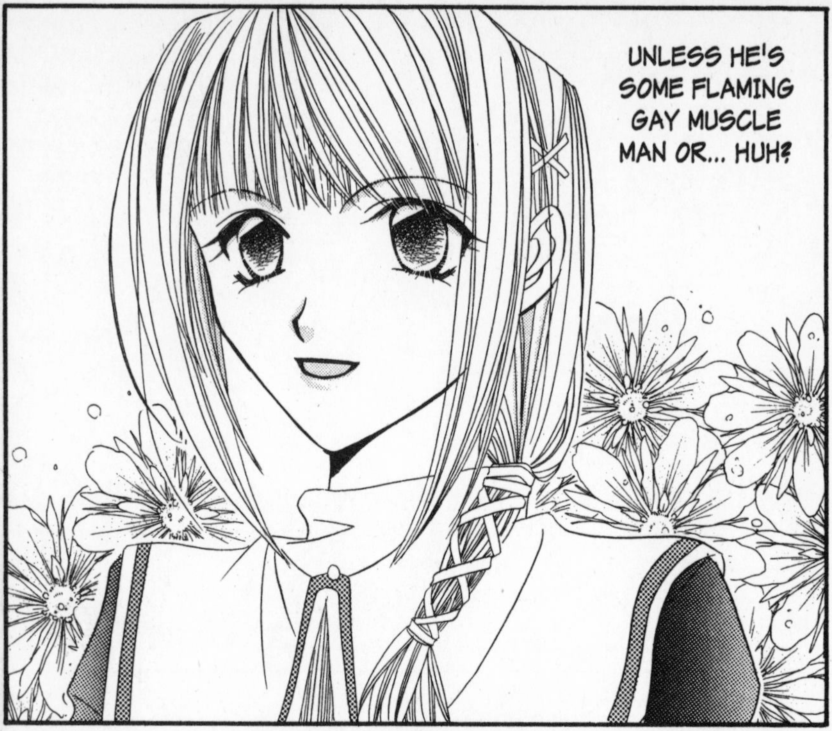
UNLESS HE'S SOME FLAMING GAY MUSCLE MAN OR... HUH?

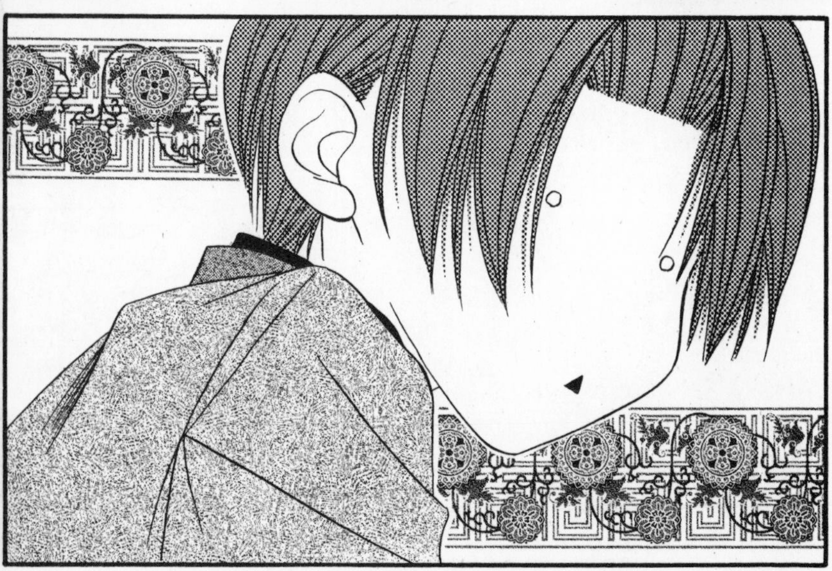

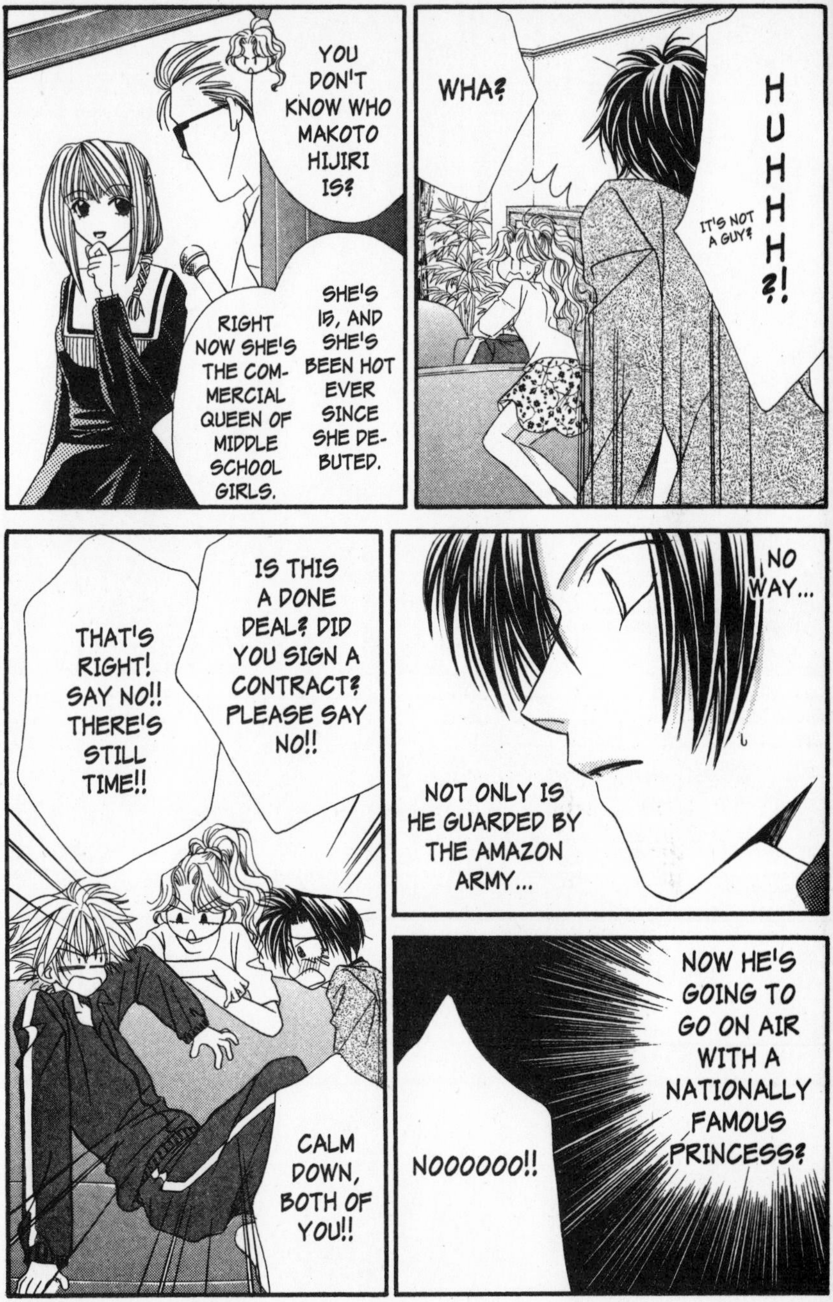
WHA?
HUHHH?!
IT'S NOT A GUY?
YOU DON'T KNOW WHO MAKOTO HIJIRI IS?
SHE'S 15, AND SHE'S BEEN HOT EVER SINCE SHE DEBUTED.
RIGHT NOW SHE'S THE COMMERCIAL QUEEN OF MIDDLE SCHOOL GIRLS.
NO WAY...
NOT ONLY IS HE GUARDED BY THE AMAZON ARMY...
NOW HE'S GOING TO GO ON AIR WITH A NATIONALLY FAMOUS PRINCESS?
NOOOOOO!!
IS THIS A DONE DEAL? DID YOU SIGN A CONTRACT? PLEASE SAY NO!!
THAT'S RIGHT! SAY NO!! THERE'S STILL TIME!!
CALM DOWN, BOTH OF YOU!!

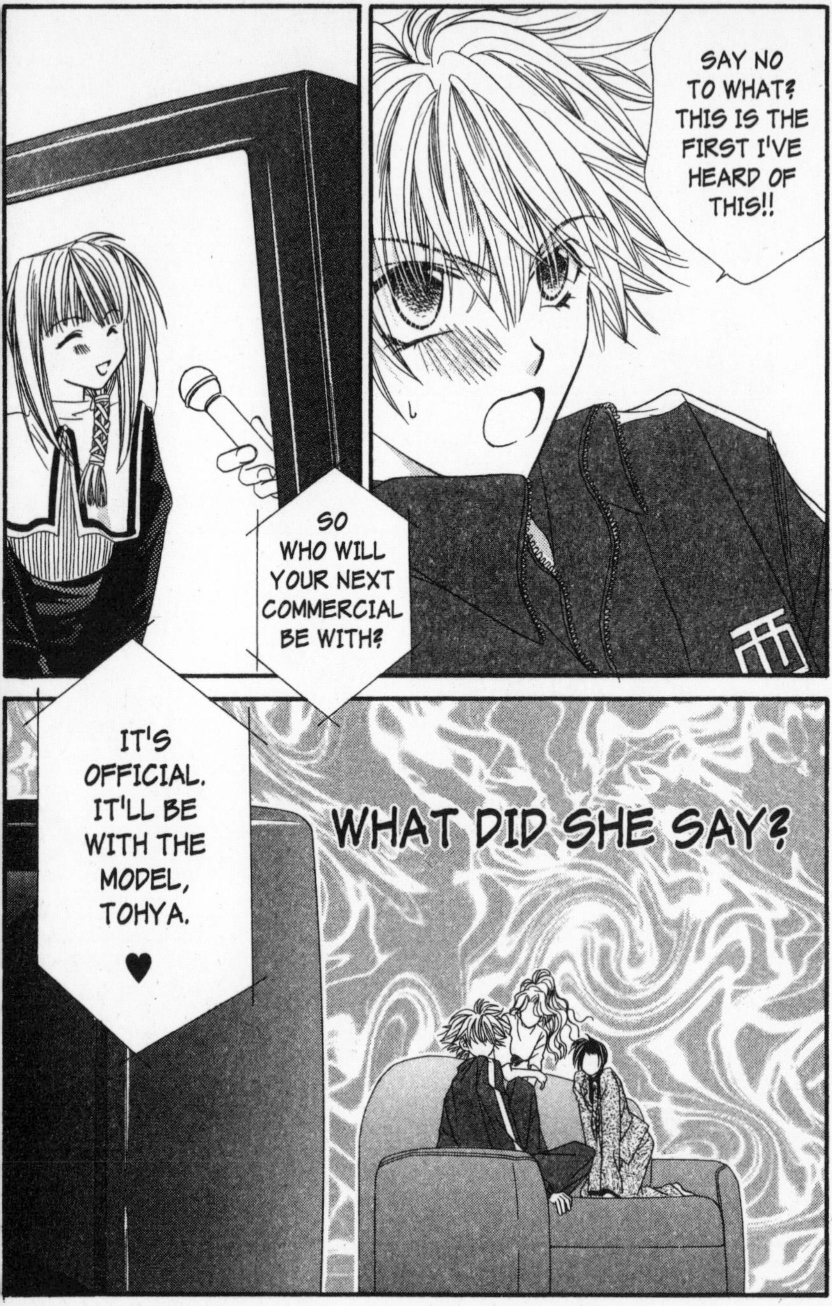
SAY NO TO WHAT? THIS IS THE FIRST I'VE HEARD OF THIS!!
SO WHO WILL YOUR NEXT COMMERCIAL BE WITH?
IT'S OFFICIAL. IT'LL BE WITH THE MODEL, TOHYA. ♥
WHAT DID SHE SAY?

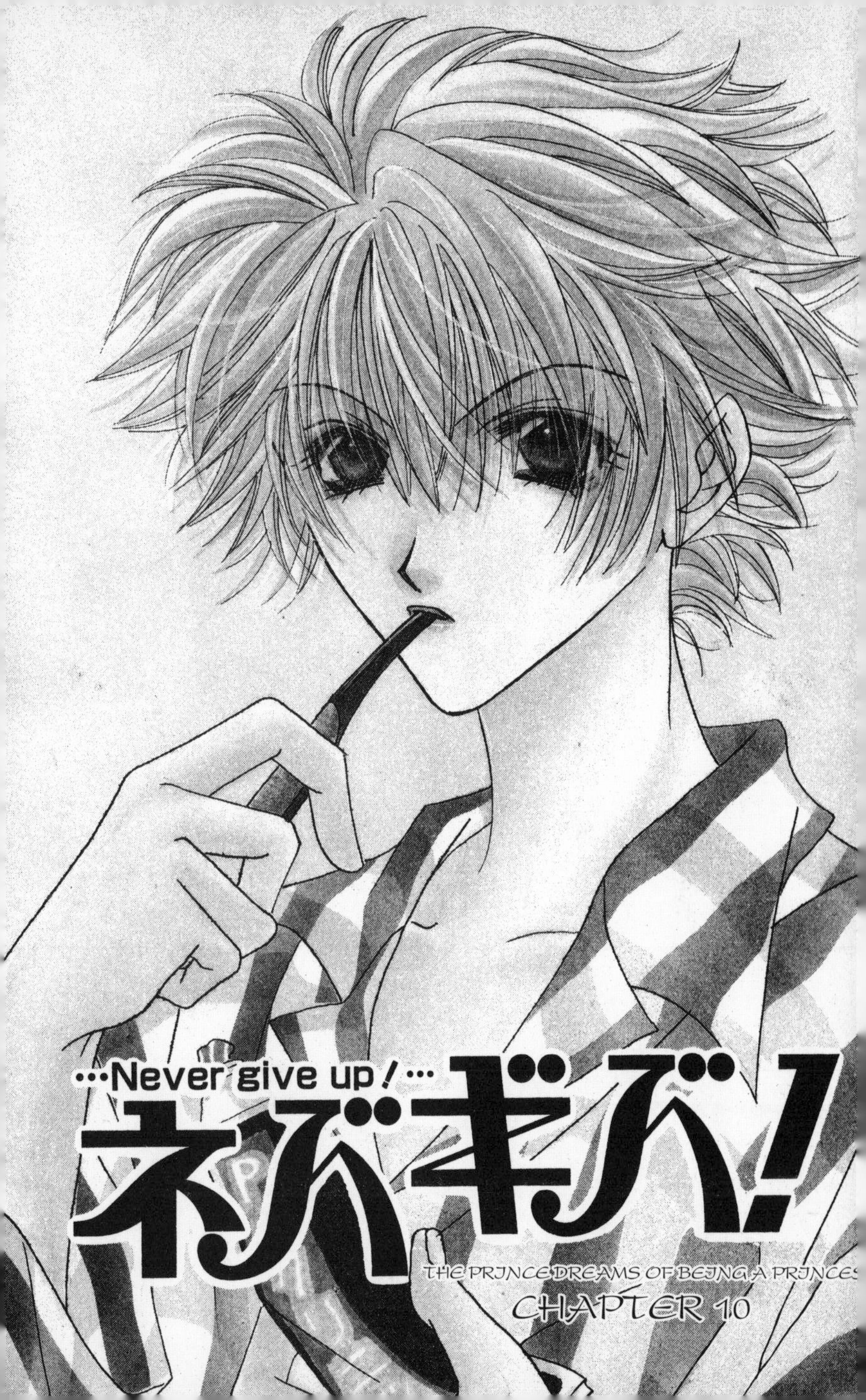
···Never give up!···
ネバギバ!
THE PRINCE DREAMS OF BEING A PRINCES
CHAPTER 10

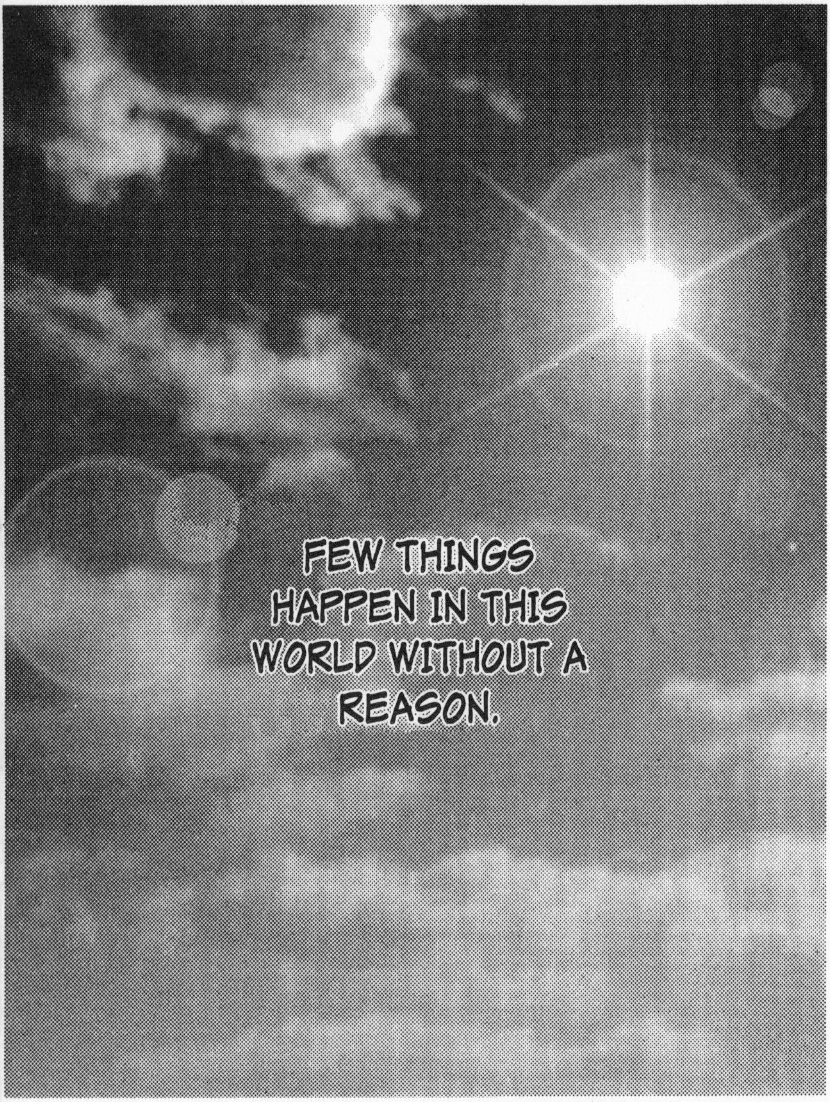
FEW THINGS HAPPEN IN THIS WORLD WITHOUT A REASON.

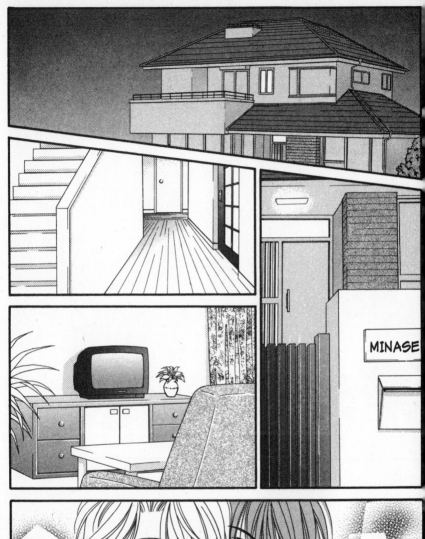

MINASE

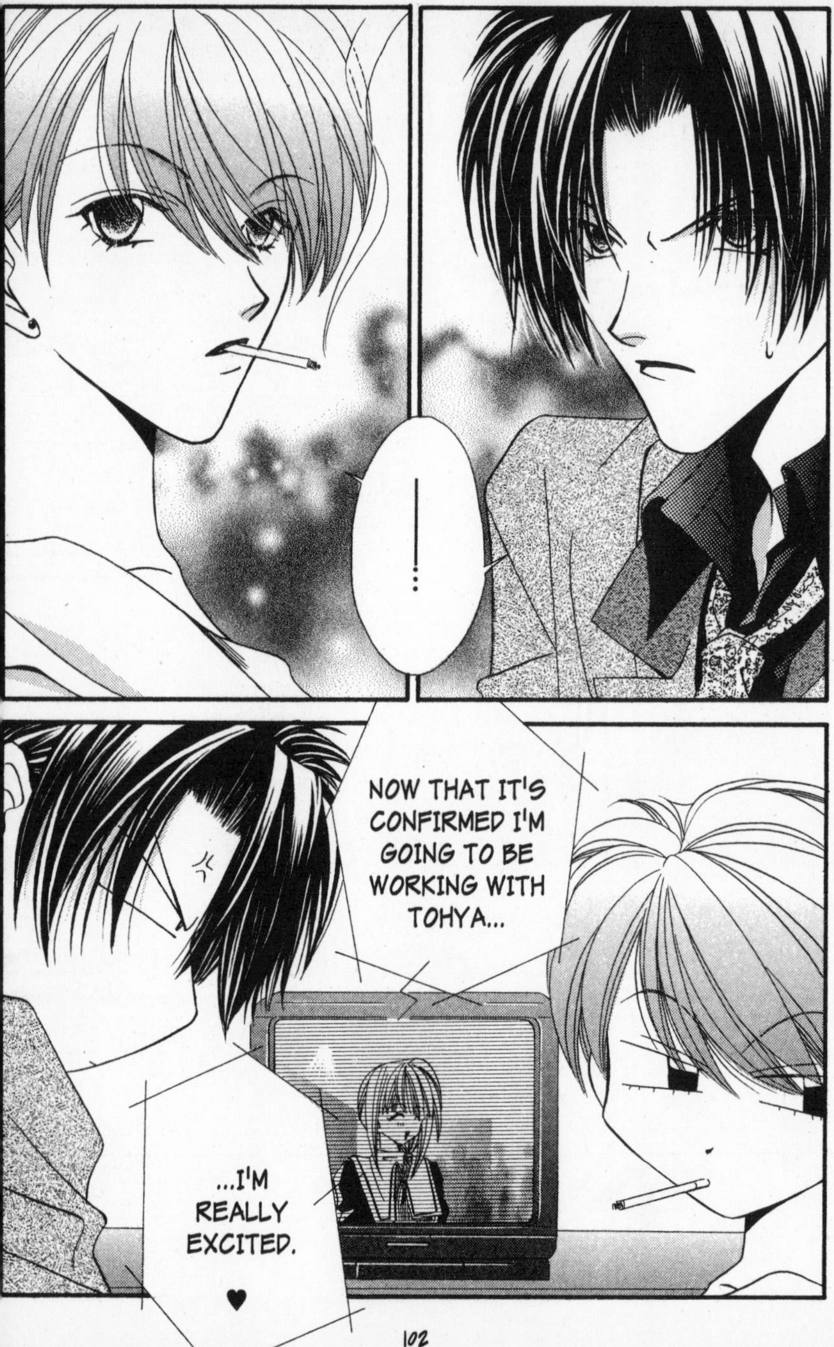

......
NOW THAT IT'S CONFIRMED I'M GOING TO BE WORKING WITH TOHYA...
...I'M REALLY EXCITED. ♥

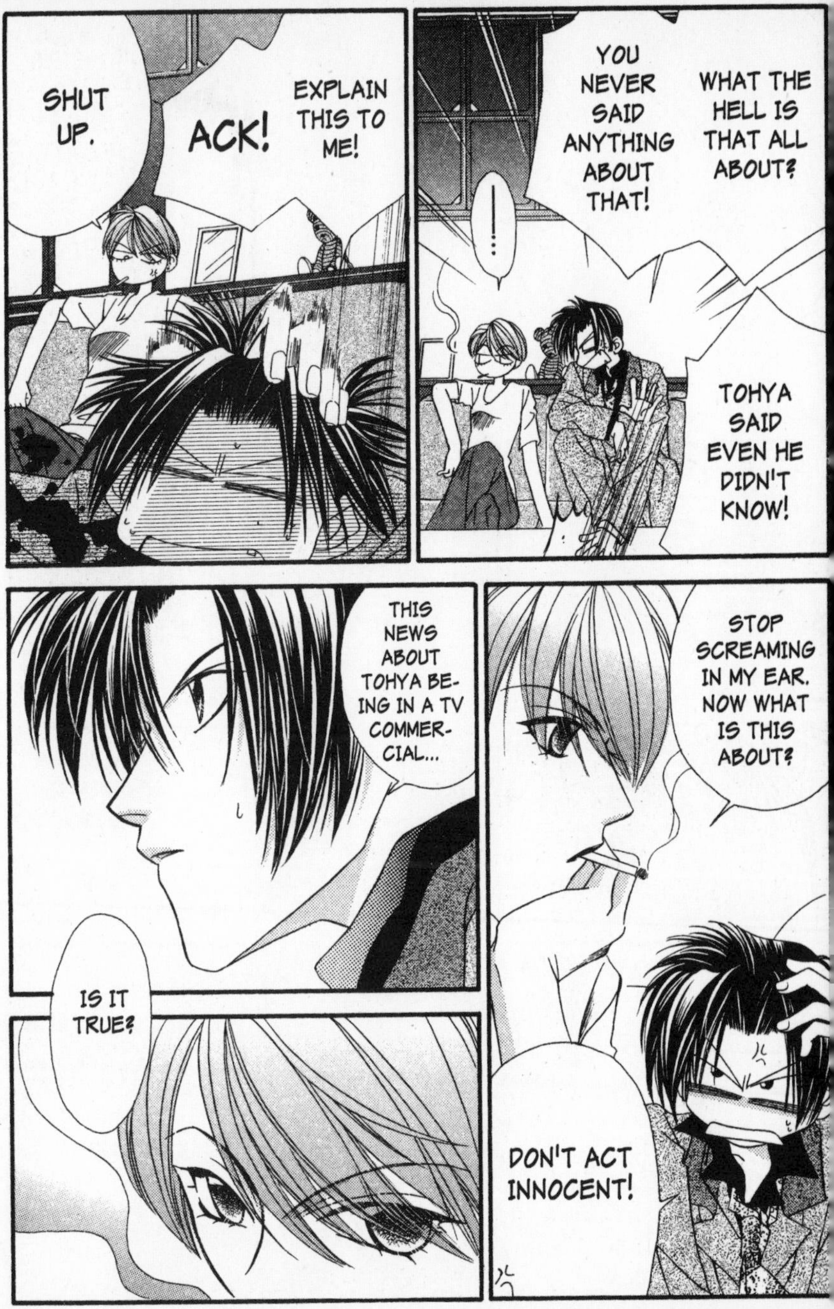
WHAT THE HELL IS THAT ALL ABOUT?
YOU NEVER SAID ANYTHING ABOUT THAT!
!...
TOHYA SAID EVEN HE DIDN'T KNOW!
EXPLAIN THIS TO ME!
ACK!
SHUT UP.
STOP SCREAMING IN MY EAR. NOW WHAT IS THIS ABOUT?
DON'T ACT INNOCENT!
THIS NEWS ABOUT TOHYA BEING IN A TV COMMERCIAL...
IS IT TRUE?

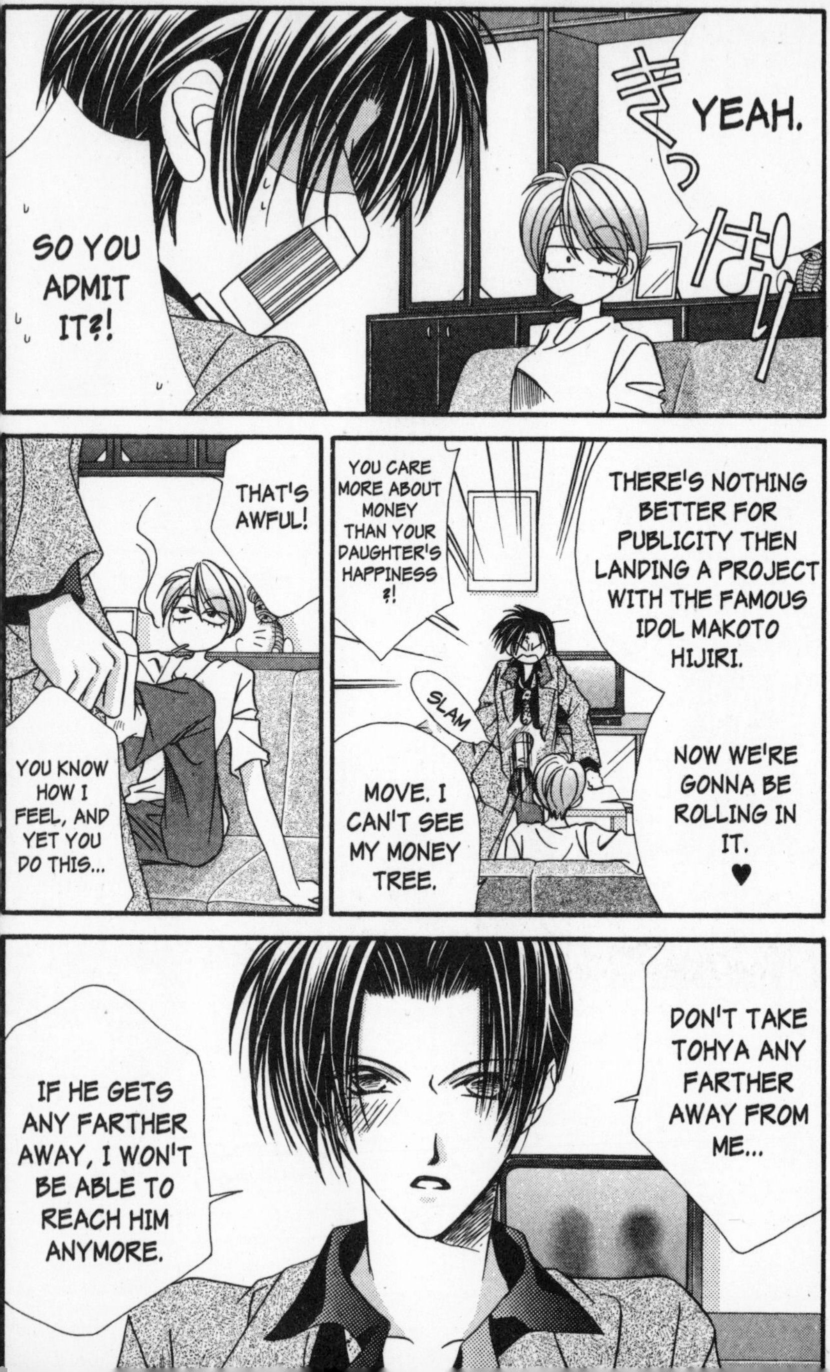
きっぱり
YEAH.
SO YOU ADMIT IT?!
THERE'S NOTHING BETTER FOR PUBLICITY THEN LANDING A PROJECT WITH THE FAMOUS IDOL MAKOTO HIJIRI.
YOU CARE MORE ABOUT MONEY THAN YOUR DAUGHTER'S HAPPINESS?!
NOW WE'RE GONNA BE ROLLING IN IT. ♥
SLAM
MOVE. I CAN'T SEE MY MONEY TREE.
THAT'S AWFUL!
YOU KNOW HOW I FEEL, AND YET YOU DO THIS...
DON'T TAKE TOHYA ANY FARTHER AWAY FROM ME...
IF HE GETS ANY FARTHER AWAY, I WON'T BE ABLE TO REACH HIM ANYMORE.

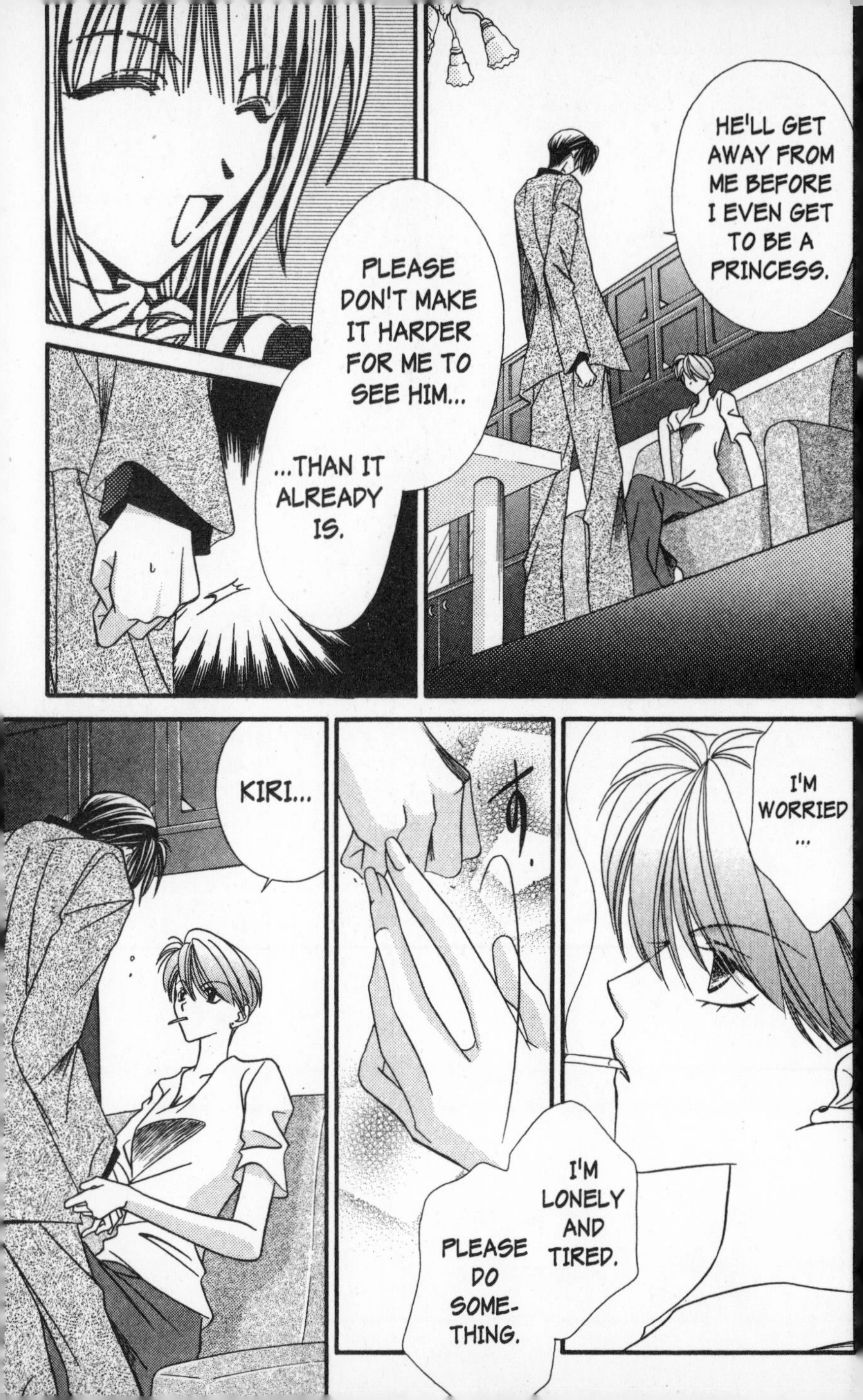
HE'LL GET AWAY FROM ME BEFORE I EVEN GET TO BE A PRINCESS.
PLEASE DON'T MAKE IT HARDER FOR ME TO SEE HIM...
...THAN IT ALREADY IS.
I'M WORRIED...
I'M LONELY AND TIRED.
PLEASE DO SOME-THING.
KIRI...

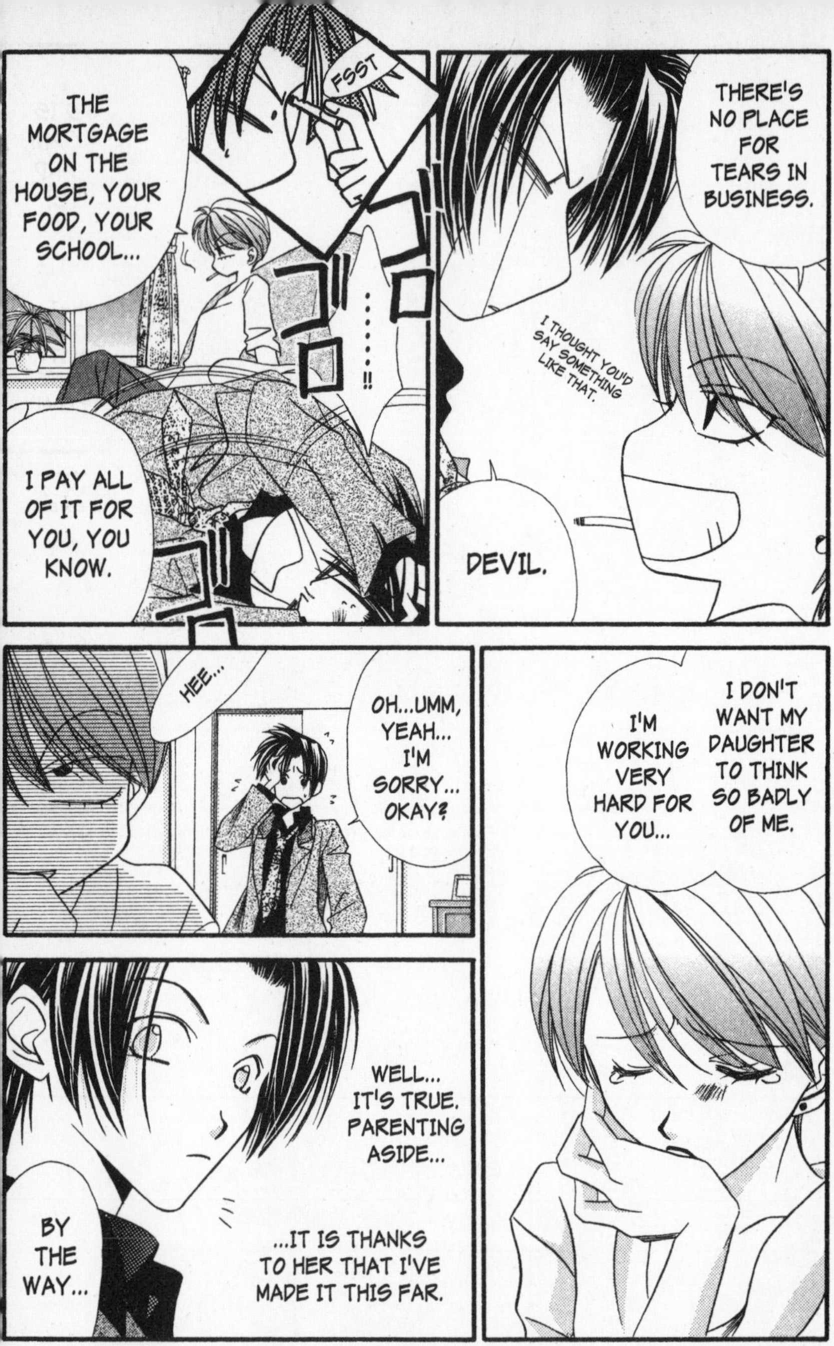
THERE'S NO PLACE FOR TEARS IN BUSINESS.
I THOUGHT YOU'D SAY SOMETHING LIKE THAT.
DEVIL.
FSST
THE MORTGAGE ON THE HOUSE, YOUR FOOD, YOUR SCHOOL...
......!!
I PAY ALL OF IT FOR YOU, YOU KNOW.
I DON'T WANT MY DAUGHTER TO THINK SO BADLY OF ME.
I'M WORKING VERY HARD FOR YOU...
HEE...
OH...UMM, YEAH... I'M SORRY... OKAY?
WELL... IT'S TRUE. PARENTING ASIDE...
...IT IS THANKS TO HER THAT I'VE MADE IT THIS FAR.
BY THE WAY...

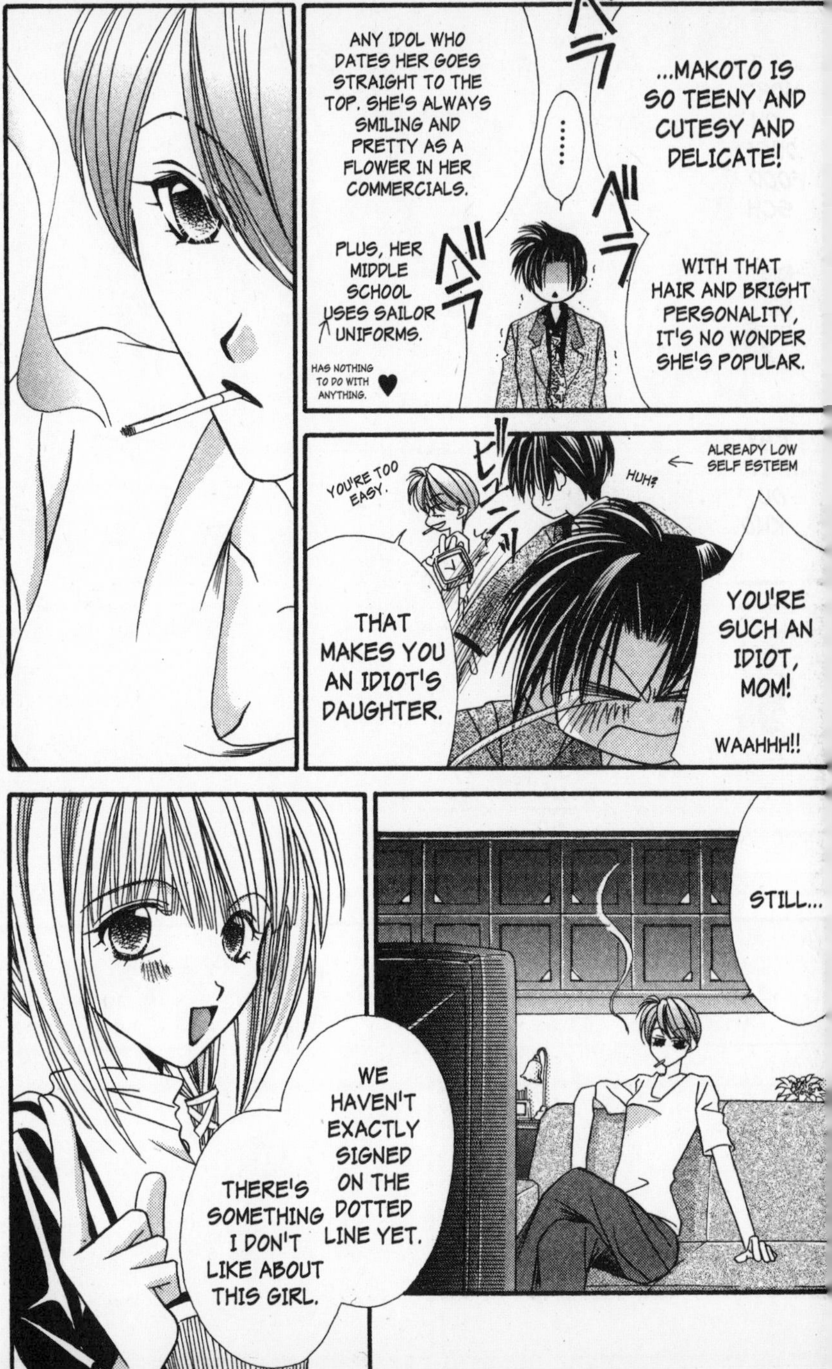
...MAKOTO IS SO TEENY AND CUTESY AND DELICATE!
ベラ ベラ ベラ
WITH THAT HAIR AND BRIGHT PERSONALITY, IT'S NO WONDER SHE'S POPULAR.
......
ANY IDOL WHO DATES HER GOES STRAIGHT TO THE TOP. SHE'S ALWAYS SMILING AND PRETTY AS A FLOWER IN HER COMMERCIALS.
PLUS, HER MIDDLE SCHOOL USES SAILOR UNIFORMS.
HAS NOTHING TO DO WITH ANYTHING. ♥
ALREADY LOW SELF ESTEEM
YOU'RE SUCH AN IDIOT, MOM!
WAAHHH!!
HUH?
YOU'RE TOO EASY.
THAT MAKES YOU AN IDIOT'S DAUGHTER.
STILL...
WE HAVEN'T EXACTLY SIGNED ON THE DOTTED LINE YET.
THERE'S SOMETHING I DON'T LIKE ABOUT THIS GIRL.

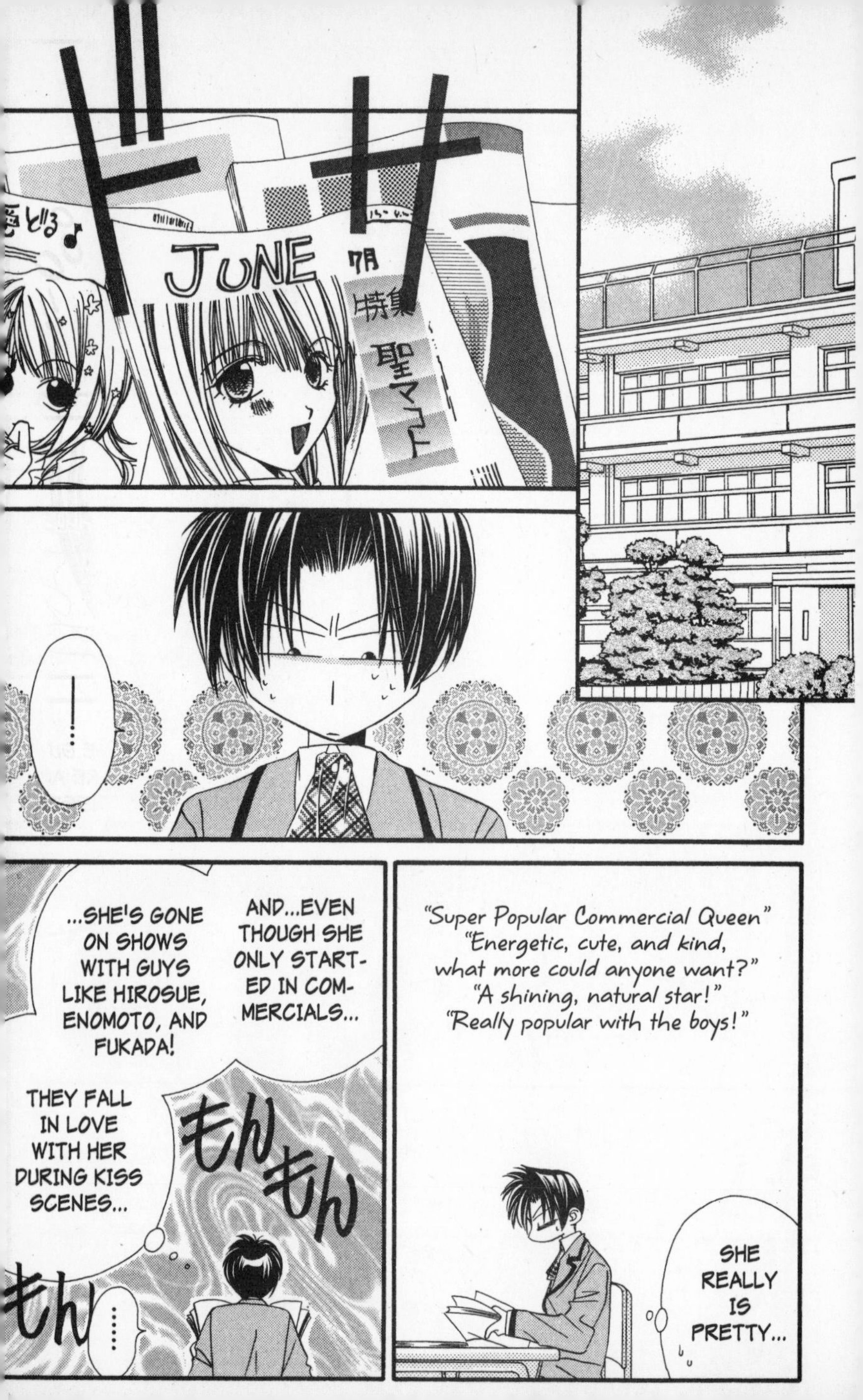

ドサ
JUNE
7月
特集
聖マコト
…!
"Super Popular Commercial Queen"
"Energetic, cute, and kind, what more could anyone want?"
"A shining, natural star!"
"Really popular with the boys!"
SHE REALLY IS PRETTY...
AND...EVEN THOUGH SHE ONLY START-ED IN COM-MERCIALS...
...SHE'S GONE ON SHOWS WITH GUYS LIKE HIROSUE, ENOMOTO, AND FUKADA!
THEY FALL IN LOVE WITH HER DURING KISS SCENES...
もん
もん
もん
......

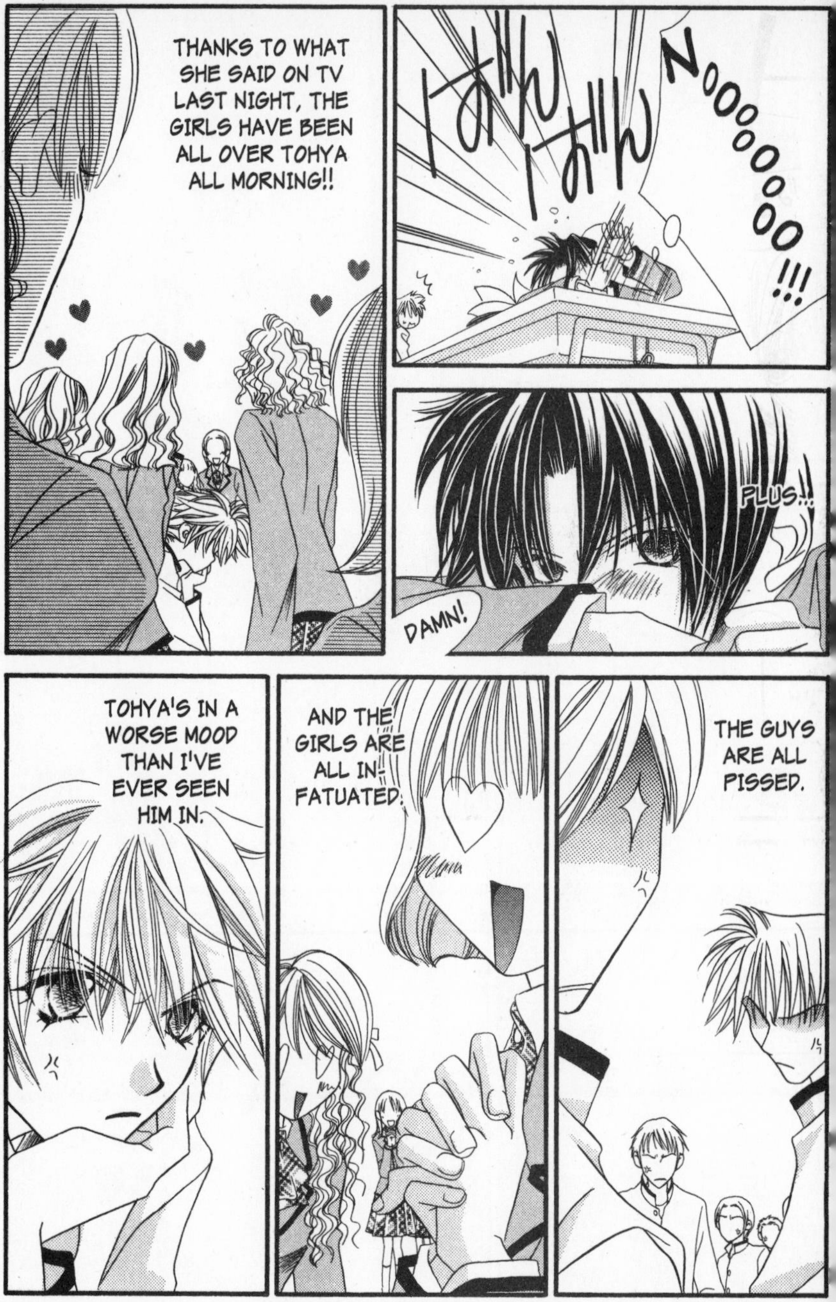
NOOOOOOOO!!!
PLUS!!
DAMN!
THANKS TO WHAT SHE SAID ON TV LAST NIGHT, THE GIRLS HAVE BEEN ALL OVER TOHYA ALL MORNING!!
THE GUYS ARE ALL PISSED.
AND THE GIRLS ARE ALL IN-FATUATED.
TOHYA'S IN A WORSE MOOD THAN I'VE EVER SEEN HIM IN.

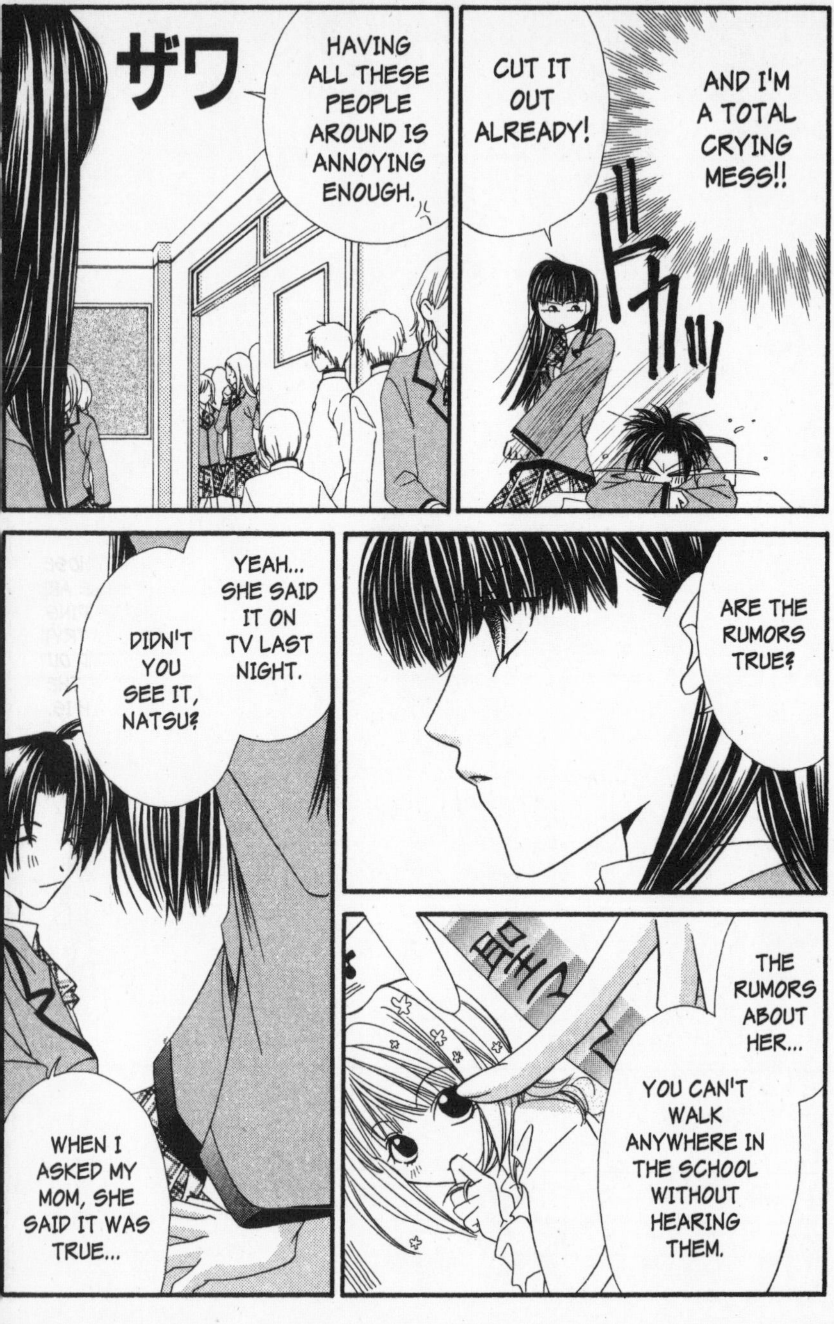
AND I'M A TOTAL CRYING MESS!!
CUT IT OUT ALREADY!
ドカッ
HAVING ALL THESE PEOPLE AROUND IS ANNOYING ENOUGH.
ザワ
ARE THE RUMORS TRUE?
THE RUMORS ABOUT HER...
YOU CAN'T WALK ANYWHERE IN THE SCHOOL WITHOUT HEARING THEM.
YEAH... SHE SAID IT ON TV LAST NIGHT.
DIDN'T YOU SEE IT, NATSU?
WHEN I ASKED MY MOM, SHE SAID IT WAS TRUE...

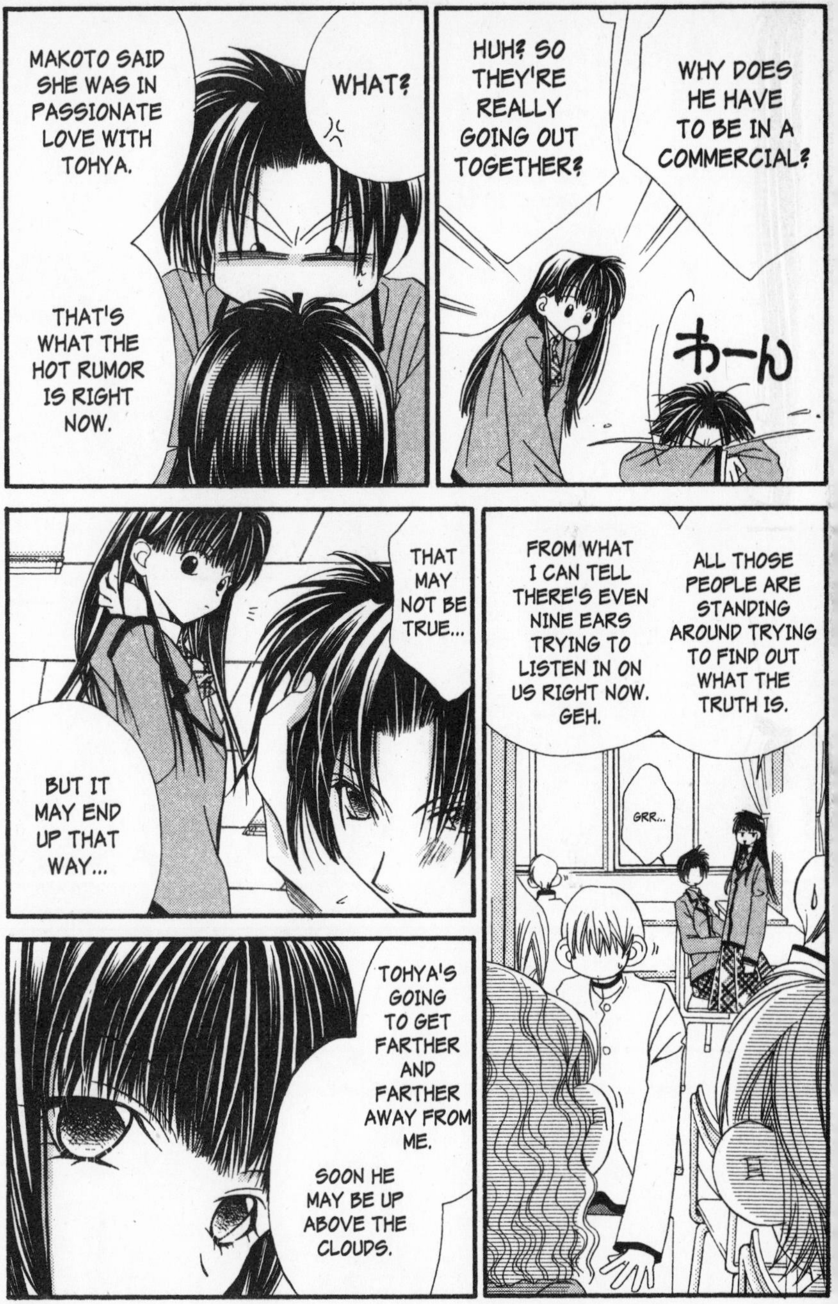
WHY DOES HE HAVE TO BE IN A COMMERCIAL?
HUH? SO THEY'RE REALLY GOING OUT TOGETHER?
わーん
WHAT?
MAKOTO SAID SHE WAS IN PASSIONATE LOVE WITH TOHYA.
THAT'S WHAT THE HOT RUMOR IS RIGHT NOW.
ALL THOSE PEOPLE ARE STANDING AROUND TRYING TO FIND OUT WHAT THE TRUTH IS.
FROM WHAT I CAN TELL THERE'S EVEN NINE EARS TRYING TO LISTEN IN ON US RIGHT NOW. GEH.
GRR...
THAT MAY NOT BE TRUE...
BUT IT MAY END UP THAT WAY...
TOHYA'S GOING TO GET FARTHER AND FARTHER AWAY FROM ME.
SOON HE MAY BE UP ABOVE THE CLOUDS.

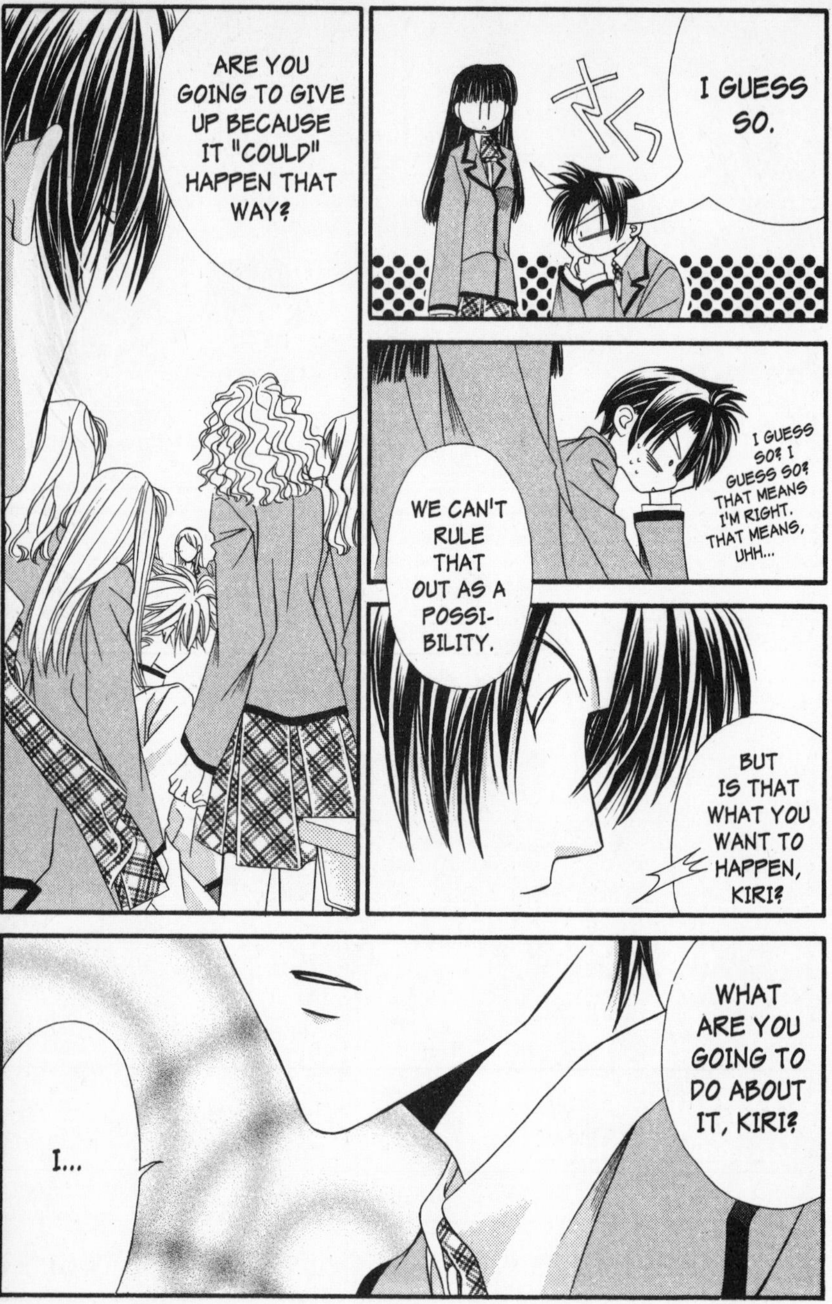
さくっ
I GUESS SO.
I GUESS SO? I GUESS SO? THAT MEANS I'M RIGHT. THAT MEANS, UHH...
WE CAN'T RULE THAT OUT AS A POSSI-BILITY.
BUT IS THAT WHAT YOU WANT TO HAPPEN, KIRI?
ARE YOU GOING TO GIVE UP BECAUSE IT "COULD" HAPPEN THAT WAY?
WHAT ARE YOU GOING TO DO ABOUT IT, KIRI?
I...

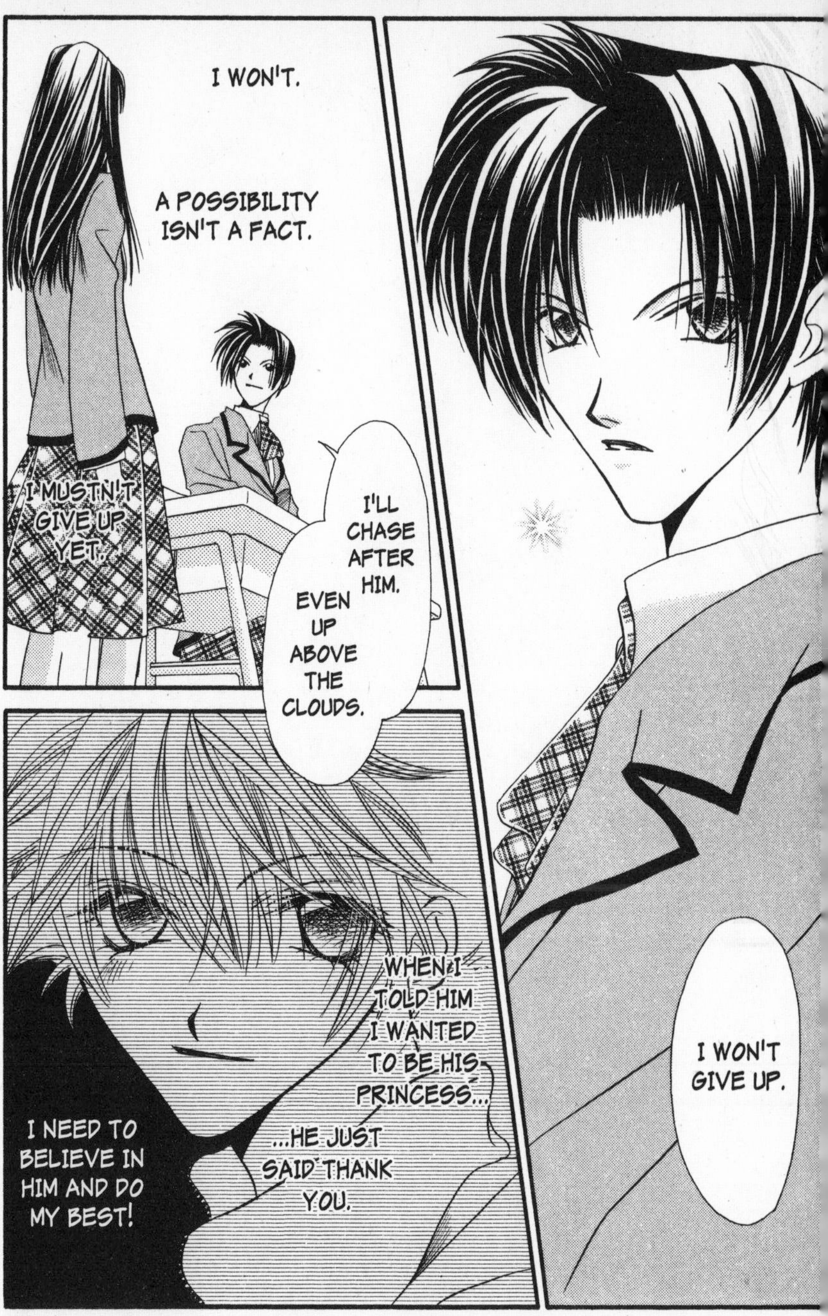
I WON'T GIVE UP.
I WON'T.
A POSSIBILITY ISN'T A FACT.
I'LL CHASE AFTER HIM. EVEN UP ABOVE THE CLOUDS.
I MUSTN'T GIVE UP YET.
WHEN I TOLD HIM I WANTED TO BE HIS PRINCESS...
...HE JUST SAID THANK YOU.
I NEED TO BELIEVE IN HIM AND DO MY BEST!

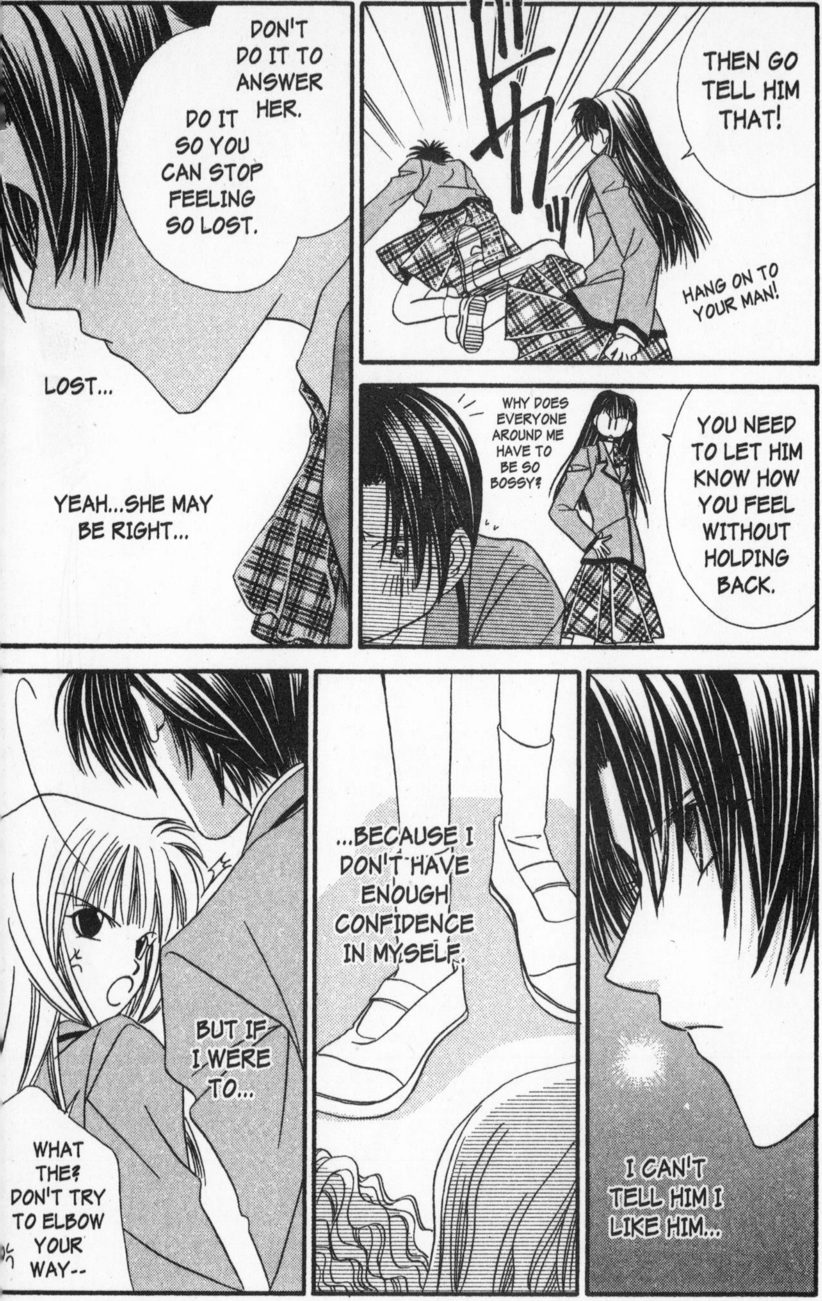
THEN GO TELL HIM THAT!
HANG ON TO YOUR MAN!
YOU NEED TO LET HIM KNOW HOW YOU FEEL WITHOUT HOLDING BACK.
WHY DOES EVERYONE AROUND ME HAVE TO BE SO BOSSY?
DON'T DO IT TO ANSWER HER.
DO IT SO YOU CAN STOP FEELING SO LOST.
LOST...
YEAH...SHE MAY BE RIGHT...
I CAN'T TELL HIM I LIKE HIM...
...BECAUSE I DON'T HAVE ENOUGH CONFIDENCE IN MYSELF.
BUT IF I WERE TO...
WHAT THE? DON'T TRY TO ELBOW YOUR WAY--

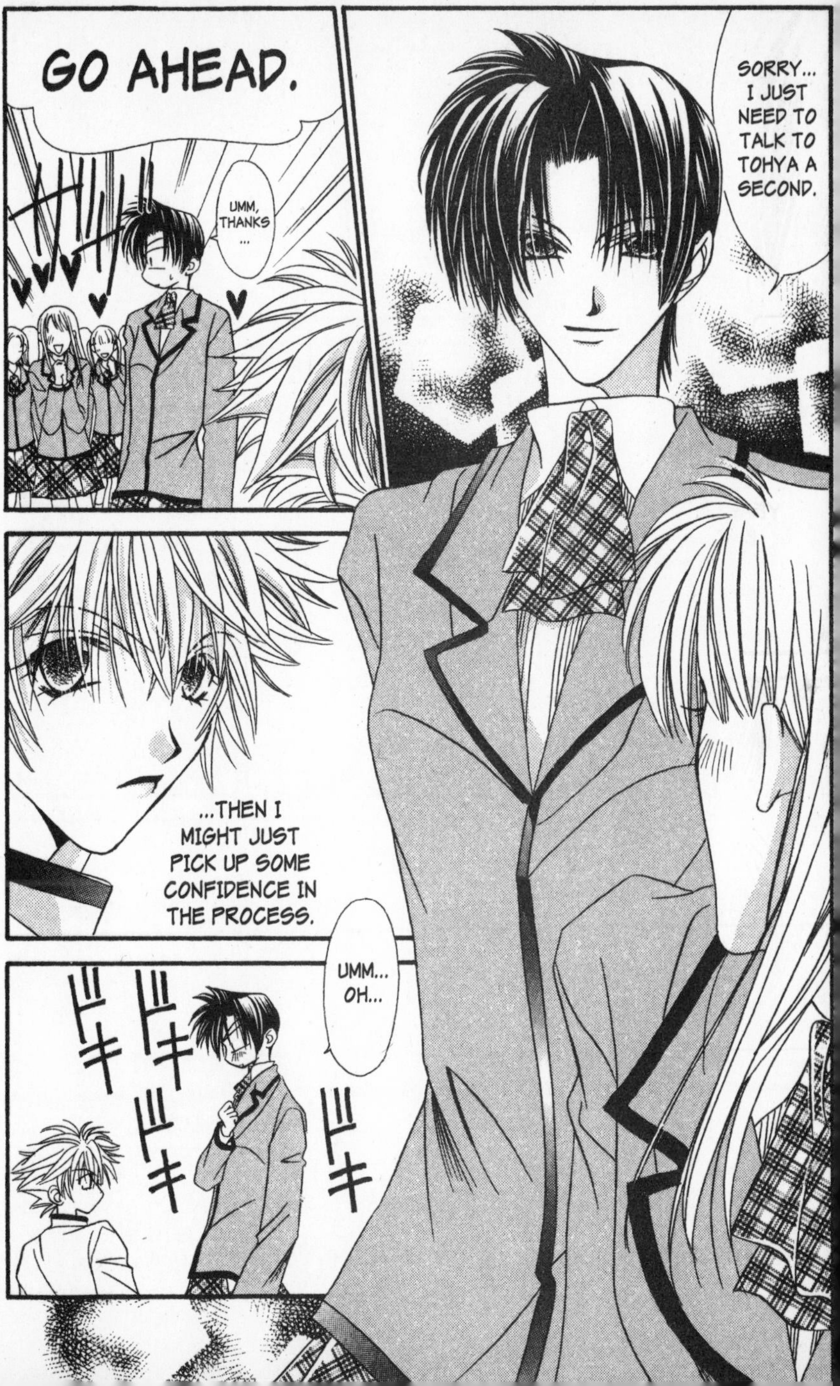
SORRY... I JUST NEED TO TALK TO TOHYA A SECOND.
GO AHEAD.
UMM, THANKS ...
...THEN I MIGHT JUST PICK UP SOME CONFIDENCE IN THE PROCESS.
ドキ
ドキ
ドキ
UMM... OH...
ドキ

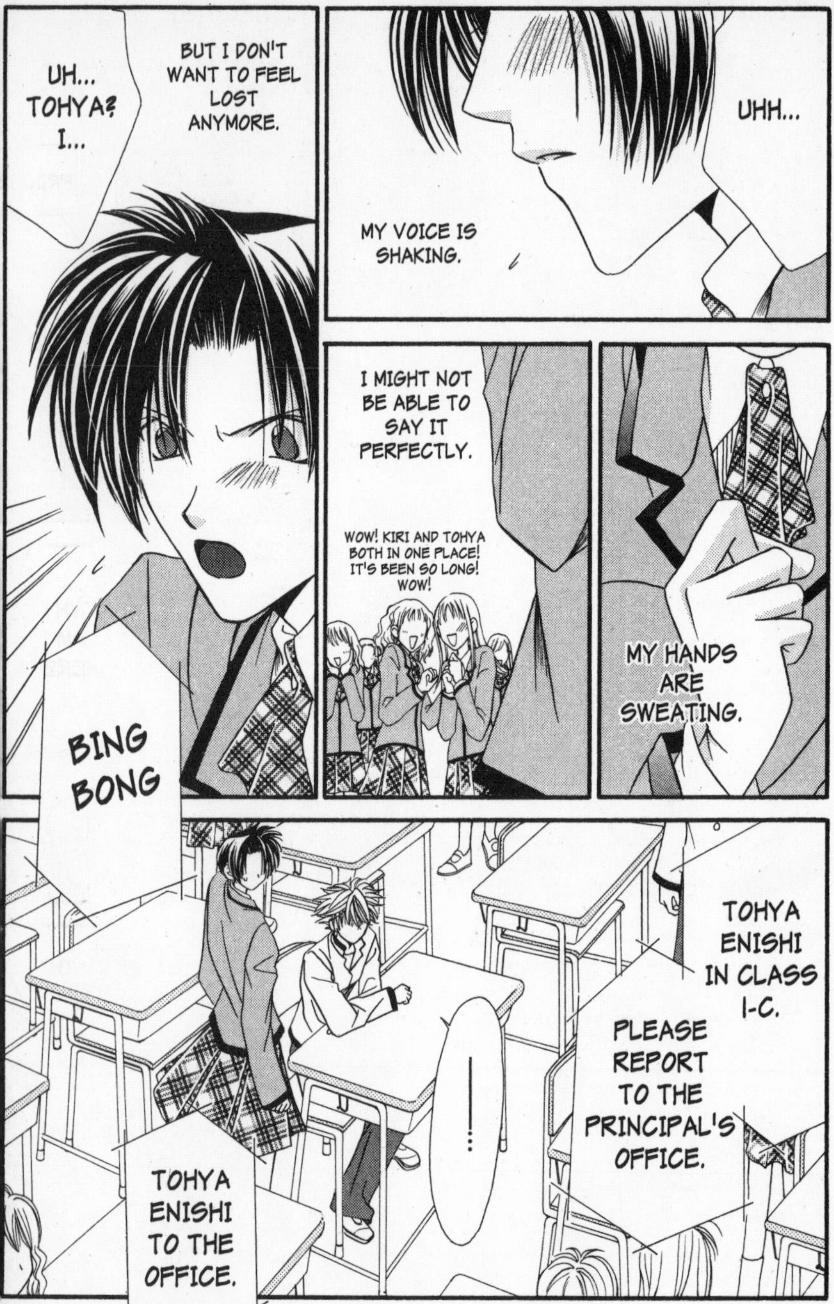
UHH...
MY VOICE IS SHAKING.
MY HANDS ARE SWEATING.
I MIGHT NOT BE ABLE TO SAY IT PERFECTLY.
WOW! KIRI AND TOHYA BOTH IN ONE PLACE! IT'S BEEN SO LONG! WOW!
BUT I DON'T WANT TO FEEL LOST ANYMORE.
UH... TOHYA? I...
BING BONG
TOHYA ENISHI IN CLASS I-C.
PLEASE REPORT TO THE PRINCIPAL'S OFFICE.
......
TOHYA ENISHI TO THE OFFICE.

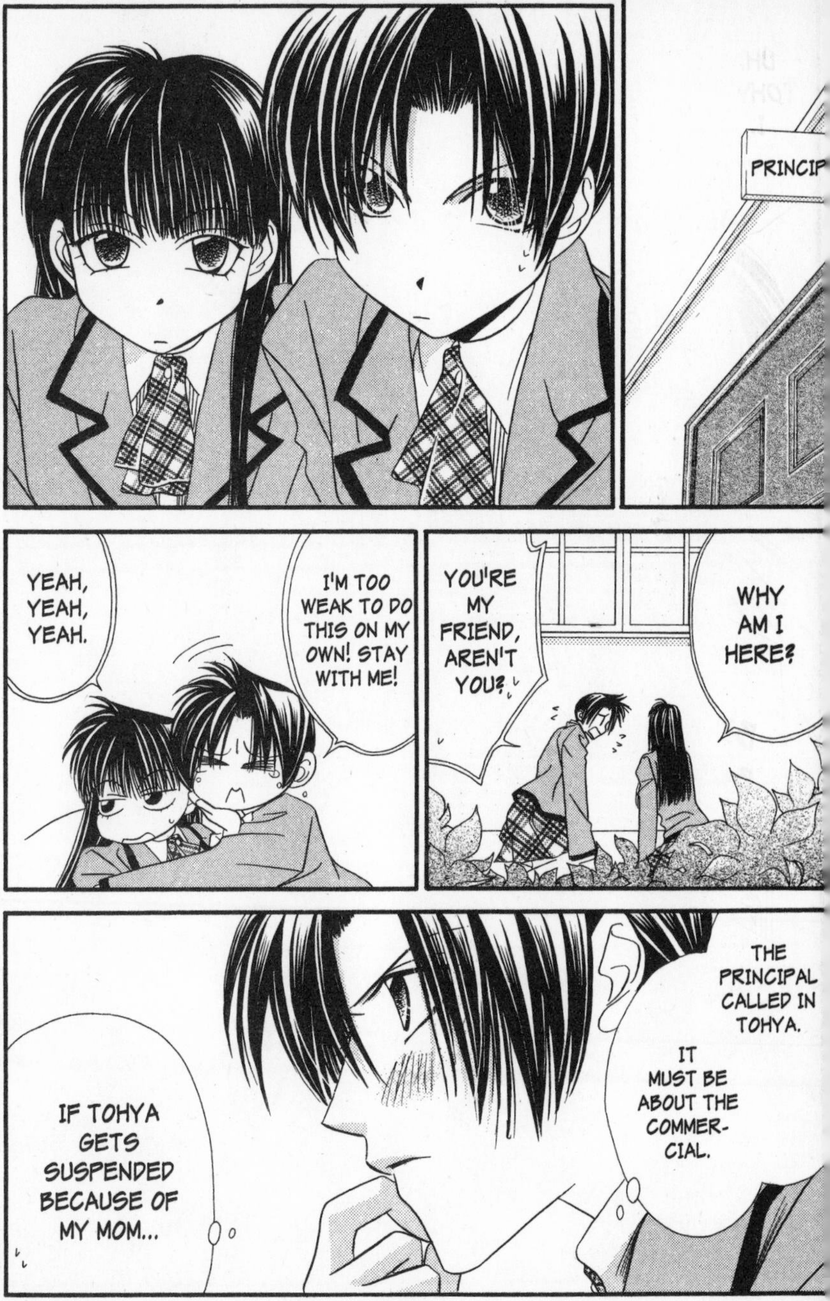

PRINCIP
WHY AM I HERE?
YOU'RE MY FRIEND, AREN'T YOU?
I'M TOO WEAK TO DO THIS ON MY OWN! STAY WITH ME!
YEAH, YEAH, YEAH.
THE PRINCIPAL CALLED IN TOHYA.
IT MUST BE ABOUT THE COMMER-CIAL.
IF TOHYA GETS SUSPENDED BECAUSE OF MY MOM...

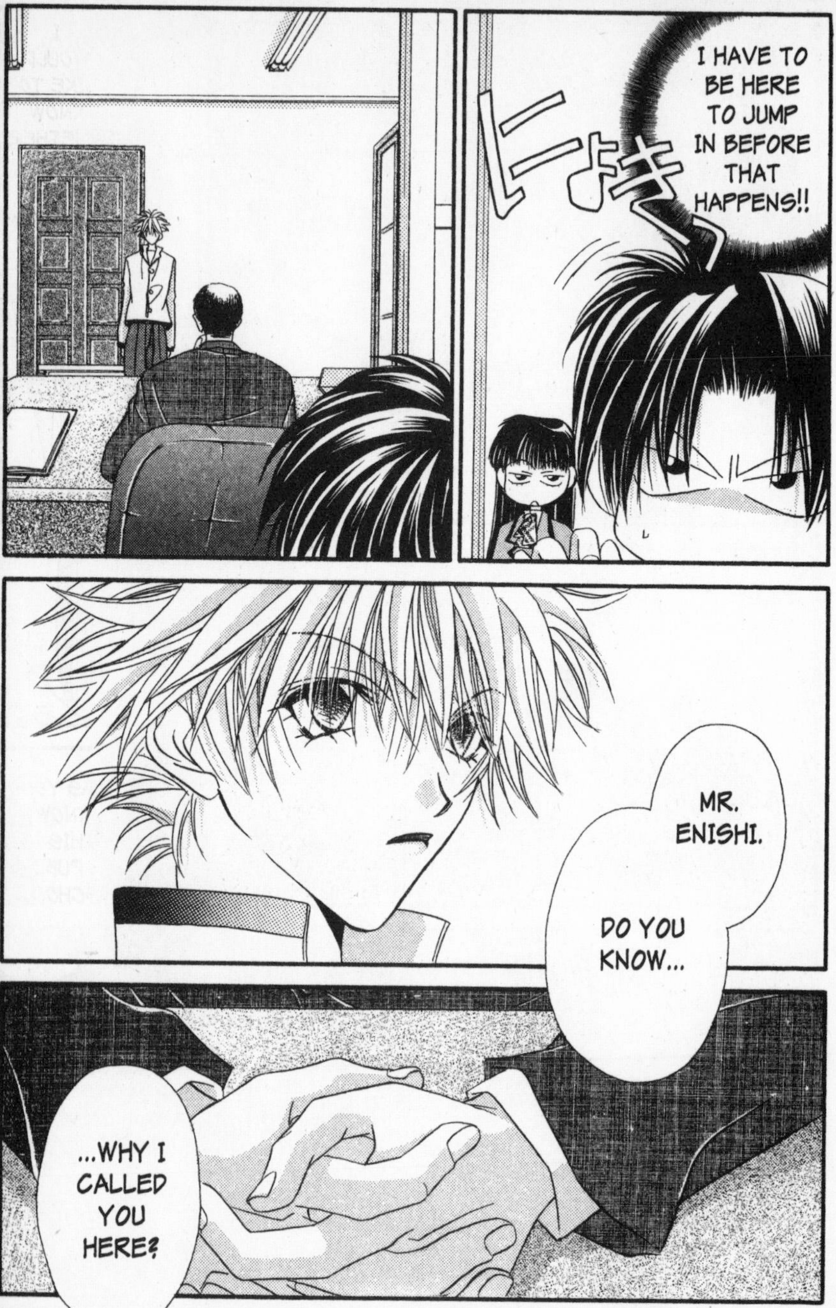
I HAVE TO BE HERE TO JUMP IN BEFORE THAT HAPPENS!!
MR. ENISHI.
DO YOU KNOW...
...WHY I CALLED YOU HERE?

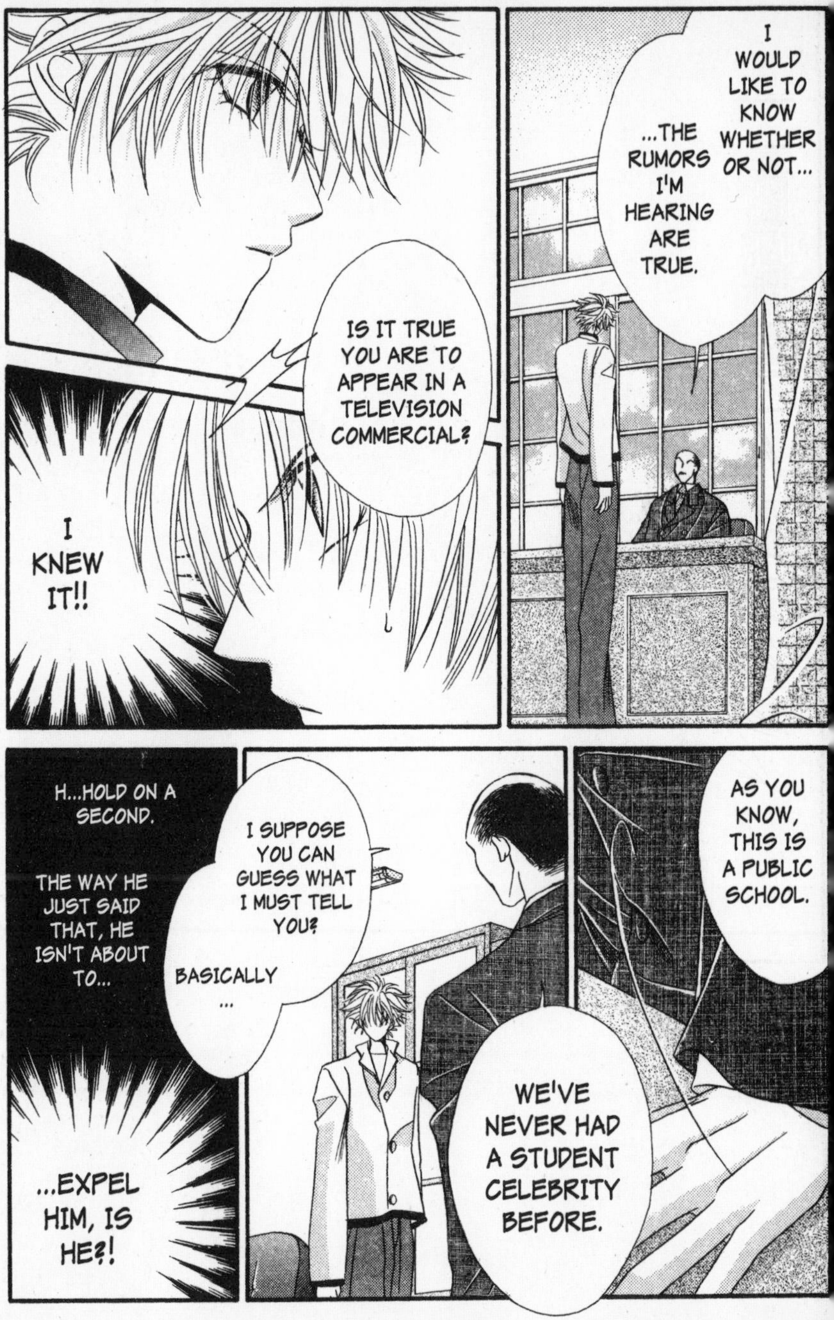
I WOULD LIKE TO KNOW WHETHER OR NOT...
...THE RUMORS I'M HEARING ARE TRUE.
IS IT TRUE YOU ARE TO APPEAR IN A TELEVISION COMMERCIAL?
I KNEW IT!!
AS YOU KNOW, THIS IS A PUBLIC SCHOOL.
WE'VE NEVER HAD A STUDENT CELEBRITY BEFORE.
I SUPPOSE YOU CAN GUESS WHAT I MUST TELL YOU?
BASICALLY ...
H...HOLD ON A SECOND.
THE WAY HE JUST SAID THAT, HE ISN'T ABOUT TO...
...EXPEL HIM, IS HE?!

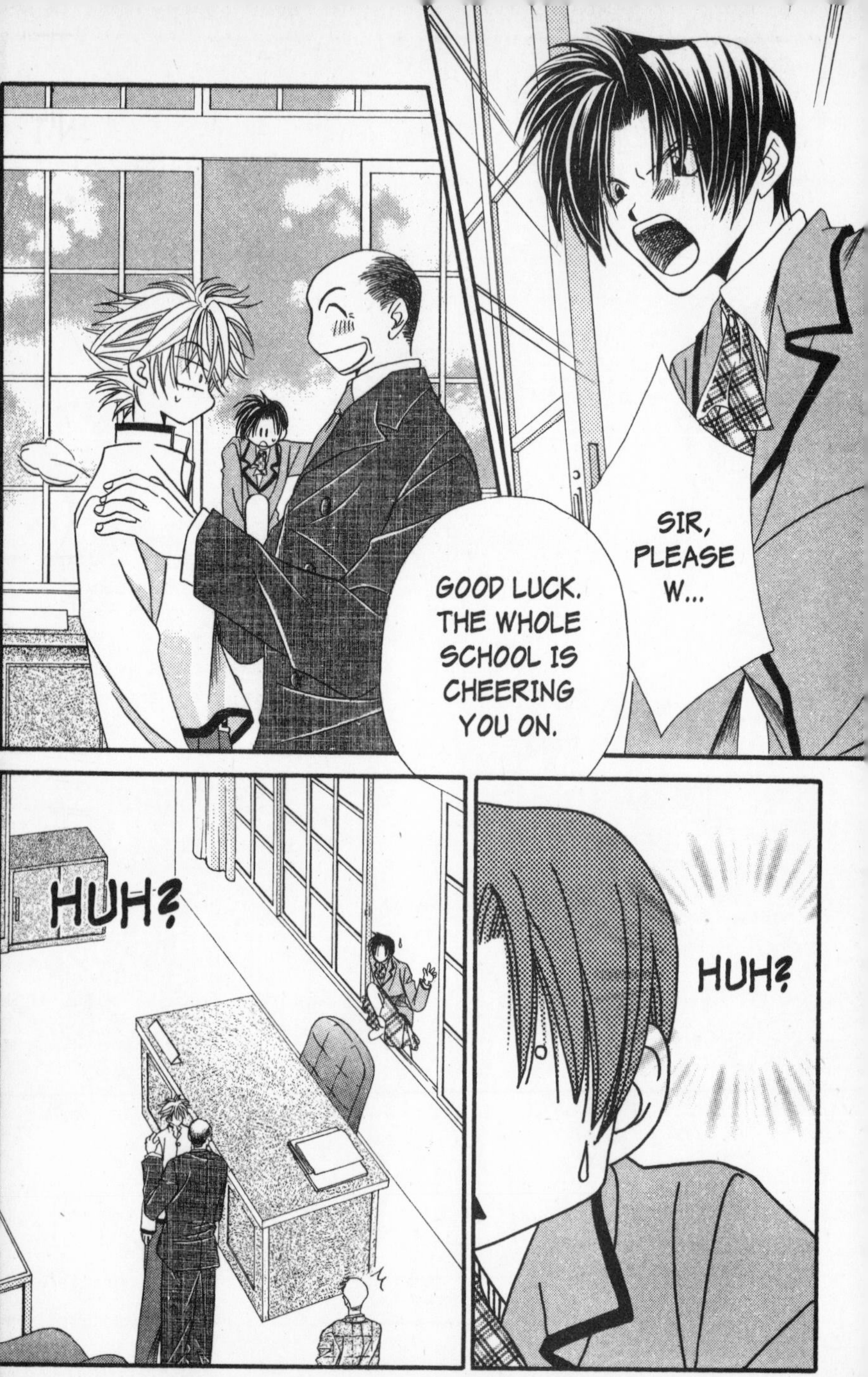
SIR, PLEASE W...
GOOD LUCK. THE WHOLE SCHOOL IS CHEERING YOU ON.
HUH?
HUH?

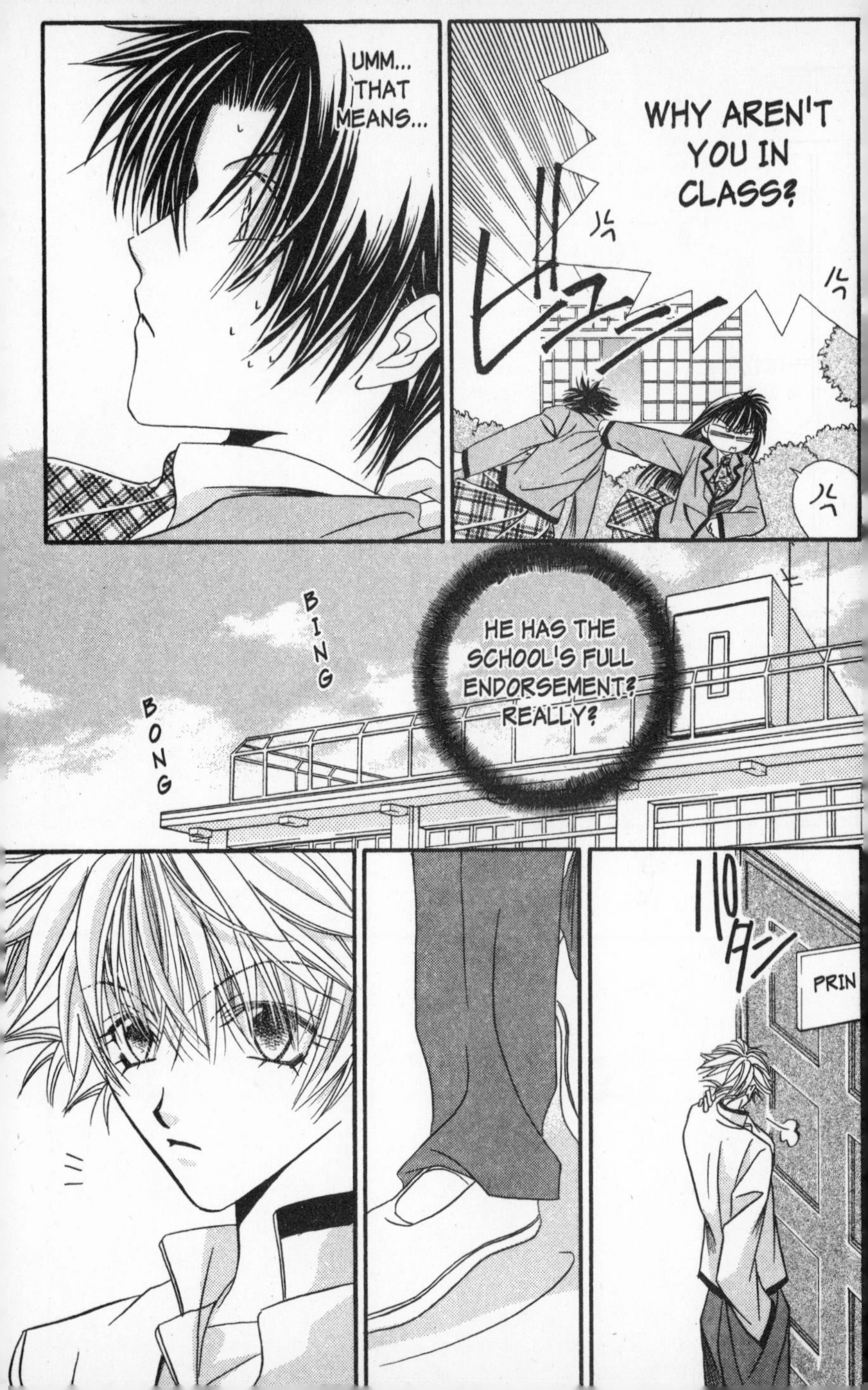
WHY AREN'T YOU IN CLASS?
UMM... THAT MEANS...
HE HAS THE SCHOOL'S FULL ENDORSEMENT? REALLY?
BING
BONG
PRIN

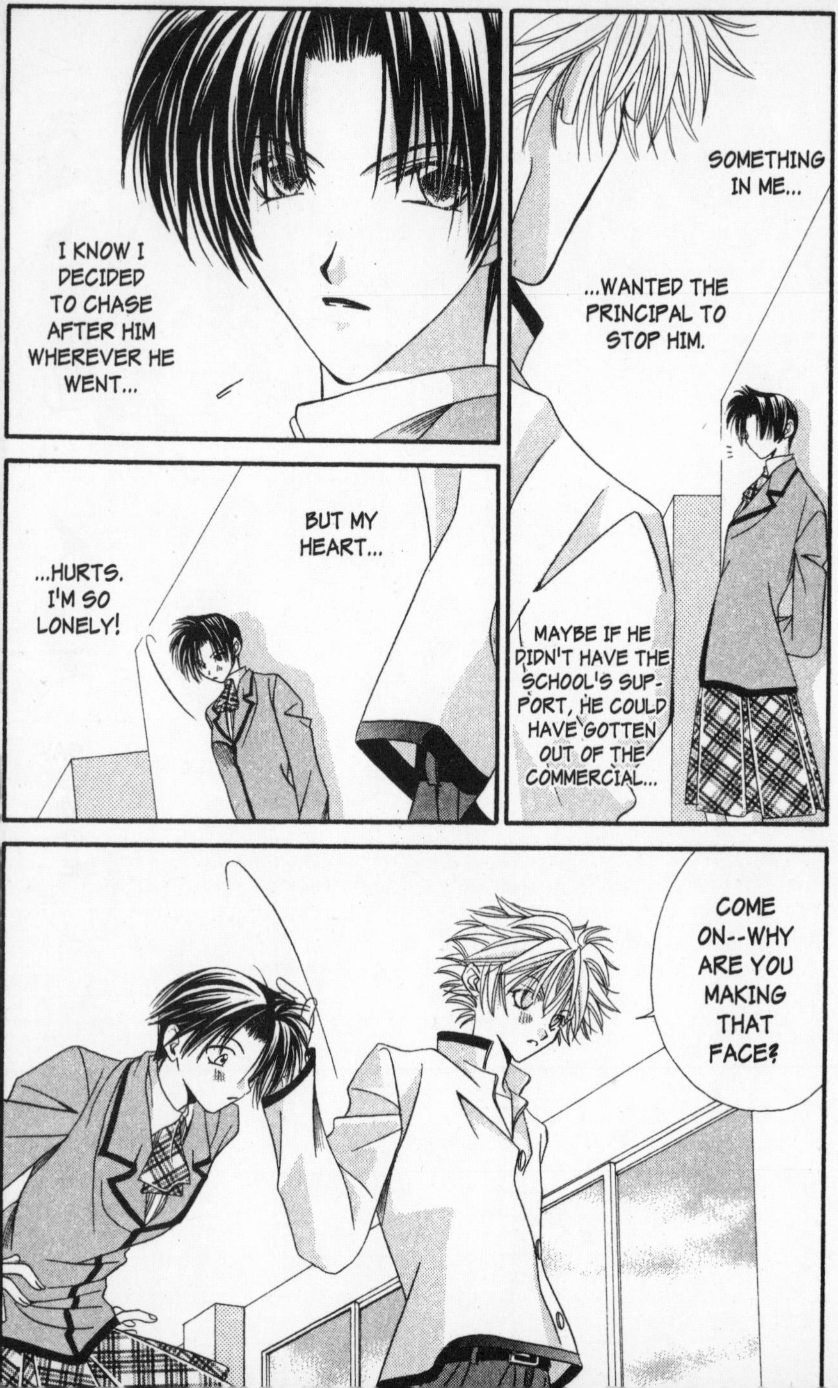
SOMETHING IN ME...
...WANTED THE PRINCIPAL TO STOP HIM.
MAYBE IF HE DIDN'T HAVE THE SCHOOL'S SUP-PORT, HE COULD HAVE GOTTEN OUT OF THE COMMERCIAL...
I KNOW I DECIDED TO CHASE AFTER HIM WHEREVER HE WENT...
BUT MY HEART...
...HURTS. I'M SO LONELY!
COME ON--WHY ARE YOU MAKING THAT FACE?

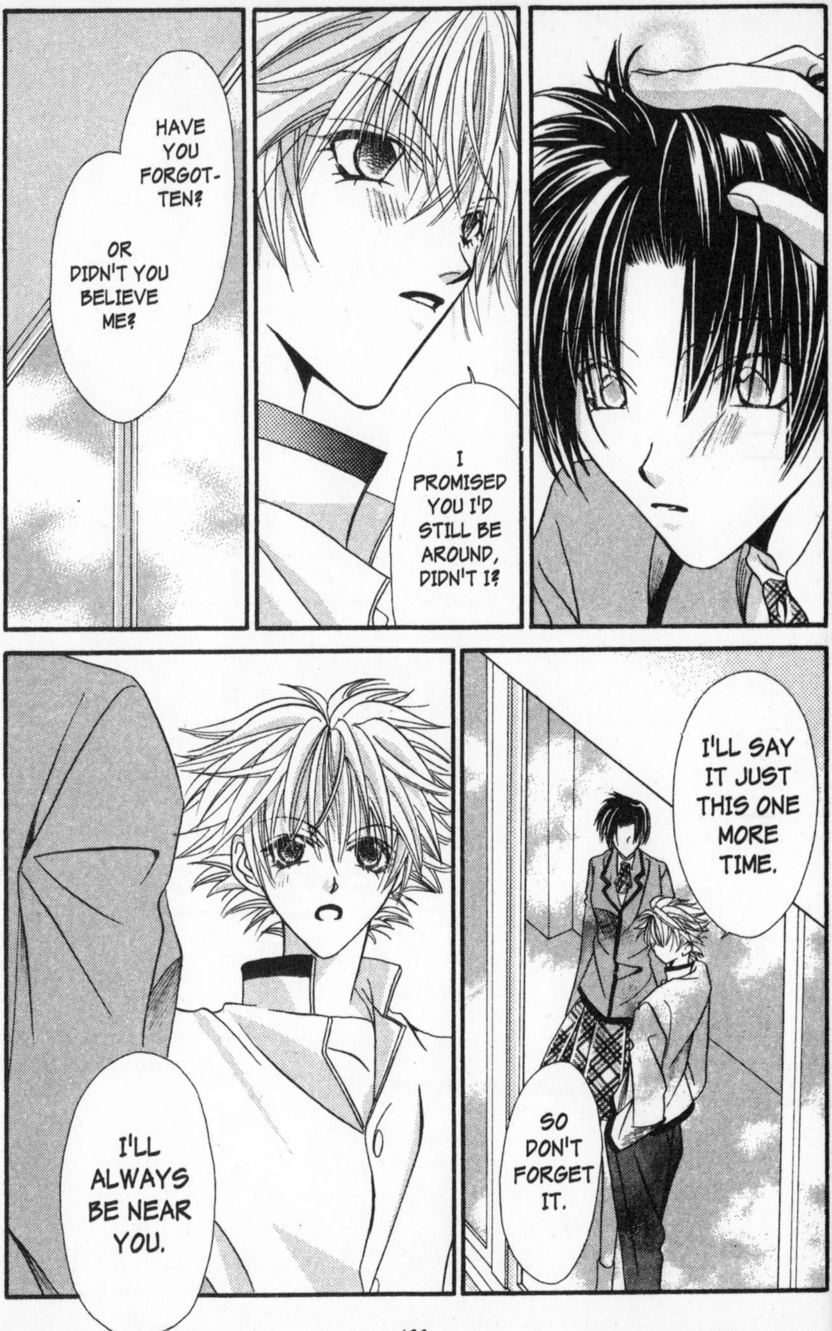
I PROMISED YOU I'D STILL BE AROUND, DIDN'T I?
HAVE YOU FORGOTTEN?
OR DIDN'T YOU BELIEVE ME?
I'LL SAY IT JUST THIS ONE MORE TIME.
SO DON'T FORGET IT.
I'LL ALWAYS BE NEAR YOU.

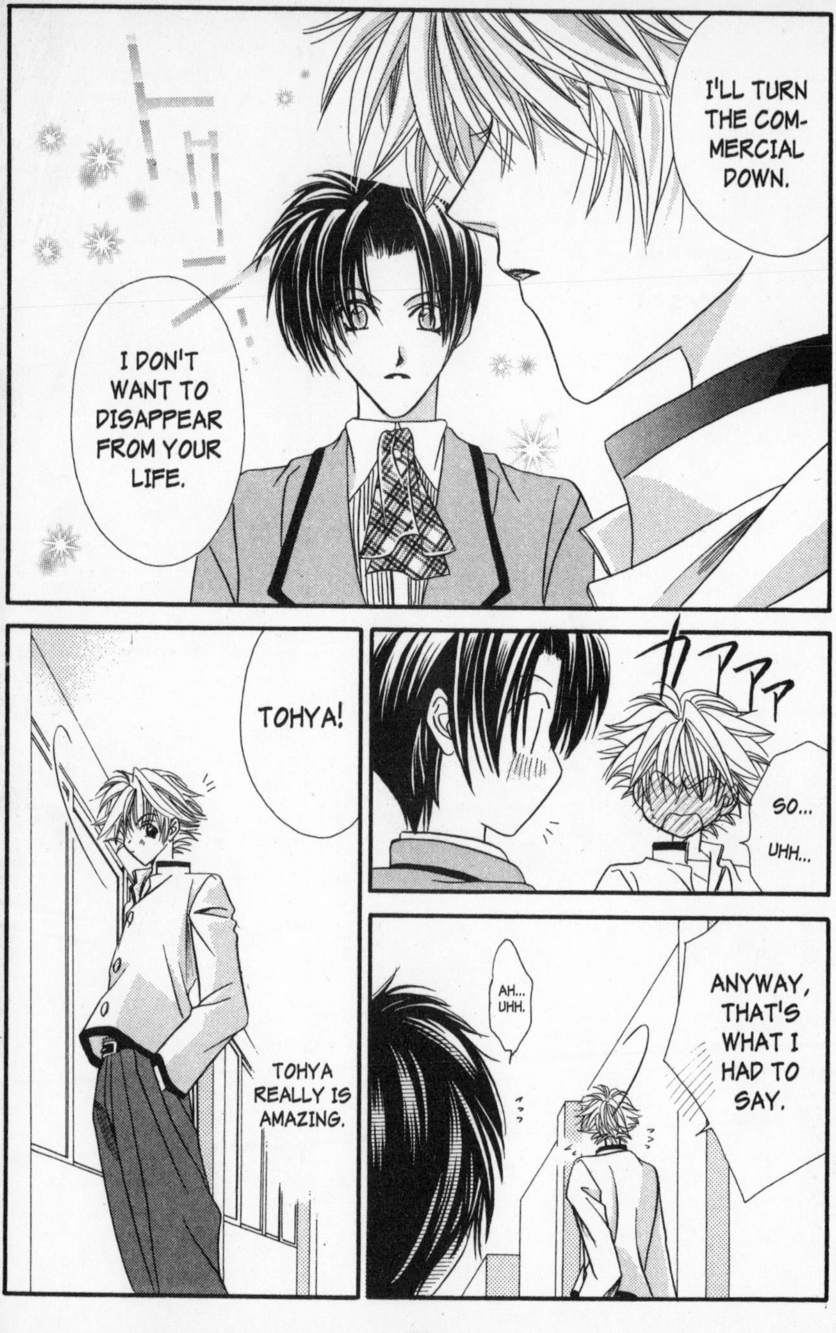
I'LL TURN THE COM-MERCIAL DOWN.
I DON'T WANT TO DISAPPEAR FROM YOUR LIFE.
SO... UHH...
ANYWAY, THAT'S WHAT I HAD TO SAY.
AH... UHH.
TOHYA!
TOHYA REALLY IS AMAZING.

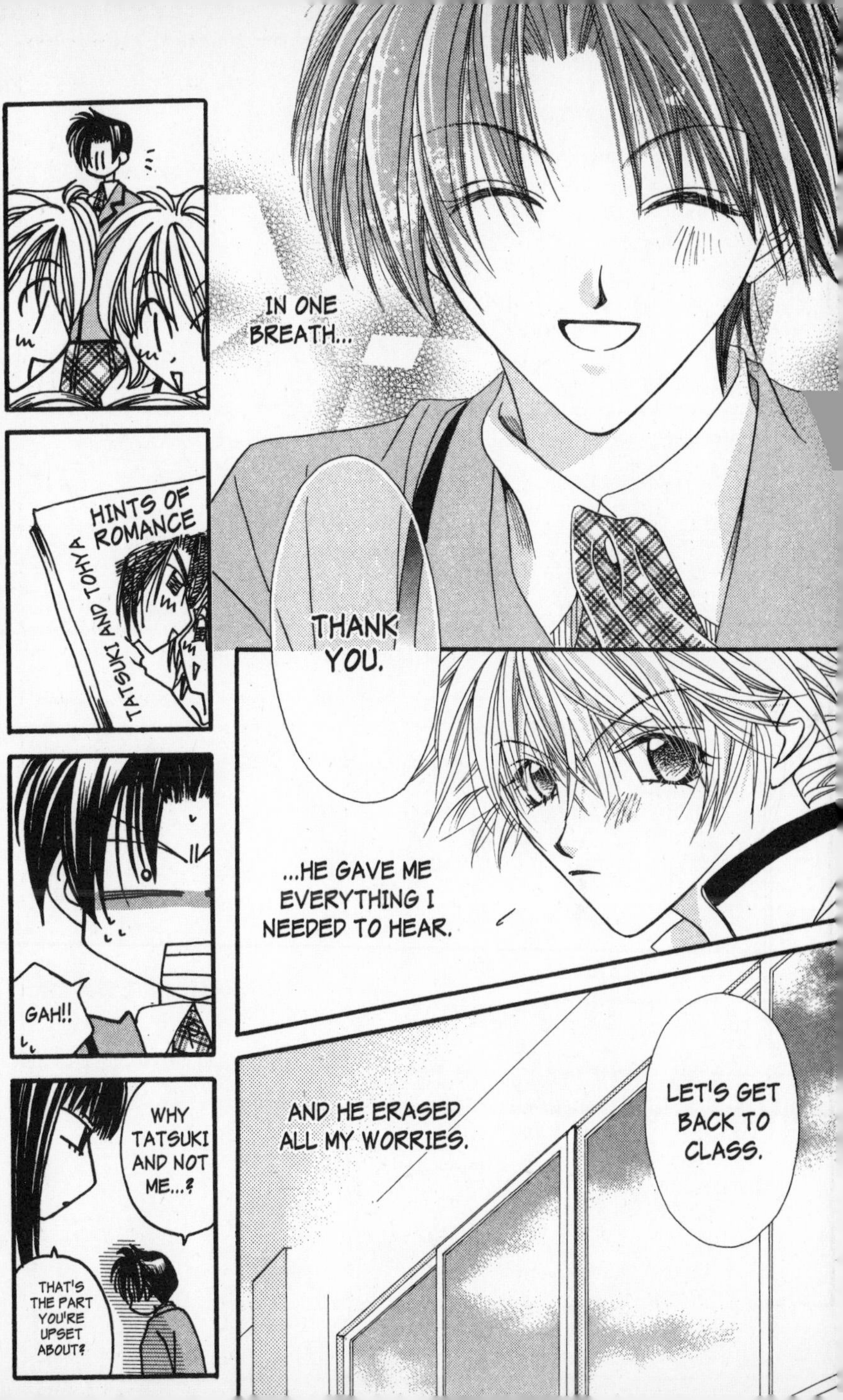
IN ONE BREATH...
THANK YOU.
...HE GAVE ME EVERYTHING I NEEDED TO HEAR.
LET'S GET BACK TO CLASS.
AND HE ERASED ALL MY WORRIES.
HINTS OF ROMANCE
TATSUKI AND TOHYA
GAH!!
WHY TATSUKI AND NOT ME...?
THAT'S THE PART YOU'RE UPSET ABOUT?

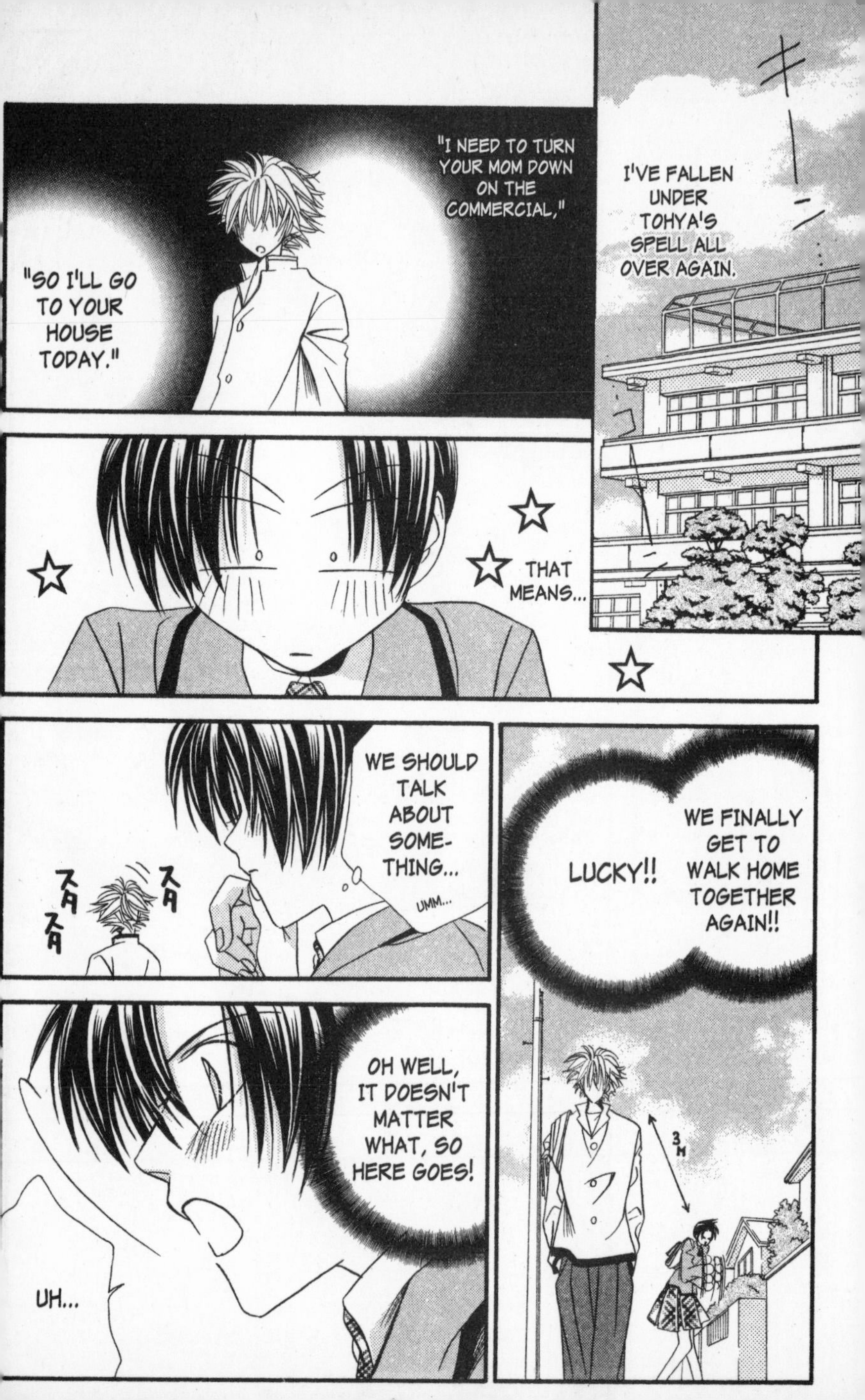
I'VE FALLEN UNDER TOHYA'S SPELL ALL OVER AGAIN.
"I NEED TO TURN YOUR MOM DOWN ON THE COMMERCIAL,"
"SO I'LL GO TO YOUR HOUSE TODAY."
THAT MEANS...
WE FINALLY GET TO WALK HOME TOGETHER AGAIN!!
LUCKY!!
3 M
WE SHOULD TALK ABOUT SOME-THING...
UMM...
スタ
スタ
スタ
OH WELL, IT DOESN'T MATTER WHAT, SO HERE GOES!
UH...

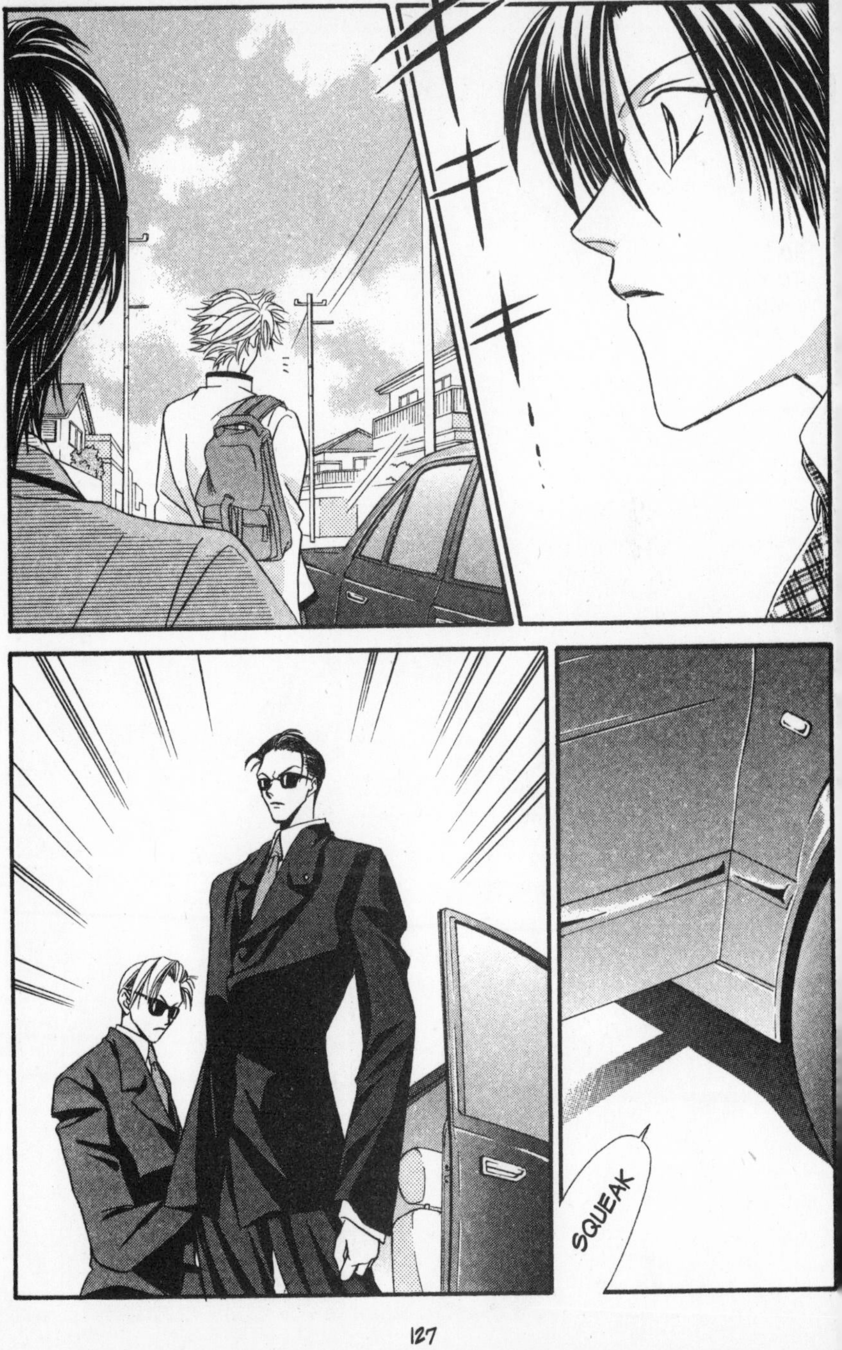
SQUEAK

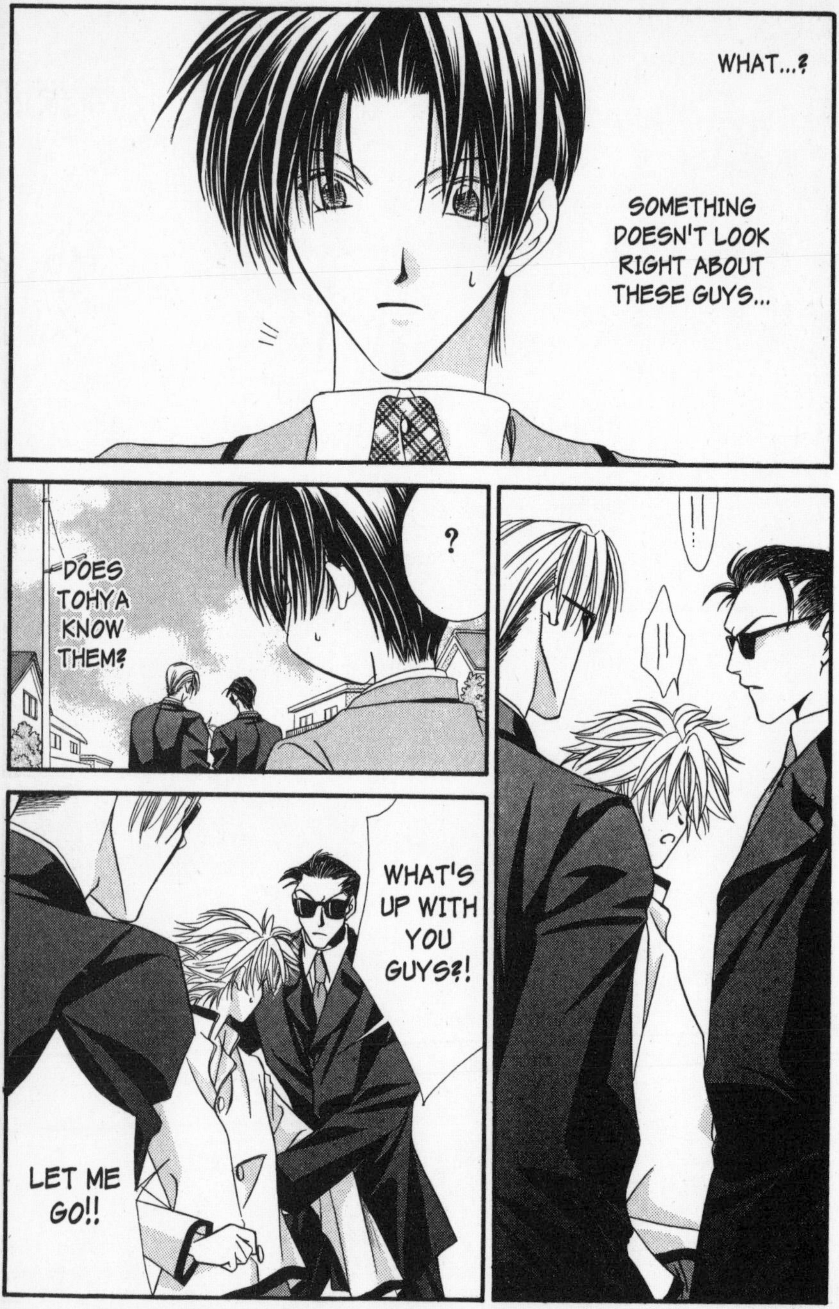
WHAT...?
SOMETHING DOESN'T LOOK RIGHT ABOUT THESE GUYS...
!...
!!
?
DOES TOHYA KNOW THEM?
WHAT'S UP WITH YOU GUYS?!
LET ME GO!!

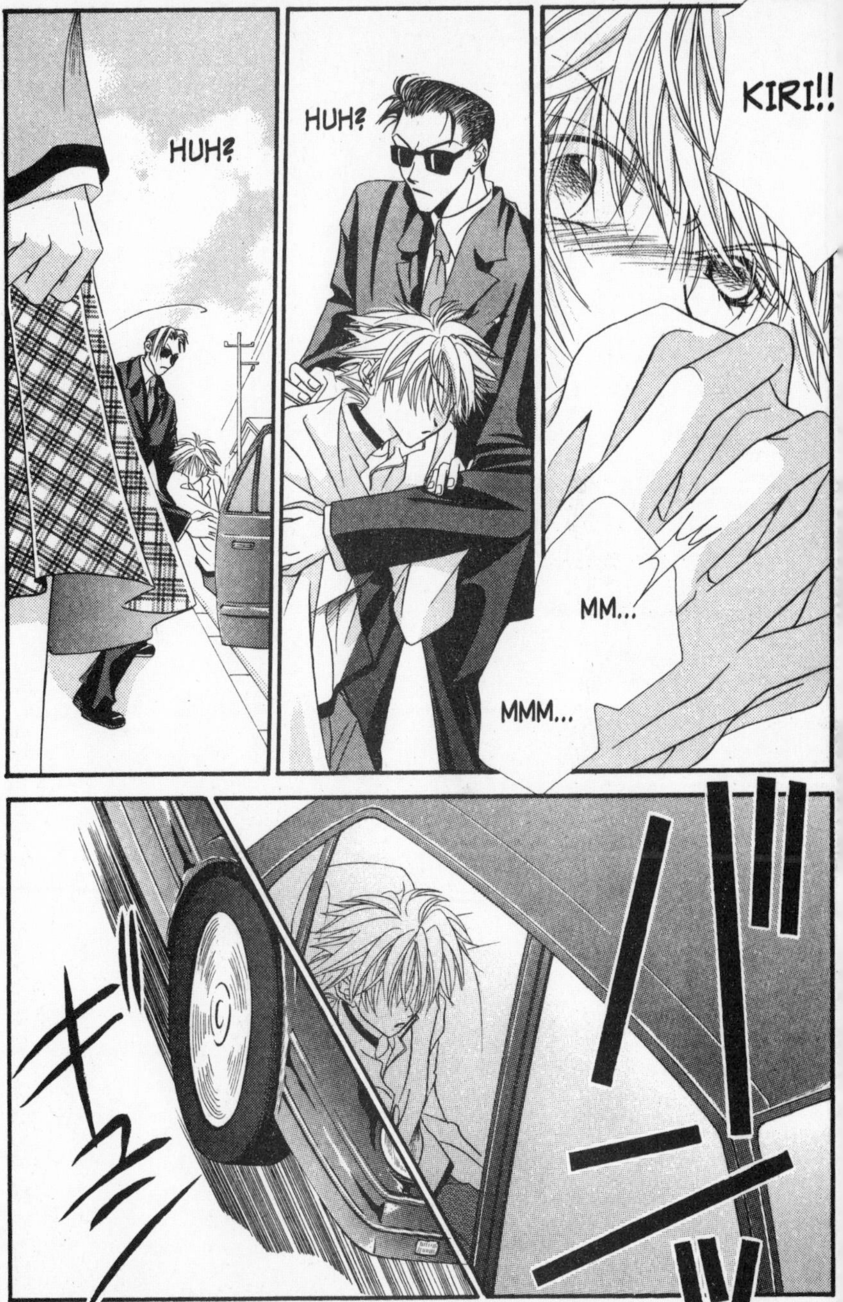
KIRI!!
MM...
MMM...
HUH?
HUH?

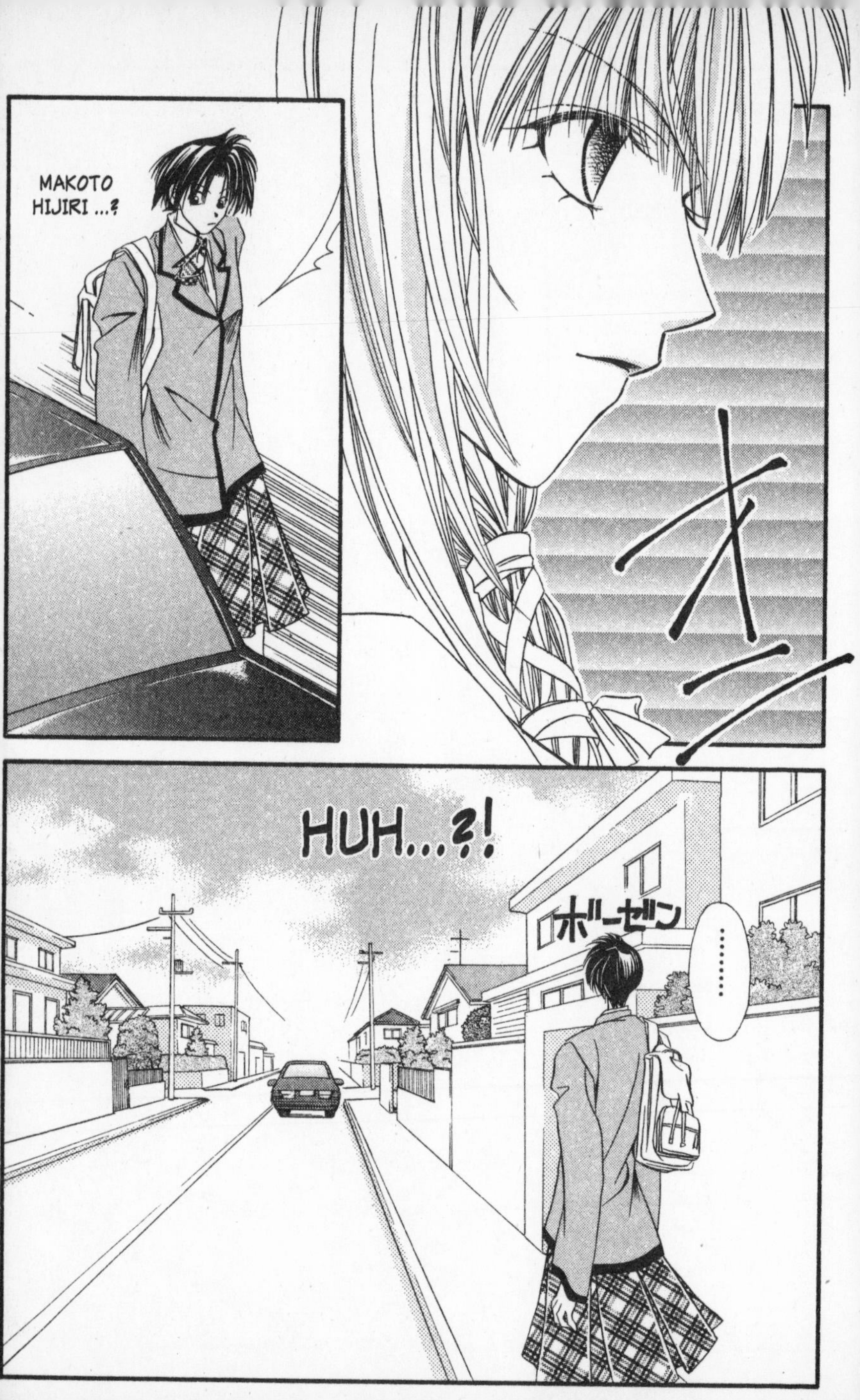
MAKOTO HIJIRI ...?
HUH...?!
ボーゼン
......

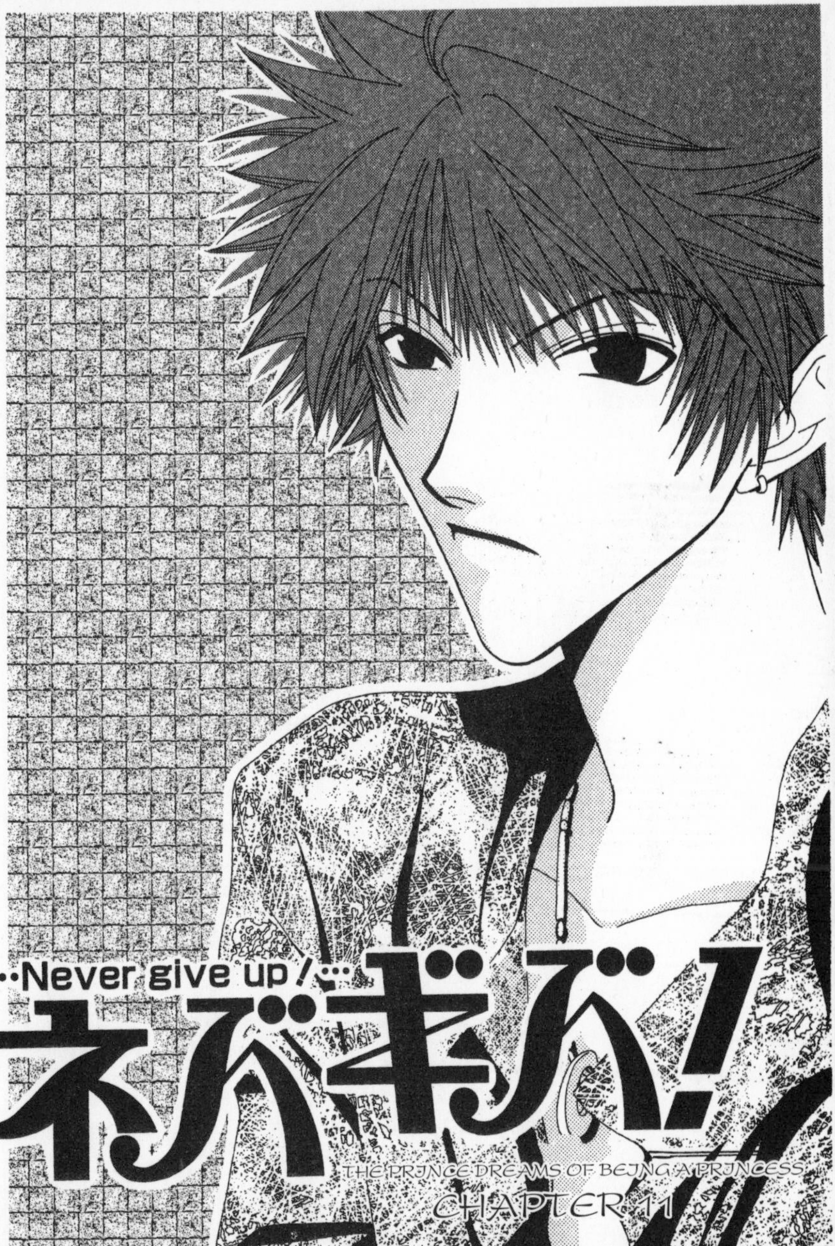
…Never give up!…
ネバギバ!
THE PRINCE DREAMS OF BEING A PRINCESS
CHAPTER 11

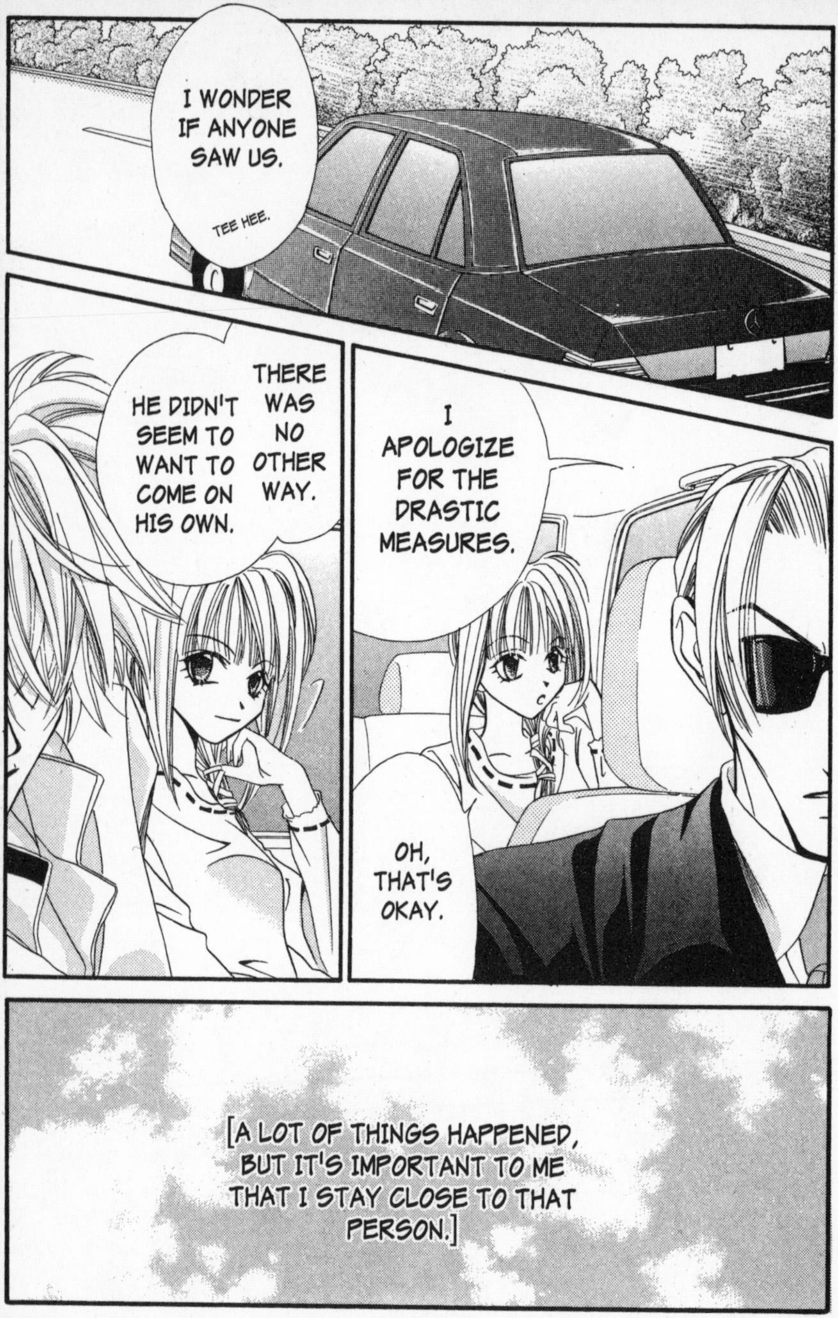
I WONDER IF ANYONE SAW US.
TEE HEE.
I APOLOGIZE FOR THE DRASTIC MEASURES.
OH, THAT'S OKAY.
THERE WAS NO OTHER WAY.
HE DIDN'T SEEM TO WANT TO COME ON HIS OWN.
[A LOT OF THINGS HAPPENED, BUT IT'S IMPORTANT TO ME THAT I STAY CLOSE TO THAT PERSON.]

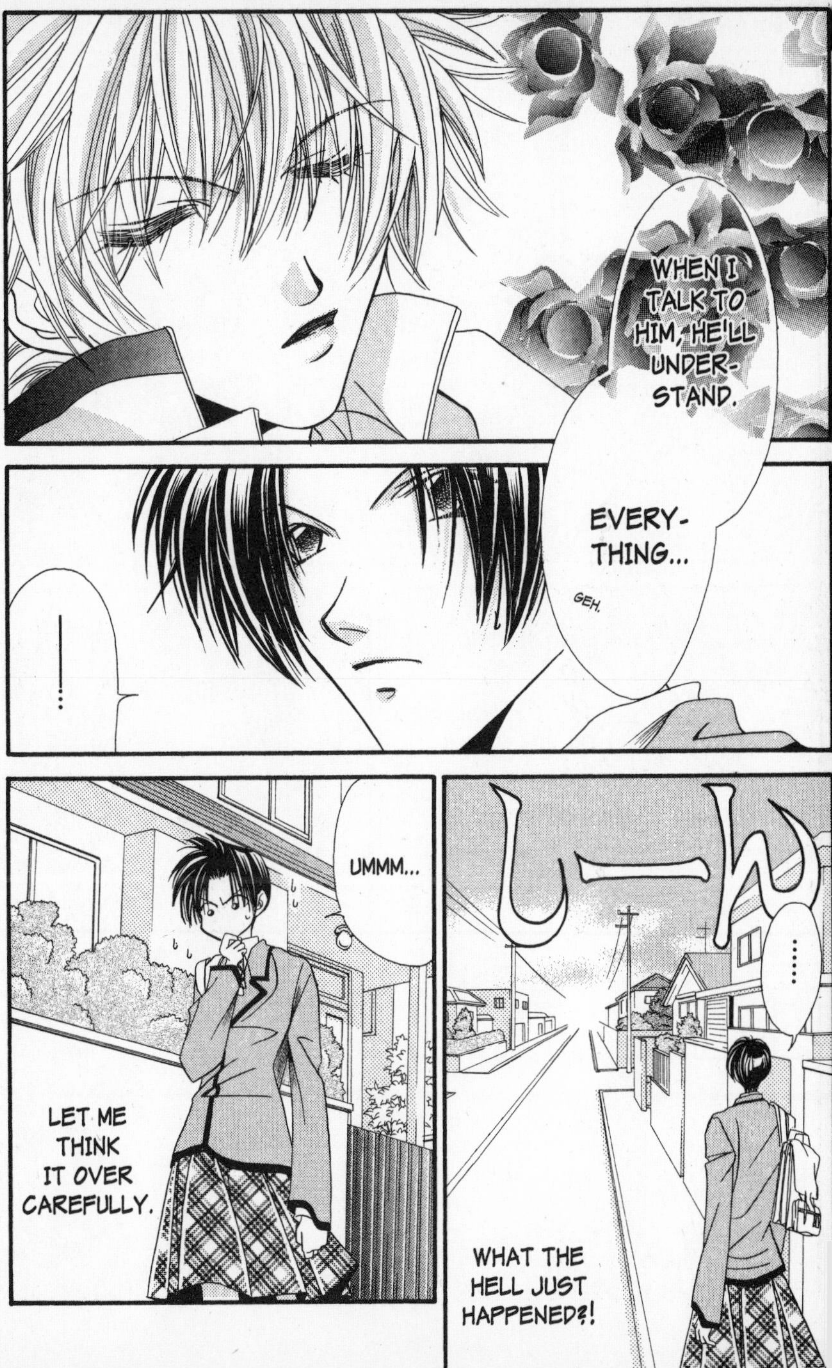
WHEN I TALK TO HIM, HE'LL UNDER-STAND.
EVERY-THING...
GEH.
......
しーん
......
WHAT THE HELL JUST HAPPENED?!
UMMM...
LET ME THINK IT OVER CAREFULLY.

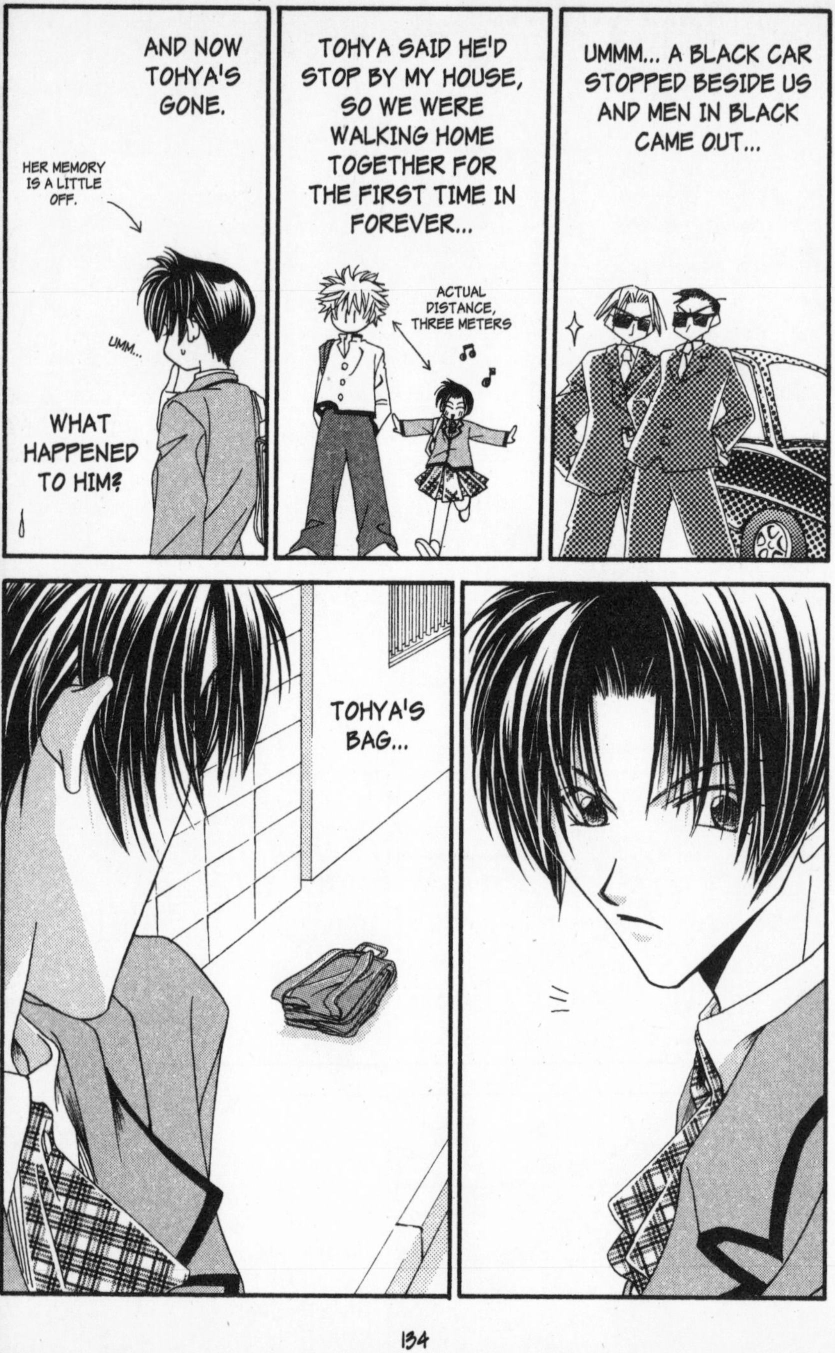
UMMM... A BLACK CAR STOPPED BESIDE US AND MEN IN BLACK CAME OUT...
TOHYA SAID HE'D STOP BY MY HOUSE, SO WE WERE WALKING HOME TOGETHER FOR THE FIRST TIME IN FOREVER...
ACTUAL DISTANCE, THREE METERS
AND NOW TOHYA'S GONE.
HER MEMORY IS A LITTLE OFF.
UMM...
WHAT HAPPENED TO HIM?
TOHYA'S BAG...

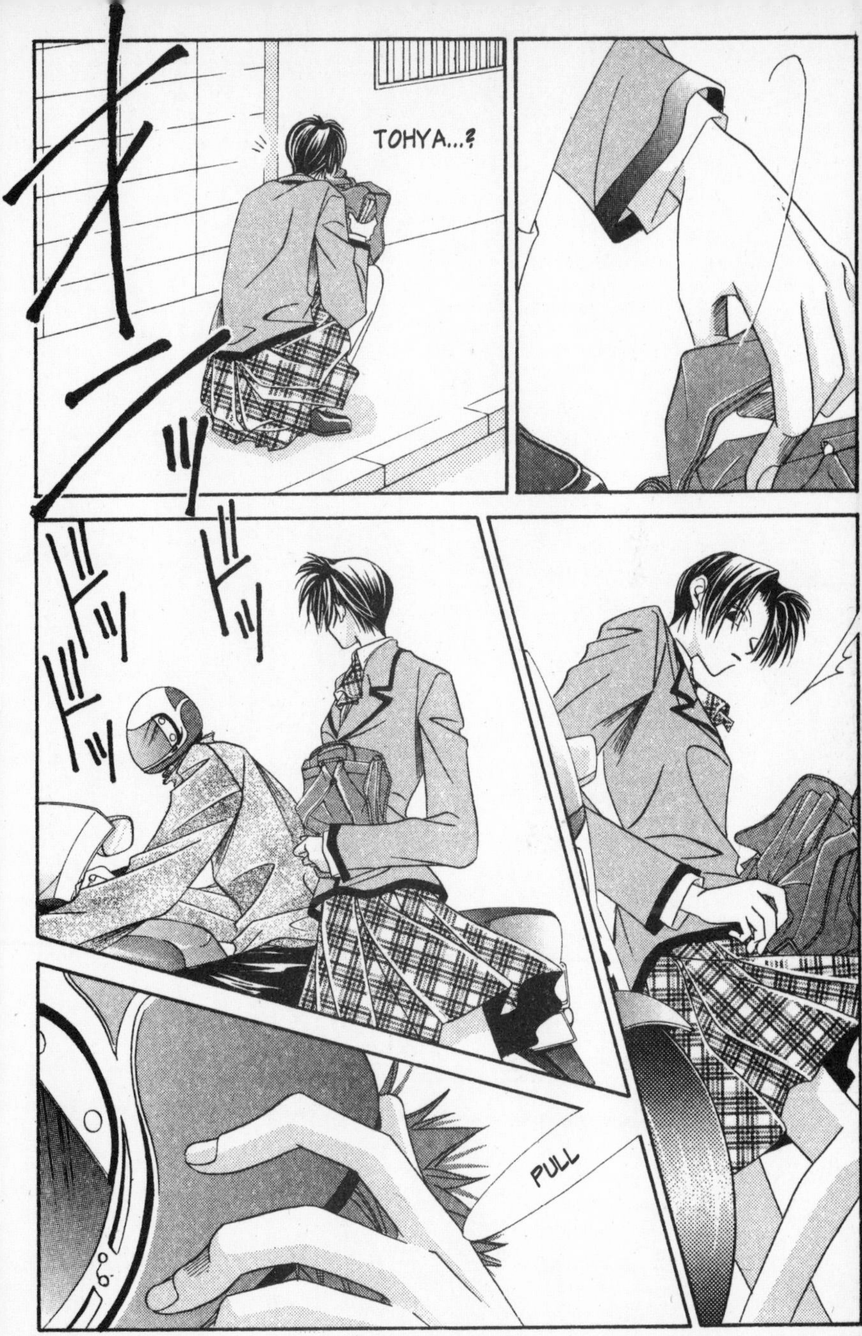
TOHYA...?
PULL

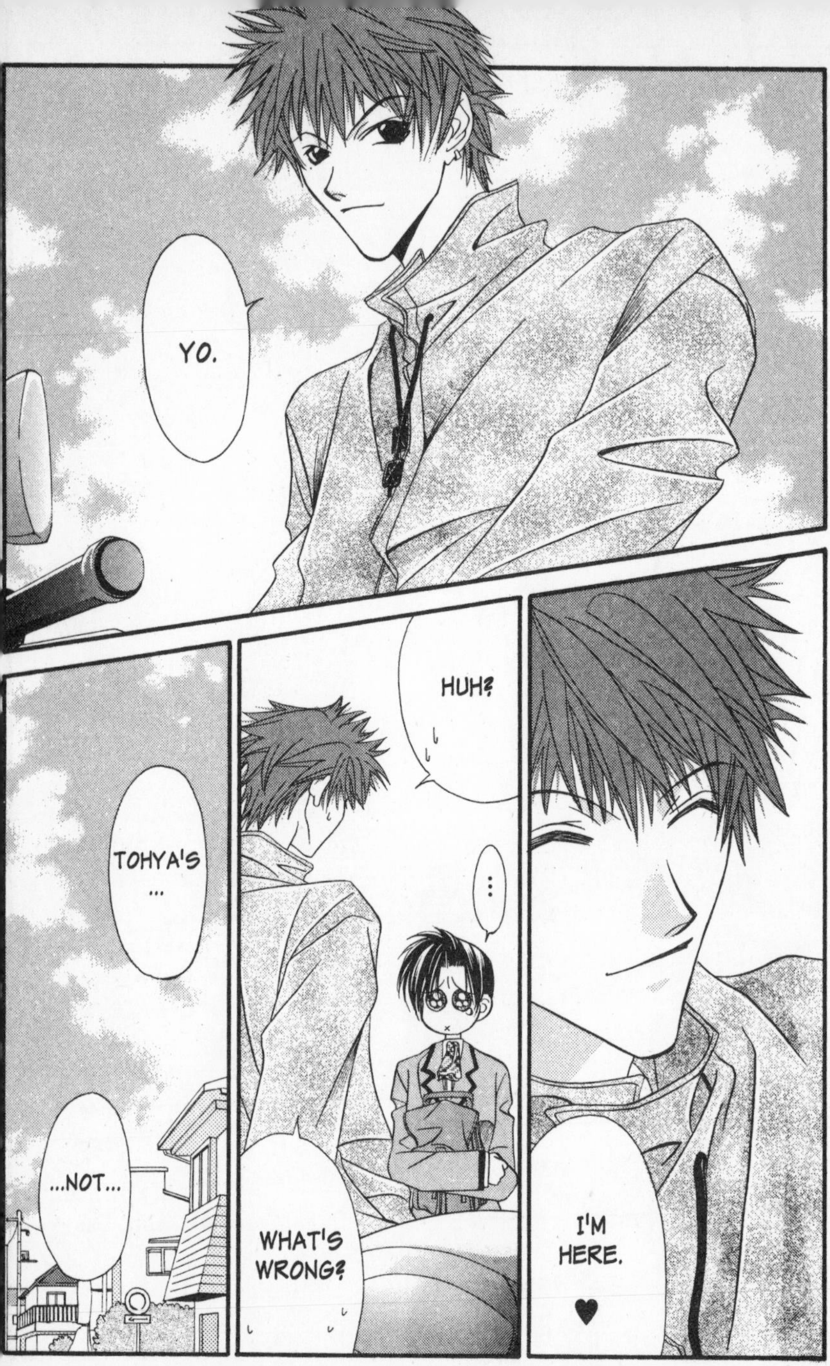
YO.
I'M HERE. ♥
HUH?
...
WHAT'S WRONG?
TOHYA'S ...
...NOT...

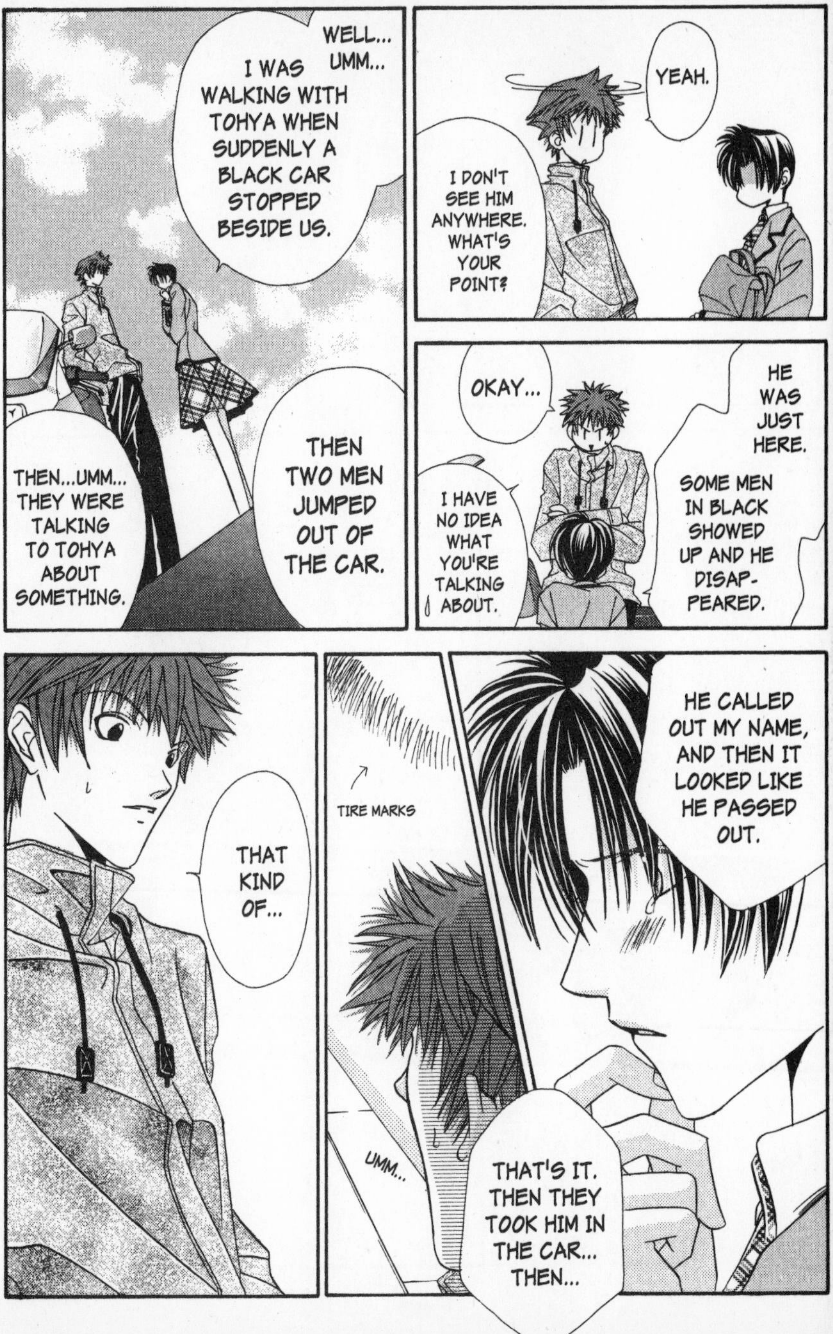
YEAH.
I DON'T SEE HIM ANYWHERE. WHAT'S YOUR POINT?
HE WAS JUST HERE.
SOME MEN IN BLACK SHOWED UP AND HE DISAP-PEARED.
OKAY...
I HAVE NO IDEA WHAT YOU'RE TALKING ABOUT.
WELL... UMM...
I WAS WALKING WITH TOHYA WHEN SUDDENLY A BLACK CAR STOPPED BESIDE US.
THEN TWO MEN JUMPED OUT OF THE CAR.
THEN...UMM... THEY WERE TALKING TO TOHYA ABOUT SOMETHING.
HE CALLED OUT MY NAME, AND THEN IT LOOKED LIKE HE PASSED OUT.
THAT'S IT. THEN THEY TOOK HIM IN THE CAR... THEN...
UMM...
TIRE MARKS
THAT KIND OF...

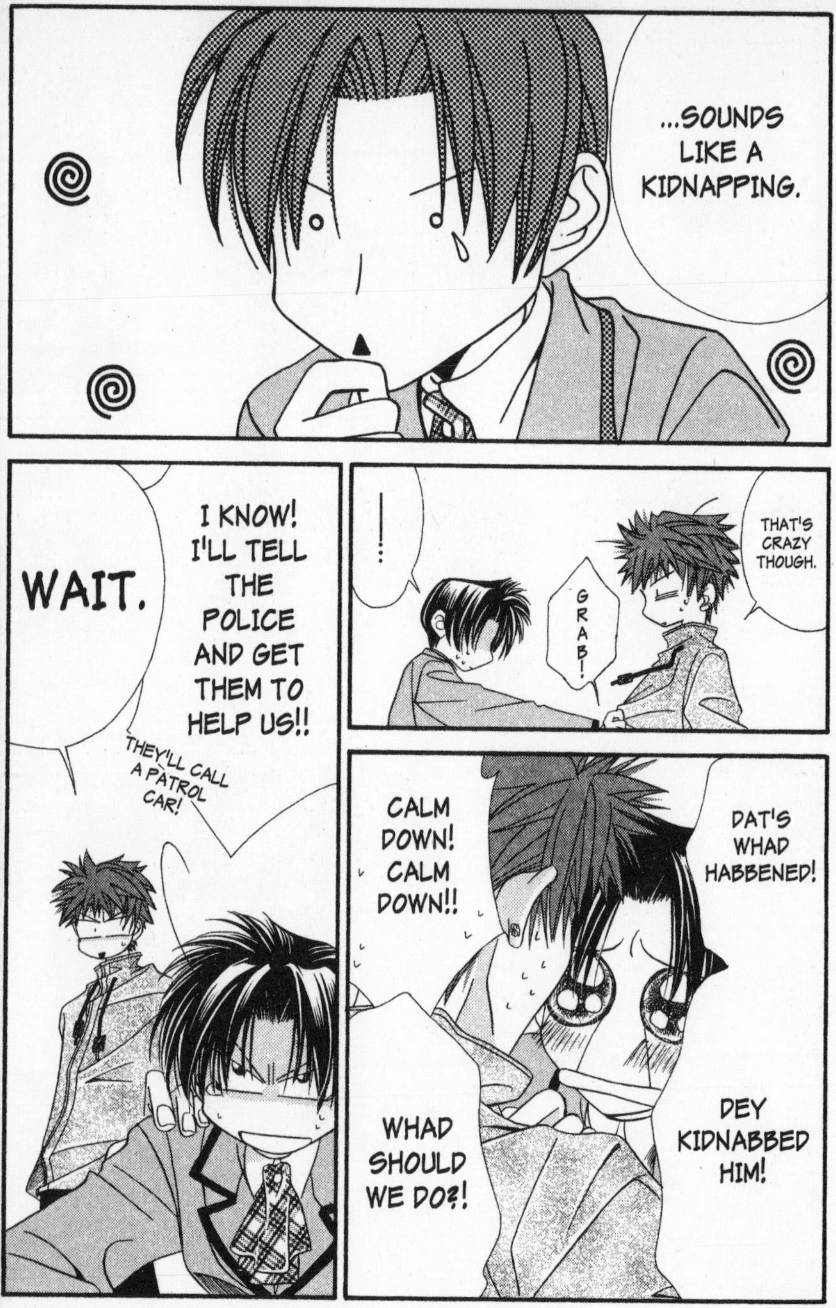
...SOUNDS LIKE A KIDNAPPING.
THAT'S CRAZY THOUGH.
GRAB!
!...
DAT'S WHAD HABBENED!
DEY KIDNABBED HIM!
CALM DOWN! CALM DOWN!!
WHAD SHOULD WE DO?!
I KNOW! I'LL TELL THE POLICE AND GET THEM TO HELP US!!
THEY'LL CALL A PATROL CAR!
WAIT.

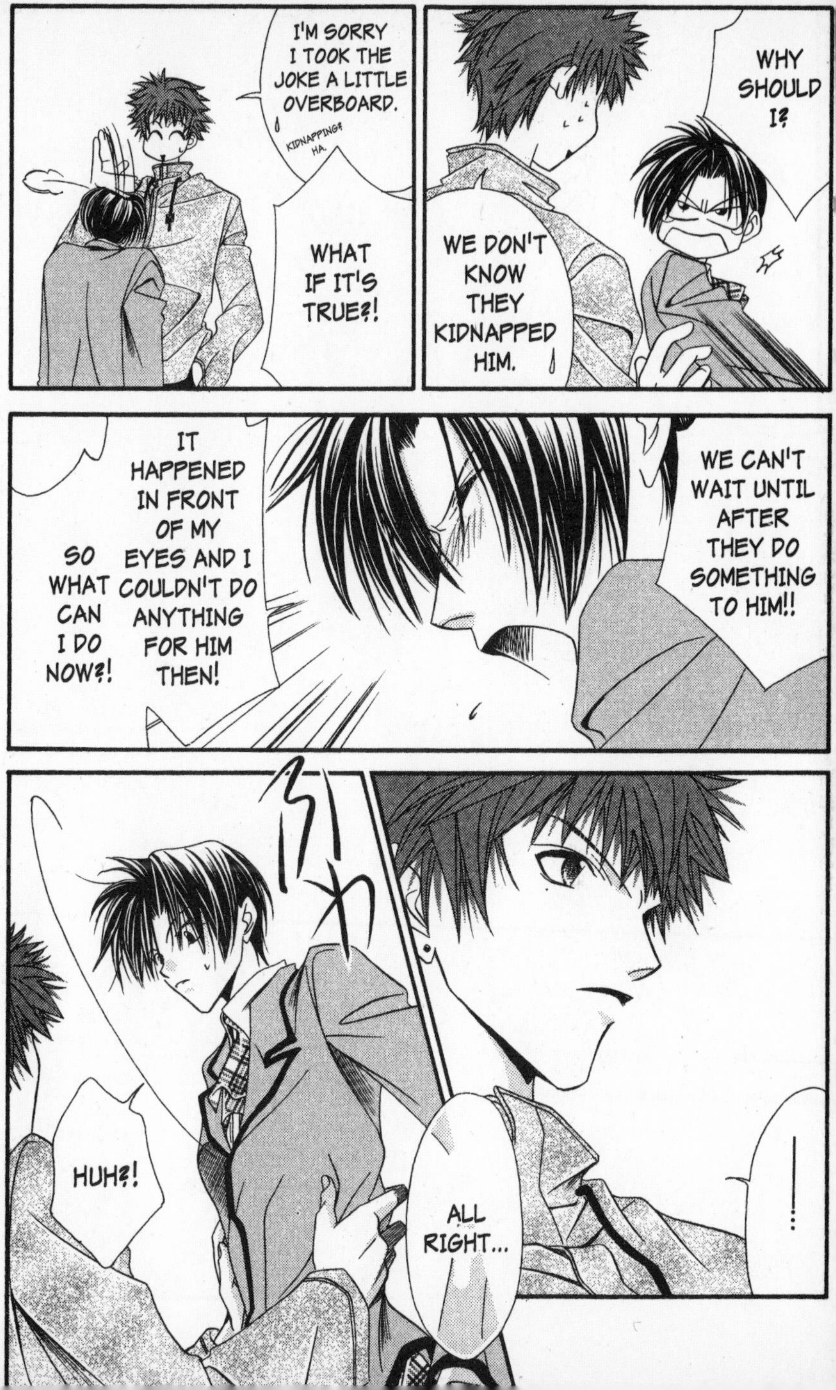
WHY SHOULD I?
WE DON'T KNOW THEY KIDNAPPED HIM.
I'M SORRY I TOOK THE JOKE A LITTLE OVERBOARD.
KIDNAPPING? HA.
WHAT IF IT'S TRUE?!
WE CAN'T WAIT UNTIL AFTER THEY DO SOMETHING TO HIM!!
IT HAPPENED IN FRONT OF MY EYES AND I COULDN'T DO ANYTHING FOR HIM THEN!
SO WHAT CAN I DO NOW?!
......
ALL RIGHT...
HUH?!

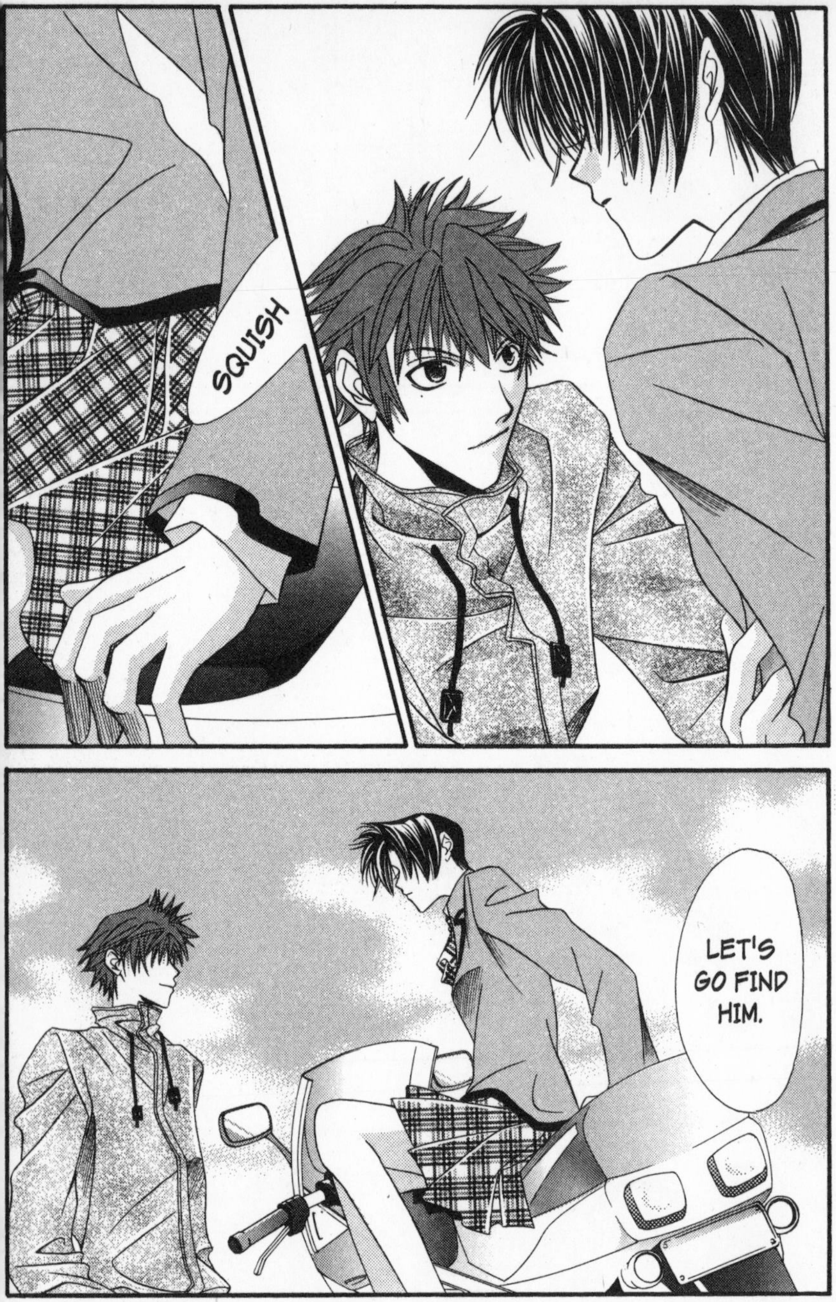
SQUISH
LET'S GO FIND HIM.

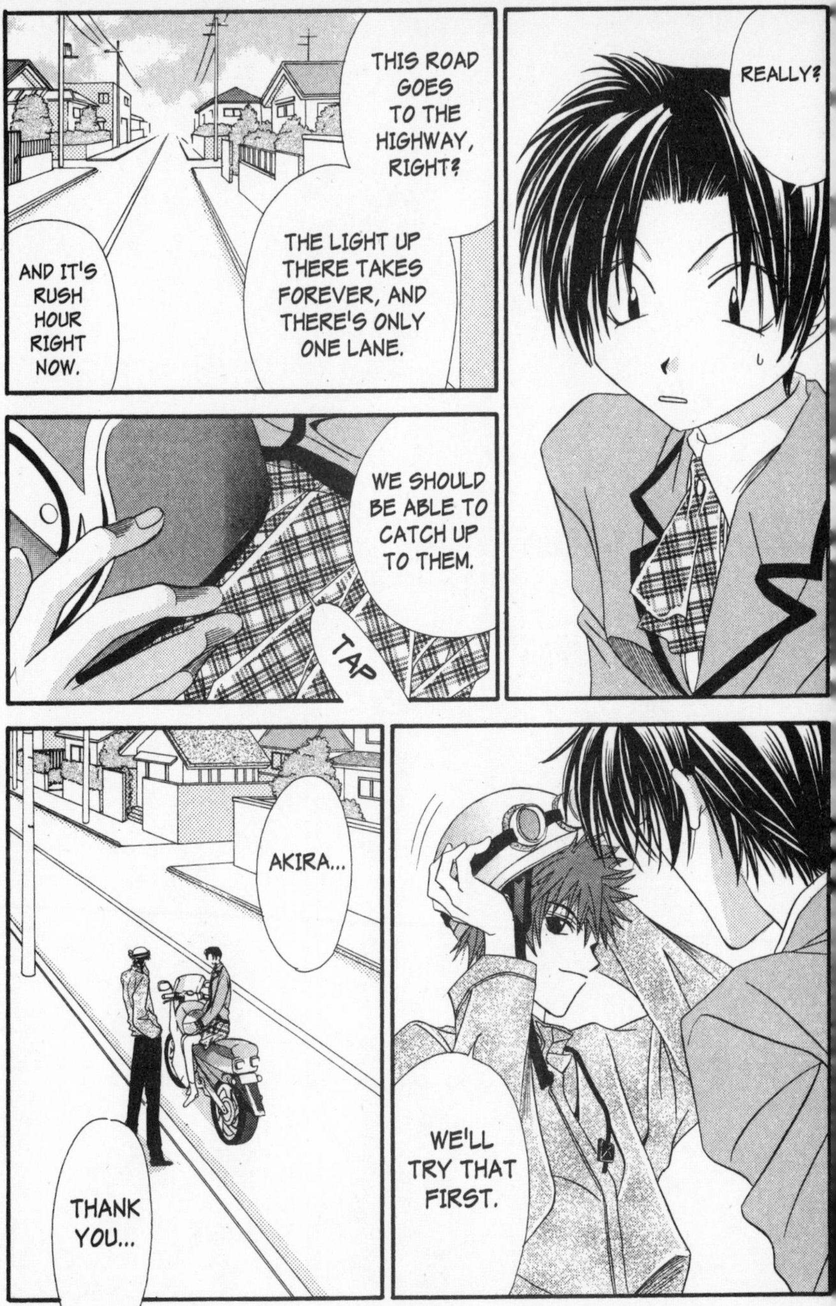
REALLY?
THIS ROAD GOES TO THE HIGHWAY, RIGHT?
THE LIGHT UP THERE TAKES FOREVER, AND THERE'S ONLY ONE LANE.
AND IT'S RUSH HOUR RIGHT NOW.
WE SHOULD BE ABLE TO CATCH UP TO THEM.
TAP
WE'LL TRY THAT FIRST.
AKIRA...
THANK YOU...

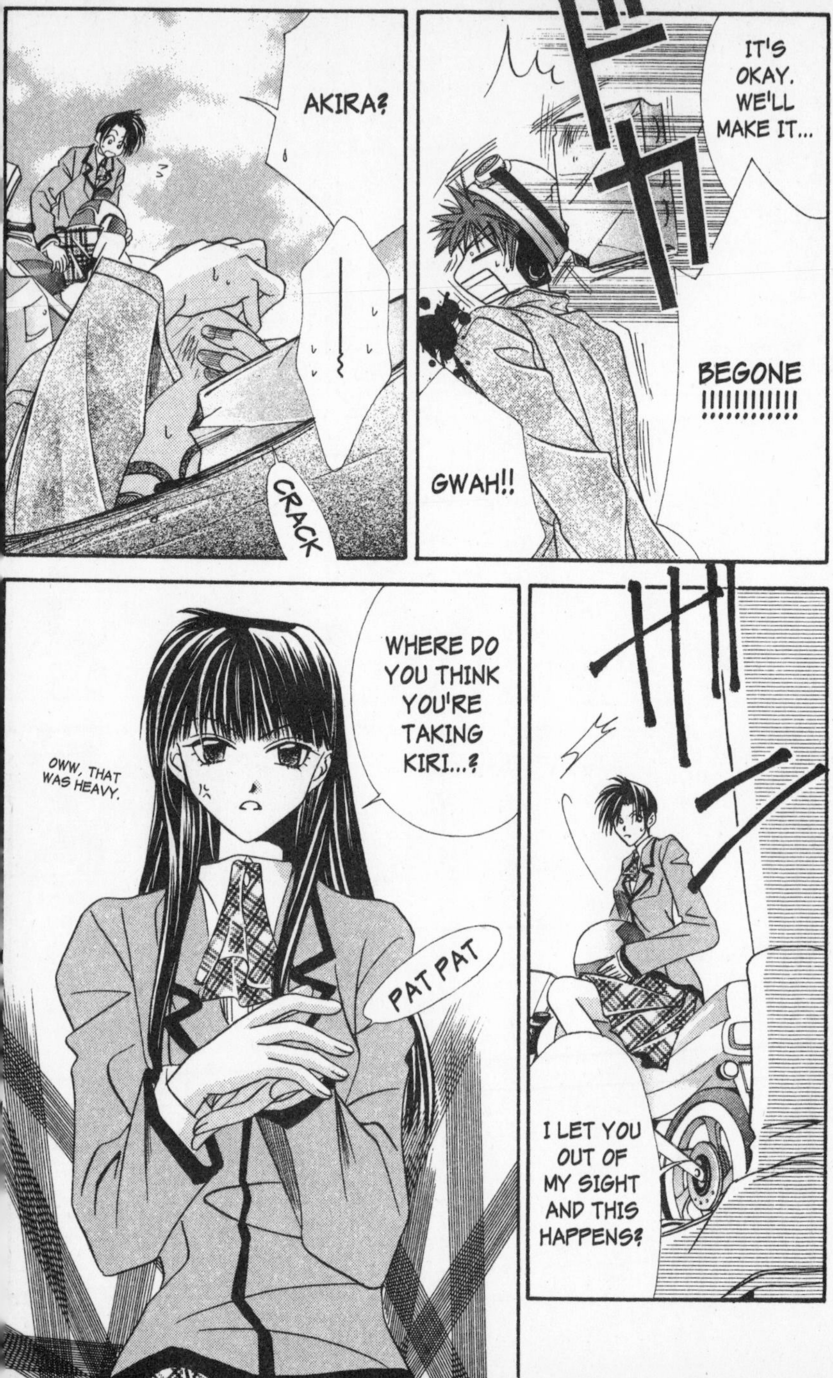
IT'S OKAY. WE'LL MAKE IT...
BEGONE !!!!!!!!!!!!!
GWAH!!
AKIRA?
CRACK
I LET YOU OUT OF MY SIGHT AND THIS HAPPENS?
WHERE DO YOU THINK YOU'RE TAKING KIRI...?
PAT PAT
OWW, THAT WAS HEAVY.

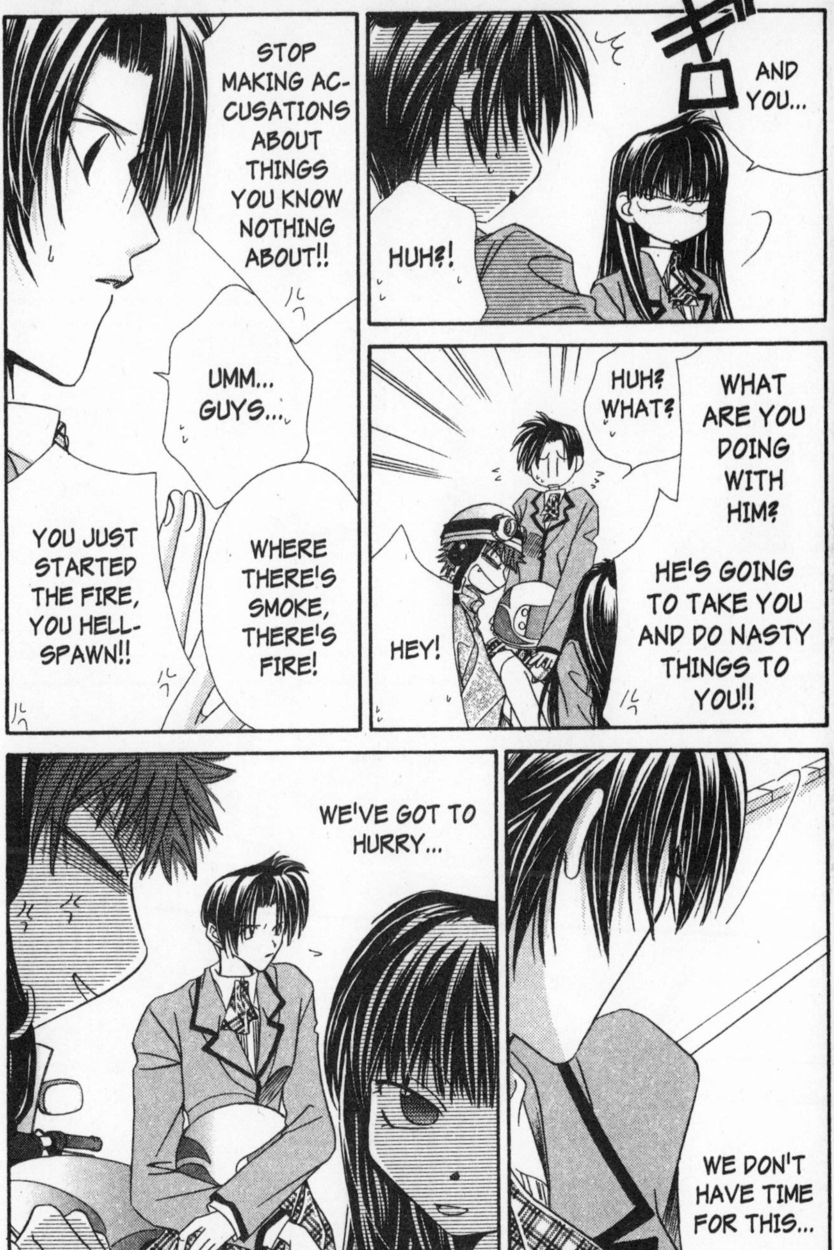
ギロ
AND YOU...
HUH?!
WHAT ARE YOU DOING WITH HIM?
HUH? WHAT?
HE'S GOING TO TAKE YOU AND DO NASTY THINGS TO YOU!!
HEY!
STOP MAKING AC-CUSATIONS ABOUT THINGS YOU KNOW NOTHING ABOUT!!
UMM... GUYS...
WHERE THERE'S SMOKE, THERE'S FIRE!
YOU JUST STARTED THE FIRE, YOU HELL-SPAWN!!
WE DON'T HAVE TIME FOR THIS...
WE'VE GOT TO HURRY...

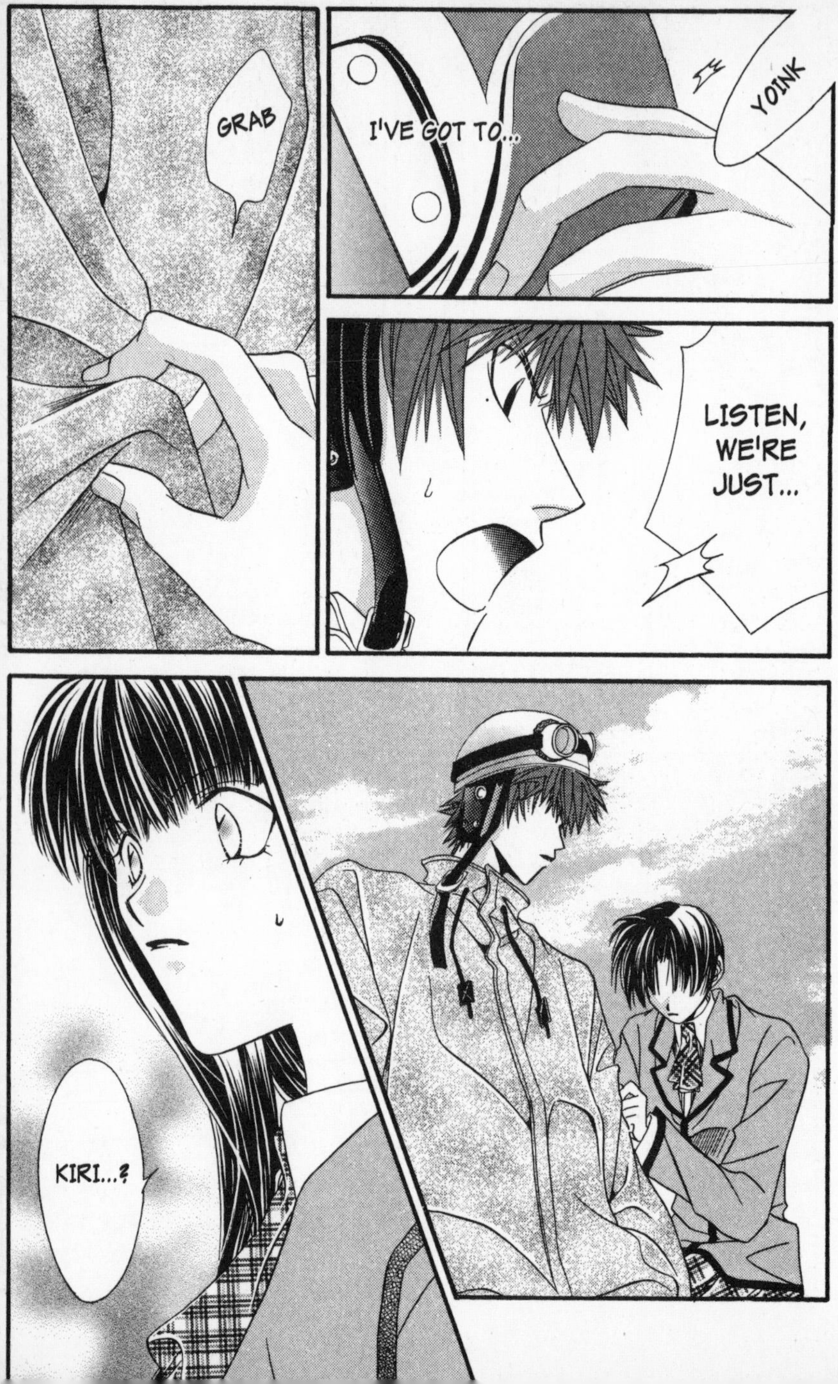
YOINK
I'VE GOT TO...
LISTEN, WE'RE JUST...
GRAB
KIRI...?

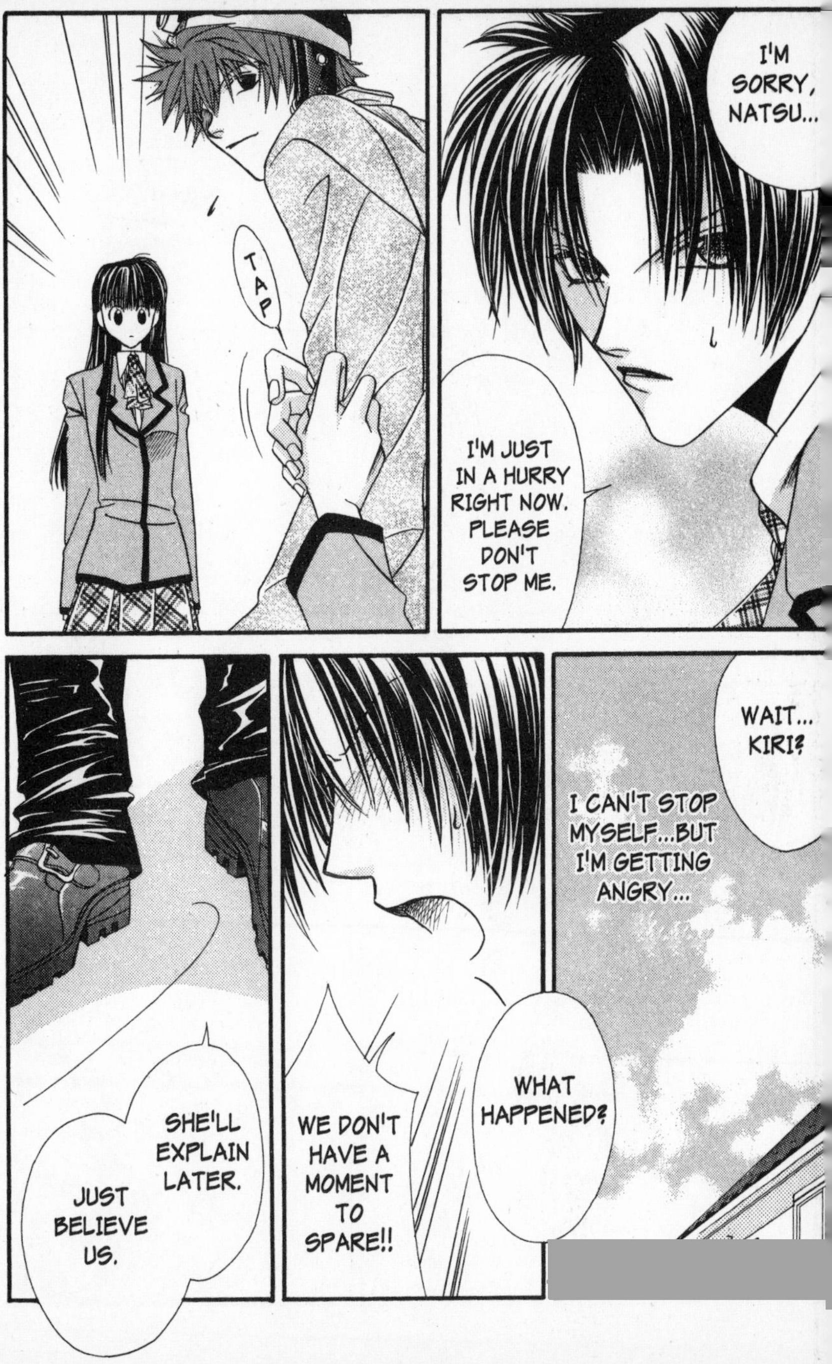
I'M SORRY, NATSU...
I'M JUST IN A HURRY RIGHT NOW. PLEASE DON'T STOP ME.
TAP
WAIT... KIRI?
I CAN'T STOP MYSELF...BUT I'M GETTING ANGRY...
WHAT HAPPENED?
WE DON'T HAVE A MOMENT TO SPARE!!
SHE'LL EXPLAIN LATER.
JUST BELIEVE US.

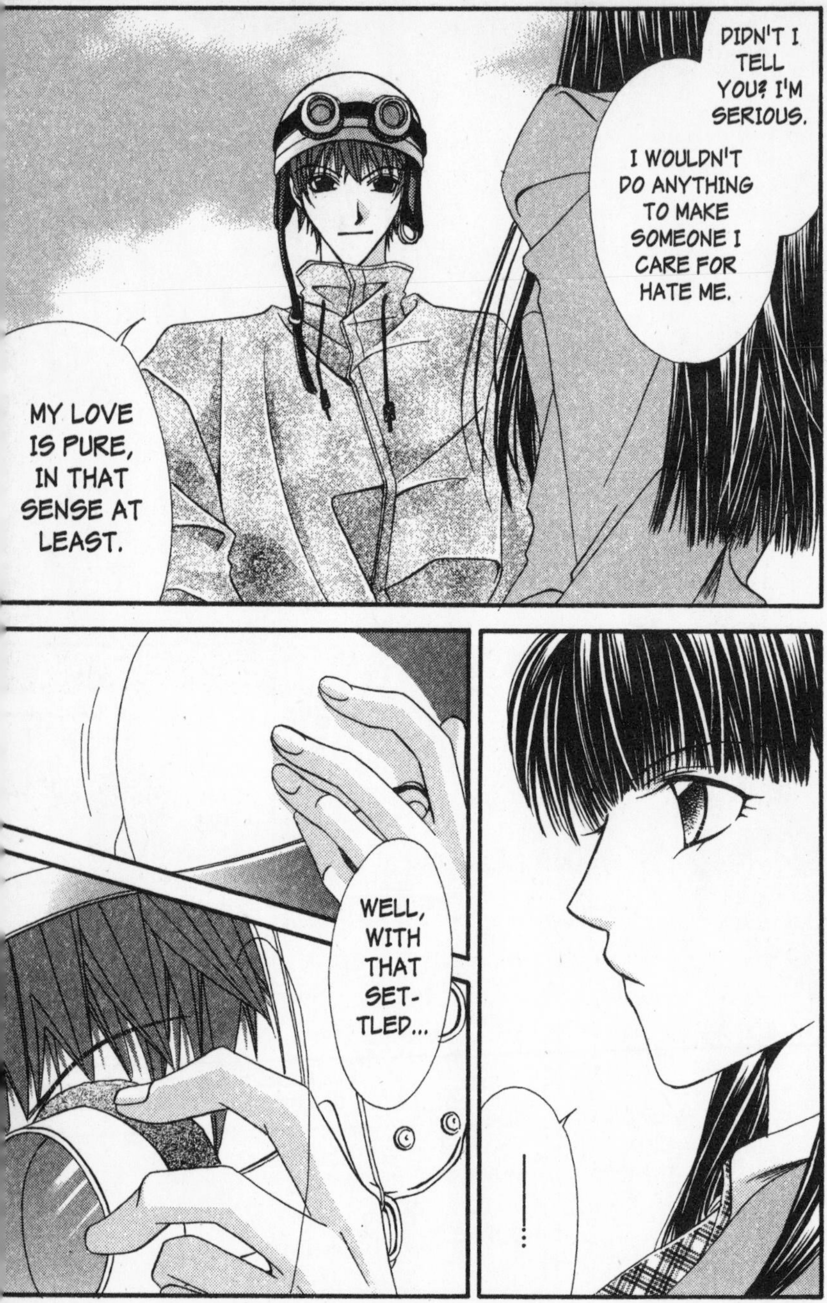
DIDN'T I TELL YOU? I'M SERIOUS.
I WOULDN'T DO ANYTHING TO MAKE SOMEONE I CARE FOR HATE ME.
MY LOVE IS PURE, IN THAT SENSE AT LEAST.
......
WELL, WITH THAT SET-TLED...

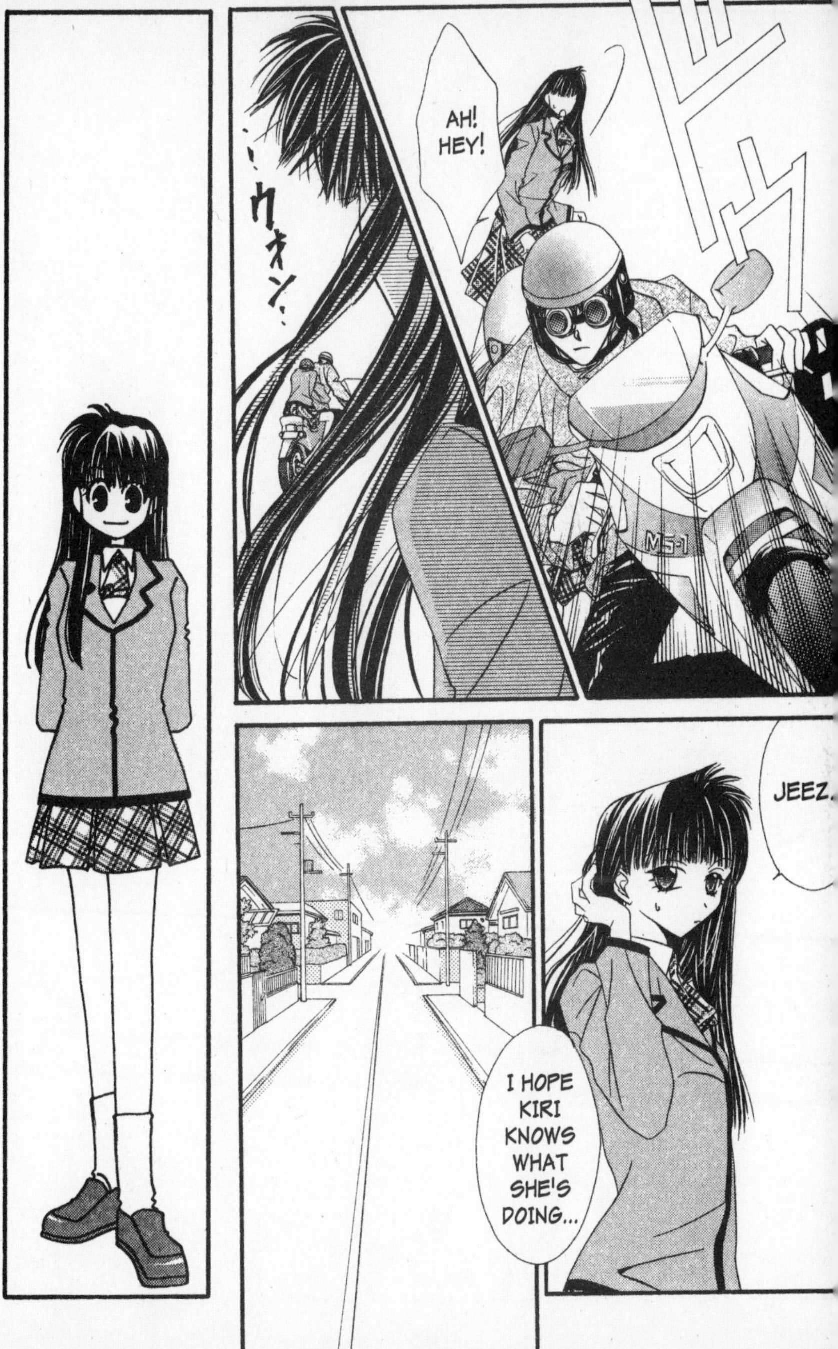
AH! HEY!
ウォン
JEEZ.
I HOPE KIRI KNOWS WHAT SHE'S DOING...

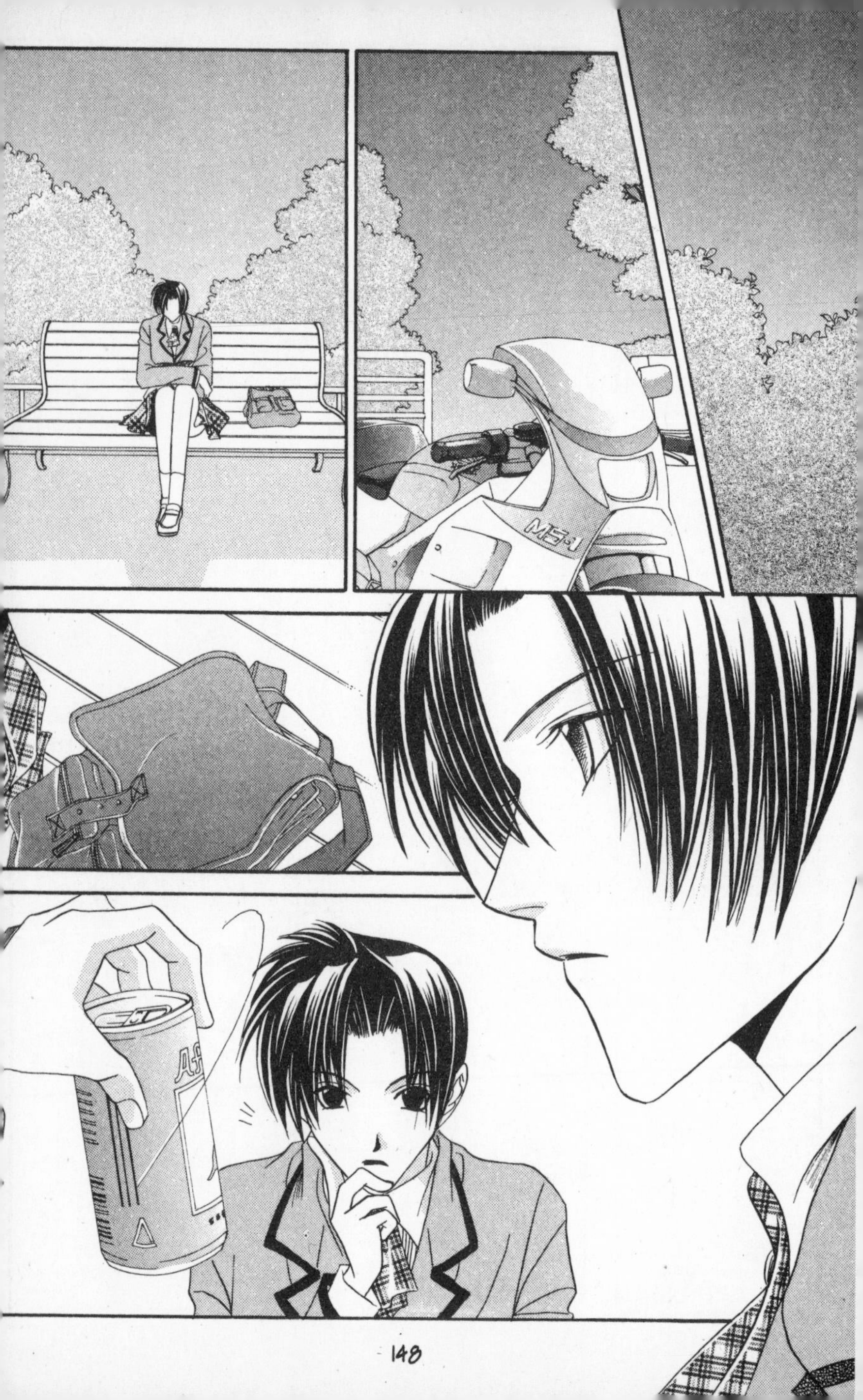

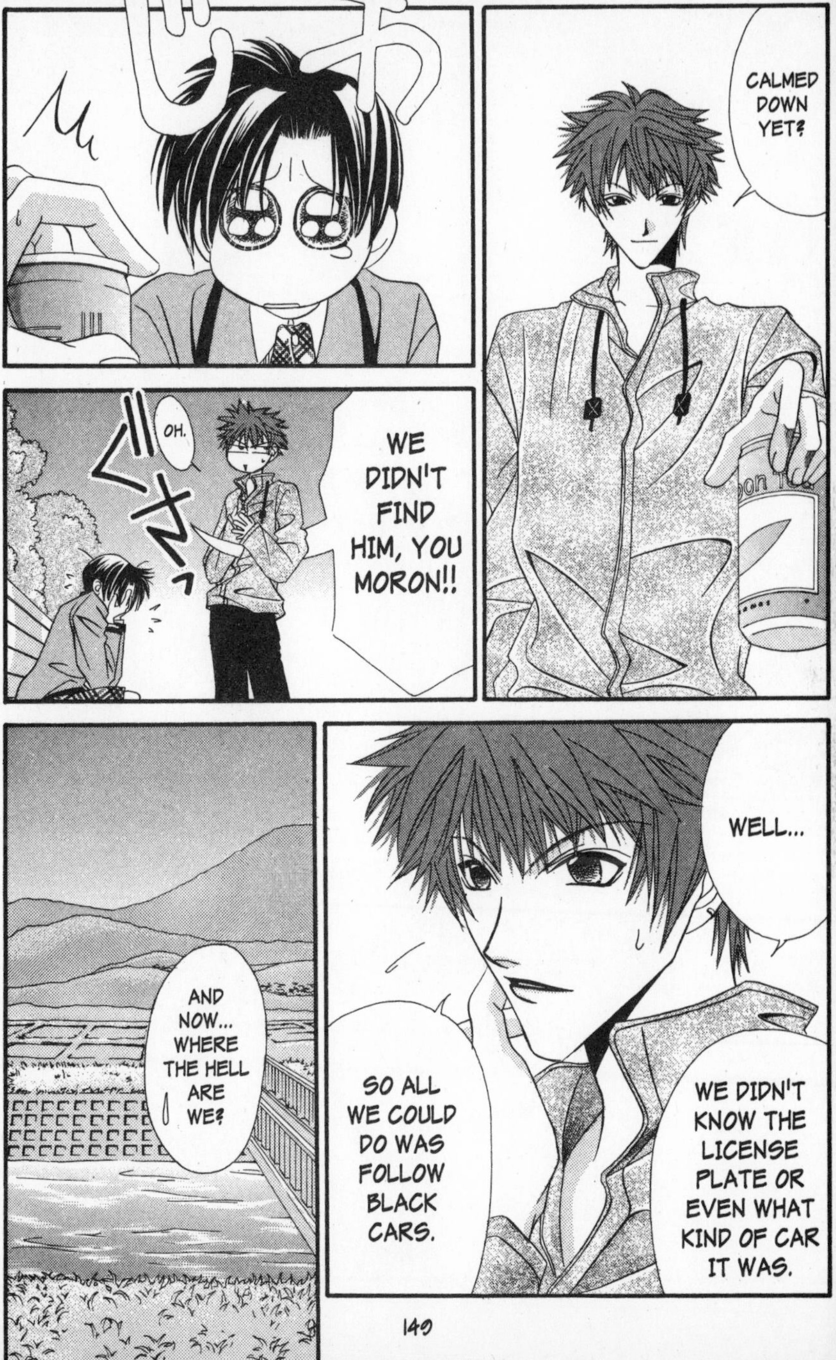
CALMED DOWN YET?
じわ
OH.
WE DIDN'T FIND HIM, YOU MORON!!
ぐさっ
WELL...
WE DIDN'T KNOW THE LICENSE PLATE OR EVEN WHAT KIND OF CAR IT WAS.
SO ALL WE COULD DO WAS FOLLOW BLACK CARS.
AND NOW... WHERE THE HELL ARE WE?

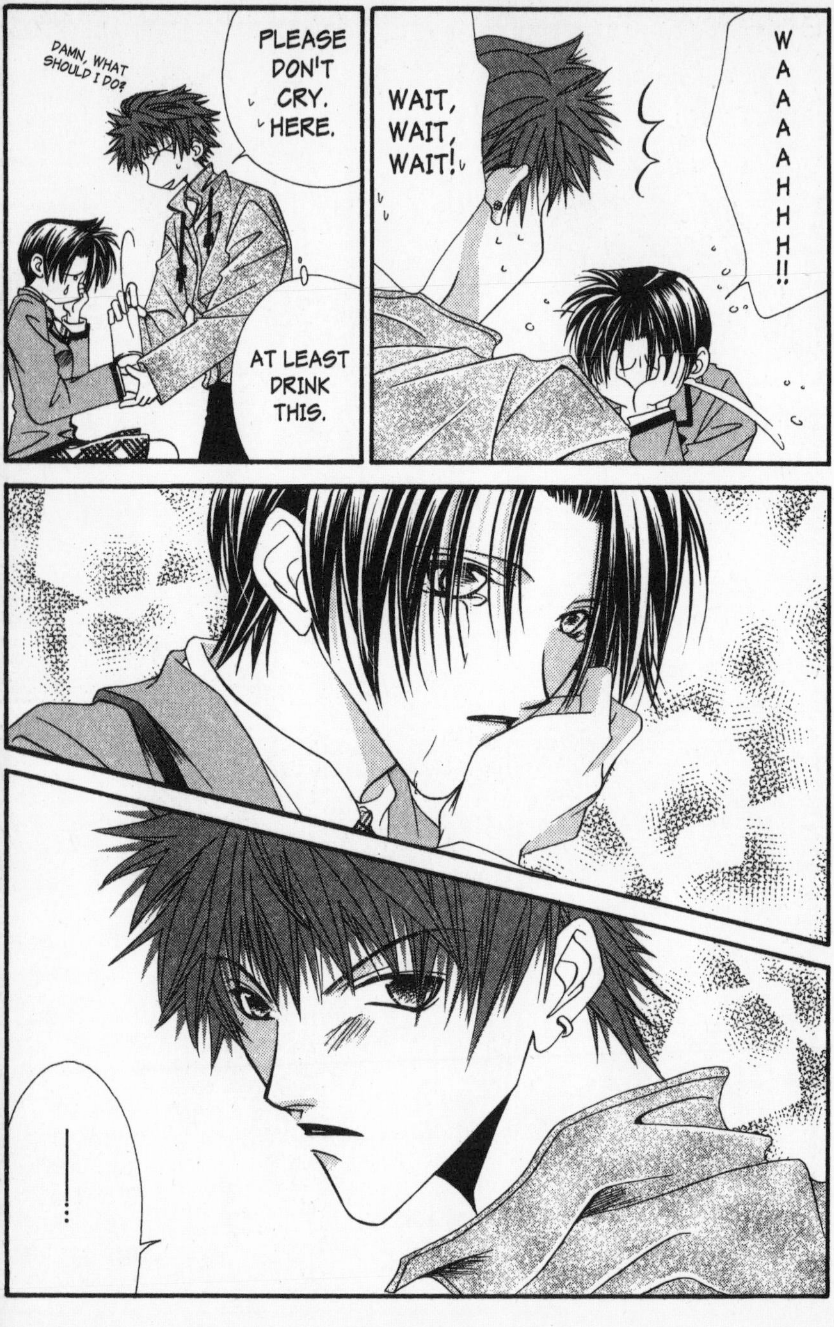
WAAAAAHHH!!
WAIT, WAIT, WAIT!
PLEASE DON'T CRY. HERE.
DAMN, WHAT SHOULD I DO?
AT LEAST DRINK THIS.
......

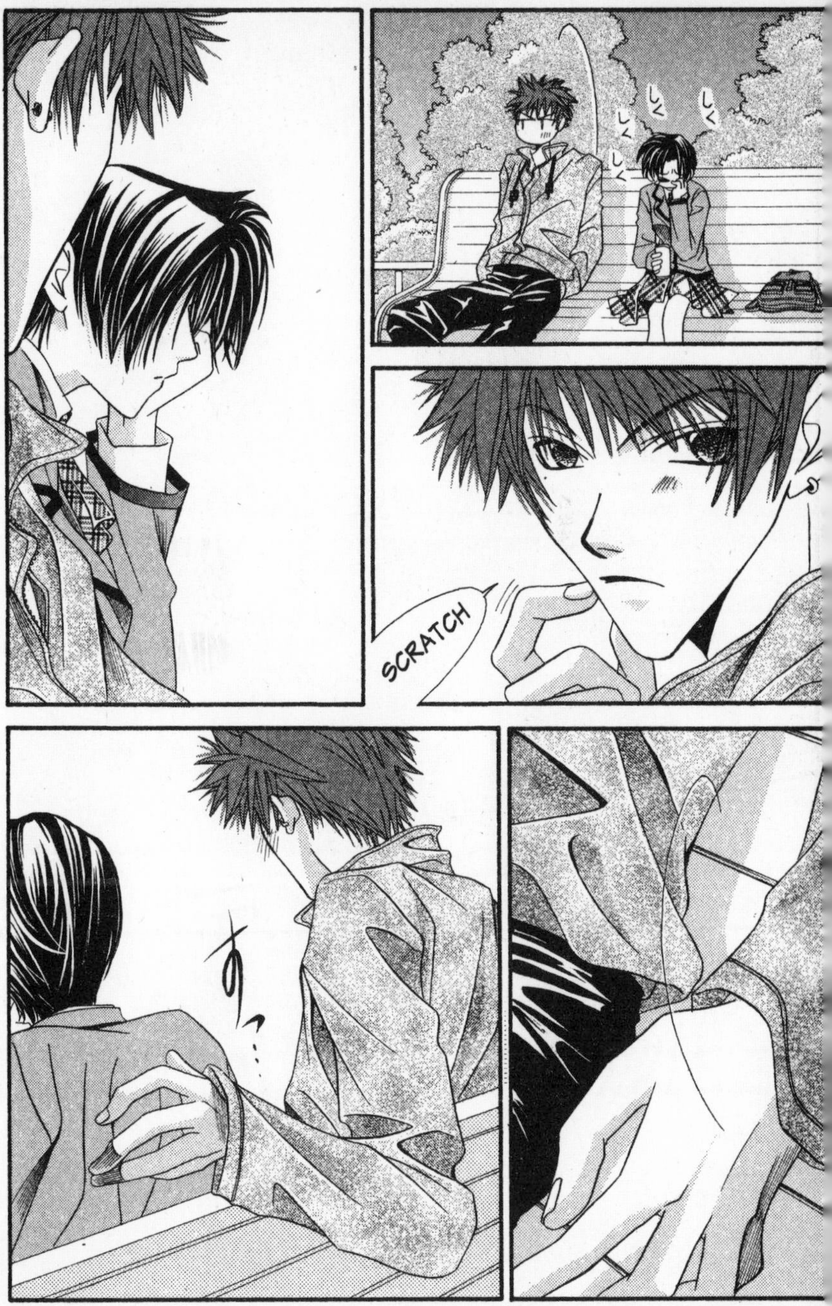
しく
しく
しく
しく
SCRATCH
すっ…

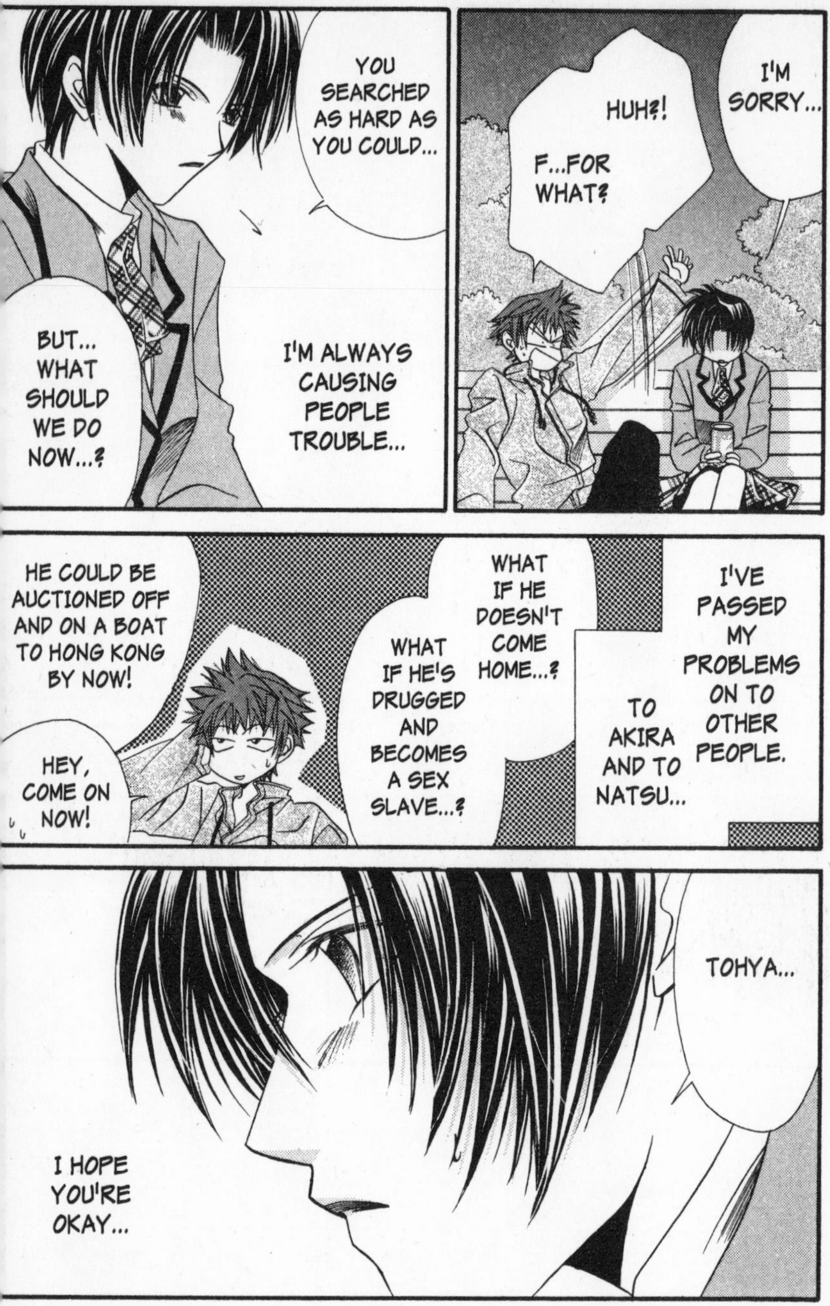
I'M SORRY...
HUH?!
F...FOR WHAT?
YOU SEARCHED AS HARD AS YOU COULD...
I'M ALWAYS CAUSING PEOPLE TROUBLE...
BUT... WHAT SHOULD WE DO NOW...?
I'VE PASSED MY PROBLEMS ON TO OTHER PEOPLE.
TO AKIRA AND TO NATSU...
WHAT IF HE DOESN'T COME HOME...?
WHAT IF HE'S DRUGGED AND BECOMES A SEX SLAVE...?
HE COULD BE AUCTIONED OFF AND ON A BOAT TO HONG KONG BY NOW!
HEY, COME ON NOW!
TOHYA...
I HOPE YOU'RE OKAY...

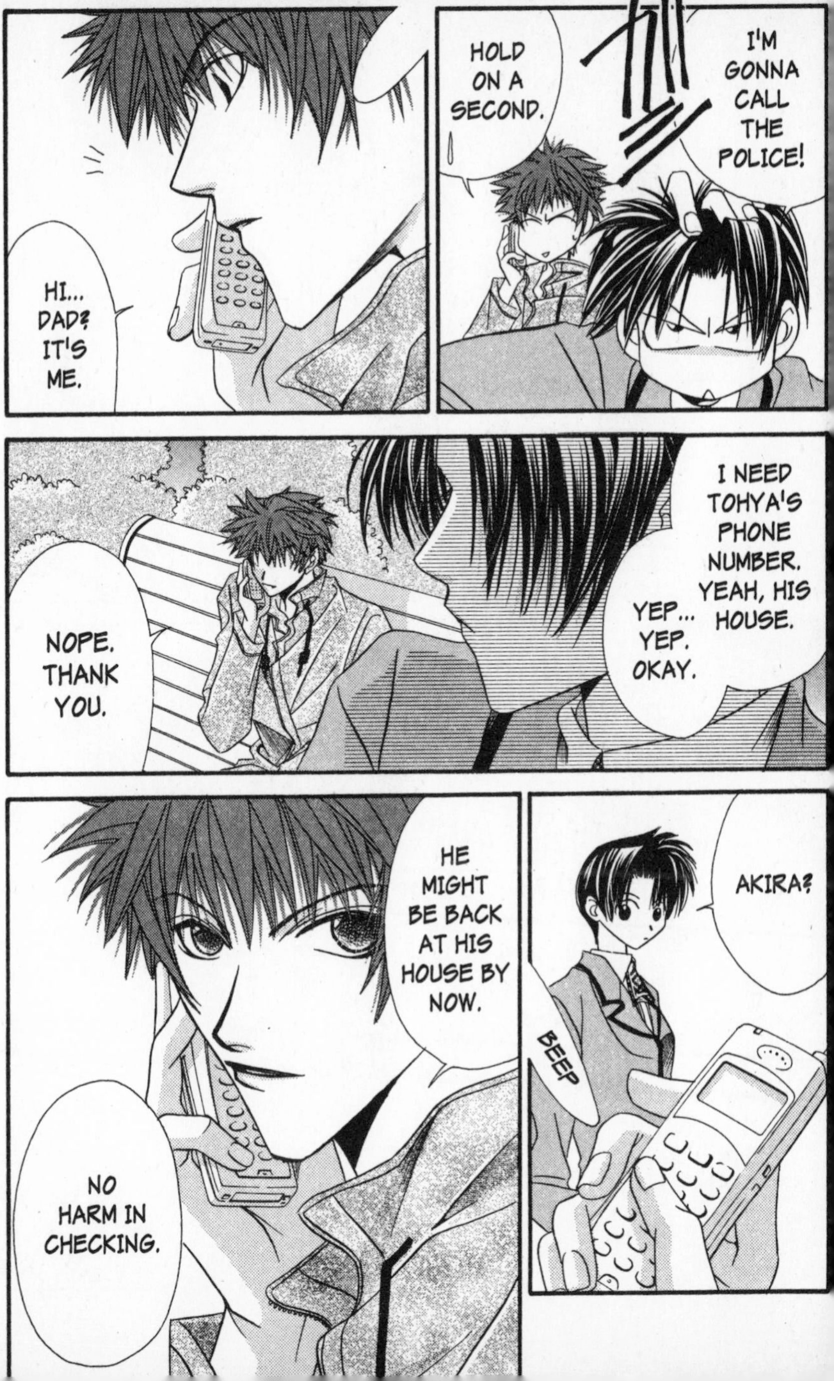
I'M GONNA CALL THE POLICE!
HOLD ON A SECOND.
HI... DAD? IT'S ME.
I NEED TOHYA'S PHONE NUMBER. YEAH, HIS HOUSE.
YEP... YEP. OKAY.
NOPE. THANK YOU.
AKIRA?
BEEP
HE MIGHT BE BACK AT HIS HOUSE BY NOW.
NO HARM IN CHECKING.

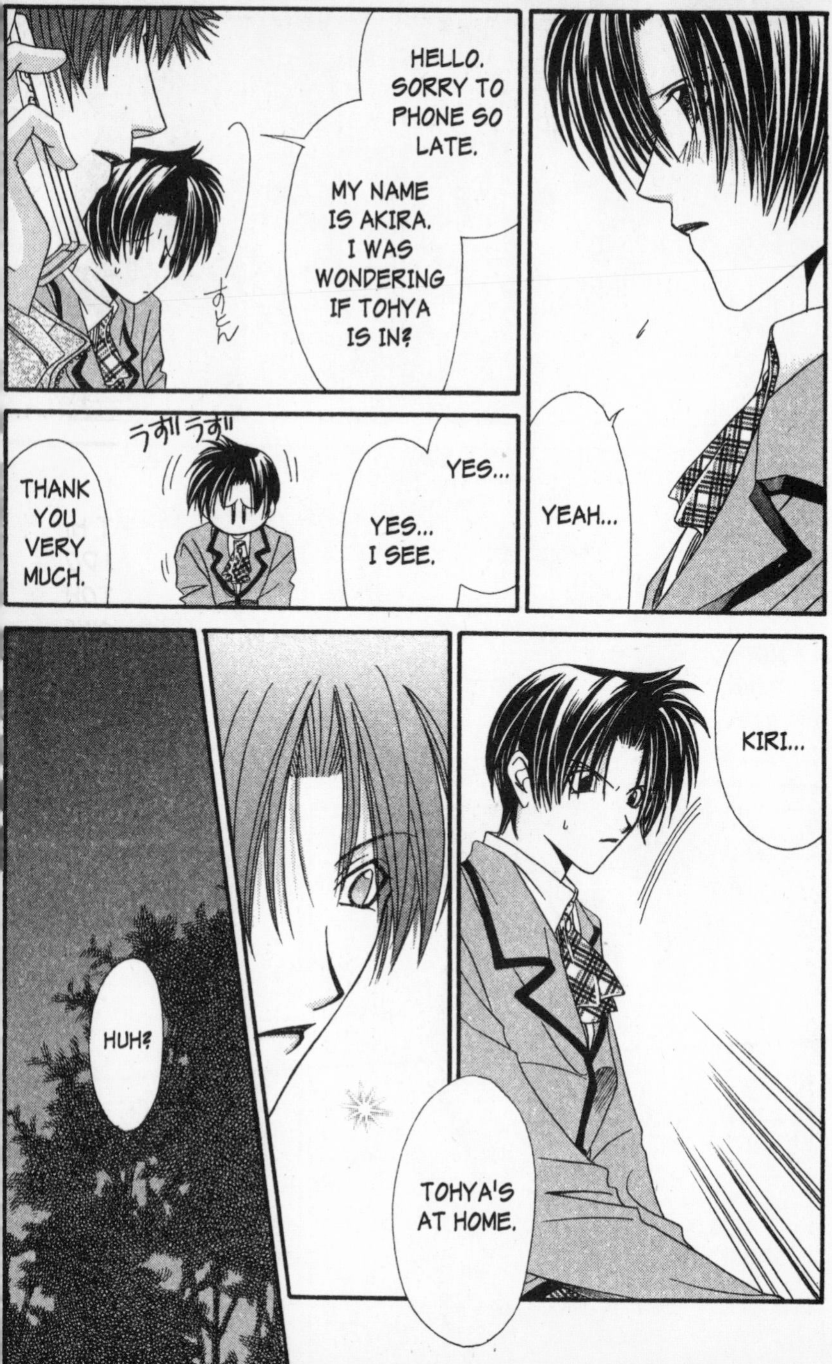
YEAH...
HELLO. SORRY TO PHONE SO LATE.
MY NAME IS AKIRA. I WAS WONDERING IF TOHYA IS IN?
すとん
YES...
YES... I SEE.
うずうず
THANK YOU VERY MUCH.
KIRI...
TOHYA'S AT HOME.
HUH?

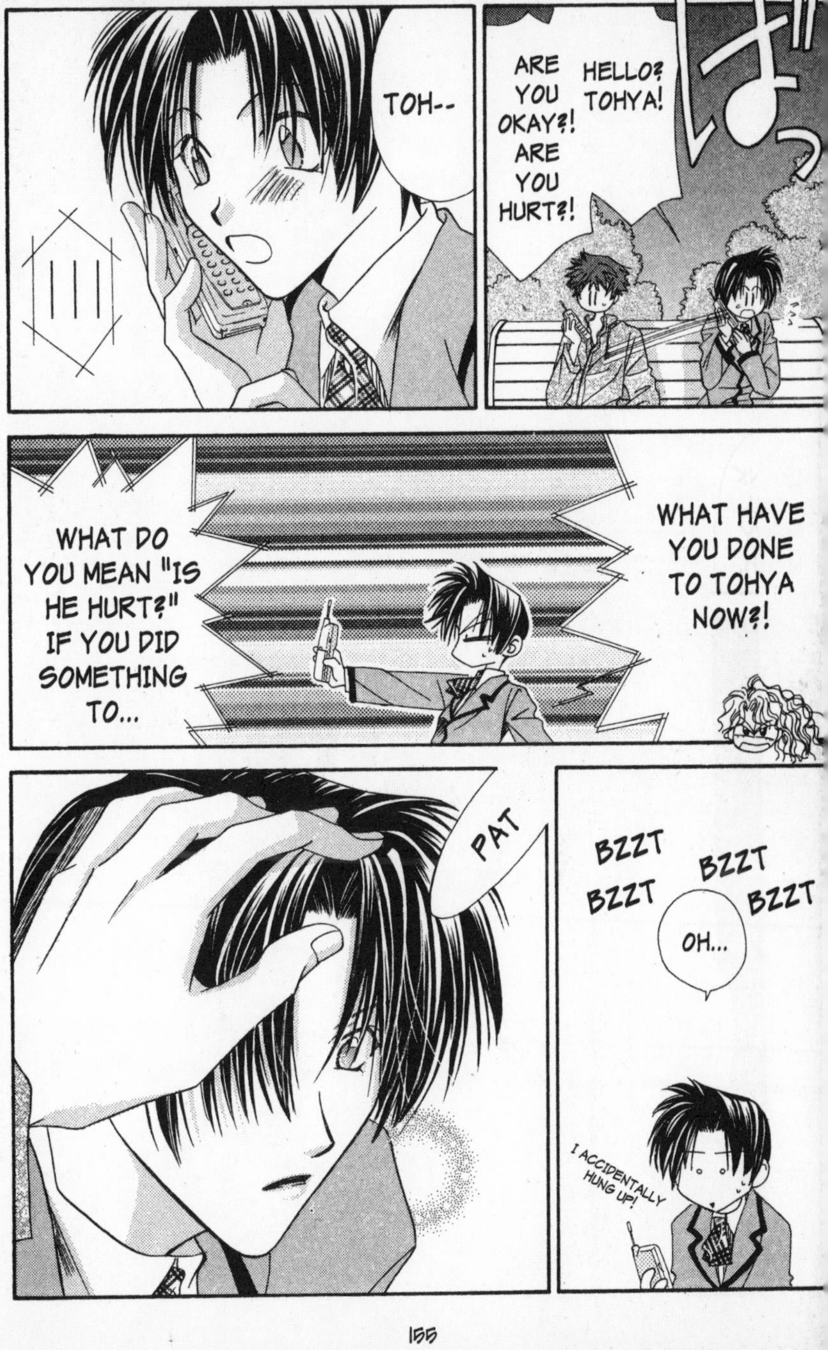
ばっ
HELLO? TOHYA!
ARE YOU OKAY?! ARE YOU HURT?!
TOH--
WHAT HAVE YOU DONE TO TOHYA NOW?!
WHAT DO YOU MEAN "IS HE HURT?" IF YOU DID SOMETHING TO...
BZZT BZZT BZZT BZZT
OH...
I ACCIDENTALLY HUNG UP!
PAT

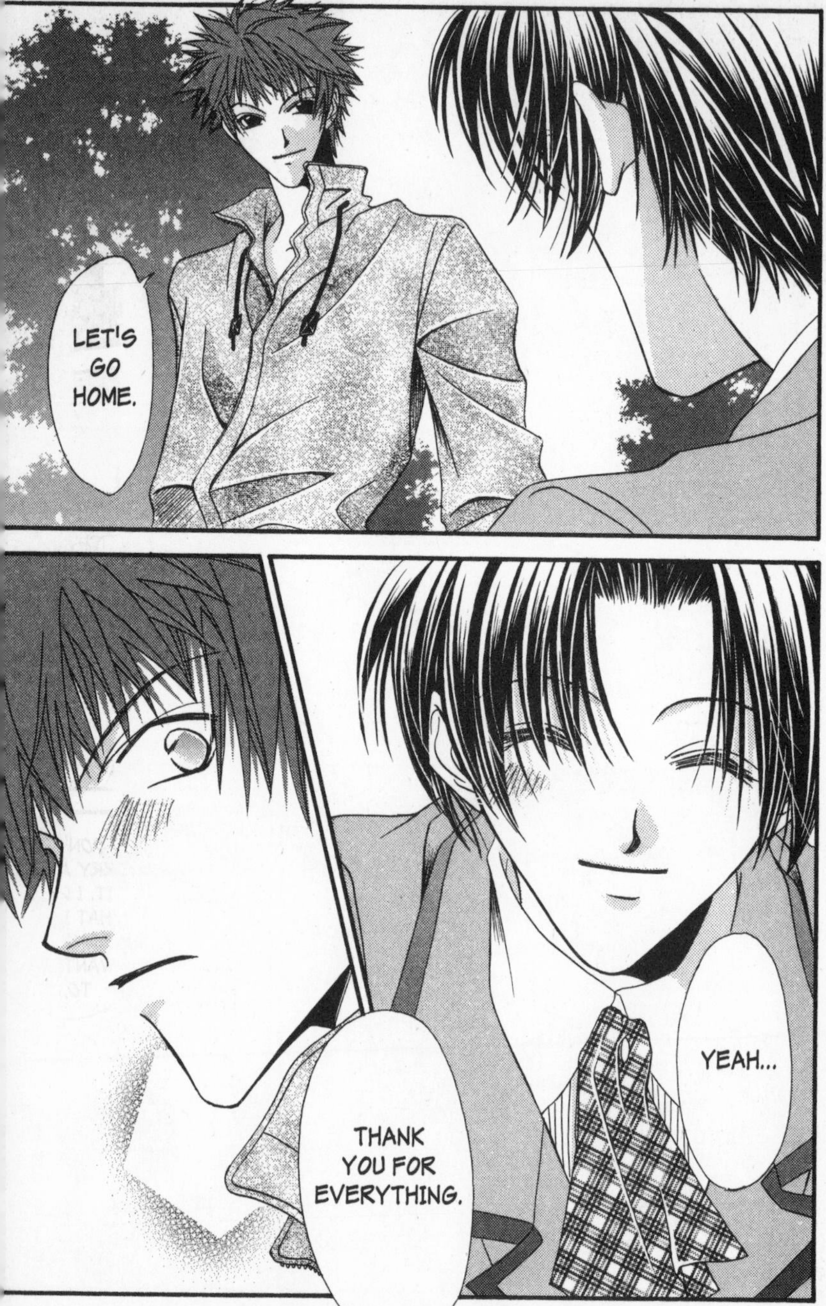
LET'S GO HOME.
YEAH...
THANK YOU FOR EVERYTHING.

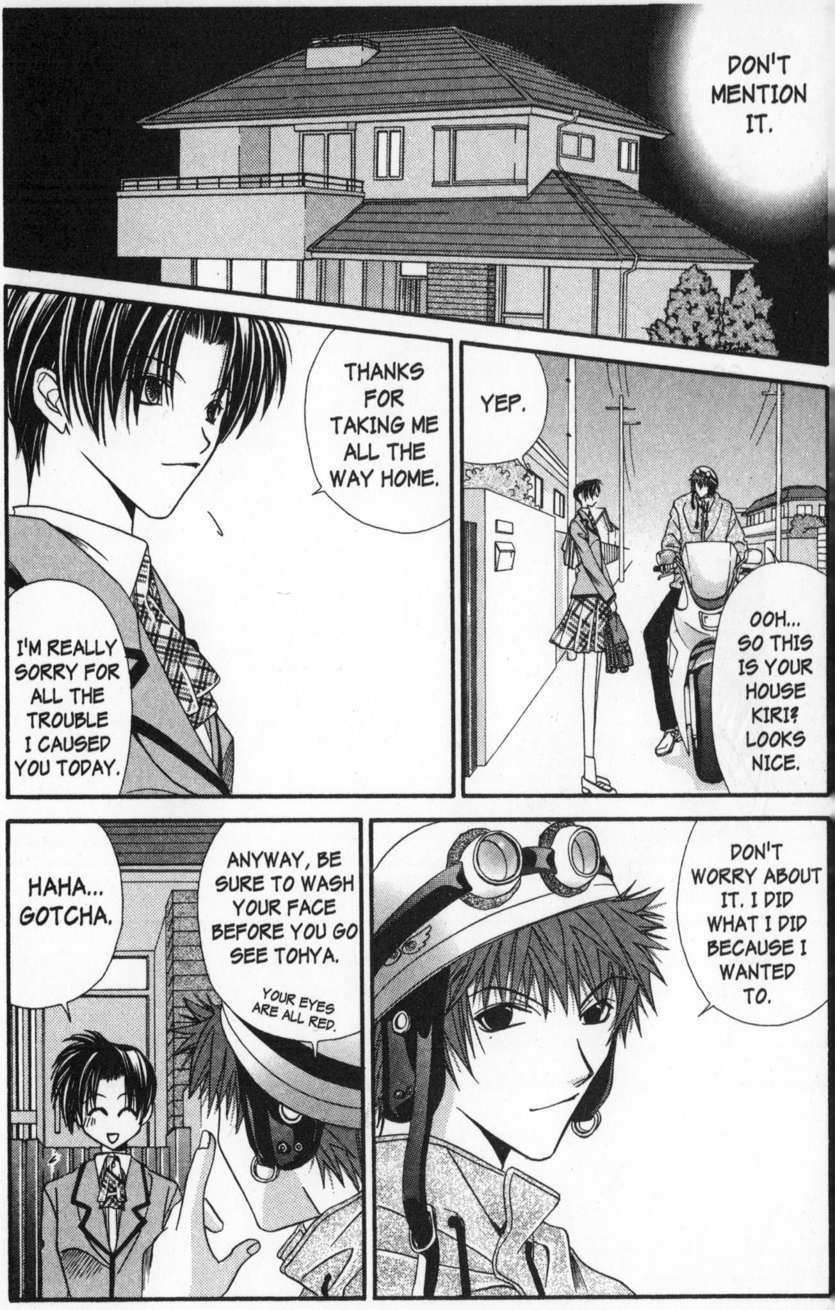
DON'T MENTION IT.
YEP.
OOH... SO THIS IS YOUR HOUSE KIRI? LOOKS NICE.
THANKS FOR TAKING ME ALL THE WAY HOME.
I'M REALLY SORRY FOR ALL THE TROUBLE I CAUSED YOU TODAY.
DON'T WORRY ABOUT IT. I DID WHAT I DID BECAUSE I WANTED TO.
ANYWAY, BE SURE TO WASH YOUR FACE BEFORE YOU GO SEE TOHYA.
YOUR EYES ARE ALL RED.
HAHA... GOTCHA.

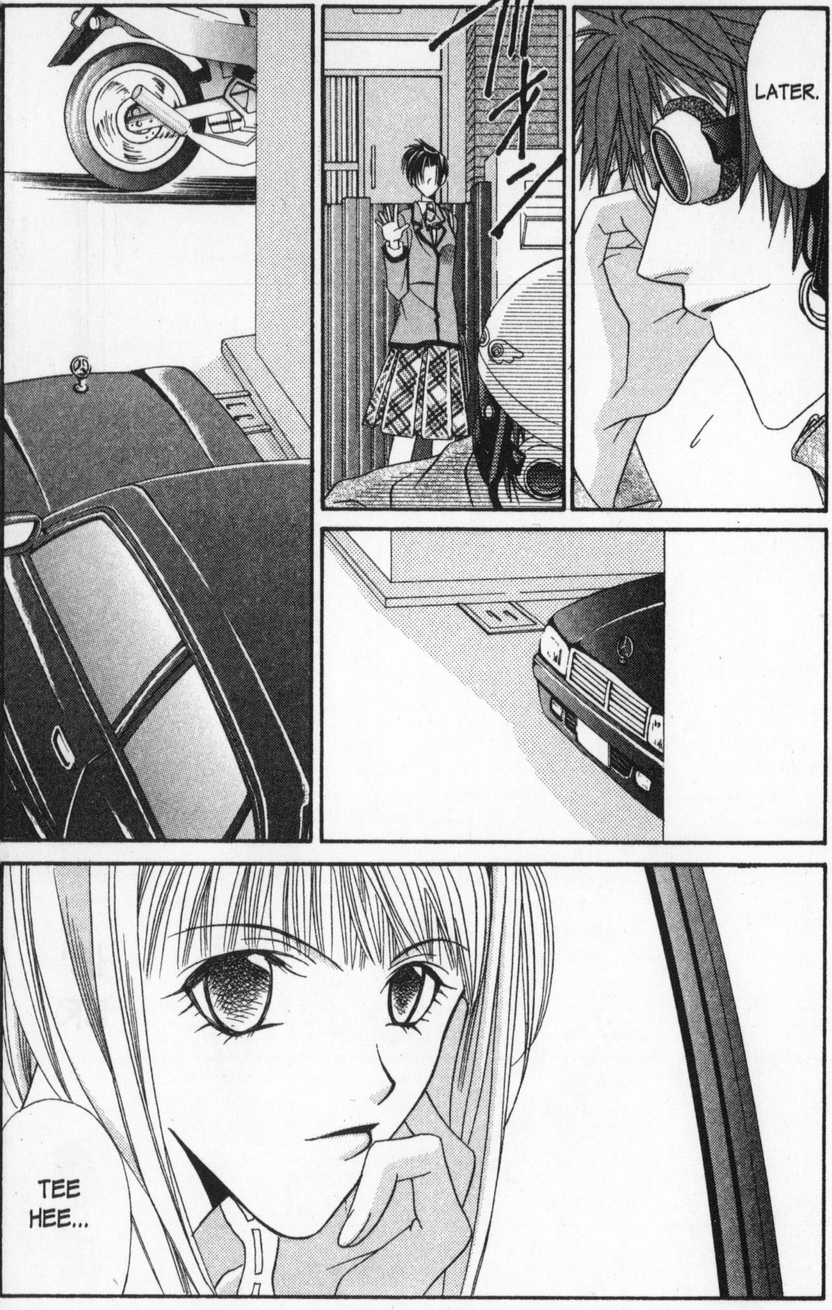
LATER.
TEE HEE...

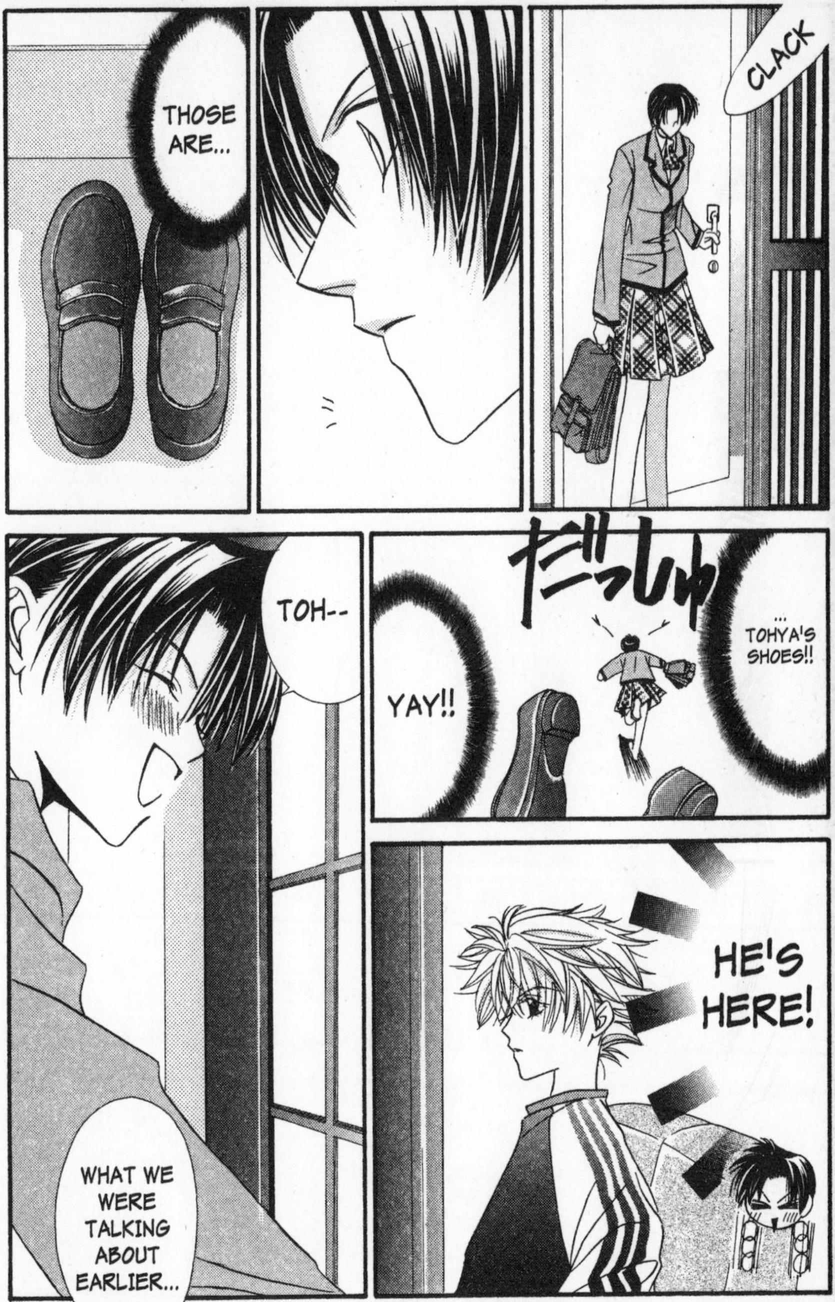
CLACK
THOSE ARE...
だっしゅ
... TOHYA'S SHOES!!
YAY!!
HE'S HERE!
TOH--
WHAT WE WERE TALKING ABOUT EARLIER...

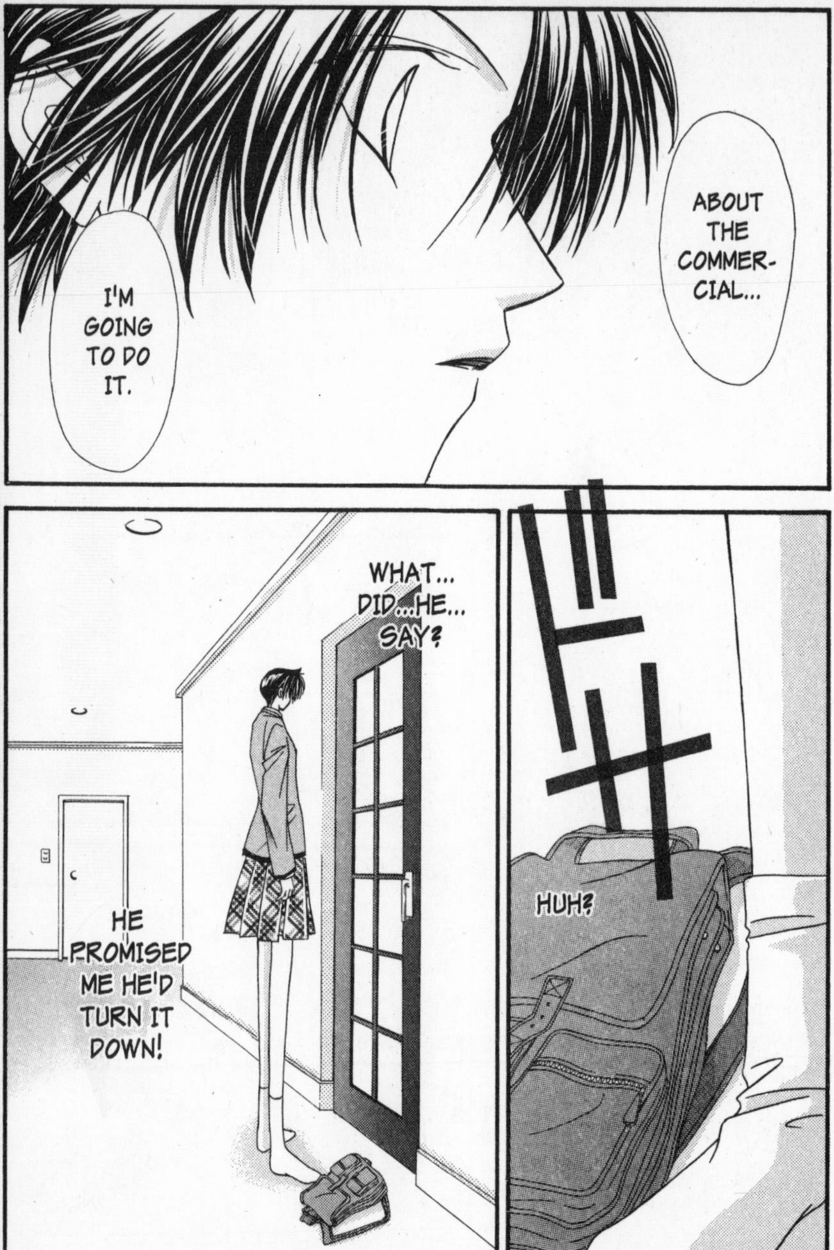
ABOUT THE COMMER-CIAL...
I'M GOING TO DO IT.
HUH?
WHAT... DID...HE... SAY?
HE PROMISED ME HE'D TURN IT DOWN!

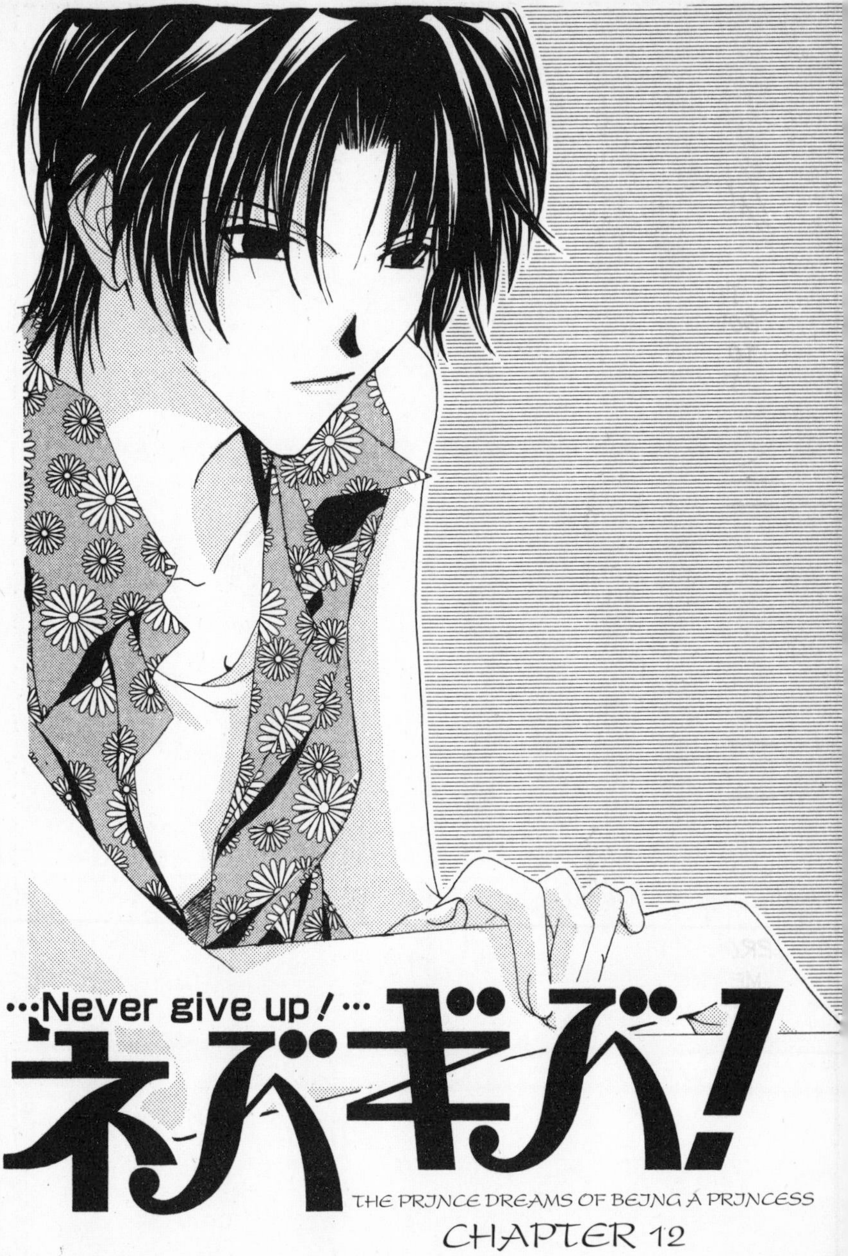

…Never give up!…

ネバギバ!

THE PRINCE DREAMS OF BEING A PRINCESS

CHAPTER 12

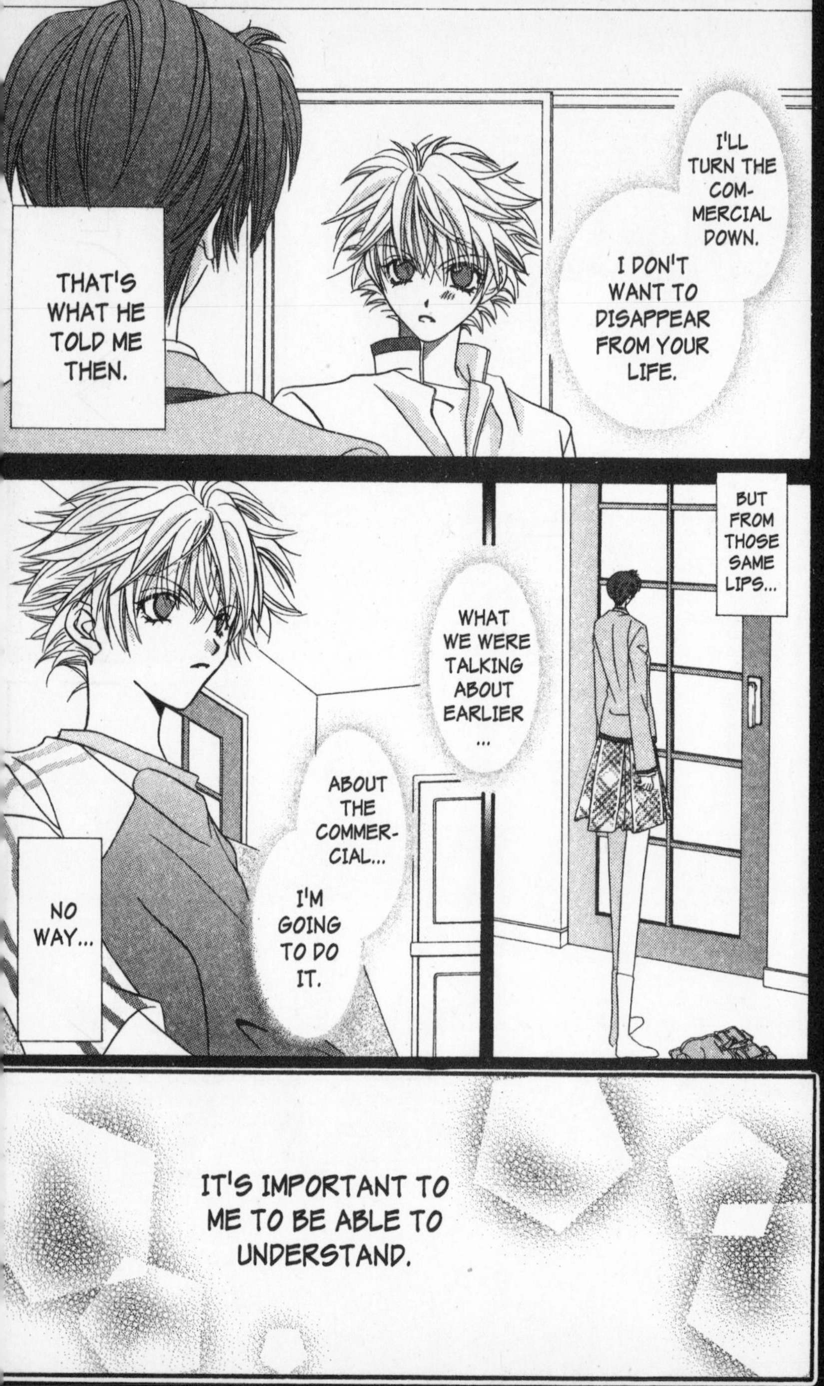
I'LL TURN THE COM-MERCIAL DOWN.
I DON'T WANT TO DISAPPEAR FROM YOUR LIFE.
THAT'S WHAT HE TOLD ME THEN.
BUT FROM THOSE SAME LIPS...
WHAT WE WERE TALKING ABOUT EARLIER ...
ABOUT THE COMMER-CIAL...
I'M GOING TO DO IT.
NO WAY...
IT'S IMPORTANT TO ME TO BE ABLE TO UNDERSTAND.

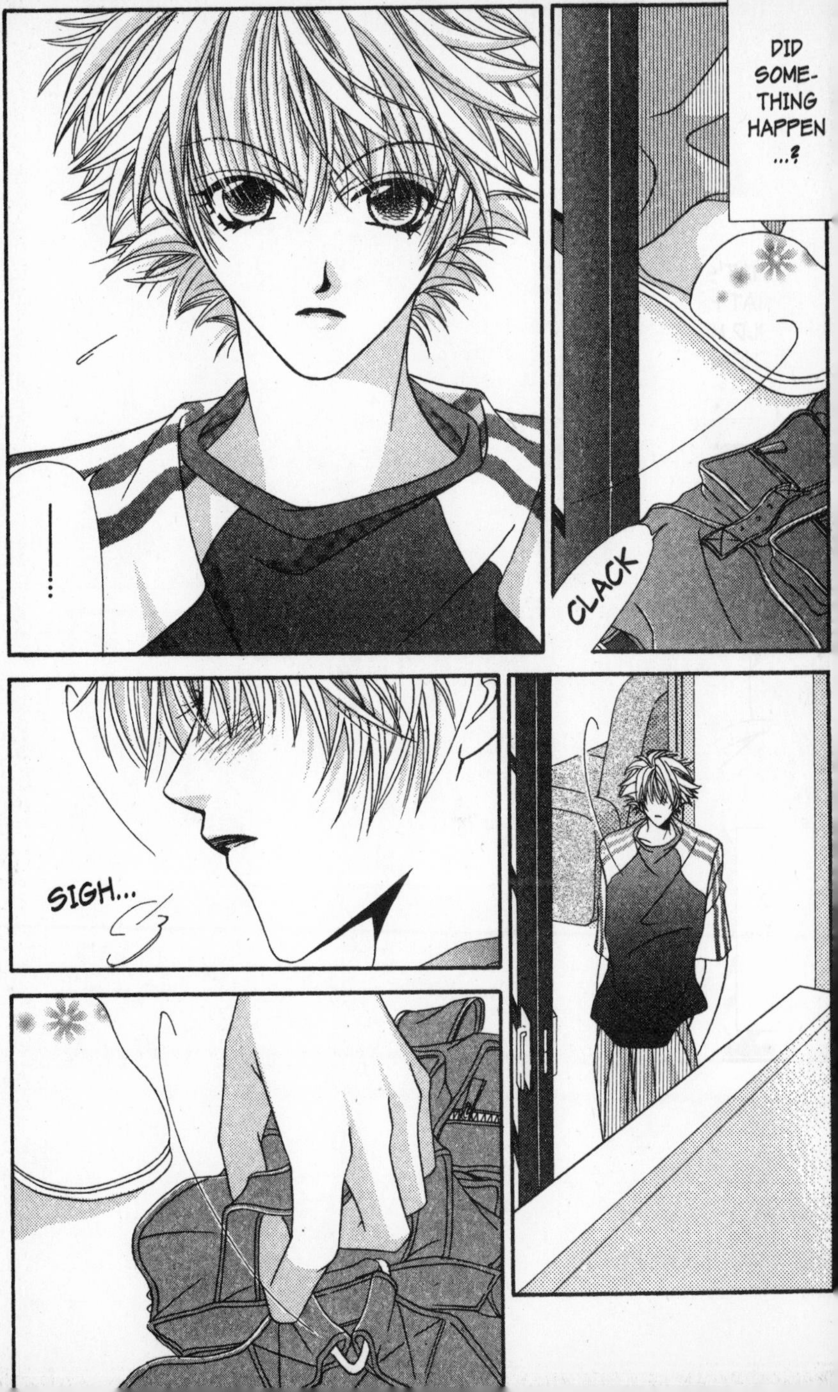
DID SOME-THING HAPPEN ...?
CLACK
......
SIGH...

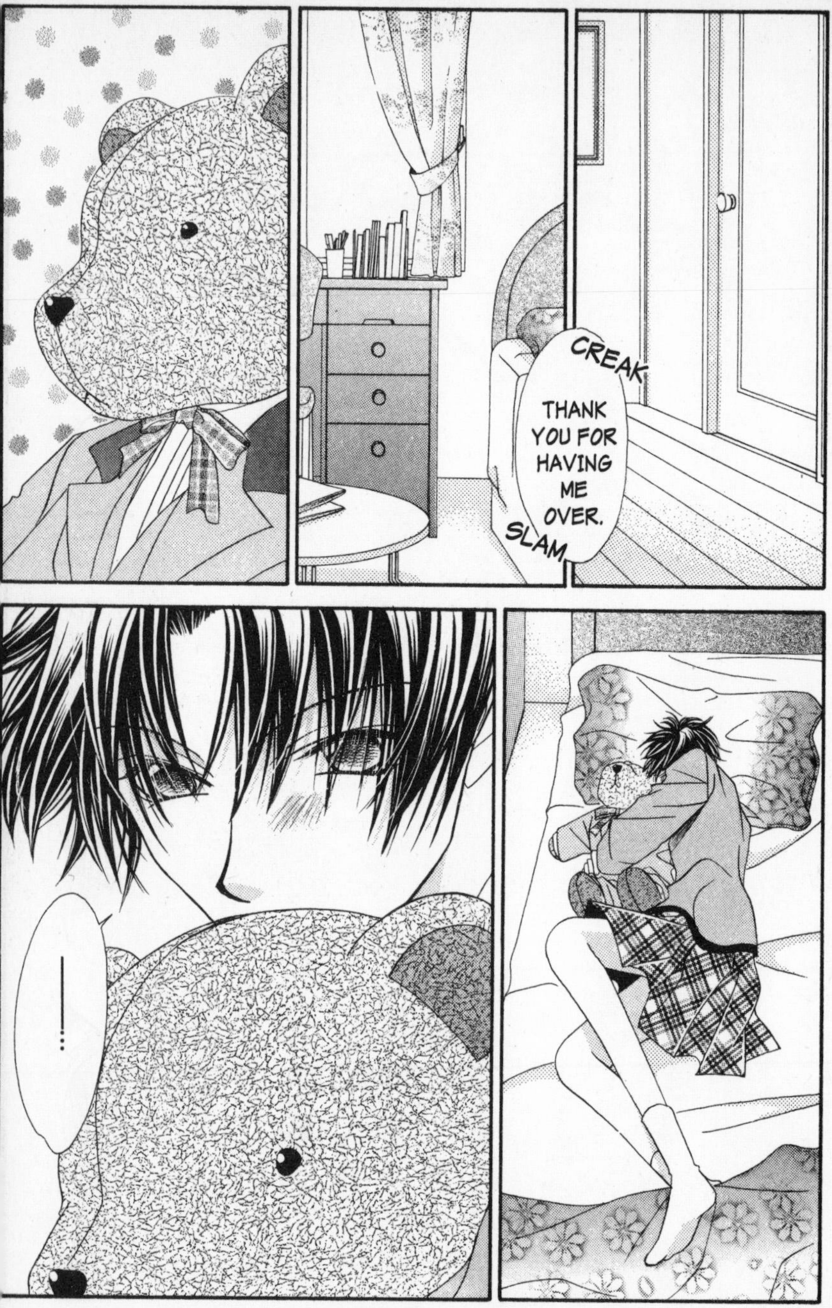
CREAK
THANK YOU FOR HAVING ME OVER.
SLAM
—...

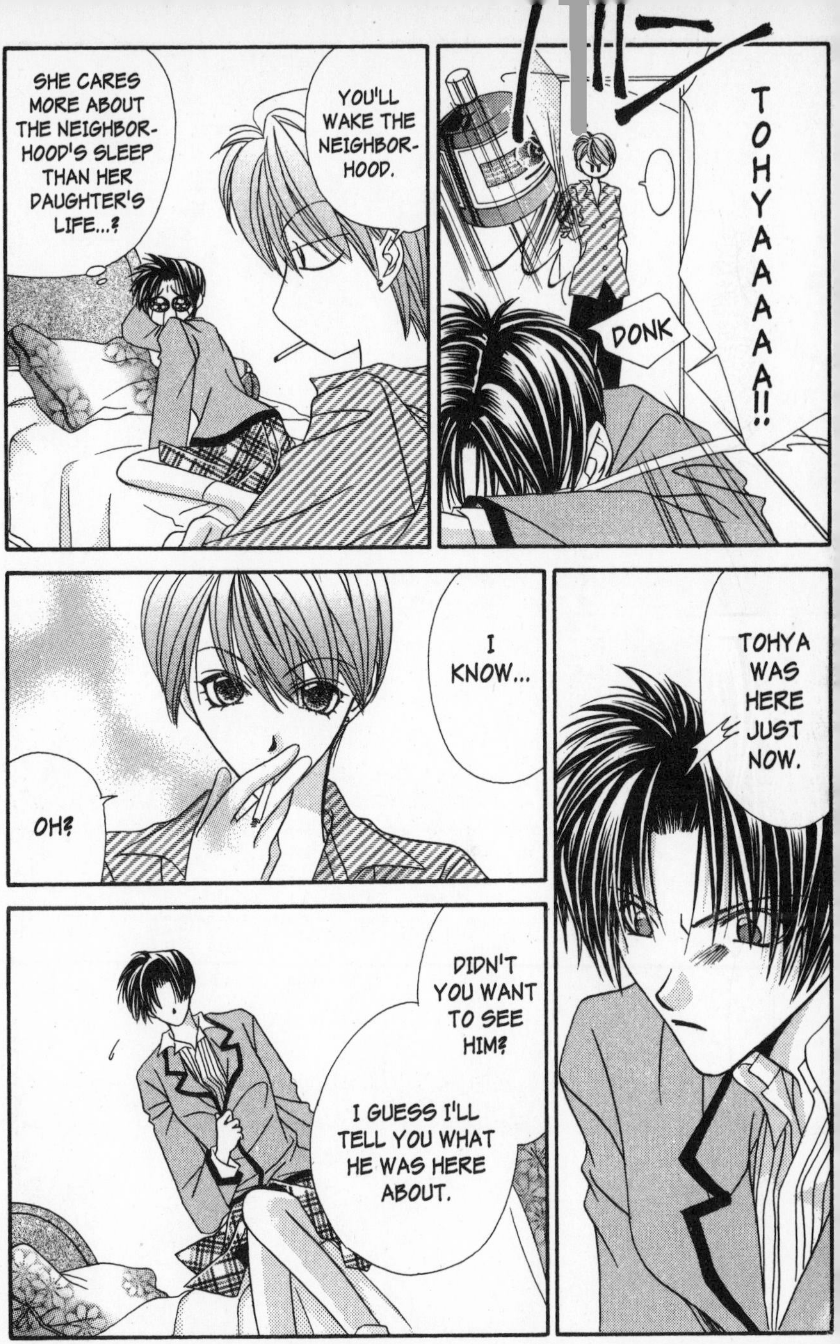
TOHYAAAAAA!!
DONK
YOU'LL WAKE THE NEIGHBOR-HOOD.
SHE CARES MORE ABOUT THE NEIGHBOR-HOOD'S SLEEP THAN HER DAUGHTER'S LIFE...?
TOHYA WAS HERE JUST NOW.
I KNOW...
OH?
DIDN'T YOU WANT TO SEE HIM?
I GUESS I'LL TELL YOU WHAT HE WAS HERE ABOUT.

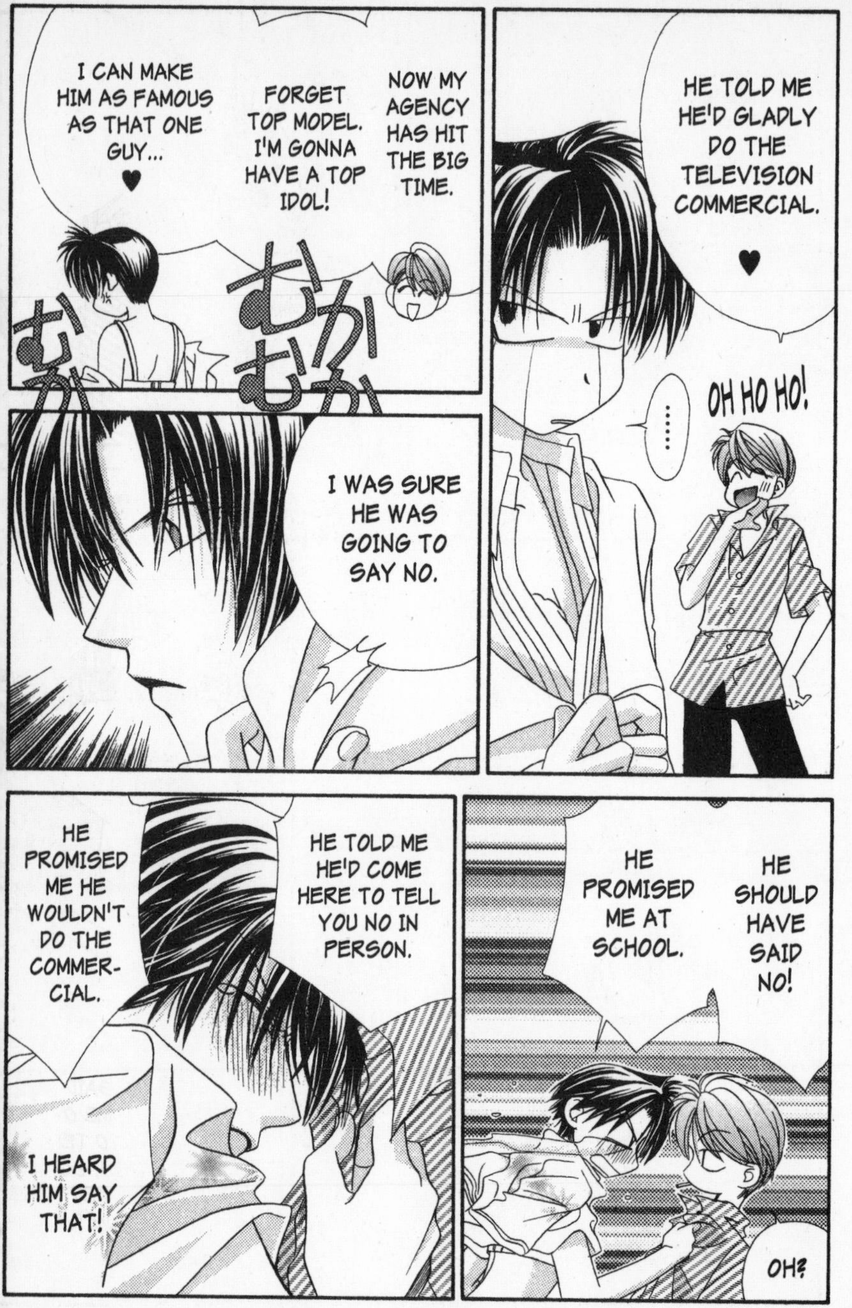
HE TOLD ME HE'D GLADLY DO THE TELEVISION COMMERCIAL. ♥
......
OH HO HO!
NOW MY AGENCY HAS HIT THE BIG TIME.
FORGET TOP MODEL. I'M GONNA HAVE A TOP IDOL!
I CAN MAKE HIM AS FAMOUS AS THAT ONE GUY... ♥
むかむか
むかむか
I WAS SURE HE WAS GOING TO SAY NO.
HE SHOULD HAVE SAID NO!
HE PROMISED ME AT SCHOOL.
OH?
HE TOLD ME HE'D COME HERE TO TELL YOU NO IN PERSON.
HE PROMISED ME HE WOULDN'T DO THE COMMER-CIAL.
I HEARD HIM SAY THAT!

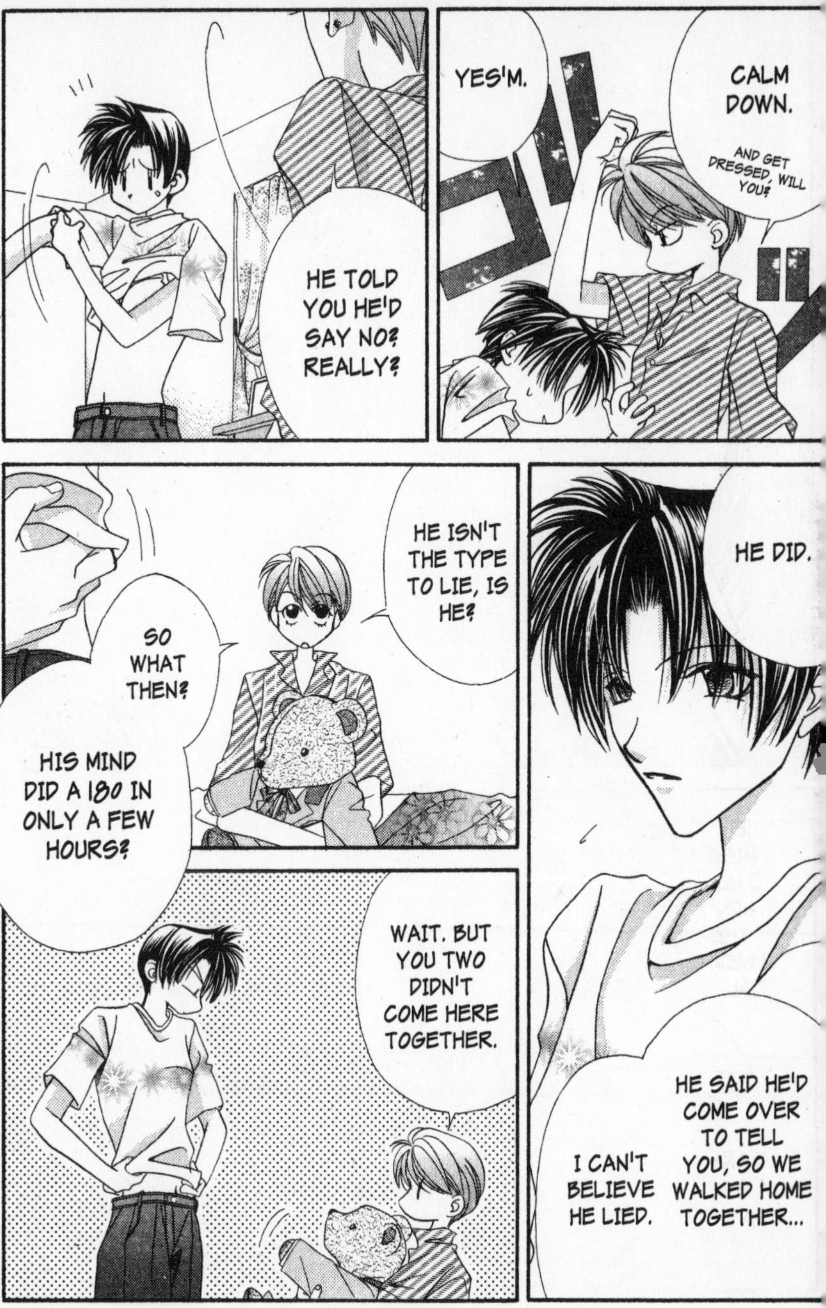
CALM DOWN.
AND GET DRESSED, WILL YOU?
YES'M.
HE TOLD YOU HE'D SAY NO? REALLY?
HE DID.
HE SAID HE'D COME OVER TO TELL YOU, SO WE WALKED HOME TOGETHER...
I CAN'T BELIEVE HE LIED.
HE ISN'T THE TYPE TO LIE, IS HE?
SO WHAT THEN?
HIS MIND DID A 180 IN ONLY A FEW HOURS?
WAIT. BUT YOU TWO DIDN'T COME HERE TOGETHER.

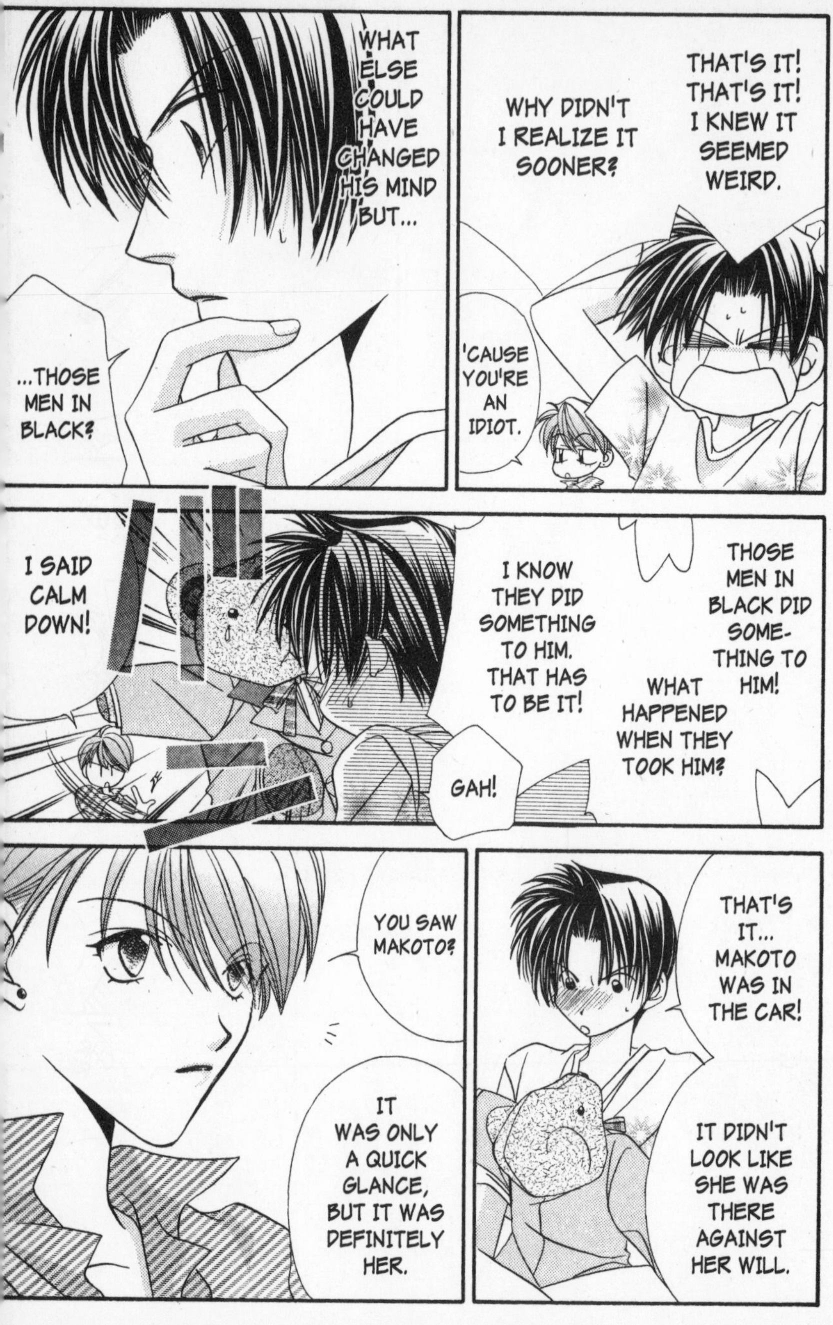
THAT'S IT! THAT'S IT! I KNEW IT SEEMED WEIRD.
WHY DIDN'T I REALIZE IT SOONER?
'CAUSE YOU'RE AN IDIOT.
WHAT ELSE COULD HAVE CHANGED HIS MIND BUT...
...THOSE MEN IN BLACK?
THOSE MEN IN BLACK DID SOME-THING TO HIM!
I KNOW THEY DID SOMETHING TO HIM. THAT HAS TO BE IT!
WHAT HAPPENED WHEN THEY TOOK HIM?
GAH!
I SAID CALM DOWN!
THAT'S IT... MAKOTO WAS IN THE CAR!
IT DIDN'T LOOK LIKE SHE WAS THERE AGAINST HER WILL.
YOU SAW MAKOTO?
IT WAS ONLY A QUICK GLANCE, BUT IT WAS DEFINITELY HER.

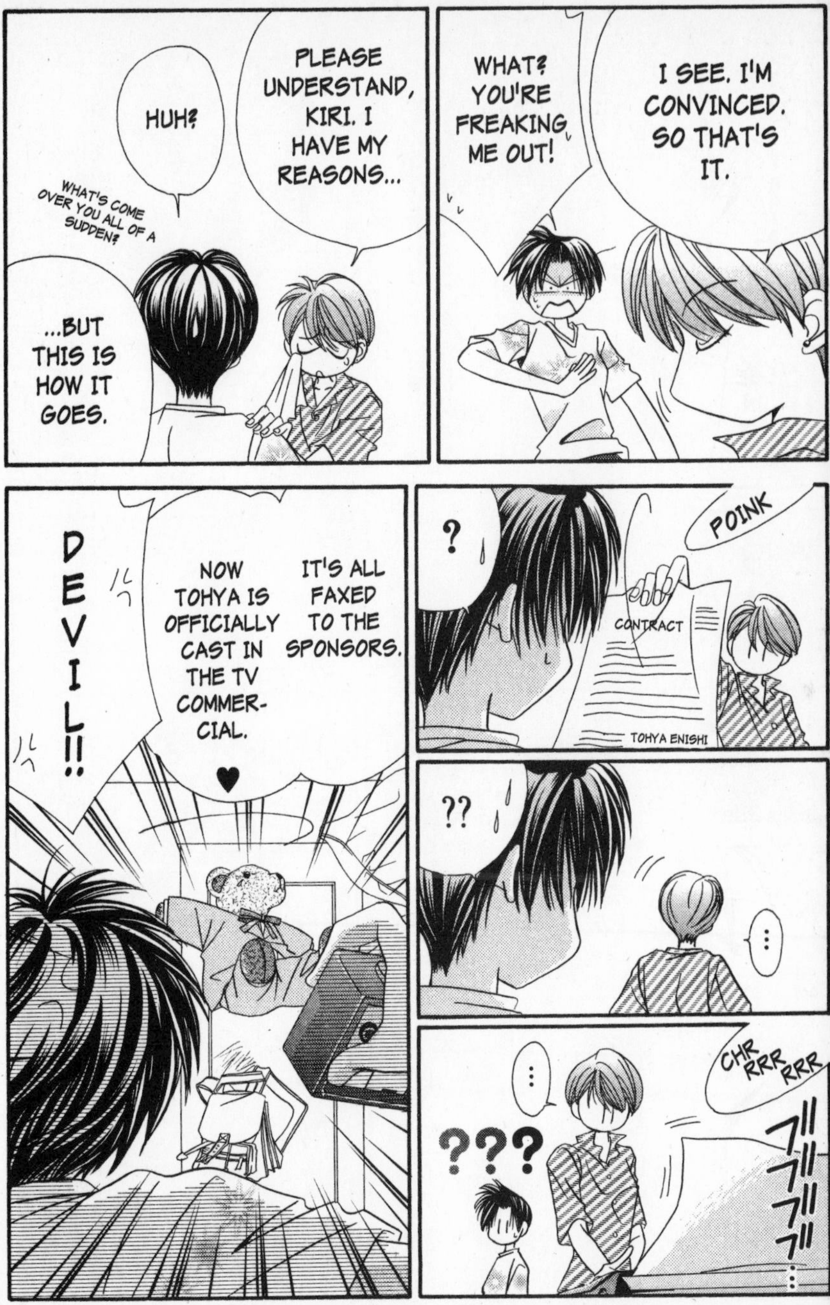
I SEE. I'M CONVINCED. SO THAT'S IT.
WHAT? YOU'RE FREAKING ME OUT!
PLEASE UNDERSTAND, KIRI. I HAVE MY REASONS...
HUH?
WHAT'S COME OVER YOU ALL OF A SUDDEN?
...BUT THIS IS HOW IT GOES.
POINK
?
CONTRACT
TOHYA ENISHI
??
...
CHR RRR RRR
...
???
ブブブブ…
IT'S ALL FAXED TO THE SPONSORS.
NOW TOHYA IS OFFICIALLY CAST IN THE TV COMMERCIAL. ♥
DEVIL!!

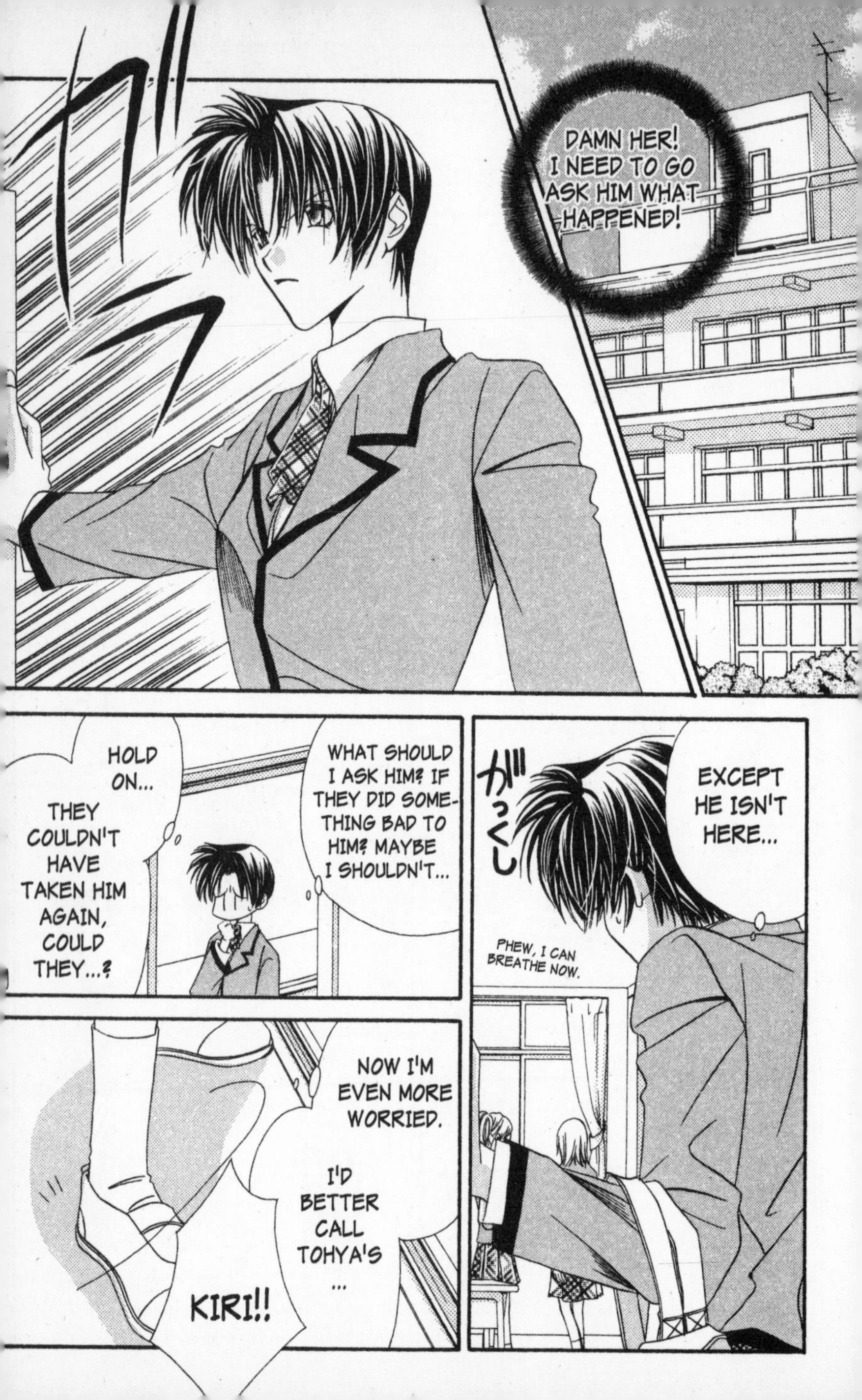
DAMN HER! I NEED TO GO ASK HIM WHAT HAPPENED!
EXCEPT HE ISN'T HERE...
がっくし
PHEW, I CAN BREATHE NOW.
WHAT SHOULD I ASK HIM? IF THEY DID SOMETHING BAD TO HIM? MAYBE I SHOULDN'T...
HOLD ON... THEY COULDN'T HAVE TAKEN HIM AGAIN, COULD THEY...?
NOW I'M EVEN MORE WORRIED.
I'D BETTER CALL TOHYA'S ...
KIRI!!

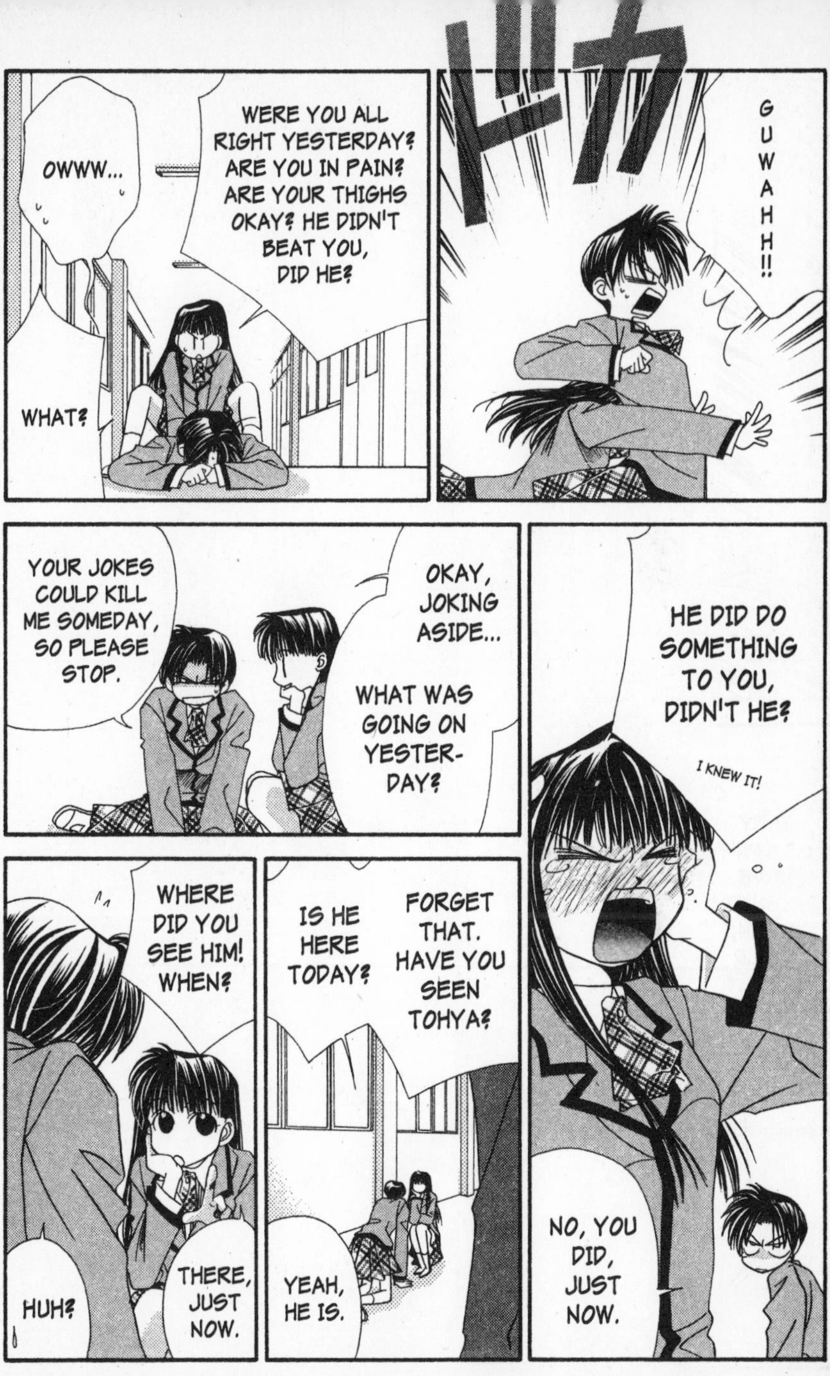

ドカ
GUWAHH!!
WERE YOU ALL RIGHT YESTERDAY? ARE YOU IN PAIN? ARE YOUR THIGHS OKAY? HE DIDN'T BEAT YOU, DID HE?
OWWW...
WHAT?
HE DID DO SOMETHING TO YOU, DIDN'T HE?
I KNEW IT!
NO, YOU DID, JUST NOW.
OKAY, JOKING ASIDE...
WHAT WAS GOING ON YESTER-DAY?
YOUR JOKES COULD KILL ME SOMEDAY, SO PLEASE STOP.
FORGET THAT. HAVE YOU SEEN TOHYA?
IS HE HERE TODAY?
YEAH, HE IS.
WHERE DID YOU SEE HIM! WHEN?
THERE, JUST NOW.
HUH?

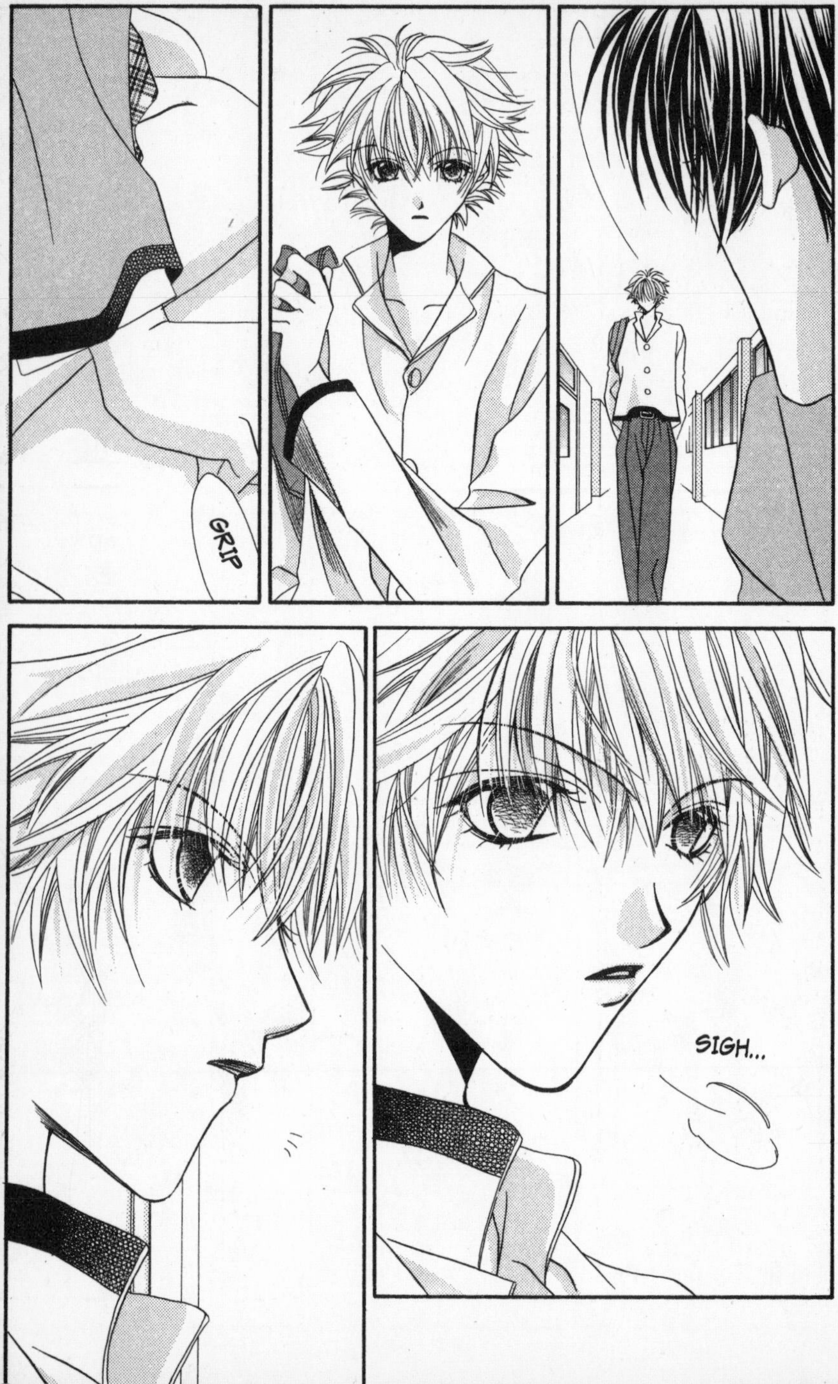
GRIP
SIGH...

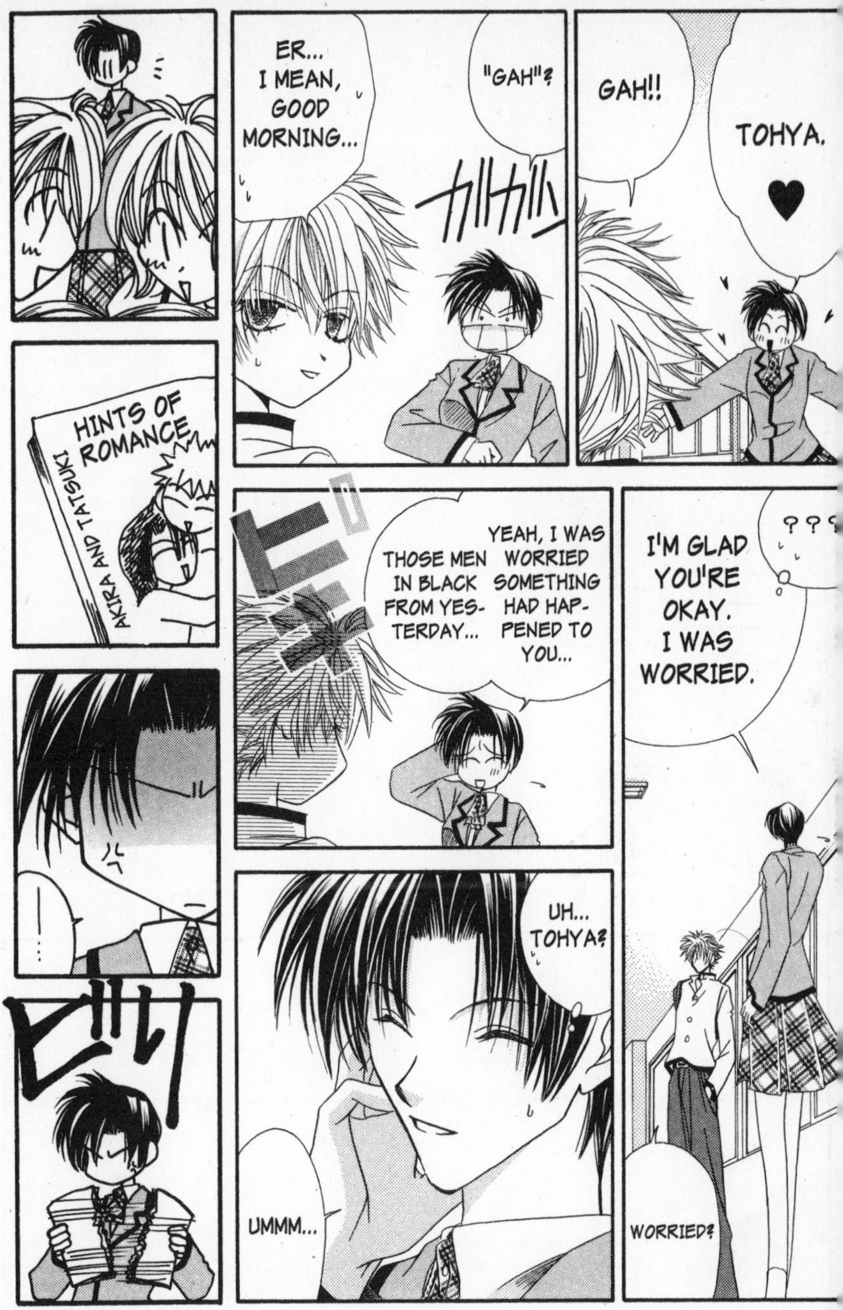
TOHYA. ♥
GAH!!
"GAH"?
ER... I MEAN, GOOD MORNING...
I'M GLAD YOU'RE OKAY. I WAS WORRIED.
???
WORRIED?
YEAH, I WAS WORRIED SOMETHING HAD HAP-PENED TO YOU...
THOSE MEN IN BLACK FROM YES-TERDAY...
UH... TOHYA?
UMMM...
HINTS OF ROMANCE
AKIRA AND TATSUKI
......

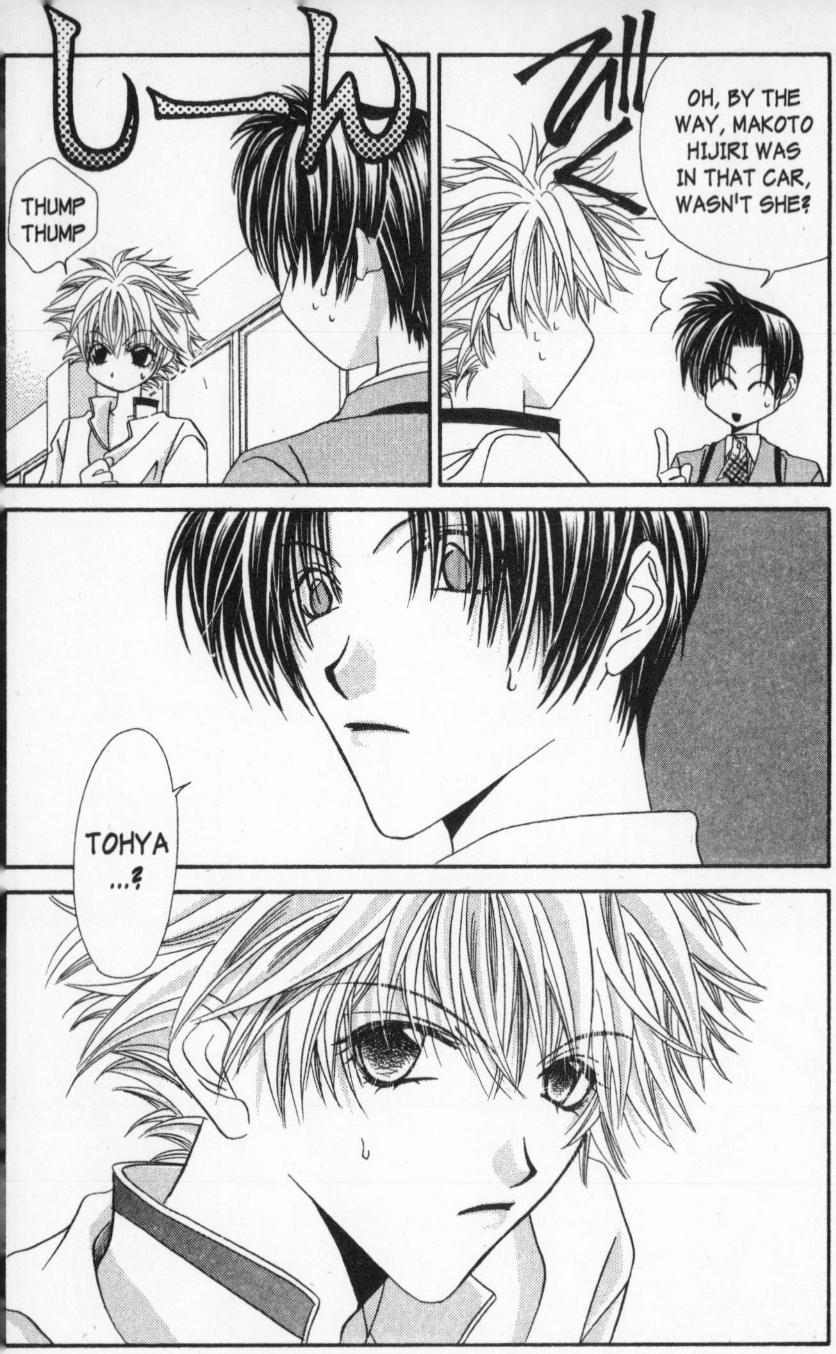
OH, BY THE WAY, MAKOTO HIJIRI WAS IN THAT CAR, WASN'T SHE?
しーん
THUMP THUMP
TOHYA ...?

DOES THAT HAVE SOME-THING TO DO... WITH YOU AGREEING TO THE COMMER-CIAL?
I'M RIGHT, AREN'T I...?
......
NOT EXACTLY ...
WAIT! WHERE ARE YOU GOING?
HOME.
HUH?
KIRI...

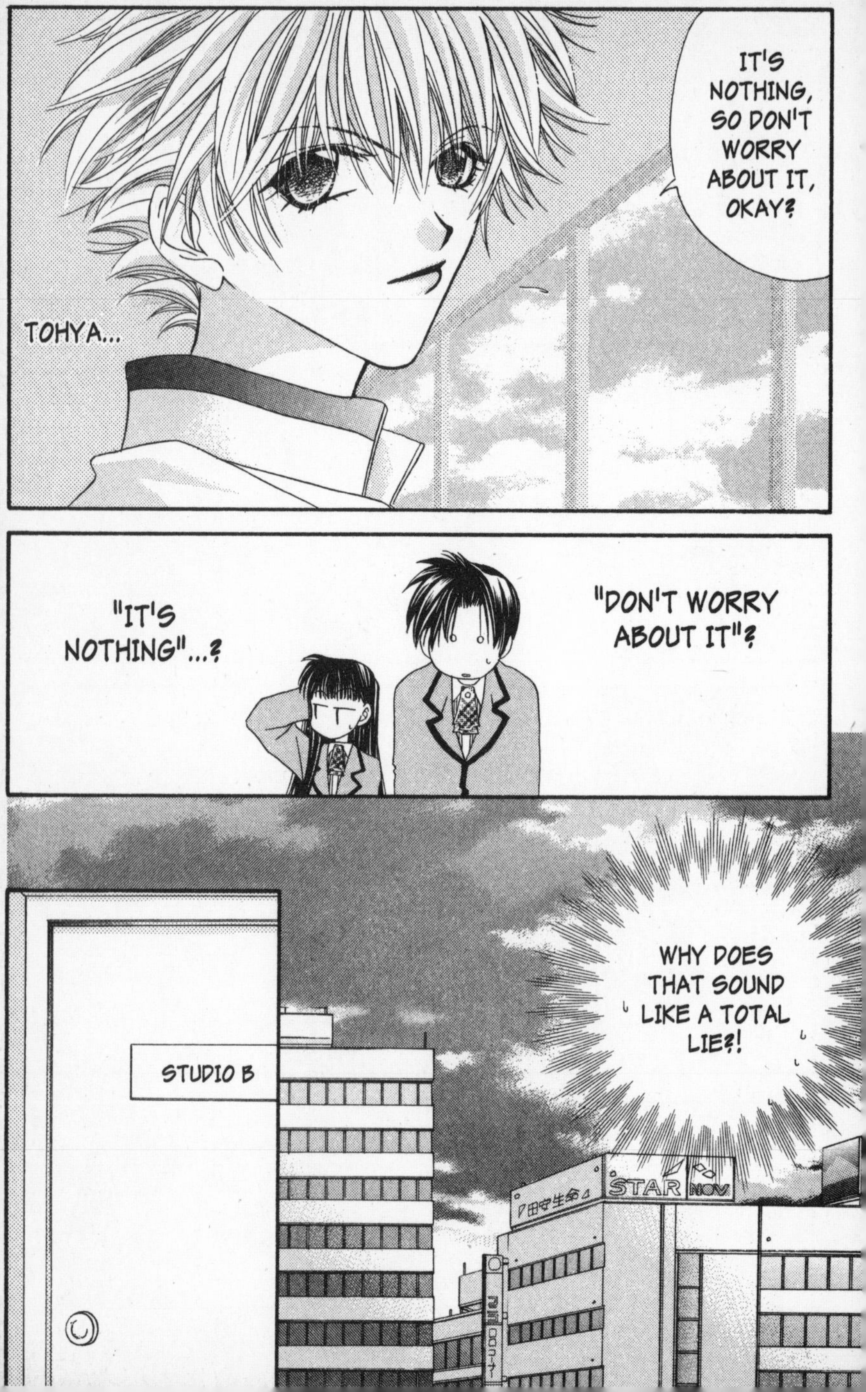
IT'S NOTHING, SO DON'T WORRY ABOUT IT, OKAY?
TOHYA...
"DON'T WORRY ABOUT IT"?
"IT'S NOTHING"...?
WHY DOES THAT SOUND LIKE A TOTAL LIE?!
STUDIO B
STAR

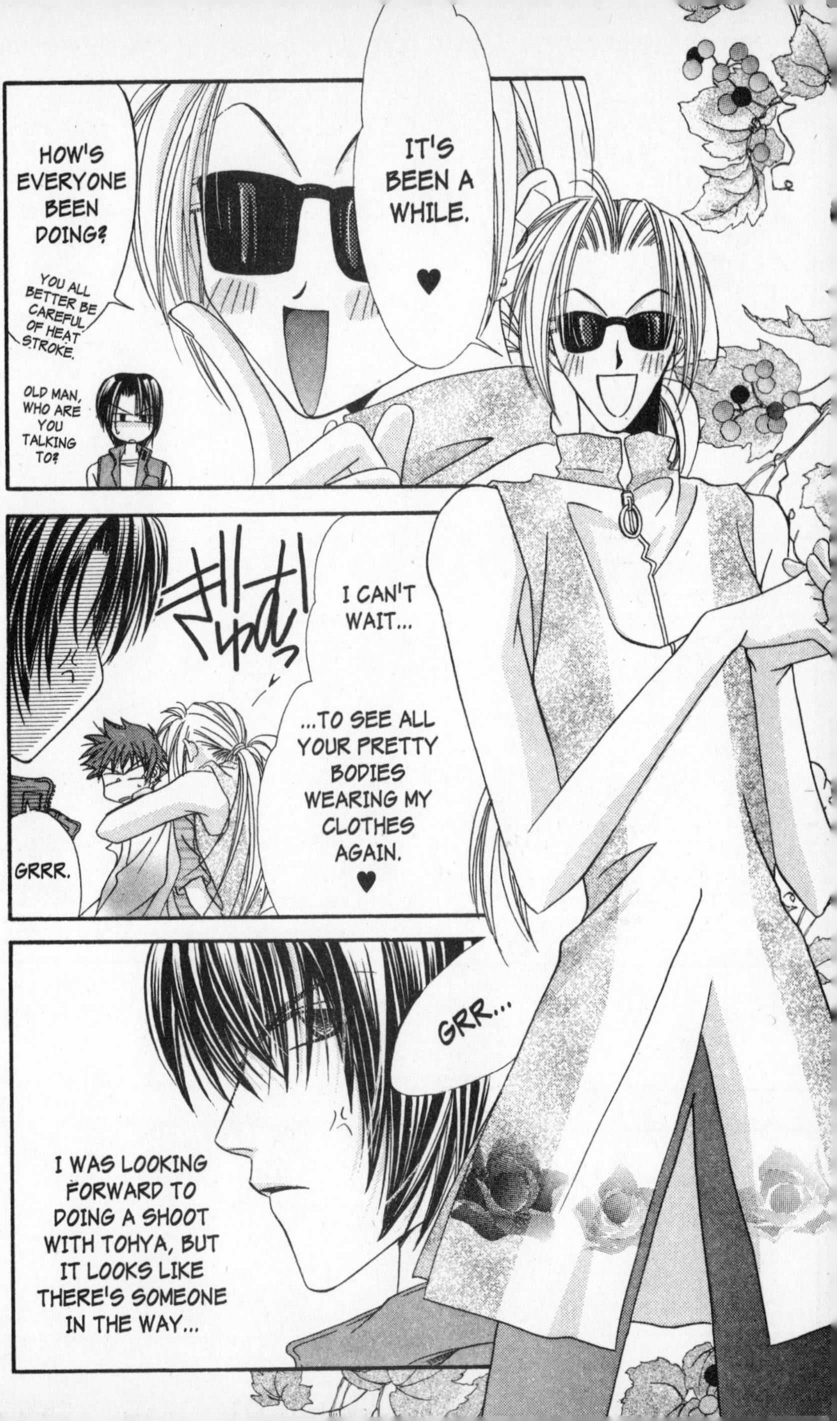
IT'S BEEN A WHILE. ♥
HOW'S EVERYONE BEEN DOING?
YOU ALL BETTER BE CAREFUL OF HEAT STROKE.
OLD MAN, WHO ARE YOU TALKING TO?
I CAN'T WAIT...
...TO SEE ALL YOUR PRETTY BODIES WEARING MY CLOTHES AGAIN. ♥
GRRR.
GRR...
I WAS LOOKING FORWARD TO DOING A SHOOT WITH TOHYA, BUT IT LOOKS LIKE THERE'S SOMEONE IN THE WAY...

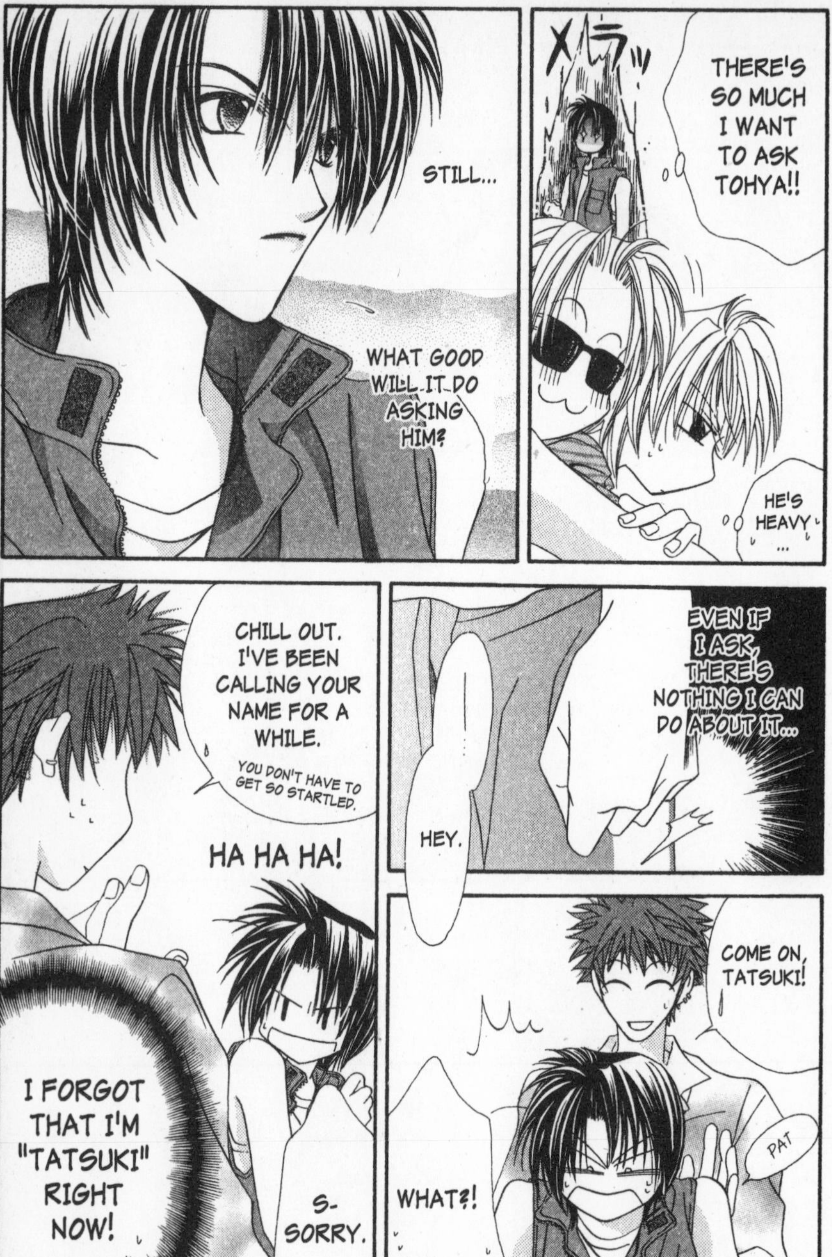
メラッ
THERE'S SO MUCH I WANT TO ASK TOHYA!!
HE'S HEAVY...
STILL...
WHAT GOOD WILL IT DO ASKING HIM?
EVEN IF I ASK, THERE'S NOTHING I CAN DO ABOUT IT...
HEY.
COME ON, TATSUKI!
PAT
WHAT?!
CHILL OUT. I'VE BEEN CALLING YOUR NAME FOR A WHILE.
YOU DON'T HAVE TO GET SO STARTLED.
HA HA HA!
I FORGOT THAT I'M "TATSUKI" RIGHT NOW!
S-SORRY.

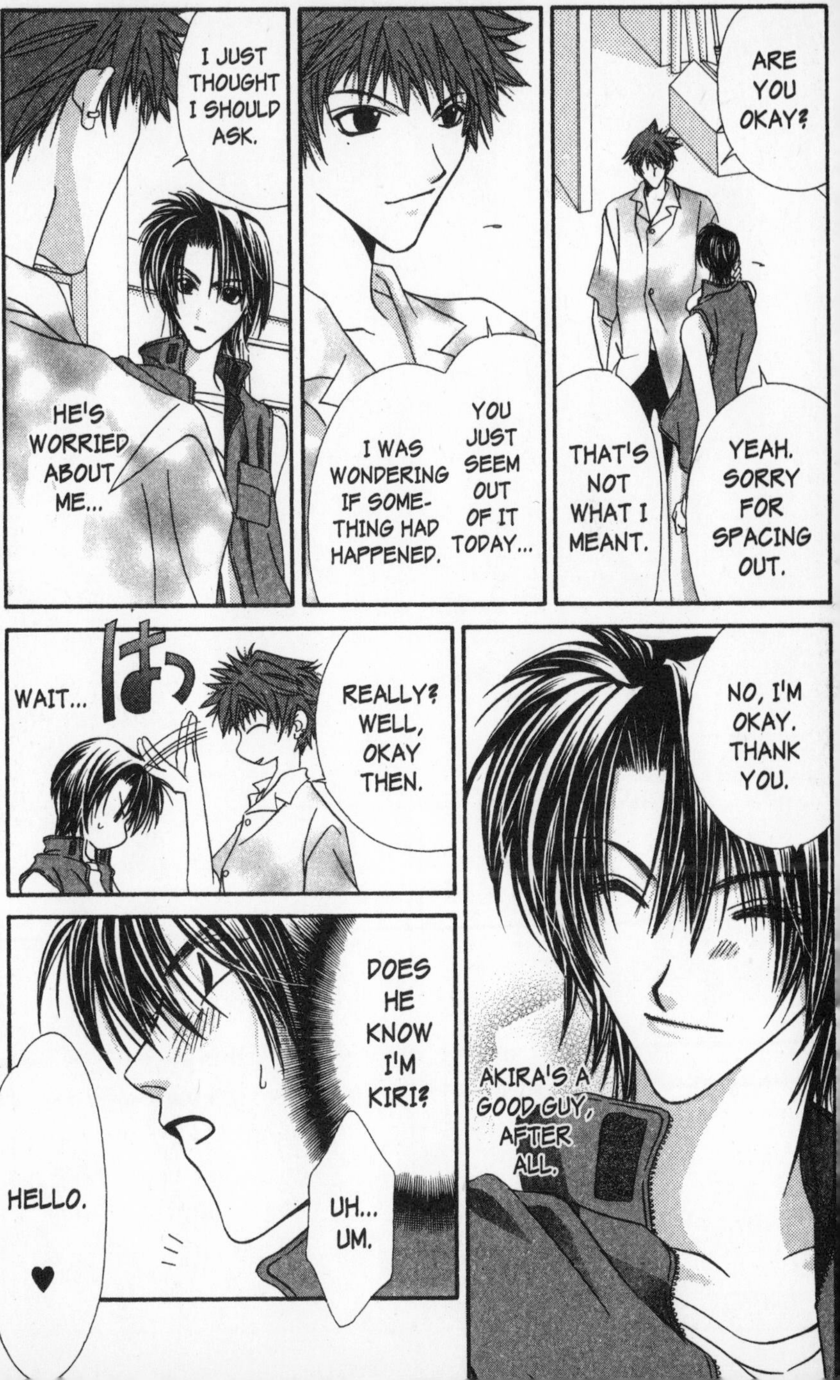
ARE YOU OKAY?
YEAH. SORRY FOR SPACING OUT.
THAT'S NOT WHAT I MEANT.
YOU JUST SEEM OUT OF IT TODAY...
I WAS WONDERING IF SOME-THING HAD HAPPENED.
I JUST THOUGHT I SHOULD ASK.
HE'S WORRIED ABOUT ME...
NO, I'M OKAY. THANK YOU.
AKIRA'S A GOOD GUY, AFTER ALL.
REALLY? WELL, OKAY THEN.
はっ
WAIT...
DOES HE KNOW I'M KIRI?
UH... UM.
HELLO. ♥

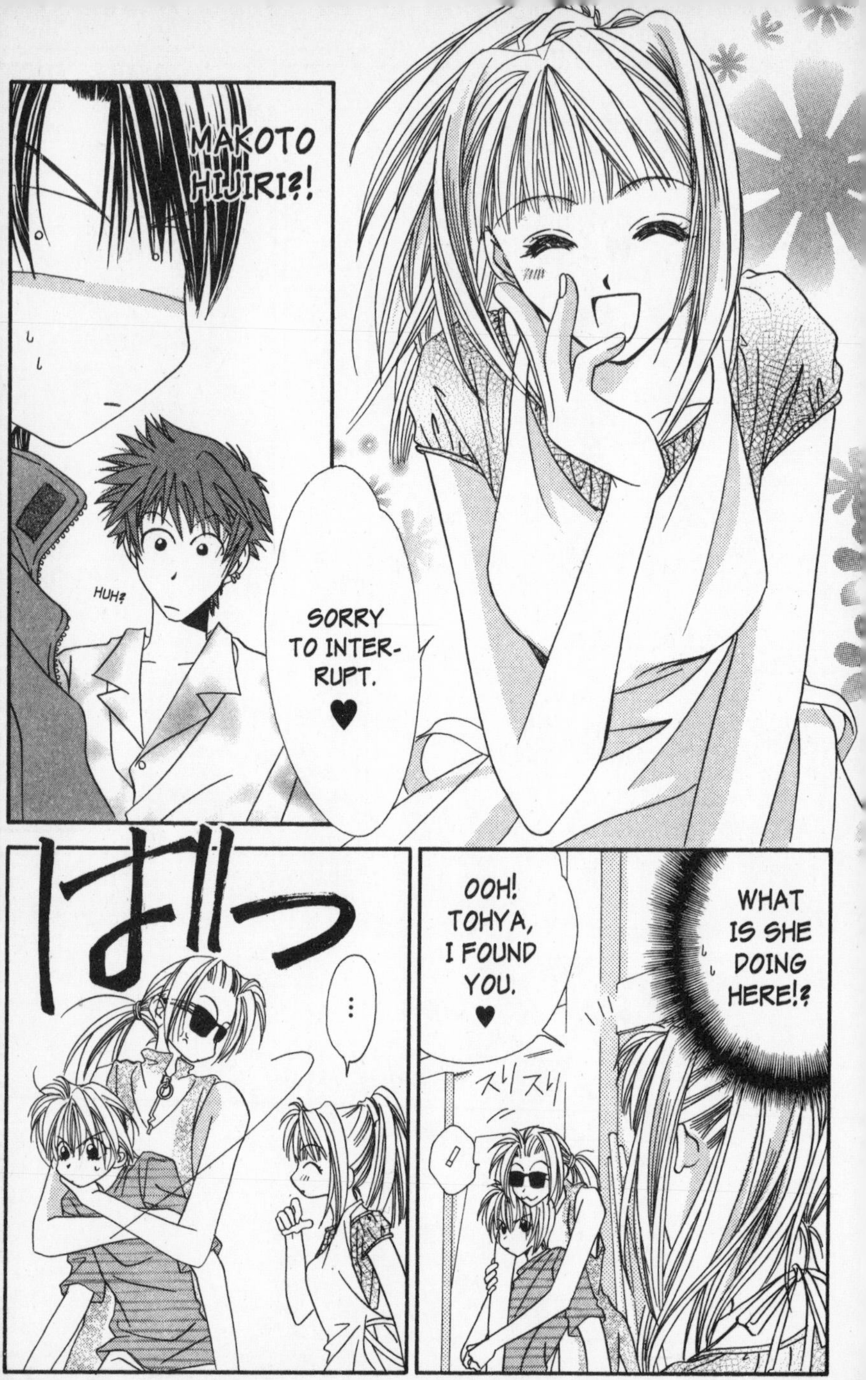
SORRY TO INTER-RUPT. ♥
MAKOTO HIJIRI?!
HUH?
WHAT IS SHE DOING HERE!?
OOH! TOHYA, I FOUND YOU. ♥
スリスリ
!
はっ
...

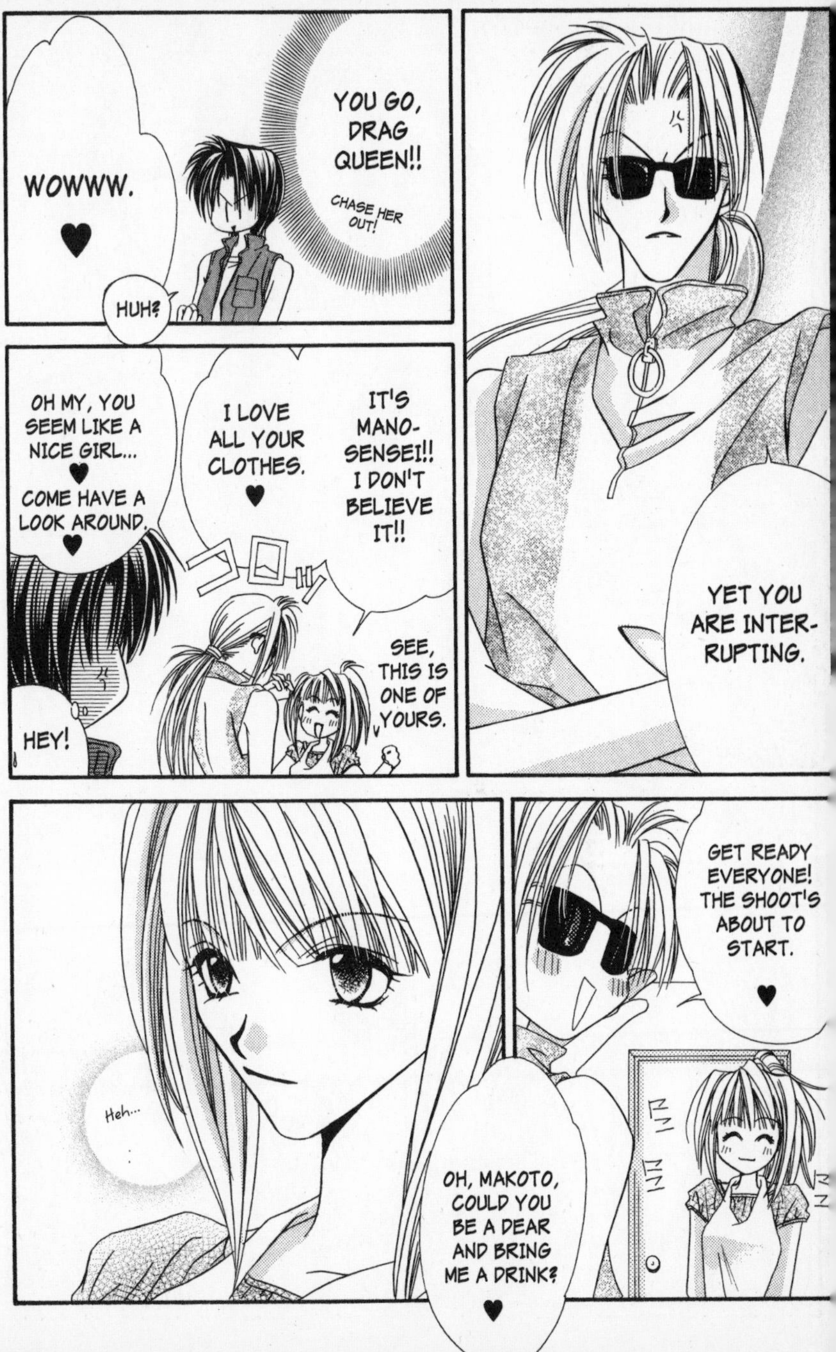
YET YOU ARE INTER-RUPTING.
YOU GO, DRAG QUEEN!!
CHASE HER OUT!
WOWWW. ♥
HUH?
IT'S MANO-SENSEI!! I DON'T BELIEVE IT!!
I LOVE ALL YOUR CLOTHES. ♥
OH MY, YOU SEEM LIKE A NICE GIRL... ♥ COME HAVE A LOOK AROUND. ♥
SEE, THIS IS ONE OF YOURS.
HEY!
GET READY EVERYONE! THE SHOOT'S ABOUT TO START. ♥
OH, MAKOTO, COULD YOU BE A DEAR AND BRING ME A DRINK? ♥
Heh...

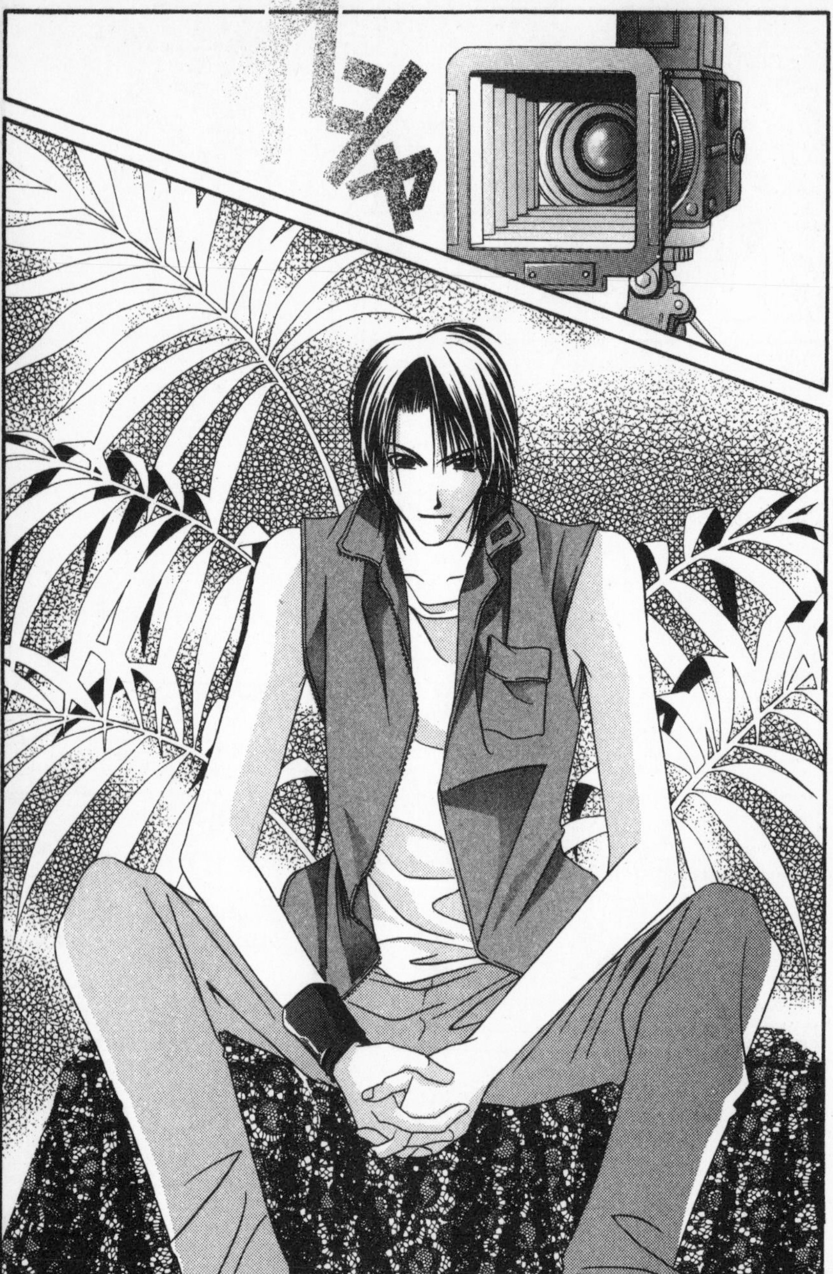

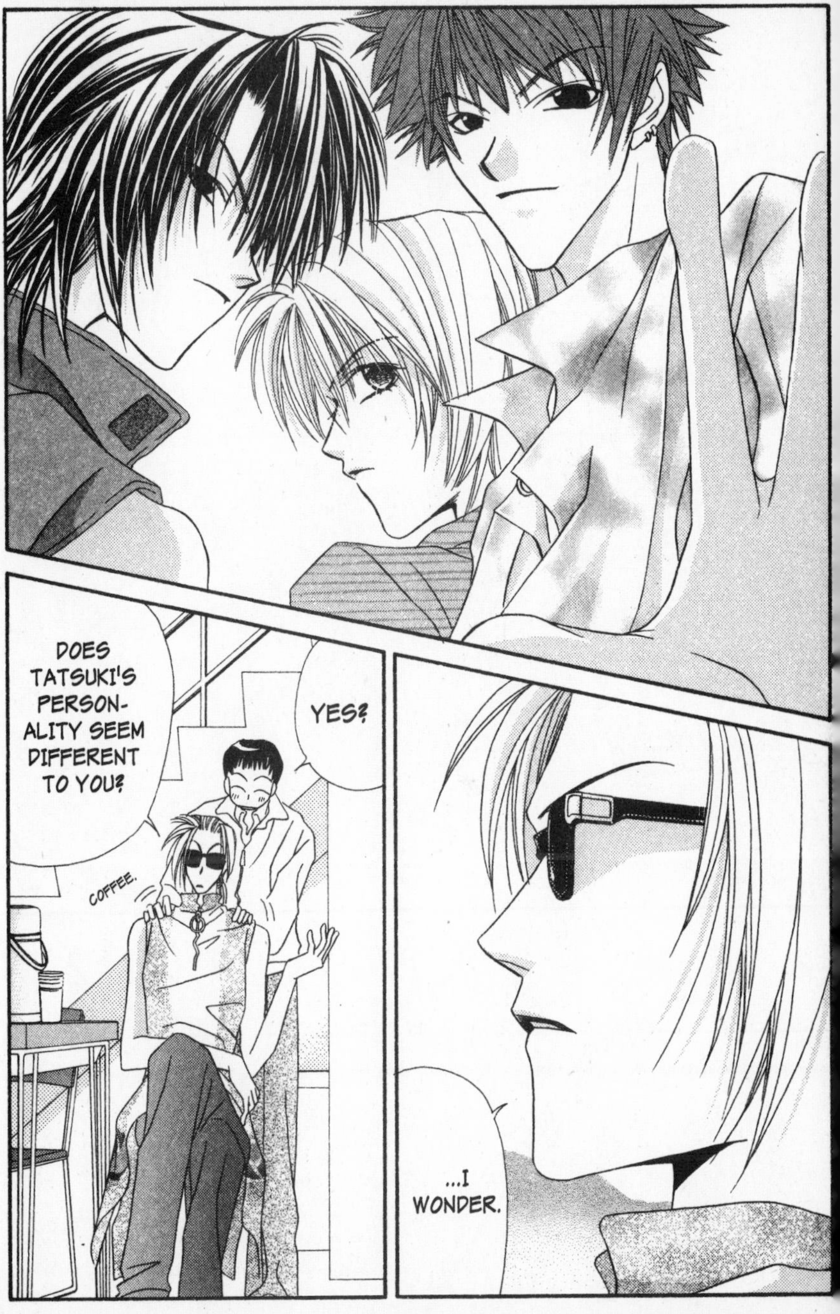
...I WONDER.
YES?
DOES TATSUKI'S PERSON-ALITY SEEM DIFFERENT TO YOU?
COFFEE.

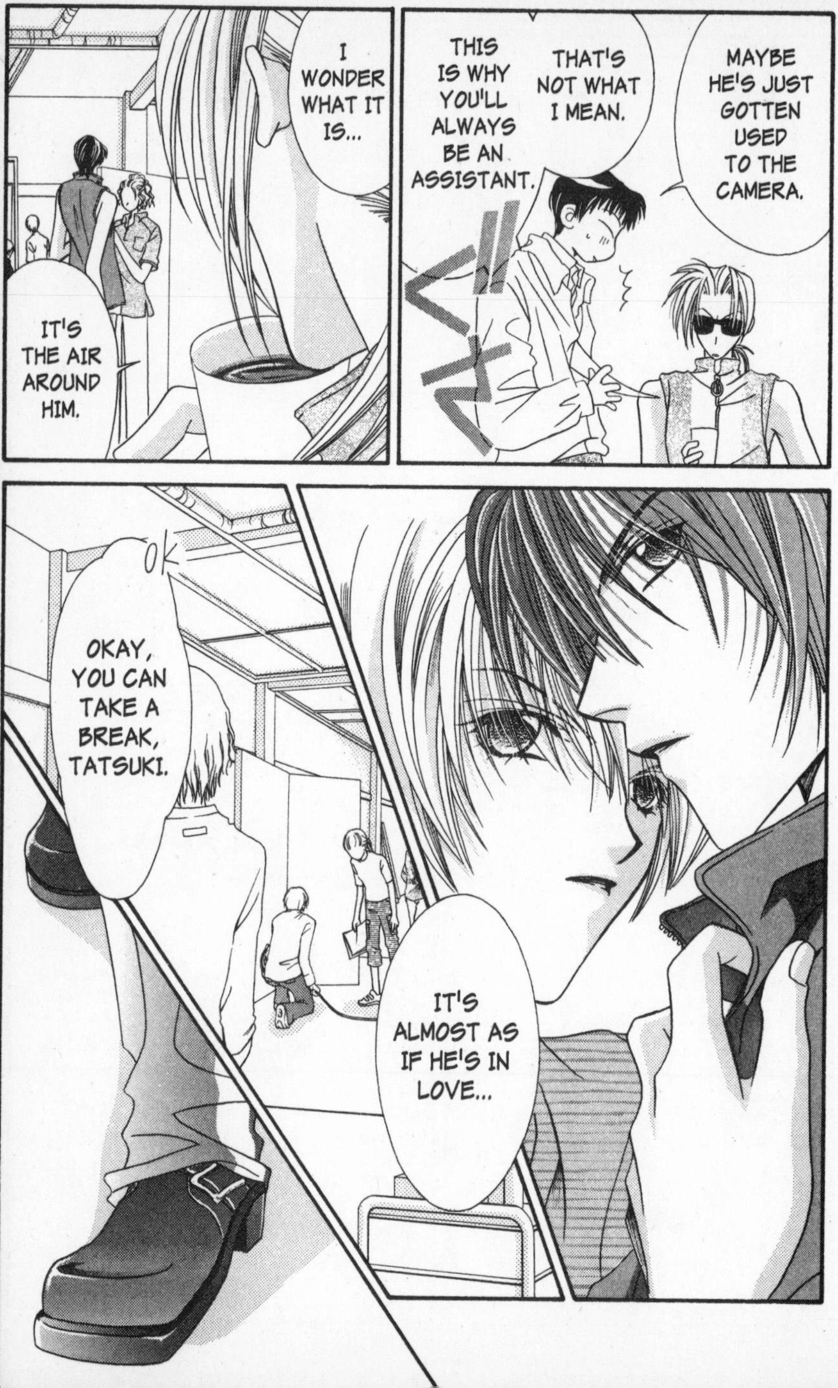
MAYBE HE'S JUST GOTTEN USED TO THE CAMERA.
THAT'S NOT WHAT I MEAN.
THIS IS WHY YOU'LL ALWAYS BE AN ASSISTANT.
I WONDER WHAT IT IS...
IT'S THE AIR AROUND HIM.
IT'S ALMOST AS IF HE'S IN LOVE...
OK
OKAY, YOU CAN TAKE A BREAK, TATSUKI.

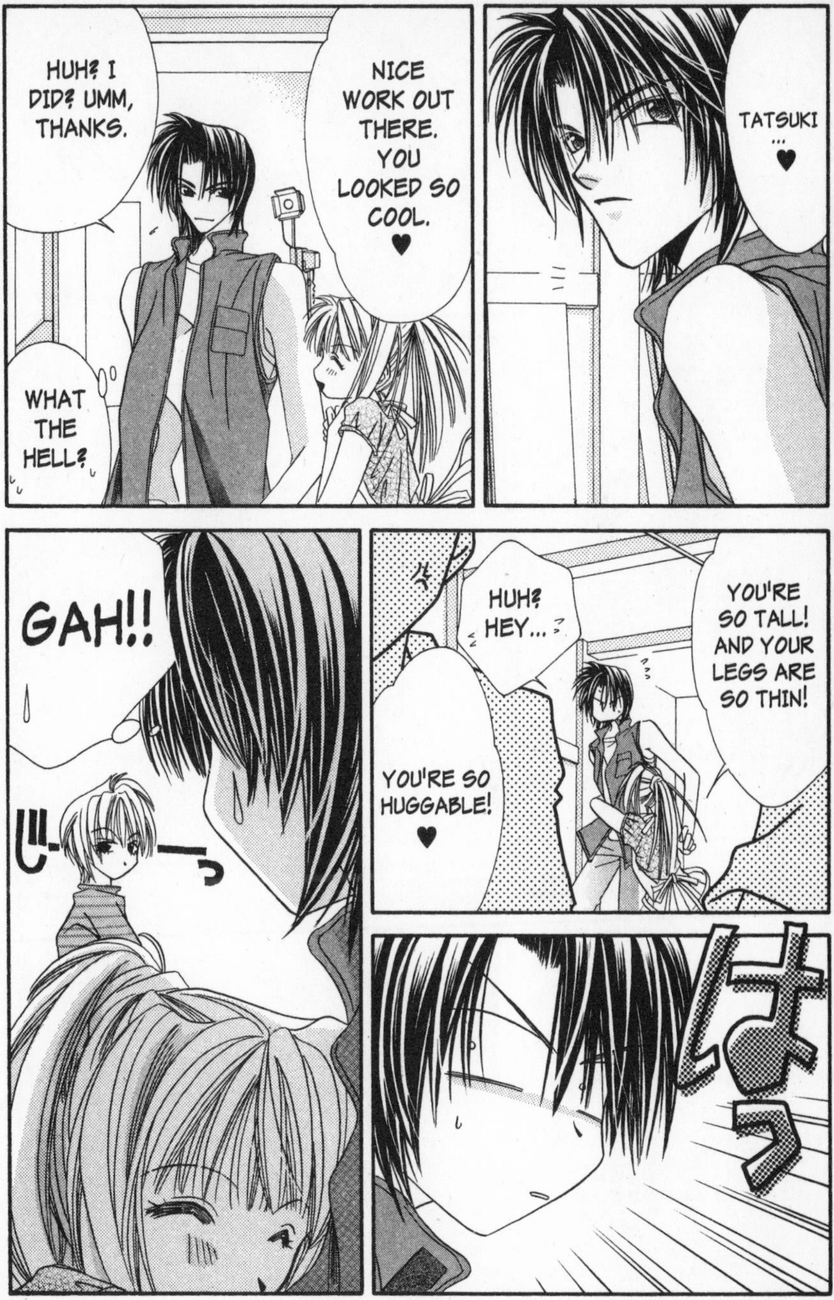
TATSUKI ... ♥
NICE WORK OUT THERE. YOU LOOKED SO COOL. ♥
HUH? I DID? UMM, THANKS.
WHAT THE HELL?
YOU'RE SO TALL! AND YOUR LEGS ARE SO THIN!
HUH? HEY...
YOU'RE SO HUGGABLE! ♥
はっ
GAH!!
じーーっ

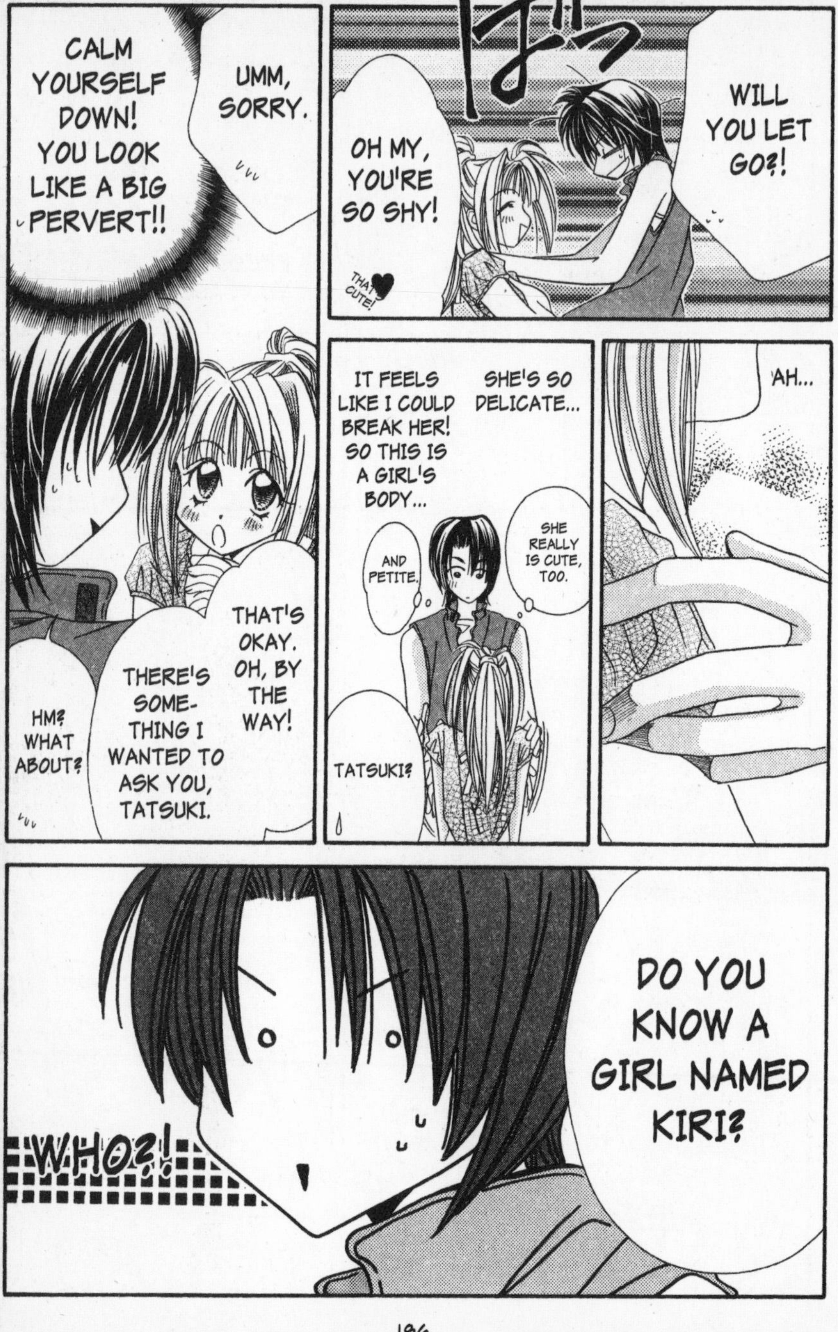
ぱっ
WILL YOU LET GO?!
OH MY, YOU'RE SO SHY!
THAT'S CUTE!
AH...
SHE'S SO DELICATE...
IT FEELS LIKE I COULD BREAK HER! SO THIS IS A GIRL'S BODY...
SHE REALLY IS CUTE, TOO.
AND PETITE.
TATSUKI?
UMM, SORRY.
CALM YOURSELF DOWN! YOU LOOK LIKE A BIG PERVERT!!
THAT'S OKAY. OH, BY THE WAY!
THERE'S SOME-THING I WANTED TO ASK YOU, TATSUKI.
HM? WHAT ABOUT?
DO YOU KNOW A GIRL NAMED KIRI?
WHO?!

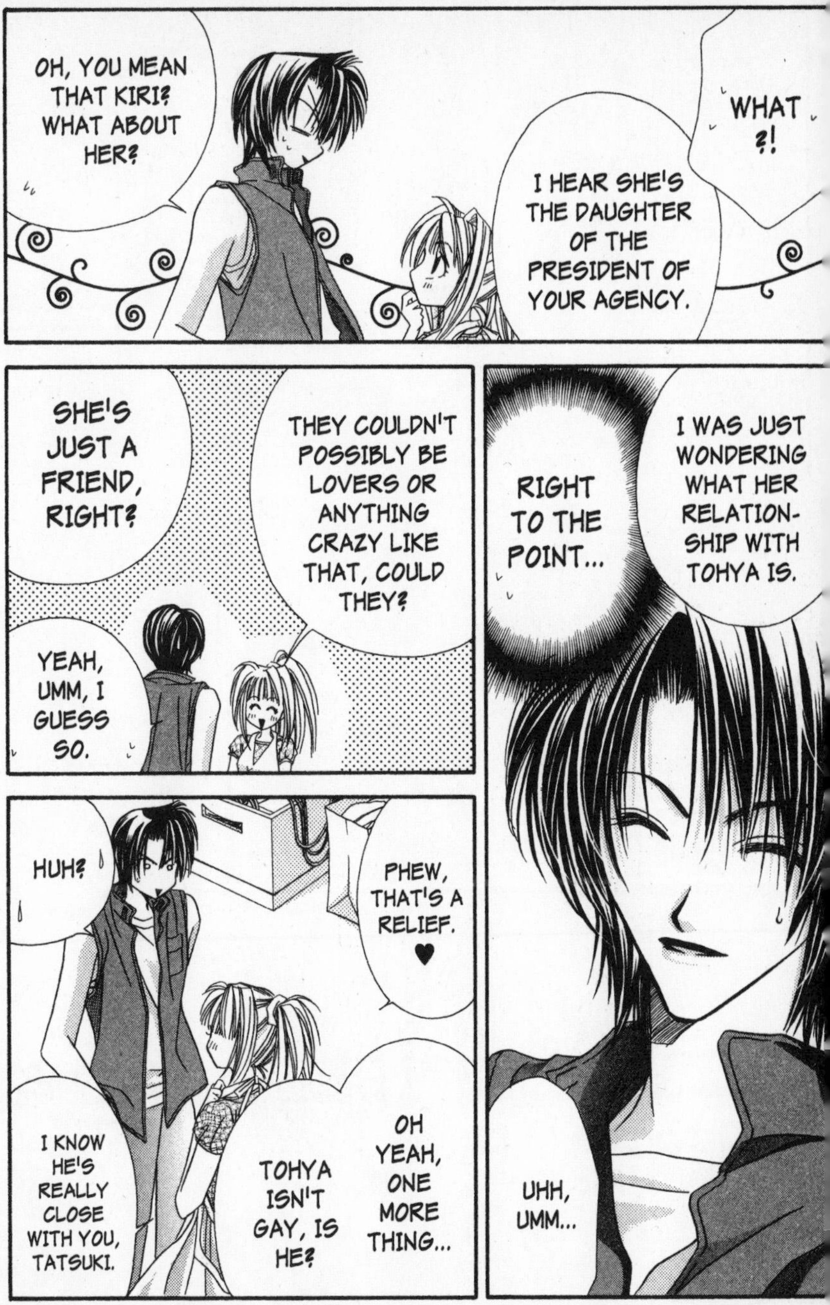
WHAT ?!
I HEAR SHE'S THE DAUGHTER OF THE PRESIDENT OF YOUR AGENCY.
OH, YOU MEAN THAT KIRI? WHAT ABOUT HER?
I WAS JUST WONDERING WHAT HER RELATION-SHIP WITH TOHYA IS.
RIGHT TO THE POINT...
UHH, UMM...
THEY COULDN'T POSSIBLY BE LOVERS OR ANYTHING CRAZY LIKE THAT, COULD THEY?
SHE'S JUST A FRIEND, RIGHT?
YEAH, UMM, I GUESS SO.
PHEW, THAT'S A RELIEF. ♥
HUH?
OH YEAH, ONE MORE THING...
TOHYA ISN'T GAY, IS HE?
I KNOW HE'S REALLY CLOSE WITH YOU, TATSUKI.

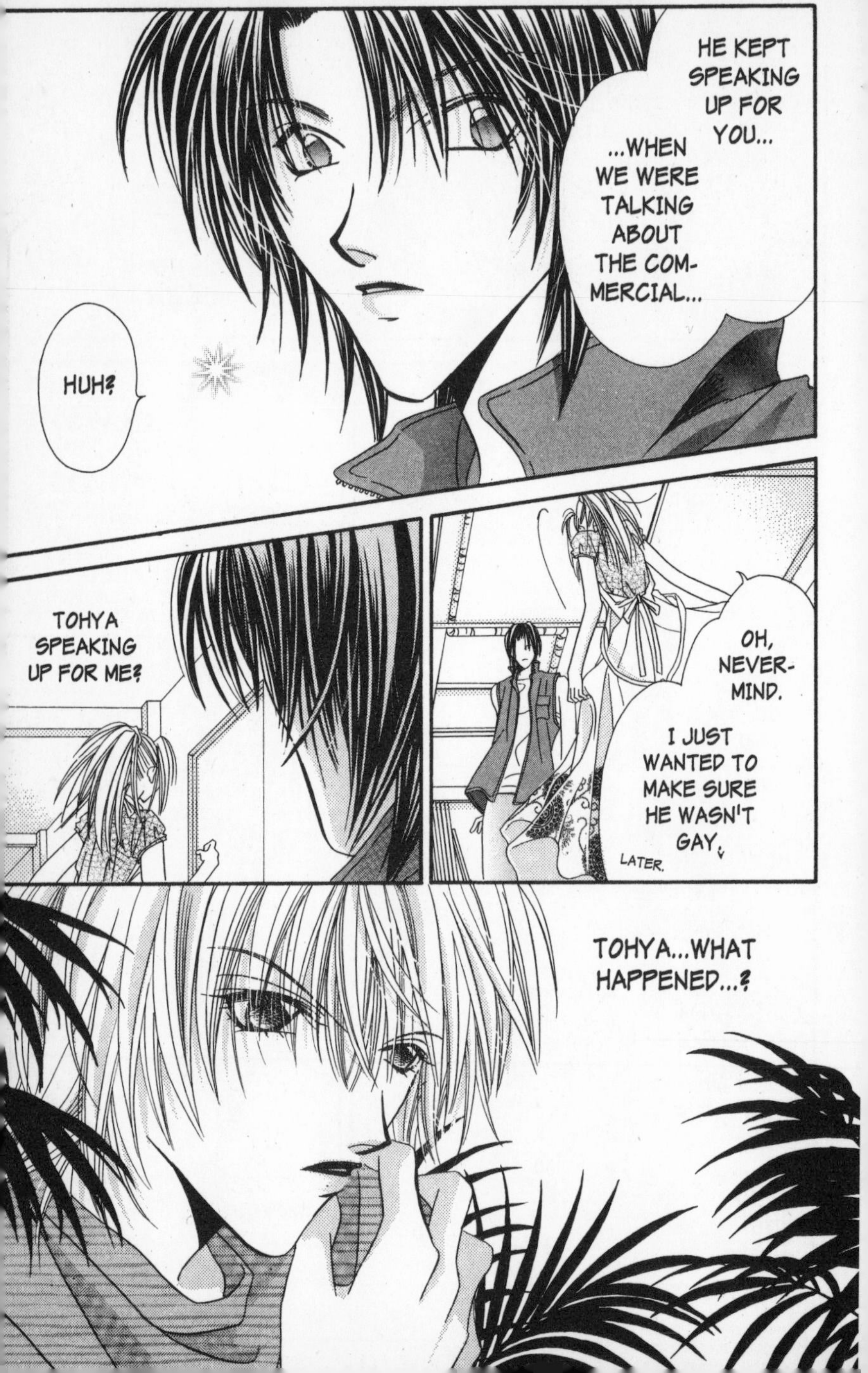
HE KEPT SPEAKING UP FOR YOU...
...WHEN WE WERE TALKING ABOUT THE COM-MERCIAL...
HUH?
OH, NEVER-MIND.
I JUST WANTED TO MAKE SURE HE WASN'T GAY.
LATER.
TOHYA SPEAKING UP FOR ME?
TOHYA...WHAT HAPPENED...?

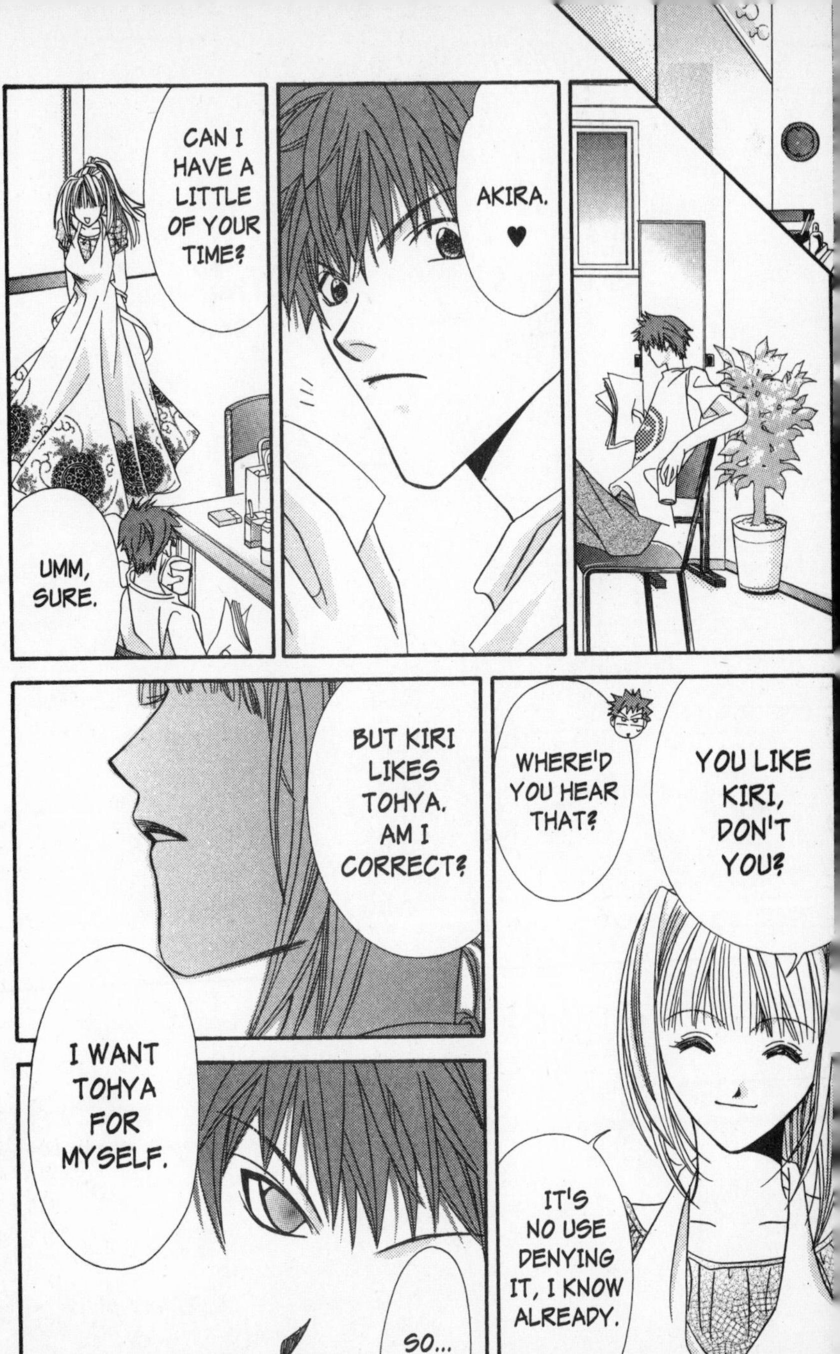
AKIRA. ♥
CAN I HAVE A LITTLE OF YOUR TIME?
UMM, SURE.
YOU LIKE KIRI, DON'T YOU?
WHERE'D YOU HEAR THAT?
IT'S NO USE DENYING IT, I KNOW ALREADY.
BUT KIRI LIKES TOHYA. AM I CORRECT?
I WANT TOHYA FOR MYSELF.
SO...

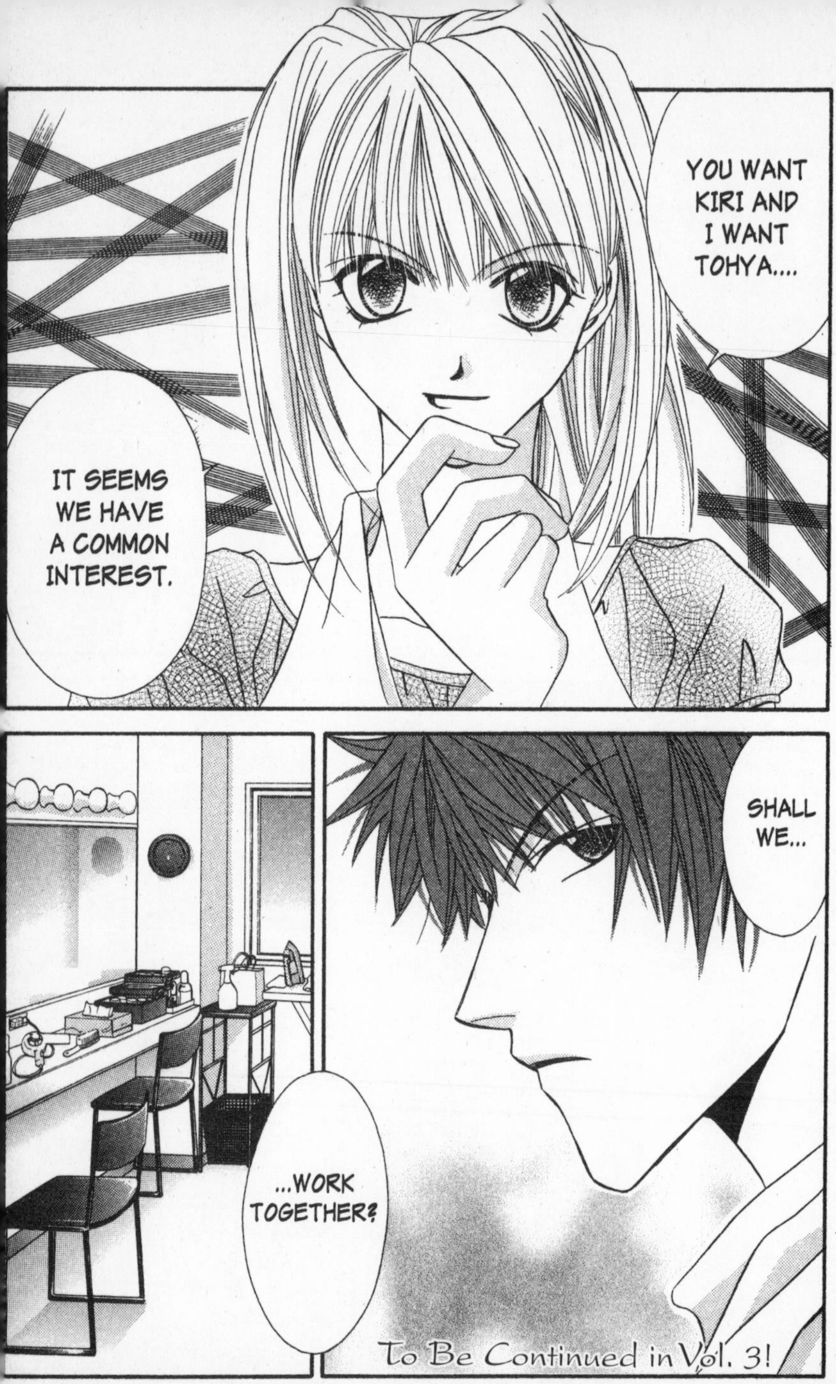
YOU WANT KIRI AND I WANT TOHYA....
IT SEEMS WE HAVE A COMMON INTEREST.
SHALL WE...
...WORK TOGETHER?
To Be Continued in Vol. 3!

AN OCCASIONAL WORD
-YOU CAN SKIP THIS-
(WAIT!)

THE PAW PRINT OF →
KURARA-CHAN'S CAT (LOL)

RECENTLY, I SAID GOODBYE TO SOMEONE VERY IMPORTANT TO ME (NO, IT WASN'T A GUY (LOL). I CRIED FOR THE FIRST TIME IN A LONG TIME. I CRIED A WHOLE LOT. JUST REMEMBERING IT NOW MAKES ME WANT TO CRY. I CRIED SO MUCH MY HEAD HURT. BUT IT'S GIVEN ME A CHANCE TO THINK AND REMEMBER WHAT'S REALLY IMPORTANT, AND LEARN THINGS I NEVER KNEW. WHAT "GOODBYE" IS. WHY WE HAVE TO LOSE THINGS DEAR TO US. PEOPLE THOUGHT THIS SOMEONE WAS TOO DEPENDENT ON ME. I THOUGHT SO TOO. I THOUGHT I'D BE ABLE TO STAND ON MY OWN JUST FINE, BUT WHAT I'VE FOUND IS THAT I WAS THE ONE DEPENDENT ON HER. BY THINKING HER NEEDED ME, AND THINKING I WAS BETTER THAN HER, I ENDED UP DIGGING MY OWN GRAVE. AND NOW THERE'S REGRET FILLING THE SPACE I MADE FOR HER. I KNOW NOW HOW RASH I WAS. THERE'S TIMES WHEN IT'S HARD TO HEAR SOMEONE SAY HER "LIKE" YOU. NO, MAYBE WHAT'S HARDER IS NOT BEING ABLE TO HONESTLY SAY "I LIKE YOU" BACK. WHEN I HEARD "I DON'T WANT TO SEE YOU AGAIN," I COULDN'T RESPOND. THERE'S ONLY ONE RESPONSE, AND IT'S SOMETHING ONE SHOULDN'T SAY. IF WE HATED EACH OTHER, IT MIGHT BE EASIER, I GUESS. BUT THAT'S NO USE. HIDING HOW WE FEEL DOESN'T HELP ANYTHING. HOW DID IT END UP LIKE THIS IS WHAT'S IMPORTANT. LOOKING BACK, I THINK IT WAS ALL BECAUSE I THOUGHT I WAS BETTER THAN HER. PLUS A LITTLE RASHNESS (LOL). THE PLACE I MADE FOR HER, ONLY HER CAN FILL. I KNOW I'LL MEET MANY MORE PEOPLE IMPORTANT TO ME, BUT THAT HOLE WILL NEVER CLOSE. I THINK IT SHOULD BE THAT WAY. IT MAKES WHAT HAPPENED BETWEEN US REAL. I LOVED HER ENOUGH TO CRY OVER HER, SO THERE'S NO WAY I'D WANT TO FORGET HER. AS TIME GOES ON, I'LL STILL LOVE HER. I THINK I'M LUCKY TO HAVE MET SOMEONE I FEEL THAT WAY ABOUT. IN THE END, I WAS A LIAR. I ACTED TOO BIG FOR TOO LONG. I GUESS YOU CAN SAY I REGRET THAT TOO. NOTHING GOOD CAN COME FROM ACTING BETTER THAN SOMEONE, IS WHAT I'VE LEARNED (LOL).

Thanks"

I WANT THESE IMPORTANT
WORDS TO REACH THE ONE
IMPORTANT TO ME.

Secrets of the Muto Household

--Hiromu's Song-- by Shinoyu

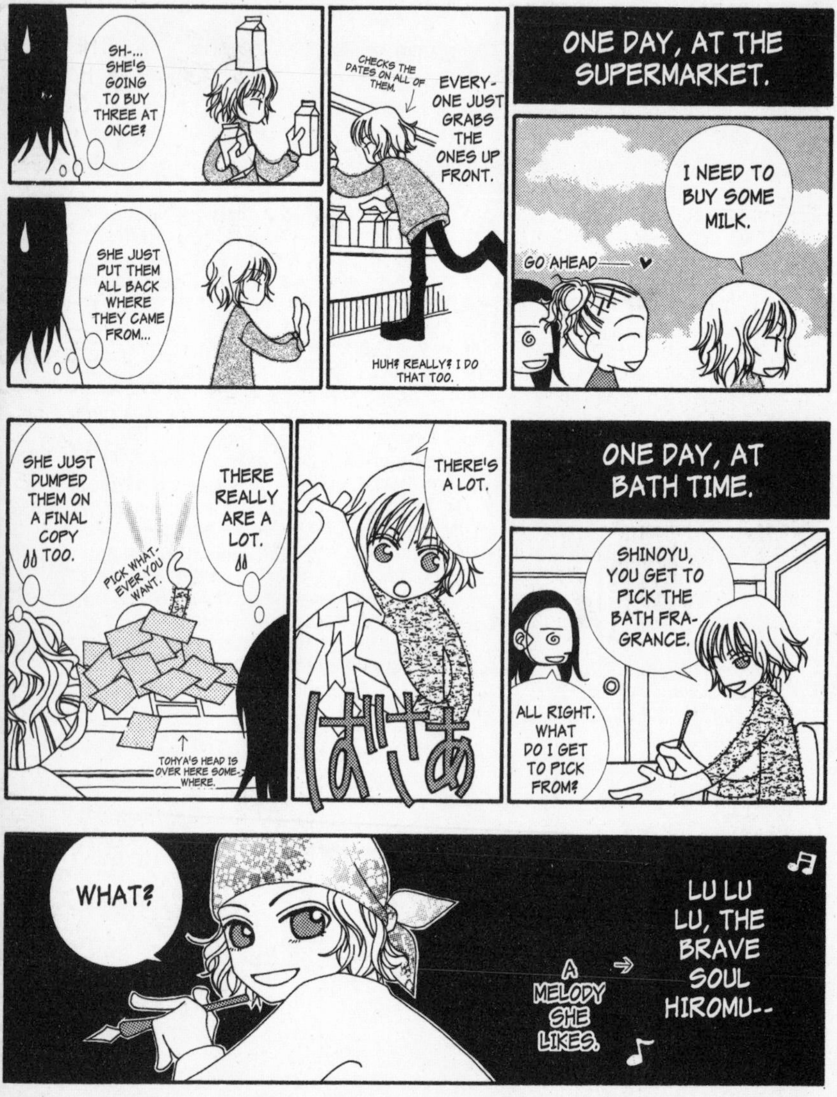
ONE DAY, AT THE SUPERMARKET.
I NEED TO BUY SOME MILK.
GO AHEAD ♥
CHECKS THE DATES ON ALL OF THEM.
EVERY-ONE JUST GRABS THE ONES UP FRONT.
HUH? REALLY? I DO THAT TOO.
SH-... SHE'S GOING TO BUY THREE AT ONCE?
SHE JUST PUT THEM ALL BACK WHERE THEY CAME FROM...
ONE DAY, AT BATH TIME.
SHINOYU, YOU GET TO PICK THE BATH FRA-GRANCE.
ALL RIGHT. WHAT DO I GET TO PICK FROM?
THERE'S A LOT.
ばさあ
THERE REALLY ARE A LOT.
SHE JUST DUMPED THEM ON A FINAL COPY TOO.
PICK WHAT-EVER YOU WANT.
TOHYA'S HEAD IS OVER HERE SOME-WHERE.
LU LU LU, THE BRAVE SOUL HIROMU--
A MELODY SHE LIKES.
WHAT?

Secrets of the Muto Household

--Hiromu's Song-- by Shinoyu

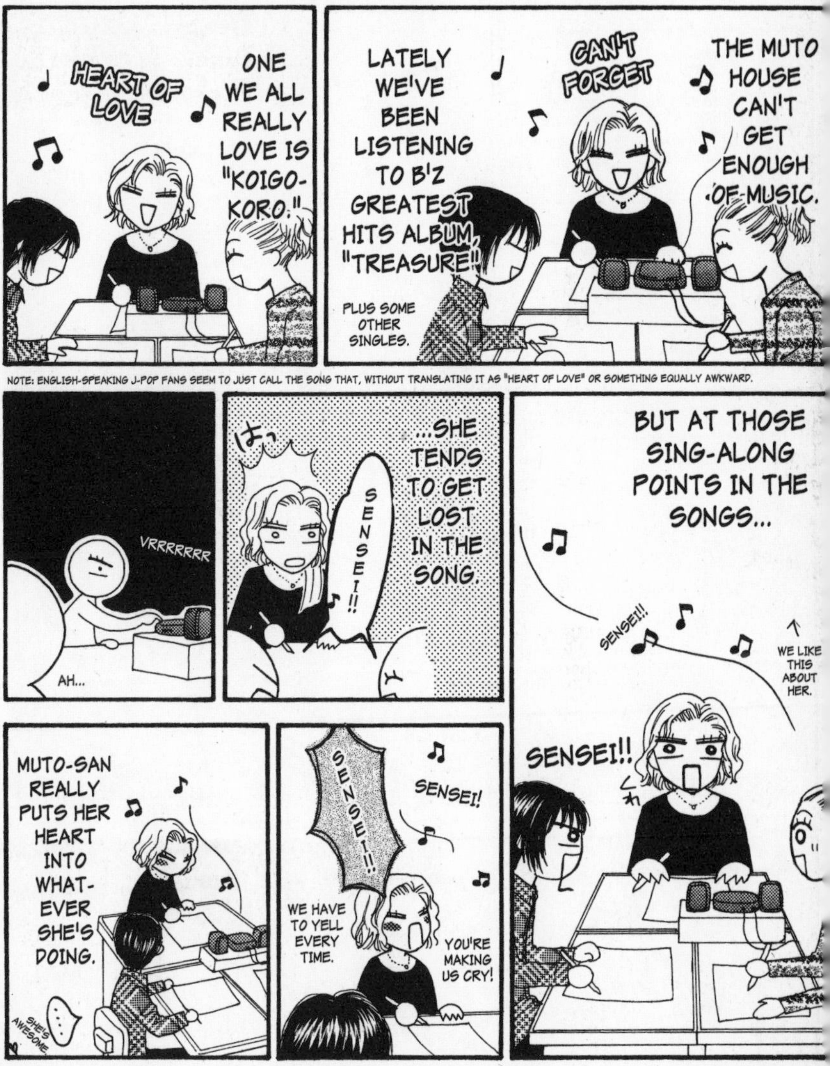
THE MUTO HOUSE CAN'T GET ENOUGH OF MUSIC.
CAN'T FORGET
LATELY WE'VE BEEN LISTENING TO B'Z GREATEST HITS ALBUM, "TREASURE"!
PLUS SOME OTHER SINGLES.
ONE WE ALL REALLY LOVE IS "KOIGO-KORO."
HEART OF LOVE
NOTE: ENGLISH-SPEAKING J-POP FANS SEEM TO JUST CALL THE SONG THAT, WITHOUT TRANSLATING IT AS "HEART OF LOVE" OR SOMETHING EQUALLY AWKWARD.
BUT AT THOSE SING-ALONG POINTS IN THE SONGS...
WE LIKE THIS ABOUT HER.
SENSEI!!
SENSEI!!
...SHE TENDS TO GET LOST IN THE SONG.
SENSEI!!
はっ
VRRRRRRR
AH...
SENSEI!
SENSEI!!
YOU'RE MAKING US CRY!
WE HAVE TO YELL EVERY TIME.
MUTO-SAN REALLY PUTS HER HEART INTO WHAT-EVER SHE'S DOING.
SHE'S AWESOME.

Secrets of the Muto Household

--Hiromu's Song-- by Shinoyu

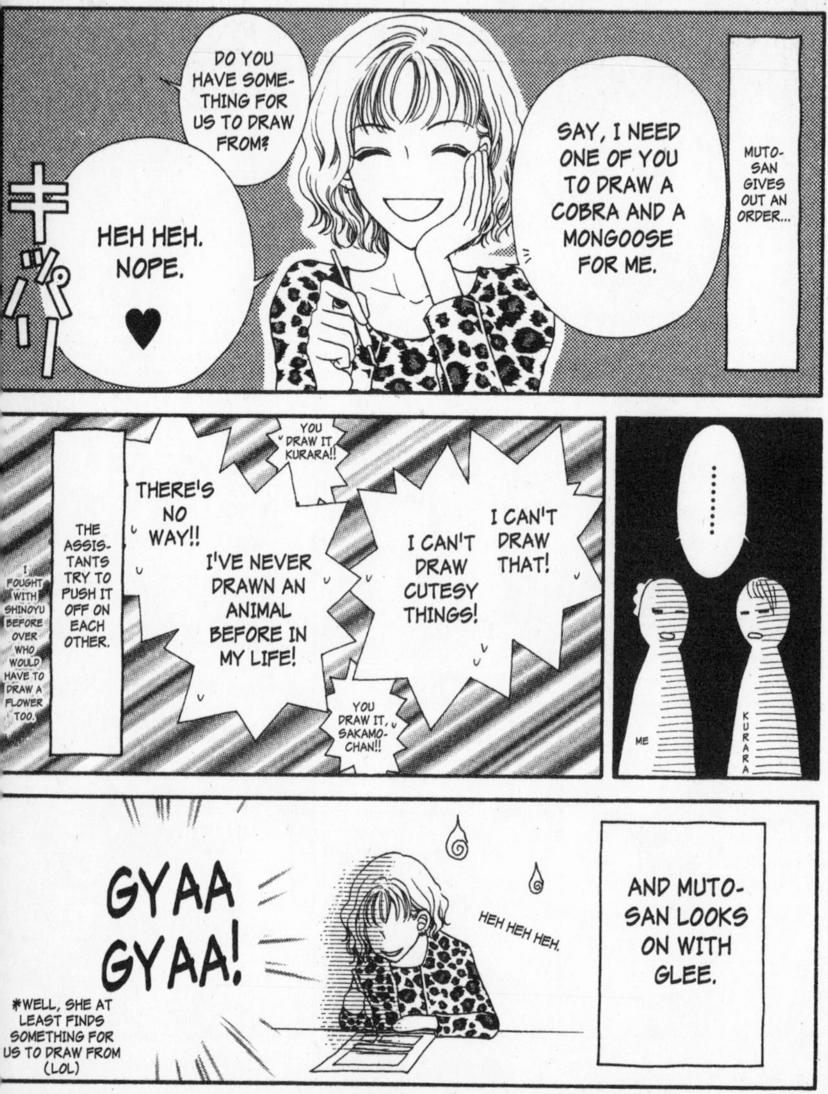

MUTO-SAN GIVES OUT AN ORDER...
SAY, I NEED ONE OF YOU TO DRAW A COBRA AND A MONGOOSE FOR ME.
DO YOU HAVE SOME-THING FOR US TO DRAW FROM?
HEH HEH. NOPE. ♥
......
ME
KURARA
I CAN'T DRAW THAT!
YOU DRAW IT KURARA!!
I CAN'T DRAW CUTESY THINGS!
THERE'S NO WAY!!
I'VE NEVER DRAWN AN ANIMAL BEFORE IN MY LIFE!
YOU DRAW IT, SAKAMO-CHAN!!
THE ASSIS-TANTS TRY TO PUSH IT OFF ON EACH OTHER.
I FOUGHT WITH SHINOYU BEFORE OVER WHO WOULD HAVE TO DRAW A FLOWER TOO.
AND MUTO-SAN LOOKS ON WITH GLEE.
HEH HEH HEH.
GYAA GYAA!
*WELL, SHE AT LEAST FINDS SOMETHING FOR US TO DRAW FROM (LOL)

Secrets of the Muto Household /End

In the next volume of...

As Makoto tries to recruit Akira to help break up Kiri and Tohya, Kiri sinks into a deep depression. When she ends up fainting at school, she's rushed to a clinic, where she gets a visit--and a kiss--from Tohya. But was it all a dream? She better decide fast: Makoto may be on to her, and she's about to find out if Tatsuki and Kiri are really one in the same!

GRENADIER

CREATED BY: SOUSUKE KAISE

TWO BIG GUNS CAN BRING PEACE TO THE WORLD...

Rushuna is a golden-haired Senshi—a gunslinger who travels the land with one purpose: to make the world a peaceful place with her high-caliber revolver and enchanting smile. However, her journey of nonviolence won't be easy and she may have to display her amazing gun skills and talent for reloading on the bounce.

THE MANGA THAT SPARKED THE POPULAR ANIME!

ACTION

OT OLDER TEEN AGE 16+

© SOUSUKE KAISE

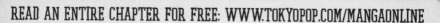

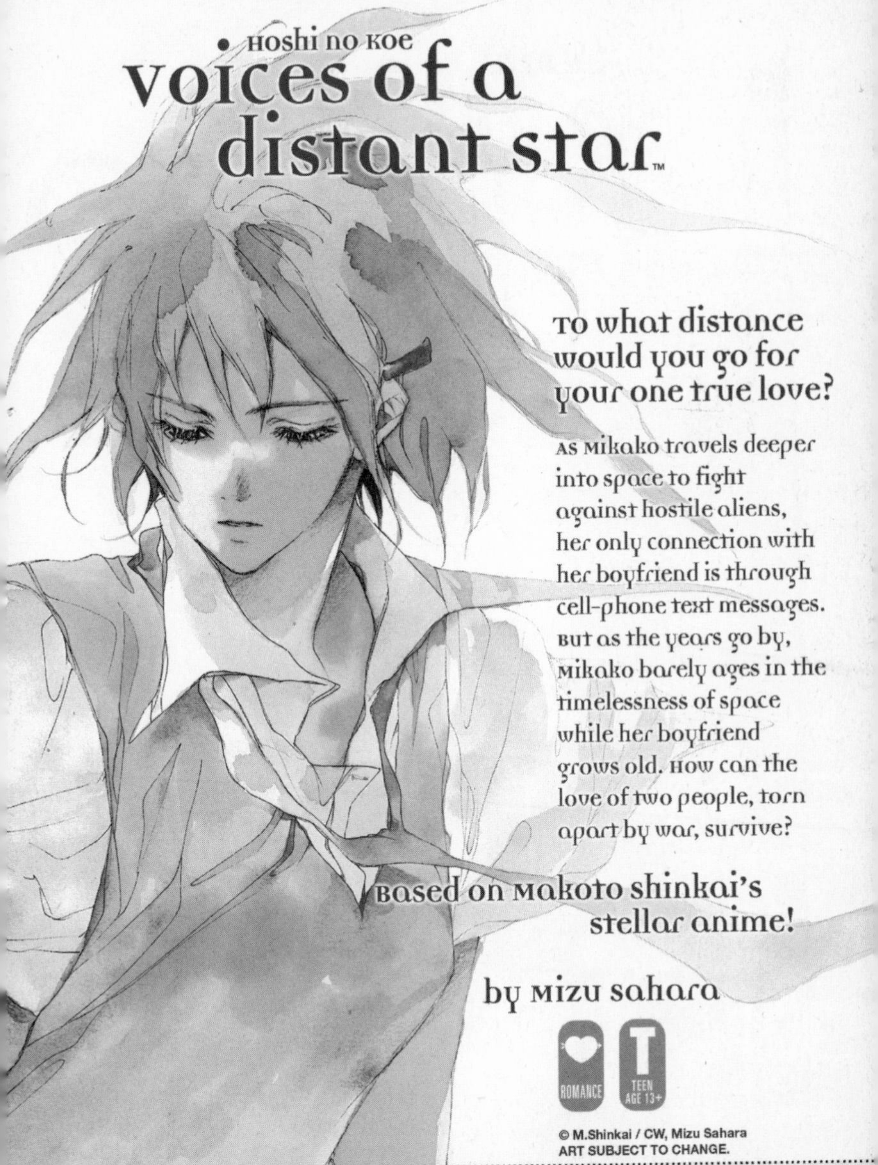
HOSHI NO KOE
voices of a distant star™
To what distance would you go for your one true love?
As Mikako travels deeper into space to fight against hostile aliens, her only connection with her boyfriend is through cell-phone text messages. But as the years go by, Mikako barely ages in the timelessness of space while her boyfriend grows old. How can the love of two people, torn apart by war, survive?
Based on Makoto Shinkai's stellar anime!
by Mizu Sahara
ROMANCE
T
TEEN AGE 13+
© M.Shinkai / CW, Mizu Sahara
ART SUBJECT TO CHANGE.

STOP!

This is the back of the book.
You wouldn't want to spoil a great ending!

This book is printed "manga-style," in the authentic Japanese right-to-left format. Since none of the artwork has been flipped or altered, readers get to experience the story just as the creator intended. You've been asking for it, so TOKYOPOP® delivered: authentic, hot-off-the-press, and far more fun!

DIRECTIONS

If this is your first time reading manga-style, here's a quick guide to help you understand how it works.

It's easy... just start in the top right panel and follow the numbers. Have fun, and look for more 100% authentic manga from TOKYOPOP®!